Noam Chomsky is one of the leading intellectual figures of modern times. He has had a major influence on linguistics, psychology, and philosophy, and a significant effect on a range of other disciplines from anthropology to mathematics, education to literary criticism.

In this rigorous yet accessible account of Chomsky's work and influence, Neil Smith analyzes Chomsky's key contributions to the study of language and the study of mind. He gives a detailed and partly historical exposition of Chomsky's linguistic theorizing, and examines the ideas (such as deep and surface structure) for which he is best known. Smith discusses the psychological and philosophical implications of Chomsky's work, and argues that he has fundamentally changed the way we think of ourselves, gaining a position in the history of ideas on a par with that of Darwin or Descartes. Finally, he examines Chomsky's political ideas and how these fit intellectually with his scholarly work. Smith argues that, despite Chomsky's own disavowal of any very close connection, there are fundamental ideas of rationality, creativity, and modularity that draw together the disparate strands of his vast output. Throughout, Smith explores the controversy surrounding Chomsky's work, and explains why he has been both adulated and vilified.

This second edition has been thoroughly updated and revised to account for Chomsky's most recent work, including his continued contributions to linguistics (in particular new developments in the Minimalist Program), his further discussion on evolution, and his extensive work on the events of September 11, 2001 and their aftermath. The bibliography and notes have been expanded to account for the rapidly growing secondary literature on Chomsky's work, as well as the many new works by Chomsky himself. It will be welcomed by students and researchers across the disciplines of linguistics, philosophy, cognitive science and politics, and anyone with an interest in the impact of Chomsky's work.

NEIL SMITH is Professor and Head of Linguistics at University College London. He is the author of *An Outline Grammar of Nupe* (1967); *The Acquisition of Phonology* (Cambridge University Press, 1973); *Modern Linguistics: The Results of Chomsky's Revolution* (with Deirdre Wilson, 1979); *The Twitter Machine: Reflections on Language* (1989); *The Mind of a Savant* (with Ianthi Tsimpli, 1995), *Language, Bananas and Bonobos* (2002), and he has edited a volume on *Mutual Knowledge* (1982). In addition, he has published around one hundred and fifty essays, articles and reviews in a wide variety of publications, including *Journal of Linguistics*, *Lingua*, *Journal of Neurolinguistics*, and *Glot International*. He was elected FBA in 1999 and an Honorary Member of the Linguistic Society of America in 2000.

Chomsky

Ideas and Ideals

Second edition

Neil Smith

CAMBRIDGE
UNIVERSITY PRESS

PUBLISHED BY THE PRESS SYNDICATE OF THE UNIVERSITY OF CAMBRIDGE
The Pitt Building, Trumpington Street, Cambridge, United Kingdom

CAMBRIDGE UNIVERSITY PRESS
The Edinburgh Building, Cambridge, CB2 2RU, UK
40 West 20th Street, New York, NY 10011–4211, USA
477 Williamstown Road, Port Melbourne, VIC 3207, Australia
Ruiz de Alarcón 13, 28014 Madrid, Spain
Dock House, The Waterfront, Cape Town 8001, South Africa

http://www.cambridge.org

First published 1999
Second edition 2004
Reprinted 2004

Printed in the United Kingdom at the University Press, Cambridge

Typeface Times 10/12 pt.   *System* LATEX 2_ε [TB]

A catalogue record for this book is available from the British Library

Library of Congress Cataloguing in Publication data
Smith, N. V. (Neilson Voyne)
Chomsky: ideas and ideals / Neil Smith. – 2nd edn.
    p.   cm.
Includes bibliographical references and index.
ISBN 0 521 83788 X (hb.) – ISBN 0 521 54688 5 (pb.)
1. Chomsky, Noam.   2. Linguistics.   I. Title.
P85.C47S64   2004
410′.92 – dc22   2004040781

ISBN 0 521 83788 X hardback
ISBN 0 521 54688 5 paperback

The publisher has used its best endeavors to ensure that the URLs for external
websites are correct and active at the time of going to press. However, the publisher
has no responsibility for the websites and can make no guarantee that a site will
remain live or that the content is or will remain appropriate.

Dedication to my friends

Dear friends, I say friends here
In the larger sense of the word:
Wife, sister, associates, relatives,
Schoolmates, men and women,
Persons seen only once
Or frequented all my life:
Provided that between us, for at least a moment,
Was drawn a segment,
A well-defined chord.

   . . . remember the time
Before the wax hardened.

From "To my friends" by Primo Levi (Levi, 1990: 5)

Contents

Preface to the second edition

Much has happened in the five years since I finished the first edition of this book. Linguistics has advanced, the cognitive sciences have exploded, the world has become ever more dangerous, and Chomsky has continued to lead a dual existence as academic and activist.

To take account of all these changes is impossible. Nevertheless, I have made many additions and amendments. First, I have corrected mistakes where I have become aware of them, and attempted to clarify points which were unclear. Second, I have updated the notes and references where that has been within my ability. As no one can be master of all the disciplines touched on here, I have concentrated on updating those sections pertaining to areas where Chomsky's recent work has been directly relevant. As a result, the bibliography contains entries for about forty new works by Chomsky himself: over fifteen new or revised books, and another twenty-five new articles. At the same time, the secondary literature on Chomsky has also burgeoned: major works have appeared by Antony & Hornstein (2003), McGilvray (1999), Mitchell & Schoeffel (2002), Winston (2002), and many others. These, as well as about a hundred other new entries are likewise included and, where relevant, I have simultaneously expanded the notes to include reference to these new items.

Third, I have attempted to give some indication of how the field and the world have changed since 1998. Chomsky has continued to produce seminal work in linguistics, and I have revised the relevant sections of chapter 2 and added some discussion of developments in Minimalism accordingly. This has entailed making a number of modifications to the first edition, where I had failed to lay the relevant groundwork for some of the issues that now occupy center-stage. I have also updated the discussion of evolution, another area where Chomsky has produced interesting new work. Most obviously, I have added a section on the events of September 11, 2001 and their aftermath – "9-11" – which have overwhelmingly preoccupied Chomsky's time and energy. These revisions and extensions have necessitated other minor changes throughout the book.

As before I have benefited from comment, criticism, and correction from colleagues and friends. In addition to those mentioned in the original acknowledgments, I am grateful for the input of *inter alia*: Misi Brody, Dick Hudson, Annette Karmiloff-Smith, Colin Phillips, Paul Postal, Geoff Pullum, and a number of reviewers, including Martin Atkinson, Gary Milsark, and especially Phillip Carr. It is reasonably certain that none of them will be entirely happy with what I have done with their contributions. I am especially grateful to Nicholas Allott, Annabel Cormack, and Ann Law, who read and commented on the entire revised manuscript. A draft of the first edition received extensive comments from Chomsky, and he later said that, while not agreeing with everything I had written, he had no serious objections. He has not seen this revised edition and is not to be blamed for my interpretation of his ideas and ideals.

As always, it is a pleasure to acknowledge the love and support of my family and friends.

Acknowledgments for the first edition

My greatest debt, both intellectual and personal, is to Noam Chomsky. Without his work, and inspiration, my career would have been radically different, and this book would obviously not have existed. In addition, he has made time over the years to talk and correspond with me, despite the overwhelming pressures of his innumerable other commitments. When I sent him the pre-final version of the manuscript, he replied with some sixty pages of comments and suggestions. If I have still misrepresented him in any way, he is not to blame. It has been a privilege to work in his shadow.

A number of colleagues and friends have discussed all or parts of the contents of this book over the five years or so that I have been preoccupied with it: Stefanie Anyadi, Misi Brody, Robyn Carston, Ray Cattell, Teun Hoekstra, Rita Manzini, Milena Nuti, Ianthi Tsimpli, Hans van de Koot, Nigel Vincent, and especially Annabel Cormack and Deirdre Wilson. Needless to say, they are not to be taken to agree with what I have written, nor to be blamed because I have sometimes failed to take their advice. Closer to home my family – Amahl, Ivan, and Saras – have inspired and supported me with sage advice, heartfelt encouragement, and good food.

Part of the work for this book was carried out while I was in receipt of a British Academy research grant, which was matched by a comparable period of sabbatical leave from University College London. I was also granted travel expenses by the Dean of the Faculty of Arts at UCL to visit Chomsky at MIT. I am grateful to the Academy and to the College for their support, and to my colleagues for shouldering my duties while I was away.

Introduction

A child of the Enlightenment. (Chomsky, 1992b: 158)

Chomsky's achievement

Why is Chomsky important? He has shown that there is really only one human language:[1] that the immense complexity of the innumerable languages we hear around us must be variations on a single theme. He has revolutionized linguistics, and in so doing has set a cat among the philosophical pigeons. He has resurrected the theory of innate ideas, demonstrating that a substantial part of our knowledge is genetically determined; he has reinstated rationalist ideas that go back centuries, but which had fallen into disrepute; and he has provided evidence that "unconscious knowledge" is what underlies our ability to speak and understand. He has overturned the dominant school of behaviorism in psychology, and has returned the mind to its position of preeminence in the study of humankind. In short, Chomsky has changed the way we think of ourselves, gaining a position in the history of ideas on a par with that of Darwin or Descartes. And he has done this while devoting the majority of his time to dissident politics and activism: documenting the lies of government, exposing the hidden influences of big business, developing a model of the social order, and acting as the conscience of the West.[2]

In this century his peers in influence are such disparate figures as Einstein, Picasso, and Freud, with each of whom he has something in common. Like Freud – but with added intellectual rigor – he has changed our conception of the mind; like Einstein, he blends intense scientific creativity with radical political activism; like Picasso, he has overturned and replaced his own established systems with startling frequency. Perhaps his greatest similarity is to Bertrand Russell, whose early work, *Principia Mathematica*, redefined the foundations of mathematics, and who devoted much of his life to political writing and activism. But while everyone knows something about mathematics, that most people have even heard of linguistics is largely due to Chomsky. His renown in linguistics, philosophy, and psychology first ensured that a few people would listen to his political views; subsequently, his political fame, or notoriety, has attracted

1

attention to his academic work, which has brought the study of language into the mainstream of scientific research, and simultaneously made it relevant to the rest of the humanities and the natural sciences.

This book is not a biography. I am concerned with Chomsky's ideas, rather than the details of his private life. This is not through lack of interest. Fascinating snippets of information emerge from his interviews:[3] endearing tales of childhood visits to a baseball match with his schoolteacher or insights about his feelings when forced to take boxing at college.[4] However, Chomsky is "really a hermit by nature"[5] and has repeatedly emphasized that his personal views are irrelevant to his scientific ideas; indeed, that "to the extent that a subject is significant and worth pursuing, it is not personalized."[6] For those who want personal glimpses beyond the following few notes, the book by Barsky (1997) and the interviews with Barsamian, MacFarquhar, and Peck are the best sources (see Bibliography).

Chomsky was born on December 7, 1928. From the age of two, he spent ten years in a progressive Deweyite school in Philadelphia, where there was a congenial emphasis on individual creativity. From there he moved on to a regimented and stifling high school, about which he claims to remember "virtually nothing."[7] Thereafter he attended the University of Pennsylvania where he met Zellig Harris,[8] a leading linguist and political theorist, who had a profound influence on his life. He graduated in 1949, with an undergraduate thesis about Modern Hebrew, that was later revised and extended as his Master's thesis.[9] That same year he married Carol Schatz,[10] a fellow student who has made a significant contribution to language and linguistics in her own right. He entered graduate school later the same year and in 1951 became one of the Society of Fellows at Harvard, from where he moved to the Massachusetts Institute of Technology (MIT) in 1955. He has been there ever since, although a large part of each year is devoted to traveling around the world giving countless lectures and interviews.

Apart from his major influence on linguistics, philosophy, and psychology, Chomsky has had a minor but not insignificant effect on a range of disciplines from anthropology to mathematics, from education to literary criticism. To understand this pervasive influence requires a grasp of the defining characteristics of Chomsky's scientific program of Generative Grammar, and some insight into the appeal of his social and political thought. What follows is an attempt to explain Chomsky's work by analyzing and putting into context the key contributions he has made to the study of language and the study of mind. This involves dealing with issues, some of them technical and profound, in linguistics, psychology, and philosophy. His work in all these areas has been systematically innovative and systematically controversial. Misunderstanding of his views is widespread in all three communities of scholars, and part of my aim is to explain why it is that he has been both adulated and vilified. In some instances the task is straightforward: the preconceptions that cause the misapprehensions are reasonably superficial and clear. In others it is harder to see why the hostility is so uncomprehending.

The book is intended to be accessible to everyone without the reader having to pursue the information given in the footnotes. However, for those who want them, detailed references, explanations, brief elaborations, and suggestions for further reading are collected together at the end of the book. In particular, all quotations are identified there and it should be possible to locate any source in a few moments. References are in all instances to Chomsky's work, unless explicit indication to the contrary is given. Much of Chomsky's work is extremely technical and I have attempted to simplify his ideas in the interest of comprehensibility. Nonetheless, I have occasionally included a brief technicality in order to make it clear to my professional colleagues what it is I am simplifying. In every case, it is worth emphasizing that the linguistic examples I cite will need mulling over, if their implications are to be fully grasped.

Chapter 1 begins by putting language and the study of language in a wider context as part of the scientific investigation of human nature. This involves a discussion of the structure of mind, with evidence drawn from studies of both normal and pathological cases of the dissociation of human faculties, and with language as the "mirror of the mind." This opening chapter is followed by a detailed and partly historical exposition of Chomsky's linguistic theorizing, which constitutes the bedrock on which the rest is built. The aim of this section is to give the reader some understanding of current theory by showing how we got where we are. An account is given of the ideas for which Chomsky is best known (deep and surface structure, for instance) and why they are no longer part of his current Minimalist framework; but most importantly, I try to give a flavor of the kind of argument that Chomsky has used in his work over the last fifty years. The next two chapters are devoted to the psychological and philosophical implications of Chomsky's work. Chapter 3 looks at the vexed question of what is meant by psychological reality, and provides evidence for it from language processing, from the child's acquisition of a first language, and from language breakdown in pathology. At the core of this chapter is a discussion of Chomsky's solution to "Plato's problem," the puzzle of how children can acquire their first language on the basis of so little evidence. Chapter 4 turns to the philosophical aspects of Chomsky's ideas, outlining his intellectual commitments to realism, mentalism, and naturalism, and explaining the controversies which have sparked so much debate in the philosophical community. The final chapter is devoted to a discussion of his political ideas and how these fit in intellectually with his "academic" work. Despite Chomsky's own disavowal of any very close connection, it is argued that there are fundamental ideas of rationality, creativity, and modularity which draw the disparate strands of his output together. The book ends with an annotated bibliography.

The task of summarizing Chomsky is daunting, and I am conscious of Leonardo da Vinci's aphorism that "abbreviators do injury to knowledge." Chomsky's output is vast: he has published nearly a hundred books, hundreds of articles, and written tens of thousands of letters. His mastery of a huge literature is awe-inspiring: in current affairs throughout the world, in politics, history, linguistics, philosophy, psychology, mathematics . . . there are few areas where he has no knowledge. To achieve this mastery of many fields demands "fanaticism" plus, in his words, the ability and dedication to "work like a maniac." It also takes immense courage, ceaseless energy, and the sacrifice of any leisure. He wrote: "It takes a big ego to withstand the fact that you're saying something different from everyone else." He views his own contribution as "pre-Galilean,"[11] though Berlinski is probably right to consider him "As big as Galileo."[12] At the end of the sixteenth century Galileo founded the experimental method which underpins the whole of modern science; at the end of the twentieth century Chomsky is generally viewed as the originator of the cognitive revolution which is beginning to extend that method to the study of the mind.

Not everyone shares this positive evaluation of him. The philosopher Richard Montague reportedly called him one of the "two great frauds of twentieth century science"[13] (the other was Einstein, so at least he was in good company); the linguist Paul Postal says that "everything he says is false . . . He will lie just for the fun of it";[14] he has been vilified as an "opportunist, . . . applauder of corruption, and apologist for government indifference to protests against war and colonialism";[15] he has been called the "great American crackpot" and "outside the pale of intellectual responsibility."[16] He has been repeatedly jailed for his political activism[17] and has frequently been the victim of death threats.[18] Even those who are basically sympathetic to his position sometimes accuse him of being simplistic, or "paranoid,"[19] or of showing "willful naïveté,"[20] and suspect that he sometimes wins arguments for the wrong reasons, wishing that he might "try admitting that, just sometimes, he has got it wrong."[21] As his wife somewhat ruefully put it: "one never wins an argument with Noam,"[22] even when, on reflection, one is convinced one is right. This polarization of opinion demands explanation, and one of the reasons for writing this book is to provide the foundations for such an explanation. Chomsky says: "You have a responsibility to explain why what you are doing is worth doing."[23] For me, his work is illuminating,[24] but I think it is under-appreciated and worth broadcasting more widely, so I have tried to distill the essence into a few brief chapters.

On heroes and influences

Most people *need* heroes to act as role models, whose exploits they can emulate or, more mundanely, simply use as a basis for defining the kind of activity it is appropriate, morally defensible, and at least partly feasible to follow. This is not the mindless homage of hero-worship, though the adulation Chomsky receives is often embarrassing.[25] Close scrutiny usually leads to the discovery that one's heroes – like everyone else in the world – have feet of clay, which can be an encouragement if it puts them on the same mundane plane as oneself. I am happy to admit that Chomsky is a hero for me. It does not follow that I always agree with him, though if I didn't agree with him on many issues, I almost certainly wouldn't have written this book: I do not identify with those who idolize political leaders because of their strength of leadership, irrespective of the direction in which they lead.

For Chomsky "Nobody is a hero,"[26] and he usually avoids answering questions about whom he admires,[27] though the list of those who have influenced him and whom he respects is lengthy. It includes anarchist thinkers like Mikhail Bakunin, Peter Kropotkin, and Rudolf Rocker; the left Marxist Anton Pannekoek; a long series of philosophers: Descartes, Humboldt, and Rousseau; John Dewey and Charles Sanders Peirce; more recently Wittgenstein,[28] Nelson Goodman, and W. v. O. Quine; linguists like Zellig Harris and Otto Jespersen; and libertarians like A. J. Muste and Bertrand Russell ("one of the very few people that I actually admire").[29] At a greater remove, it would doubtless include Galileo, Kant, and Newton. Some of the influences are less obvious than others: Ahad Ha-'am, a cultural Zionist at the turn of the century, whose work was later considered not only to be anti-Zionist, but to show "an excess of rationalism," was an early influence on both Chomsky and his parents.[30] His father, William Chomsky,[31] not only influenced him politically, but also exposed him early in life to classical Semitic philology: his book *Hebrew: the Eternal Language* (dedicated to Noam and his brother) appeared in the same year, 1957, as his son's *Syntactic Structures*, the accepted beginning of the Chomskyan revolution.

Despite his ability to overthrow the edifices he has himself created, there is a timelessness about his moral commitments and the intellectual foundations of his work, that clearly date to his childhood. His views are never adopted unthinkingly, and none of the influences is accepted uncritically. In linguistics as in politics what is striking is Chomsky's ability to see to the heart of issues; to extract that which is defensible and constructive and to dismiss that which is dishonest, immoral or irrational. In both domains he defends the insights of those whose general position he has no time for and criticizes the perceived failings of his intellectual allies. Moreover, he does it with grace and humor. Intellectually, he is perhaps closest in spirit, as well as achievement, to Darwin, who wrote to his friend and mentor Henslow: "I believe there exists, & I feel within me, an instinct for truth, or knowledge or discovery, of something [the] same nature as the instinct of virtue, & that our having such an instinct is reason enough for scientific researches without any practical results *ever* ensuing from them."[32]

1 The mirror of the mind

> One reason for studying language – and for me personally the most compelling reason – is that it is tempting to regard language, in the traditional phrase, as "a mirror of mind."
> (Chomsky, 1975a: 4)

Frogs are not like us.[1] They are better at catching flies but not, it seems, at explaining how they do it. The frog mind is narrowly specialized to control tasks such as locating small black specks, escaping predators, and finding mates, but not for reflecting on the ethics of eating insects or the issue of equal rights for toads.

This view of the limited intellectual capabilities of amphibians is unlikely to be controversial.[2] If I extended it to apes the reaction might be different, and it would clearly be false of humans. How do we know? Because humans can tell us so and the others cannot. Although having a language is not a prerequisite for having a mind, language is overwhelmingly our best evidence for the nature of mind. Language is definitional of what it is to be human, and the study of language is a way in to the study of the human, but not the frog, mind.

Despite the complexity and variety of animal communication systems, no other creature has language like ours. Although chimpanzees and bonobos[3] can be taught to manipulate an impressive array of signs and use them to communicate with us or with each other, human language, in particular the syntax of human language, is *sui generis*. As far as we know, even the singing of whales and the color communication of cuttle-fish have nothing like syntax. In one respect this uniqueness is trivial: the inherent interest of our abilities would not be diminished just because it turned out that our close genetic relatives had even more in common with us than we had previously suspected. But if we want to understand what we are – how we are unique – our linguistic ability is central, and Chomsky's work in generative grammar provides the most important and radical insights in this domain. He has achieved this by studying language with the rigor and the methodology of the hard sciences in combination with the philosophical insight of the Cartesian tradition in a way that had previously never been attempted.

In this chapter I look first at the implications of the assumption that linguistics should be part of the natural sciences, and then at the position of language in relation to the rest of cognition. This involves investigating a range of human abilities,[4] their interrelations and dissociations, the contrast between *knowledge* of language and the use of that knowledge, and taking a first glance at questions of innateness and the relation of language to thought.

Linguistics as a science

Linguistics had long been defined as the scientific study of language, but the science was restricted to taxonomy and a naïve methodology. Hockett, one of the leading figures of the American structuralism that Chomsky's revolution replaced, opens one of his early papers with the definitional claim that "linguistics is a classificatory science."[5] One of Chomsky's achievements has been to make plausible the claim that linguistics is scientific in the more interesting sense that it can provide not only explicit descriptions but also explanations for the classification. There are several strands to such a claim. The first is that linguistics provides a general theory explaining *why* languages are the way they are: each language is a particular example of a universal faculty of mind, whose basic properties are innate. The second is that the theory should spawn testable hypotheses: like a physicist or a biologist, the linguist manipulates the environment experimentally to see what happens and, crucially, he or she may be wrong. The experiments are usually not as high-tech as those in the hard sciences, but they allow for testing: if your analysis entails that English speakers should find *John speaks fluently English* as acceptable as *John speaks English fluently*, then it is wrong and must be replaced by a better one. A corollary of this emphasis on seeking testable explanations is that the central concern is *evidence* rather than *data*. Every linguist (a term which is ambiguous between theorist of language and polyglot) has suffered the question "So how many languages do you speak?" It is often hard to convince people that the answer doesn't really matter. Having a little knowledge of half a dozen languages is less useful than knowing one language with native proficiency. You may be reasonably fluent in French, for instance, without being quite sure whether the French equivalent of the unacceptable English sentence above is acceptable or not: "Jean parle couramment l'anglais." If you're not sure, your knowledge is of little more use than an unreliable balance. Even if I assure you that it is acceptable, and that this reflects a systematic difference between the two languages, this is still just another fact until I can use it as evidence for some particular theoretical assumption, at which point it may acquire vital importance for deciding between conflicting theories.

Linguistics before Chomsky (and in many cases even now) was preoccupied, like Linnaean botany or Victorian entomology, with achieving complete coverage of the respective fields. Examples are legion, from Hjelmslev's *Prolegomena*,[6] which begins with the claim that linguistic theory must permit descriptions which are "exhaustive," to current versions of Construction Grammar,[7] which criticizes the generative paradigm because "it doesn't allow the grammarian to account for absolutely everything in its terms." It is essential to collect enough data to guarantee representative coverage – missing out marsupials in a taxonomy of mammals would be a serious omission – but trying to achieve exhaustive coverage is a wild-goose chase, and such criticisms are misconceived. The set of facts is potentially infinite, but facts which can be used as evidence for some particular hypothesis are much harder to come by. Consider word order.[8]

Different languages have different word orders: in some, like English, sentences are typically of the form Subject Verb Object (SVO), so we say *Frogs eat flies*; in others, like Japanese, they are of the form Subject Object Verb (SOV), so the equivalent sentence would have the order *Frogs flies eat*; in yet others, like Arabic, they are of the form Verb Subject Object (VSO), with the order *Eat frogs flies*. Assuming that it makes sense to talk of different languages having different characteristic word orders, it was suggested some years ago that all the world's languages fell necessarily into one of these three types (SVO, SOV, and VSO). The suggestion was plausible because these are the three orders where the subject precedes the object which, given our own language background, feels logical. To test this claim it's no use just collecting more examples of languages like the ones mentioned: it's easy to find hundreds more languages that conform to the generalization. What is needed is a list of the world's languages sufficiently exhaustive to tell us whether there are any exceptions: languages with the word orders VOS, OVS, or OSV. As it happens, the suggestion was wrong: all these types do occur (although the last two in particular are extremely rare), so *all* the six logically possible orders are attested.[9] It follows that, as far as this particular observation is concerned, there is nothing more to be said. Whatever language one looks at next, it will fall into one of the six types listed, because there are no other logical possibilities, so every language will exemplify one of the possibilities we already know about. Even the signed languages[10] of the deaf manifest the same kind of word-order differences as spoken languages. Accordingly, if word order were the only consideration of interest, there would be no point in trekking off to the Highlands of New Guinea to search for another example of something we already have. Of course we still have innumerable interesting questions: why are some of these orders so rare? What other properties, if any, correlate with the word order manifested by a particular language? What happens when we consider indirect objects and adverbs, and other possible additions? It may well be that evidence about these issues will come precisely from as yet unknown languages, but to investigate these constructively we need more, and more complex, hypotheses. Our knowledge of language and languages is by now sufficiently complex that we are more likely to gain insight by looking in greater depth at well-studied languages than by looking superficially at relatively unknown ones. I spent a fascinating year learning and studying the Nupe language of Nigeria,[11] and have used the language ever since to check out various claims about the human faculty of language, but many of the things I want to check are beyond my Nupe abilities and I have to have recourse to my native intuitions in English or to the native intuitions of speakers of Nupe to settle the issue.

At this point you might rightly object that saying English is SVO is too simplistic, because many sentences diverge from this favored pattern. In *What do frogs eat?* or *Flies are what frogs eat*, the object appears at the beginning of the sentence, hence before the subject. Such orders occur systematically in English and cannot just be ignored, even if other deviations are characteristic only of poetry or archaic forms of the language and can perhaps be safely left out of consideration. For instance, in the saying *What the eye doesn't see, the heart doesn't grieve*, *the heart* is the object of *grieve*, so the expression means that what you don't see doesn't "grieve your heart." There is a sense in which such sayings are part of English, but to infer from this that English word order allows the object *either* to precede *or* to follow the verb would be grossly misleading, predicting that *Frogs flies eat* is on a par with *Frogs eat flies*; which it patently is not. Indeed, to bring the saying into conformity with their form of English, many people have changed it to *What the eye doesn't see, the heart doesn't grieve over*, thereby making *the heart* unambiguously the subject of *grieve*. This observation highlights an important and basic assumption of Chomskyan theory: the notion of language that is being investigated is the language of an individual, not the language of a community or a country or an era. This special notion is accordingly referred to as "I-language" (for "individual"),[12] and linguistics is viewed as part of cognitive psychology, an investigation of what an individual, any individual, knows in virtue of being a speaker of a language. It follows that if we are to describe accurately what our knowledge of English (or any other language) consists in, and if we are to explain why our knowledge takes the form it does and how we come by it, we need to separate out our idiosyncratic familiarity with poetic and archaic expressions and concentrate on the core knowledge reflected in our normal usage, however hard it may be to define precisely what that means.

There is a danger associated with the search for depth and explanation: looking for that narrow range of data which bear on a particular theoretical problem, one may overlook data which would be even more relevant if only one could recognize the fact. Choosing to ignore the example of *grieve* because it is archaic may deprive one of a source of useful evidence. In this situation one relies on a combination of factors to save one from egregious error: a knowledge of the literature outside one's immediate domain of interest, the correctives of colleagues and the criticisms of rivals, and serendipity. Amassing new data from as wide a range of languages as possible is a valuable enterprise, indeed an invaluable enterprise, provided that it is remembered that all data need to be analyzed and that there are no data without some kind of theory: that is, the facts need to be described within some framework that makes them useful to other linguists. Knowing that *tànkpólózì èwã èdzúzì* is the Nupe for "toads catch spiders" is of little use to you unless you know what the words mean, so that you can tell which is subject, which verb, and which object. Even the notions "subject," "verb," and "object," which I have been taking for granted, on the assumption that an example or two would make it clear what I meant, are problematic. Some linguists use them, some do not; and those who do use them need to account for the fact that the interpretation of such categories is not consistent across all sentences: there is only a partial match between the grammar and the meaning, as should be apparent from a moment's reflection on the different interpretations given to the subject *John* in *John broke a leg* and *John broke an egg*.[13]

Like physics, but unlike logic or literary criticism, linguistics is an empirical science. That is, on a Chomskyan interpretation, which takes the speaker's mentally represented grammar to be the correct focus for investigation, it makes sense to claim that one analysis is right and another wrong. Every time a linguist describes a sentence or postulates a principle, he or she is making innumerable empirically testable predictions. Those linguists who claimed that subjects precede objects in all languages were simply wrong: interestingly wrong, because the refutation of their claim has led to greater understanding of the nature of language, but wrong. By contrast, a literary critic who claims that "a song is a form of linguistic disobedience,"[14] or a logician who says that "nothing is both an X and a non-X" are not formulating hypotheses to be checked out and tested by their colleagues. The observations may be useful, insightful, even inspired, but they are not empirical.

The nature of idealization

If science aims to explain a few things rather than to describe everything, some things (such as poetic survivals) have to be left out. When Galileo[15] devised the law of uniform acceleration for falling bodies, either by dropping weights from the leaning tower of Pisa or rolling balls down an inclined plane, he ignored the effects of wind resistance and friction. In fact, we often don't even know if he carried out the experiments he described: they were thought experiments that relied for their validity as much on logical argumentation as precise observation. This was not sloppy experimental practice or ignorance of the effect of the air on falling feathers, rather it was a sensible idealization. The effect of wind resistance or friction is irrelevant to the generalization Galileo was seeking to establish. All of science is characterized by the need to exclude from consideration those factors which, while undeniably real, are not pertinent to the issue under investigation. We know that heavenly bodies are not mathematical points, but they can be treated as such for the purposes of gravitational theory. We know that Boyle's law applies to "ideal" gases,[16] and that the gases we observe appear less well-behaved, but we do not take this observation to impugn Boyle's discovery or to invalidate the idealization. In general, the role of scientific experimentation is to get us closer to the truth, to the ideal, by eliminating irrelevant extraneous considerations. In other words idealization reveals what is real, but is usually hidden from view by a mass of detail. All scientists accept the reality of the inverse-square law, whether it is being used to explain the intensity of the light reaching us from a star, of the sound reaching us from a jet engine, or the attractive force of a magnet, even though the messiness of experiments means that their measurements never mirror it exactly, giving "a distortion of reality" in Chomsky's phrase.[17]

One of the idealizing claims in linguistics that has caused the greatest misunderstanding is Chomsky's much quoted passage on the first page of his classic book *Aspects of the Theory of Syntax* that "Linguistic theory is concerned primarily with an *ideal* speaker-listener, in a completely homogeneous speech-community . . . [who] is unaffected by such grammatically irrelevant conditions as memory limitations, distractions, shifts of attention and interest, and errors (random or characteristic) in applying his knowledge of the language in actual performance."[18] There are two issues: first, is such idealization defensible? Second, if it is, which idealizations are likely to be fruitful and not beg important questions? The answer to the first question is self-evident: all science involves idealization, which "frees the explorer from irrelevant demands,"[19] and it is irrational to attempt to avoid it. When we contemplate real speaker-listeners (or gases) in their full complexity, we usually fail to see the principles which underlie their behavior, simply because of interfering factors of one kind or another. To see those (real) principles in full clarity it is necessary that some things be fruitfully ignored. A major stumbling block for many working in the humanities is that what is fruitfully ignored in the linguistic study of language may be precisely what they are interested in: the language of poetry, for instance. While acknowledging that many aspects of language remain outside the domain of scientific inquiry, Chomskyan linguistics has demonstrated that it is fruitful to incorporate some aspects into natural science. Even here a legitimate focus of argument and disagreement arises with regard to the second question: what idealizations are to be made? In *Aspects* Chomsky claimed that such phenomena as limitations of memory, tiredness, and minor variations between speakers are irrelevant to our understanding of the notion "knowledge of language." English grammars do not in general include a statement saying: "Insert 'um' here if you are tired or uncertain,"[20] even though languages differ in terms of the hesitation noises they allow, and even though the places where such phenomena can occur are not entirely random, but can provide interesting clues about language production. If you say *um* while speaking French, for instance, you give yourself away as a foreigner (the French say something like [oe]); and *um* in English is much more likely to occur after *of*, rather than before it, in phrases such as *in the middle of Texas*. Such examples of idealization are relatively unproblematic, so let's consider a somewhat more vexed case by anticipating the discussion in chapter 3 of the child's acquisition of its first language.

First language acquisition takes place within a particular window of opportunity known as the critical period,[21] which lasts for a few years and ends (at the latest) at puberty. Given what we know about children's development, it sometimes comes as a shock to read that first language acquisition is idealized to "instantaneity."[22] How can a process which extends over several years be sensibly treated as though it took no time at all? The paradox is only apparent not real. Although there is a striking uniformity across children learning their first language in respect of the stages of development they go through, they do nonetheless differ from each other. For instance, in the course of mastering the system of negation,[23] one child may form negative sentences by using an initial *no*, while another may use a final *no*, giving the contrast between *no like cabbage* and *like cabbage no*. Despite this developmental difference, both children will end up with the same system of negation in which they use the correct adult form: *I don't like cabbage*. As far as we can tell, the early difference in the children's systems has *no* effect at all on the grammar they end up with. If the focus of our interest is on what's known as "the logical problem of language acquisition" – children's transition from apparently having no knowledge of a language to being able to speak and understand it like adults – then we have support for the idealization to instantaneity, which says that the different stages children go through in the language acquisition process are of no import to their ultimate psychological state. Of course, it may turn out that this surprising claim is false. It might be that sufficiently sophisticated tests of grammaticality judgment, or investigations of neural firing, or subsequent historical changes in the language concerned, showed that the two children's grammars were crucially different, and different in ways that could explain other mysterious facts about knowledge of language. It's possible, but there is (as yet) no evidence, and the idealization is accordingly justified: it leads us to an understanding of one aspect of the real system we are studying.

There is of course no guarantee that the idealizations made are the most fruitful ones or even that they are not pernicious. Chomsky talks of "the dangers of illegitimate idealization that isolates some inquiry from factors that crucially affect its subject matter, a problem familiar in the sciences."[24] Many sociolinguists feel that Chomsky's idealization to the homogeneity of the speech community – that is, that there is no significant variation from speaker to speaker – comes in the "illegitimate" category. A recent example is provided by the pained claim that "the idealization program in practice means that at least for now we should not be studying any community where we perceive a considerable degree of 'mixing' or 'impurity'."[25] That is, of course, essentially all communities, with the implication being that nothing should be studied. This would obviously be ridiculous, but fortunately it reveals a deep misunderstanding. We should study whatever promises to cast light on the hypothesis we are currently entertaining, and variational data may well cast such light when properly interpreted. The force of Chomsky's idealization is that the variation is not necessary to an understanding of the human language faculty. In particular, it is not the case, contrary to what the writer goes on to say, that we have only a "limited range of data":[26] we are drowning in data; what we need is clearly articulated hypotheses for which some subset of these data can constitute evidence. If the hypothesis one is interested in itself crucially involves variation, then obviously the idealization to homogeneity is pernicious, but Chomsky is preoccupied with the general properties of the language faculty: what we, as speakers of any language, know and how we come by that knowledge. No one denies that there is variation, but to claim that we need to "look for ways of documenting it in order to understand language as part of the human condition"[27] is doubly misleading: first, because it suggests that such documentation will provide understanding; second, because no theory of "the human condition" which would throw up testable hypotheses is suggested. Worse, there is an implicit suggestion that it would be impossible for a child to learn language unless it was confronted with the contradictory information of dialect mixture, false starts and the like. This seems inherently implausible and no evidence for such a claim is ever presented.[28] Despite these strictures, I shall suggest in chapter 4 that variation does in fact have philosophical implications which are relevant to Chomsky's program.

While idealization is necessary, it must be emphasized that idealizing away from, for instance, speech errors, still allows one to use performance mistakes such as slips of the tongue as *evidence* for the nature of the knowledge that is the focus of enquiry. All our claims about the nature of our linguistic knowledge, like our claims about quantum physics or molecular biology, have to be supported by evidence, and where that evidence comes from is limited only by our imagination and ingenuity. On the assumption that our knowledge of language in part determines how we say what we do say: that "the rules of grammar enter into the processing mechanisms,"[29] malfunctions of the system can provide evidence for the nature of the rules of grammar. Vicki Fromkin illustrates this possibility on the basis of the regular formation of the past tense in English.[30] The usual rule is that you add *-ed* to the verb, producing *talked* from *talk*, *kissed* from *kiss*, and so on, though for a considerable number of irregular verbs, there are complications: *come* gives *came* rather than *comed*, and we say *left* rather than *leaved*. She then cites a host of slips of the tongue involving over-regularization such as *the last I knowed about it, he haved to have it, if he swimmed,* indicating that normal adult speakers of the language don't just access a store of learned items, but that they actually use a rule of the kind that linguists, for independent reasons, posit as part of the grammar. The example is elementary, but it puts into perspective the objection that the Chomskyan framework ignores a crucial range of data. In fact, a major and innovative characteristic of Chomsky's linguistics is its exploitation of the previously neglected fact that we are able to recognize immediately that some sentences are ungrammatical: we have what one might call "negative knowledge." Hamlet can tell Ophelia that *I loved you not,* but we know we have to say *I didn't love you*; Othello can ask Desdemona *Went he hence now?*, which we understand easily enough, though we know we have to rephrase it in current English as "Did he go?" We can say equally well both *I asked the way to the school* and *I inquired the way to the school,* but whereas *I asked the number of people in the class* is fine, *I inquired the number of people in the class* is odd. We should be as surprised by the fact that we have these intuitions as by the fact that apples fall down not up, or that the sea has waves. Newton was not the first to notice apples falling, but his insight that *why* apples fall is in need of an explanation led ultimately to his theory of gravity. Chomsky was not the first to notice the elementary facts I have cited here, but his insight that our intuitions can tell us something profound about the human mind is of comparable importance.

Common sense

The similarity of linguistics to the other sciences becomes salient as soon as one tries even to demarcate the field of study. Our common-sense understanding of the world gives a useful hint as to the domains that we might expect to be illumined by scientific research, but there should be no expectation that the categories of common sense should carry over intact to a scientific theory. The case of language is no different in this respect from the case of physics or biology. We do not deride physical theories because physicists' ideas about sunsets deviate from common sense, or biological theories because they do not provide an account of the general properties of pets. Likewise we should not attack linguistic theories because they have no room for traditional notions of "language," as revealed in such usage as *Chinese is the oldest language,* or *The English language has been spoken in Britain for 1000 years,* or *She uses the most appalling language.* These remarks may be true, and they are clearly about language, but they are not observations of linguistics, because they follow from no linguistic theory. More importantly, it is almost certainly the case that there is *no* theory of "language" in the sense in which it is being used in these examples. Similarly, *The book fell off the table* is a statement about the physical world, but it is not a statement couched in the language of physics, and there are no physical laws[31] which would enable one to differentiate such a remark from *The book fell on the floor*: an observation that could truly describe exactly the same situation. Here too, it is almost certainly the case that there is no physical theory of books or of falling: these are just not domains which lend themselves to theory construction, however salient they may be to us as humans. The other side of this coin is that linguists, again like physicists, need to use concepts and vocabulary that are alien to non-linguists or non-physicists. The technical terminology of generative grammar can be as startlingly opaque as the vocabulary of quantum physics; only the mathematical underpinning is less forbidding. In both domains science and common sense frequently come apart, but they share the need to break problems down into a manageable size.

Modularity

Humans are complex. From this it follows by virtue of the meaning of "complex" that we have internal structure, and the mind is one part of that structure. But the mind itself is not an undifferentiated general-purpose machine: it is compartmentalized in such a way that different tasks are subserved by different mechanisms. The mind is "modular."[32] Sight and smell, taste and touch, language and memory, are all distinct from each other, from our moral and social judgment, and from our expertise in music or mathematics. In many cases, we even have a good idea of where in the brain these different functions of the mind are localized, though the question of localization is independent of the fact of their modular status. Even if we did not know which bit of the brain was responsible for interpreting the messages from our eyes and ears, we would still have no hesitation in separating vision from hearing.

It has been recognized for two thousand years that the language faculty can be selectively impaired as the result of damage to different parts of the brain,[33] but it is only since the middle of the nineteenth century that we have had systematic evidence for the "lateralization" of language:[34] that is, that our linguistic ability is largely the preserve of the left hemisphere of the brain, while visuo-spatial abilities are largely the responsibility of the right hemisphere. In each case it is necessary to generalize: both language and vision are so rich and diverse that it would be naïve to expect a single simple relation between mind and brain. Parts of the visual system responsible for the perception of color, shape, and motion involve interaction among many parts of the brain,[35] and face processing appears to show some sharing of responsibilities between the hemispheres, with the right side concentrating on holistic patterns and the left on individual features. Similarly, different linguistic functions are typically localized differently, with the left hemisphere taking the major responsibility for syntax, but semantic and pragmatic processes also invoking the right hemisphere. Irrespective of the detail of their neural localization, it is uncontroversial that different parts of the brain are "domain-specific" in that they are dedicated to sight, to smell, and to the other senses. It would make little sense to postulate abstract structures that are neutral as between sight and taste, for instance, as the incoming stimuli are radically different in kind, and the representations the mind constructs out of them are likewise idiosyncratic: there is little[36] in common between the perception of purple and the smell of soap.

In Jerry Fodor's influential work (inspired in part by Chomsky's),[37] human cognition is treated in terms of a basic dichotomy between the "central system" and a number of "input systems." The senses – taste, sight, smell, hearing, and touch – are dedicated input systems each of which constitutes one module (or cluster of modules) of the mind, and feed into the central system, which is responsible for rational thought, problem solving and what philosophers call the "fixation of belief." (Such beliefs need not be profound. On the basis of the smell of burning, the sight of smoke and one's memory of similar past events, one comes to *believe* that the toast is burning.) Fodorian modules have a number of well-defined characteristics: they are specialized for particular domains, they operate fast and mandatorily (one has no choice but to hear sounds one is exposed to), they are "hard-wired" with a particular part of the brain dedicated to each, their structure and function are largely innately determined, and they are "informationally encapsulated"; that is, they operate without interference from central control. Fodor makes two further controversial claims not shared by Chomsky:[38] that language is an input system analogous to those devoted to the senses, and that the central system is essentially unstructured and putatively uninvestigable. The reason for this pessimism about the central system is that you can solve problems by drawing on your knowledge from every conceivable domain: the celebrated physicist Richard Feynman got his initial inspiration for solving a problem in quantum theory from seeing a cafeteria plate wobble as someone tossed it spinning in the air. If you can make a connection between "the axial wobble of a cafeteria plate and the abstract quantum-mechanical notion of spin,"[39] it seems likely that your mind can make connections of any conceivable kind. We presumably don't have bits of our brain specialized for dealing with spinning plates, still less for quantum mechanics, so this suggests a construct of awesome complexity. Nevertheless, the pessimistic conclusion is unnecessary; a more appropriate one is that the central system, while internally structured, must allow essentially unlimited interaction among its components in a way that Fodorian modules definitely do not.

The most important criterion for modularity in Fodor's sense is informational encapsulation, which says that the internal workings of any module are oblivious to the workings of the central system. The classic example is provided by the

Müller-Lyer optical illusion, in which two lines, flanked by inward or outward
pointing arrow-heads are displayed:

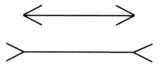

The visual system perceives the lower line as longer than the upper line. Even if
you take a ruler and convince yourself that the two lines are indeed of identical
length, your eyes still interpret them as being different. That is, the working
of the visual system is impervious to the explicit knowledge provided by the
central system. Examples of this kind are legion: for instance, the visual system seems to have two distinct modes, one accessible to consciousness and
one not.[40] When we move around in the world, with the unerring accuracy
characteristic of normal unthinking activity, our movements are subserved by
a system inaccessible to conscious control, indeed (as with the centipede in
the rhyme) consciousness makes things worse. In an interesting experiment,
subjects were presented with two discs in an array where a visual illusion (the
Titchener illusion[41]) made judgment of their relative size problematic, and were
asked to grasp the left-hand disc if it was larger than the right hand one. Subjects
were consistently wrong in their conscious visual judgment of how large the
disc was, but measurements of their grasping hand as it reached for the disk
demonstrated that unconsciously they must know the correct size, because the
configuration of their hands reflected the actual size of the disc with considerable
accuracy.

   A linguistic example of such encapsulation comes from research on memory
by Dan Schacter and his colleagues.[42] Subjects were first read a list of words and
were subsequently presented with a written list containing some of the words
they had heard and some they had not. Judgments in such experiments are
notoriously unreliable. If you have heard *sharp, point, prick*, and *pain*, you are
likely to "remember" hearing *needle*, even if you have not in fact heard *needle*
at all. But your brain really does know. Schacter used a PET[43] scan to monitor
the flow of blood in different regions of the brain while subjects were deciding
whether or not they had heard the words before. This showed equivalent activity
near the hippocampus[44] both for words that had been heard and for those that
had not. But for those words that *had* been heard previously, there was additional
activity in the left temporo-parietal region, an area responsible for processing
auditory information. The hippocampus is generally associated with memory,
the major preserve of the central system, and the left temporal lobe is the major
locus of the language faculty. It seems then that the internal workings of the
language module are inaccessible to the central system in precisely the way
modularity predicts.

Chomsky's work over several decades has provided a wealth of evidence that the language faculty does indeed constitute a separate module, akin in many respects to any other organ of the body. Moreover, he has provided more, and more rigorous, evidence about the precise internal structure of this module than has been provided for any other domain (except perhaps vision[45]). However, it is important to differentiate his position from Fodor's with respect to the two ancillary claims mentioned above. First, language is not merely an input system, in the way that vision or taste are, but is crucially also an *output* system geared to the expression and communication of thought.[46] Moreover, this output system is obviously correlated with the input system: no one can speak only one language and understand only another, different one. What is common to the two systems is necessarily part of a cognitive, central system; hence much of language is "central." Second, the "central system" (to the extent that it makes sense to postulate a single entity of this kind) is itself intricately structured: it is multiply modular in that a number of human abilities which go beyond the limits of purely sensory perception are apparently independent of each other. For instance, we have separate mechanisms underlying our ability to recognize faces, to provide moral judgments, and to evaluate social relations.

There are other areas in which Chomskyan and Fodorian modularity diverge. Chomsky suggests that the language faculty interprets everything the external world throws at it, not just well-formed sentences and phrases, but even the squeaking of a door.[47] This rather startling suggestion implies a view of language which is incompatible with the domain-specificity of (Fodorian) modularity. As Chomsky observes, the principles of language and the principles of vision seem to be "entirely distinct."[48] On Fodor's account this distinctness means that the systems are sensitive to different kinds of input. On Chomsky's account, each system may have access to a wider range of inputs, but what it can do with that input is determined by the differences in the principles that characterize that module. As the language system is in part parasitic on the auditory or visual system (for spoken or signed language respectively) it is difficult to decide at what stage the sensitivity to a particular form of stimulus makes the transition from auditory/visual representations to linguistic representations, or indeed whether the linguistic system plays any role in integrating information into the central system. As numerous writers have observed, coughs can be used with communicative intent, much as language can, so Chomsky's position is part of a long tradition. It is also coherent, and there is no doubt that one processes the squeak of a door or the swaying of a tree branch. However, I know of no evidence that such processing involves the linguistic system as such, unless the central system's operating language (the language of thought[49]) is largely the same as the natural language one knows, in which case such processing does involve the linguistic system, even if only trivially so.

One might object that this multiplication of autonomous modules is unnecessary, and that life would be simpler if we were provided with a single general-purpose processor. It might seem simpler, but we know that it would also be wrong. For example, evidence that humans come into the world supplied with a face-recognition module is now overwhelming.[50] Thus infants a few hours old respond preferentially to faces and "learn" to recognize them with markedly greater speed, generality, and facility than they recognize animals or plants. Likewise, there is very considerable evidence for a "theory-of-mind" module, whose operation is prerequisite to the understanding of other people, and whose absence (e.g. in autism[51]) gives rise to a range of pathological behaviors. For instance, autistic children (and indeed normal children at an early age) are incapable of recognizing the fact that another person's representation of the world may differ from their own, and so systematically misinterpret situations involving false belief. The classic demonstration of this is given by the Sally-Anne task.[52] In one version of this test, the subject and another observer watch while the experimenter hides a toy. The observer is then sent out of the room and, in full view of the subject, the toy is moved from its first position and hidden in a new position. After ensuring that the subject was aware of where the toy was first hidden and of when the observer was last present, he or she is then asked where the observer will look for the toy on returning to the room. From about the age of four, normal people indicate the first hiding place. Children under the age of four, and autistic subjects, usually indicate the second hiding place, *where the toy actually is*. That is, they are unable to entertain the idea that someone else could have a representation of the world which deviates from reality, they cannot understand "false belief." The standard explanation for this phenomenon is in terms of the absence or malfunctioning of the theory-of-mind module (more accurately a theory of other minds), a component of the mind that enables you to take someone else's point of view irrespective of whether that point of view conforms to reality.

It is an interesting empirical issue to determine the relations, mental and physical, among the various components of the human organism. Is the theory-of-mind module autonomous or dependent on the language faculty (or *vice versa*)?[53] Is the language faculty autonomous or dependent on intelligence, or age, or eye color, or something else? The range of possibilities is vast. Fortunately the range of evidence is also vast. The best comes from dissociations, especially double dissociations.

Double dissociation

Respiration and digestion, locomotion and reproduction are clearly independent of each other, and are served by autonomous if interacting organs. This independence is seen most clearly when things go wrong in illness or disease.

Breathing problems do not necessarily hamper one's digestion; asthmatics can have children; marathon runners may be infertile: the functions "dissociate." As with the workings of the body, so with the workings of the mind: dissociation is not restricted to the body below the neck. One can be blind without being deaf, deaf without being blind, and so on for all the faculties with which we are endowed. Because our ears and eyes are separate organs, the dissociation of deafness and blindness is unsurprising, even though the cause of deafness or blindness may in some cases be due to damage to a different organ, the brain. That is, we expect the failure of a particular component to lead to a particular deficit, even if, in the case of the brain, the complexity is so great that we may see a variety of different symptoms arising from the failure of a single part.

More interestingly, these faculties are themselves independent of intelligence. Despite their disability, the deaf and the blind have the same intellectual capacity as the hearing and the sighted: the *Oxford English Dictionary* definition of *deaf* as "dull, stupid; absurd" is happily marked as obsolete. This independence of different faculties is often masked, as the damage that causes blindness or deafness may simultaneously affect other abilities, but the occurrence of the gifted blind and the retarded sighted demonstrates that the senses and the intellect can dissociate in either direction: they are "doubly dissociable."[54]

The notion of double dissociation is important. If we consider the correlation of two properties, say sex and hemophilia, there are four logically possible combinations: being male and hemophilic, being male and non-hemophilic, being female and non-hemophilic, and being female and hemophilic. In fact, the last category is non-existent: although females can transmit hemophilia to their male offspring, they are themselves never sufferers. In other words, being female entails being non-hemophilic, there is only a single dissociation not a double dissociation, and the properties are only partially independent of each other.

An example of double dissociation can be found in certain pathological reactions to faces. To identify someone as your wife, for instance, involves the interaction of (at least) two components: the visual system, in particular the module responsible for face recognition, and some mental procedure responsible for the cognitive and emotional reaction to the output of this system, a representation in one's memory of the face of the person concerned. In certain rare pathological conditions, either one of these strands may be impaired. In prosopagnosia, the perceptual process of face recognition is defective, and sufferers exhibit bizarre behavior of the kind documented in the title case study in *The Man Who Mistook His Wife for a Hat*. Oliver Sacks's patient was unable to distinguish faces from similarly shaped entities, but as soon as he heard his wife's voice, he could recognize her for who she was; it was only one part of his visual system, in particular his processing of faces, that was defective, and his memory and emotional responses were otherwise fine. The converse of this case is provided by Capgras's Delusion.[55] In this equally rare condition, the face-recognition process is perfect, but it evokes *no* emotional response and the identification of the person "recognized" is therefore disbelieved by the central system. That is, the sufferer is convinced that the person whom he has recognized *looks like* his wife, but is simultaneously convinced that this person is an impostor, because there is no appropriate emotional response. The outcome can be extreme, even resulting in an attack on the person who is deemed to be impersonating the one whose face has been recognized. Unlike the case of hemophilia, the two properties in this example are independent of each other, so that all four logical combinations occur, though someone with both prosopagnosia and Capgras's Delusion would be in such a parlous condition that it might be hard to determine what was wrong with them. In principle, however, it would be possible even then to determine the facts of the matter by brain-imaging techniques, which could identify different sources for the disabilities.

Evidence for modularity can also be found in the normal case and not just when things go wrong. Our senses, our language, and all our cognitive abilities can dissociate. Intelligence is no guarantee of morality; emotional depth and sensitivity can coexist with aesthetic dullness. It is as though there were many independent but interacting organs concentrated in the head. Chomsky has strikingly suggested that, just as the heart and the rest of the circulatory system are organs with their own structure and functions, language is a kind of "mental organ" interacting with other mental organs.[56] Like the circulatory system, language is common to the species; like the circulatory system, it develops largely under genetic control, rather than being the fruit of learning or manipulation; like the circulatory system it is subject to impairment or failure independently of other organs. If this analogy is correct, the autonomy of language, and hence its dissociability from other faculties of mind, is predicted.

This observation is important because there is a long tradition which views language as a manifestation of intelligence and hence not dissociable from it. The most clearly expressed views of this type are those of Jean Piaget and his followers, who argued that there are cognitive prerequisites to the acquisition, and hence to the possession, of language.[57] The idea was that the normal development of language was parasitic on the prior mental development of such abilities as "seriation" and "conservation." In order to acquire such linguistic structures as correct word order or the passive, children were supposed to have reached a level of cognitive development at which they could carry out tasks such as putting items in ascending order of size (seriation), or judging that the amount of liquid poured from a tall thin glass into a short fat one remained the same (conservation). Such views are no longer tenable, as there are many cases of the double dissociation between linguistic and cognitive functioning which demonstrate their autonomy.[58] Two kinds of case will suffice as illustrations.

William's syndrome is a condition (infantile hypercalcemia) in which children have a variety of genetically conditioned physical characteristics: "an elfin-like face, with heavy orbital ridge, temporal dimples, full cheeks, retroussé nose, flat nasal bridge, flared nostrils, stellate iris pattern, wide mouth, and irregular dentition," according to the standard account.[59] These physical characteristics co-occur with a striking contrast between their general cognitive functioning and their linguistic ability. Typically, William's syndrome children have an IQ in the "mild to moderate" range of disability, but are extremely fluent in their use of complex language patterns. In early discussion of William's syndrome children, leading experts claimed that: "components of language functioning are achieved in William's syndrome in the absence of the purported cognitive underpinnings."[60] That is, these children display a mastery of language patterns – the use of passive constructions, comparatives, and so on – that had been supposed to be dependent on the prior intellectual achievement of being able to order physical items in a series, or pass conservation tasks. But they fail such cognitive tasks, demonstrating that the level of intelligence required for language acquisition had been grossly overestimated. In brief, linguistic ability and intellectual ability dissociate. Since those early claims it has become apparent that the asymmetry between language and cognition which is typical of William's syndrome is much less drastic than was previously thought. Annette Karmiloff-Smith points out first, that William's syndrome children are typically less severely cognitively impaired than was believed; second that there are "subtle impairments to all aspects of their language as well as the relation between language and other aspects of cognition."[61] While these observations make the claim of dissociation less clear-cut, it still seems to be true that there is no direct correlation between intelligence and knowledge of language.

Persuasive evidence of this is provided by the case of a man that Ianthi Tsimpli and I have documented over many years.[62] Christopher is a flawed genius. He lives in sheltered accommodation because he is unable to look after himself. He cannot reliably find his way around, and he has poor hand–eye coordination, so that everyday tasks like shaving or doing up his buttons are tedious chores. He fails to conserve number (a task which is within the capabilities of most five-year-olds),[63] and he has many of the characteristics of autism. Yet he can read, write, translate, and communicate in some twenty or more languages. Christopher is a *savant*: someone with general disability but, in Howe's felicitous phrase, "fragments of genius."[64] More particularly, he is a clear example of the dissociation of intelligence from linguistic ability.

The converse situation to these two cases, that is, where the language faculty is impaired in the presence of normal intelligence, is both more frequent and better documented. Examples occur as the result of either disease or genetic defect. The simplest and most common case is provided by stroke victims who lose their language ability but may retain other intellectual functions.[65]

Someone suffering from aphasia in this way may manifestly retain his or her intelligence in the absence of linguistic ability. A developmental example of linguistic disability in the presence of normal intelligence can be seen in the now widely documented cases of children with Specific Language Impairment (SLI).[66] There is a huge variety of manifestations of the condition, but the major generalization is that these children have great difficulty learning the linguistic processes that are characteristic of the adult language (and that their unaffected contemporaries master with ease), even though they can understand the conceptual correlates of these linguistic processes. For example, time and tense are related but not equivalent; so an SLI child might show perfectly normal understanding of the temporal relations marked by the use of *yesterday*, *today*, and *tomorrow*, but say things like *What did fell off the chair?*, *Which cat Mrs. White stroked?*, *Which coat was Professor Plum weared?*, showing a seriously defective control of the tense system. Their comprehension is fine, their grammar is deficient.

Modules and quasi-modules

One of the reasons why Chomsky has consistently dissociated himself from Fodor's view of modularity is because he does not share Fodor's pessimism about the inscrutability of the central system. Although Chomsky has spoken only in general terms about the properties of such domains as moral judgment, face recognition, and theory of mind, he is sympathetic to the claim that the central system should be fractionated roughly along the lines described above. To account for such a picture, Ianthi Tsimpli and I suggested a distinction between "modules," corresponding roughly to Fodor's input systems, and "quasi-modules,"[67] relating to domains like mathematics,[68] moral judgment, and theory of mind. Like modules, quasi-modules are domain-specific, they operate fast and mandatorily, they are subserved by particular neural architecture, and hence they allow for the manifestation of double dissociation. For instance, autistic people, who are characterized by a defective theory of mind, may be of normal intelligence but be unable to carry out false-belief tasks; whereas sufferers from Down's syndrome characteristically have severely reduced intelligence and delayed language, but have no problem with theory-of-mind tasks.[69]

Despite these parallels, quasi-modules differ in two ways from modules. First, they don't just provide input to the central system, they are rather sub-parts of the central system; second, as a corollary of this, the vocabulary over which their operations are defined is (at least in part) conceptual rather than perceptual. Just as different Fodorian modules are partly defined in terms of the stimuli they are sensitive to – light waves for vision or sound waves for audition – so quasi-modules are partly defined by the kind of representation they are sensitive to.[70] In the current context, the relevant representations are "second-order" or "meta-representations,"[71] in the sense that they don't just express a belief but, in the process of expressing their own belief, they attribute a belief to someone else. It might appear that this theory-of-mind quasi-module is just "central" with no more to be said about it, but its domain of operation is more circumscribed than this suggests, and circumscribed in just the way input systems are. Consider one example: theory-of-mind processes are domain-specific in that only a subset of second-order representations are relevant to them. Some second-order representations attribute not beliefs but simply alternative points of view in the literal spatial sense: if I went round to your side of the table, I could see the cards in your hand that I cannot now see. Virtually all people, including autistic subjects, can adopt the perspective of someone who happens to be situated in a different location; what is hard or impossible for autists is the attribution of beliefs, in particular false beliefs, to other people.

Examples of pathological dissociations of the kind described here are rare, though as in the physical sciences, extreme cases may provide us with the deepest insights. Nature's experiments enable us to understand the effects of the relevant variables in a way that is necessary to all scientific inquiry, but which it would be unethical to manipulate deliberately. Such cases are particularly valuable in helping us to tease apart whether we are dealing with mental as opposed to physical impairment, as the human organism is so tightly integrated that deficits of one kind tend to co-occur with deficits of the other. Even when we are convinced that we are dealing with mental phenomena, such dissociations shed light on the more general issue of the possible interdependence of modular functions and general cognitive processes.

Intelligence and "learning"

No one ever raises the question whether there are "cognitive prerequisites" to vision or smell or face recognition. A certain level of cognitive ability is essential for tasks like playing chess which involve learning, but there are no such prerequisites for developing the ability to see or touch. That is, we do not "learn" how to see in color or in 3-D, even though the development of three-dimensional vision takes place only around the age of sixteen to eighteen weeks. We obviously need some visual input for the process whereby we become able to see in this way to be triggered: being brought up in total darkness will guarantee that one sees not at all, hence not in 3-D or in color. Similarly, we need to be exposed to faces for the appropriate development of the face-recognition module to be triggered; and we need to be exposed to examples of language in order to acquire normal knowledge of a language. But none of this involves the kind of cognitive activity required to learn how to play chess or solve differential equations, or understand linguistics.[72]

One of the many areas where common sense and scientific understanding part company is in the role ascribed to "learning," a concept which has a role in every-day discourse, but is entirely irrelevant in domains where we are able to develop scientific theories. It is a truism that words in common use like "liquid" and "life" fail to correspond to well-defined terms in biology or physics. Glass may techni-cally be a liquid because of its ability to flow, but this certainly doesn't jibe with everyday notions of liquid. In the case of "learning," Chomsky's claim is not just that the lay and scientific notions differ in the way that lay and scientific notions of "liquid" differ, but that nothing in science corresponds to the lay notion of "learn," nor should be expected to. That is, on the assumption that modular abili-ties develop on the basis of our genes and our environment, there is no role left for traditional notions of learning. It follows that, to the extent that various versions of modularity are tentative steps towards a scientific understanding of human abilities, we should not expect to find evidence for anything akin to learning.

Modularity (or the process of modularization[73]) has the evolutionary benefit that it results in an organism which has at its disposal a range of abilities which it can deploy independently of intelligence. The case of language is somewhat different from that of other putative modules in that it is evident from the existence of languages other than our own that a certain amount of language is acquired on the basis of interaction with the environment: it is "learnt." However, as we shall see in more detail later, the most fundamental aspects of language are universal, suggesting that they can be factored out of the learning equation. In these areas we do not expect there to be differences between individuals, whether they are speakers of different languages or the same language. To give a simple example: we do not need to learn that our language contains nouns and verbs: all languages contain nouns and verbs. What we need to learn is which noises our language associates with particular examples of them. To the extent that language is a module then, we would expect learning to be irrelevant to its development. This is part of the claim, mentioned in the Introduction, that we all know the same unique human language. To clarify and elaborate what is involved in this claim, it is necessary to look more closely at what "knowledge of language" consists of and, in particular, at one of the contrasts for which Chomsky is best known: the distinction between "competence" and "performance."

Competence and performance

How is it that you can read this book? An obvious answer is because you know English. An equally obvious answer is because the light is on. These two explanations for an apparently trivial ability can illuminate a fundamental dichotomy: the difference between our knowledge of language and our use of that knowledge; between our competence and our performance.[74]

Your knowledge of the grammar and vocabulary of English, your competence as a speaker of English, is prerequisite to your understanding this sentence; the exercise of this competence is made possible by the fact, among many others, that the light is on.

Competence and grammar

Competence is, in principle, independent of performance. As the result of an accident or a stroke, people are often rendered speechless and appear to lose their language faculty, yet they may subsequently recover and show no ill-effects of their trauma.[75] Those who appear to regain their language in this way must be assumed to have retained their competence even while mute: knowledge can be preserved in the absence of the ability to exercise that knowledge. This is not logically necessary: an English speaker might recover from a stroke knowing Japanese or Swahili, but even to entertain the possibility makes its implausibility obvious. A less extreme case is provided by people who stutter or have an untreated cleft palate. Their condition may make them difficult to understand, or it may reduce them to frustrated silence, but their knowledge of language is typically indistinguishable from that of unaffected individuals. This autonomy of knowledge from the exercise of that knowledge does not alter the fact that our performance usually provides much of the evidence as to what our competence is, though it does provide some justification for the fact that modern generative linguistics idealizes away from many performance considerations and concentrates on the study of competence, leaving the study of performance to pragmatics, psychology, the medical sciences, and a range of other disciplines.

The investigation of competence is challenging because our knowledge of language is both complex and largely unconscious. Few people capable of understanding this sentence could give you a linguistic analysis of it, so the question of how such knowledge can be studied permits of no easy answers. Fortunately, although the knowledge itself is tacit, the fruits of that knowledge are available to both public inspection and private introspection: we can observe the performance of others or offer our own intuitions. It may take the example of a stroke victim to make us aware of the complexity and subtlety of our language faculty, but not all mismatches between our knowledge and the exercising of it are so drastic, and even elementary observation can give us insight into what precisely it is we know when we know a language. It is worth emphasizing that reliance on intuition is not a retreat from the usual canons of scientific rigor: "intuition" is simply another word for "judgment," with no mystical or unscientific overtones. There is no difference in principle between our linguistic judgment about sentences of our native language and our visual judgment about illusions such as the Müller-Lyer arrows. It is simply a fact that we perceive the lines as different in length, and psychologists try to devise theories of visual perception that explain this fact. Likewise, it is simply a fact that we judge the sentence *they are flying planes* as ambiguous,[76] and linguists try to devise theories of competence that explain why.

Rules

To know a language is to have a mentally represented grammar, standardly viewed as consisting of a set of rules which conspire to define the individual's competence.[77] The linguist's task is first to establish that such rules exist and then to formalize them so that they account for all the complexities that go to make up our knowledge of language. These rules are not the stipulations of school-room pedagogues, enjoining you not to split infinitives or use *hopefully* to mean "I hope." They are rather the set of generalizations describing what it is you know when you know a language, and some of which you may lose, temporarily or permanently, if you have a stroke.

Any native speaker of English knows that *I speak English fluently* and *I speak fluent English* are acceptable, but that *I speak fluently English* is wrong. You may never have come across an example like this before (except earlier in this chapter), or you may have heard innumerable such examples and know that it is a typical foreigner's mistake. You may even demur, because of the possibility of saying: *I speak quite fluently all the languages of Western Europe and most of those of North Asia*, but you nonetheless know that *I speak fluently English* is not acceptable in the way the longer sentence is. That we know this without having been explicitly taught it, and can extend the judgment to new, previously unheard, examples provides the initial evidence that our knowledge of language is rule-governed. We can't just have memorized a huge list of words and sentences that we dredge up from our memory on the appropriate occasion; rather, we must have command of a set of rules that constitute our grammar, and by reference to which we can produce or understand or make judgments on any of an infinite set of sentences. Indeed, as no memory has infinite storage capacity, even our ability to include numbers in the sentences we use is sufficient to demonstrate that we could not rely just on memory. You have presumably never before heard or read that *The surface area of the asteroid Ceres is 5,172,783 square kilometers*, but you have no difficulty in understanding it and, if you are suitably informed, knowing that it is false. Such examples illustrate what Chomsky calls the "creative"[78] aspect of language use: not in the sense of poetic creativity, but in the sense that the sentences involved, although made up of elements that are familiar, are newly created on the spur of the moment and range over an infinite domain.

The foreigner's mistake above is hardly profound, but the possibility of describing something as a mistake is itself profoundly significant, as it entails the existence of the rules by reference to which the mistake is so characterized. As a corollary, it follows that not all the utterances one may hear have the same status: being spoken or written down is no guarantee of being correct. The fact that someone may, as a slip of the tongue, say: *The advantage to be gained from letting teenagers organize their own affairs are overwhelming* (with *are* instead of *is*) doesn't mean that there is no rule requiring the verb to agree with the subject. Rather, it highlights the observation that performance data constitute only one piece of evidence about the nature of one's competence, a piece of evidence that has to be evaluated in conjunction with others, most notably the intuitions of the native speaker. A parallel can be provided from mathematics: if someone multiplies 17 by 33 incorrectly, this is no proof of their ignorance of the laws of arithmetic, still less of the need to change those laws to turn the mistake into a correct calculation.

Equally compelling evidence that our use of language is creatively rule-governed comes from examples of over-generalization, particularly prominent in the speech of children acquiring their first language. As adults we can say either *This teddy is his* or *This is his teddy*, so it's not surprising when two-year-olds generalize *This teddy is mine* to produce *This is mine teddy*.[79] That examples such as this deviate from the norms of the adult language shows that they could not be simply imitated from the child's parents, but must result from a generalization (a rule) induced by the child itself. Such rules are part of our individual knowledge of language and, as the child language example shows, this knowledge can be idiosyncratic and different from the adult pattern that the child is acquiring. In any one community the rules that we know are largely shared, but they are properties of the *individual, internal* to his or her head. To reflect this fact our mentally represented grammar is now referred to as our I-language, our individual, internal language, as opposed to the E-language outside our heads, external to us.[80] Whether E-language corresponds to a domain for which one can construct a scientific theory is dubious.

I-language and E-language

When generative grammar was being first developed, a language was defined as a set of sentences,[81] generated by the rules of a grammar, where "generated" is a term taken over from mathematics and just means formally or rigorously described. *I speak English fluently* would be generated, and so be part of the language; *I speak fluently English* would not be generated, and so would not be. Chomsky's early work included a demonstration that any such definition of a language could not have a decisive role to play in linguistic theory. There was a temptation among engineers, mathematicians, logicians, and psychologists to assume that a set of sentences had some absolute status independent of the individuals speaking the language concerned; that there was an E-language: some definable entity external to the individual that corresponded to the everyday idea of "English."[82] If such social or supra-personal constructs as E-languages were coherent and consistent, they might be the appropriate domain for political, mathematical, or logical statements, but if they are supposed to reflect the individual human capacity for language, they are neither coherent nor definable. By contrast, I-languages, with their explicitly psychological status, are the appropriate domain for statements about individual knowledge, and they have the advantage of being coherently definable. That is, the apparently narrower domain of I-language is amenable to scientific investigation in a way that E-language is not.

However controversial the details of Chomsky's linguistic analyses and the philosophical conclusions he builds on them, it is not at issue that people can make judgments about the well-formedness of sentences of their language. It is equally uncontroversial that these judgments may be colored by considerations that go beyond the strictly grammatical and that speakers of the same language may differ from each other in their intuitions. Crucially, however, it is usually feasible to separate the strictly linguistic determinants of our intuitions from the non-linguistic ones, so devising a theory of this part of the knowledge of an individual, while complex, is possible. In contrast, devising a theory of the knowledge of a community of such individuals with their different interests, commitments and habits borders on the quixotic.

It is time to recapitulate a little. We have domains of three different sizes: the species, the community, and the individual. Language is a species characteristic:[83] despite superficial differences from language to language and from individual to individual, humans appear to be essentially identical in their linguistic endowment. Abstracting away from pathological cases, every child brings the same mental apparatus to bear on the task of acquiring its first language, and as a result all languages have essentially the same properties, and all languages can provide comparable insight into the human mind. Although the species attribute, instantiated in individuals, is mainly visible in its use for communication, the social groups in which this communication occurs have virtually no linguistically definable properties. We have then a situation in which the individual, in whom knowledge resides, is an appropriate focus for scientific inquiry.[84] By implication, the species (that is, the universe of such individuals) is likewise an appropriate focus, as what is common to all individuals constitutes the innate linguistic endowment that is typical of human beings. But the intermediate social, or geo-political notion of language in the traditional sense has no status and no role to play in a scientific linguistics.

This individualist-cum-universalist view has been central since Chomsky's earliest work, and the difference between E-language and I-language was implicit in *The Logical Structure of Linguistic Theory*, completed in 1955, but only published two decades later. Unfortunately, this delay in publication meant that people's early ideas about generative grammar were derived almost exclusively from *Syntactic Structures* (1957) which, despite its seminal role, was basically a set of notes for an undergraduate course at MIT and started out with a statement of the orthodox position that Chomsky was attacking. As a result, many people failed to differentiate what Chomsky was attacking and what he was proposing. In the orthodoxy that Chomsky was arguing against, the focus was the language viewed as a set of sentences or well-formed formulae (WFFs); in all Chomsky's work over half a century the focus of investigation has been the speaker's knowledge of language. This is in turn a reflection of the general change of emphasis in the cognitive revolution from "the study of behavior and its products (such as texts), to the inner mechanisms that enter into thought and action."[85] Concentration on I-language implies that the claim that the main task of a grammar is to generate all and only[86] the well-formed sentences of a language is incoherent, as the notion of language implicit in such a formulation is not definable. An I-language is what underlies our ability to produce and understand utterances of sentences on appropriate occasions; it could not itself be that set of sentences. Indeed, Chomsky has argued repeatedly that "there isn't the slightest reason to believe that there is any such concept as WFF for natural language."[87] It may be appropriate for formal (logical) languages, or for arithmetic, but not for human languages. Moreover, this does not represent a gap in our understanding of human language: no one has proposed generalizations that could be captured only if some such notion were devised.[88]

The internalist position denies the validity of treating a language in terms of sets of sentences which are either "good" or "bad." This has the further significant implication that our judgments of well-formedness need not be absolutely clear-cut; and, more interestingly, we can have intuitions about the relative ill-formedness of sentences none of which would be included within the grammar under E-language assumptions.[89] Consider constructions of the sort known as "parasitic gaps,"[90] exemplified by *This is the man John hired without speaking to*. Such examples occur infrequently in either writing or speech, but we all have intuitions about them. In the present case most people agree that the example is fine even if stylistically not wonderful. In contrast, the example *This is the man John hired before he spoke to* is generally deemed to be unacceptable. It may take a moment or two for this to register: all the words are common and the intended message is clear enough, but the sentence as a whole is odd. It seems unexceptionable to say simply that one is grammatical and the other is ungrammatical – one is a sentence of the language and the other is not. Matters are not so straightforward, however, when we turn to further examples like: *This is the man John interviewed before reading the book you gave to* and *This is the man John interviewed before announcing the plan to speak to*. Chomsky argues that the second is less unacceptable than the first, even though neither is entirely well-formed.[91] My own judgment tends to be the reverse, but what matters is that such intuitional nuances are inexplicable (whichever way they go) if we insist on a strict demarcation between the completely grammatical and the completely ungrammatical. If attention is restricted to "fully acceptable" sentences, this judgment, which may reflect deep-seated principles of grammatical organization, is ruled out of consideration *a priori*.

Appealing to examples as complex as these often strikes non-linguists as bordering on obscurantism: a frequent objection is that "no one would actually say anything like that," or "no corpus of real utterances would contain such examples." This reflects an unmotivated preoccupation with facts of performance, viewed as some kind of collection (or possible collection) of data in the world. The examples cited here are unlikely to occur in everyday speech, but the same applies to most of the sentences it is possible to construct: language is creative. There is no requirement in science that the phenomena used as evidence should occur spontaneously under natural conditions. The major findings of particle physics have been based on hugely complex experiments carried out using more and more powerful (and expensive) accelerators. To make progress in such a field, it is necessary to study extreme conditions. Similarly, to understand language it is sometimes necessary to study extreme examples. Just as nature's unusual experiments, such as William's syndrome children or the polyglot *savant*, may be more revelatory of deep-seated principles than examples of everyday people, so may esoteric linguistic examples be the best means of gaining insight into the principles of grammar; in particular, they may be the only ones which are sufficiently rich and complex to choose between rival theories. Parasitic gaps, and variations on them, have been exploited in this way by more than one linguist in support of competing theoretical claims.

This is another example of where common sense and science part company; again with interesting parallels with the hard sciences. The tension between common-sense understanding and scientific explanation can be illustrated by another episode from the history of physics. The validity and relevance of alchemy[92] were as self-evident to Newton and his contemporaries as their irrelevance is to us with our preconceptions of what is scientific. As a result, modern commentators have difficulty, even embarrassment, in accounting for why an archetypal genius like Newton should have spent so much time on an irrelevant unscientific pursuit. We have comparable alchemical preconceptions about language. Concentrating on E-language (or imagining that one is concentrating on E-language) is like concentrating on alchemy. There is a huge amount of data, a long tradition of scholarship which has given rise to a wealth of apparent generalizations, and a dead-end. The analogy is appropriate for a further reason: most people now agree that there is no such field of inquiry as alchemy, and Chomsky argues that there is no such thing as E-language. He introduced the term in *Knowledge of Language* to cover any notion of language that isn't

I-language, but with the caveat, widely ignored, that there is no such thing.[93] There is a common conception that what one hears, the data of performance, must be (utterances of) sentences of E-language, but this makes no more sense than specifying how much a sentence weighs. There is no linguistic theory that provides for sentences to weigh anything.[94] Similarly, there is no linguistic theory of E-language, distinct from I-language, which makes claims about the data of performance. One observes phenomena and categorizes them according to the constructs of one's theory: as utterances of nouns or verbs, as examples of ambiguity or rhyme, and so on. These are all terms developed for I-language, and in the absence of an alternative theory of E-language, it is meaningless to categorize phenomena as falling under it. There is a more surprising conclusion lurking beneath the surface here: the real aim of work in science is to understand theories, not the world.[95] The world is too complex to be directly understood, the best we can do is come up with tentative theories of certain subdomains and hope to understand them.

We turn next to the performance half of the competence–performance dichotomy.

Performance, parsing, and pragmatics

Given a distinction between competence and performance, it is necessary to specify how the two interact. In particular, we need to know what the division of responsibility between them is in accounting for the linguistic observations we make. It is not always self-evident whether we should treat a perceived mistake as arising from someone's having a different grammar, a matter of competence, or from their carelessness, a matter of performance. Our I-language is neutral as between speaking and hearing:[96] there is no reason to believe that the knowledge we draw on in constructing a sentence we wish to utter is significantly different from the knowledge we draw on in decoding the utterances we hear, and no one can speak only one language and understand only a different one. Our knowledge is neutral, but our exploitation of that knowledge is not. Producing an utterance uses processes distinct from those deployed in perceiving an utterance. Part of understanding what someone says then involves the use of a device which identifies the words you hear, and works out the structural relations among them. This requires not just the grammar, but an additional device known as a parser.

Parsing considerations

The parser must have access to the rules of the I-language, but for an interesting range of cases it must come up with representations which differ from those produced by these rules. The clearest example of such a mismatch (and hence evidence for the existence of a parser distinct from the grammar) is provided by "garden path" sentences.[97] These are sentences involving a local ambiguity, where one interpretation is more plausible or more frequent than the other, and the hearer is then misled into constructing the wrong analysis. Classic examples are: *The cotton clothing is made of grows in Mississippi* and *Mary persuaded her friends were unreliable*.[98] In each case the hearer or reader is inveigled by the parser into thinking that a particular sequence (*cotton clothing*, *her friends*) is a linguistic unit (a constituent) when, according to the grammar, it is not; and this fact only becomes apparent after part of the sentence has been wrongly decoded. (If the sentence remains ambiguous to the bitter end, as with *It's too hot to eat* for instance, it is said to be globally ambiguous rather than just locally ambiguous.)

A second piece of evidence which indicates the need for the separation of grammar and parser comes from sentences which, while in conformity with the rules and principles of the I-language, are opaque to the parser. This opacity may be due either to length and complexity, with academic prose being the worst offender, or to problems occasioned by particular types of structure, with "center-embedding" being the best known. No one has any difficulty processing sentences like *Dogs bite* or *Dogs I like don't bite*, but even the four-word example *Dogs dogs bite bite* is quite impenetrable, and the notorious *Oysters oysters oysters split split split* is totally impossible.[99] There is nothing wrong with the meanings: in the former case roughly, "dogs that are bitten by other dogs will themselves tend to bite," and in the relevant respects it has the same grammatical structure as the transparent *Dogs I like don't bite*. But because of the repetition of identical elements in a particular configuration, our processing device is sabotaged. The sentence is grammatical but unparseable, indicating that the grammar and the parser must be distinct.

A third reason for thinking that a parser is needed is provided by the converse of the preceding examples: there are many sequences which are not part of the I-language at all, but which are successfully parsed and given an interpretation by the hearer: "ungrammatical"[100] sentences of the kind we have already seen; neologisms like "barking up the right tree," utterances in languages or dialects different from one's own, and so on.

Despite the claim that the parser and the grammar are distinct, it is plausible to suppose that the properties of each have affected the other over evolutionary time, leading to an interesting convergence between them. One domain where this is probably the case is in the need for "look-ahead."[101] Locally ambiguous sentences can be disambiguated by looking ahead to what is coming next, but while the speaker presumably knows what he or she is planning to say, it is not obvious how such a facility is available to the hearer. Utterances are produced in real time and one has no choice when parsing but to wait for the disambiguating words. On hearing *Mary persuaded her friends*, you may leap to the premature conclusion that you are processing a sentence like *Mary persuaded her friends to come*, and it is only when that hypothesis fails when you hear *were*, that you start again and work out that you are really confronted with something equivalent to *Mary persuaded her that friends were unreliable*. Accordingly, in imitation of the limitations of the hearer, parsers are often so constructed that they are forbidden to look ahead. Such limitations are paralleled in recent developments in the minimalist theory of grammar, which similarly avoid the possibility of look-ahead.[102] It is not then surprising that various authors have attempted to deny the difference between grammars and parsers, making do with a single entity.[103]

Assuming for the moment that the need for a parser distinct from the grammar is established, not much else about it is clear. Traditionally, parsers have been rule-based, with different properties depending on the rules of the language they are serving. But over the last twenty years specific rules have been largely superseded by general principles, and it could be that "parsers are basically uniform for all languages."[104] We will return to parsing considerations in chapter 3, when we have looked more closely at the grammar which parsers must interact with.

Pragmatic considerations

Even when one has parsed a sentence and given it a linguistic structure in accordance with the rules of the I-language, the task of interpretation is only beginning. The ambiguous sentence *It's too hot to eat* that I cited earlier has at least three grammatical parsings (strictly speaking, it is really three sentences). Whether it is interpreted as a remark about the weather, about the dog that is too hot to eat its food, or the food that is too hot for the dog to eat, depends on considerations of relevance: you choose the interpretation which best fits the context.[105] If uttered on a sweltering day around dinner time, the first interpretation is most likely; if the dog yelps and runs from its steaming dish, the last one is more plausible. These interpretations are parasitic on the grammar, but are not determined by the grammar; rather they are the result of an inferential process which presupposes a grammatical analysis. Arriving at the appropriate interpretation is itself still not the end of the story. Assuming that you have correctly inferred that the last of the three meanings was intended, you still have to decide what the speaker intended to convey by uttering it. Was he or she suggesting you cool the food down, comfort the dog, apologize? Such implications, or "implicatures" as they are called,[106] are again dependent on considerations of what is most relevant. As before, they presuppose knowledge of language, but go beyond it to exploit the inferential resources of the central system. Chomsky has little to say about such performance considerations or about "pragmatic competence"[107] more generally, but it is necessary to distinguish them in order to keep the contrasts he does discuss clear.

Competence and performance versus I-language and E-language

It is important to keep separate two distinctions: that between I-language and E-language, and that between competence and performance.[108] It is easiest to see the difference in the contrast between E-language and performance. The term E-language has been used to refer both to artificial systems like set theory or the propositional calculus and to natural languages when viewed as sets of sentences. In the former case notions of performance are simply irrelevant: no one speaks or listens to set theory, and performance is anyway defined as the use of one's knowledge of a natural language. Even if it is objected that this definition is undesirable, it should be clear that the equation of E-language and performance could not be right as E-language is potentially infinite, and no one's performance can be infinite. The germ of truth that underlies the misapprehension is that E-language is also used to characterize the 1930s structuralist position of Leonard Bloomfield that a language is "the totality of utterances that can be made in a speech community."[109] Utterances are the fruits of performance, so there is apparently a close relation between E-language and performance. But while performance data provide some of the evidence for the nature of I-language, there is no need, perhaps (as I suggested above) no possibility, of making the additional claim that these data constitute an entity in their own right – an E-language. As an example, consider the importance of performance errors in investigating competence: spontaneous speech is "a highly fragmented and discontinuous activity,"[110] but this discontinuity can provide evidence for the nature of our knowledge: pauses do not occur at random, but fall either at grammatical boundaries or, more interestingly, mark the cognitive effort of planning what one is going to say. Giving these data the status of an E-language is an unnecessary further step with no attendant benefits and, in the case of "ungrammatical" utterances, a step that would give rise to an incoherent construct, consisting of both grammatical and ungrammatical sequences.

There has been equal confusion concerning the difference between competence and I-language. Chomsky has sometimes distinguished "grammatical competence" ("knowledge of form and meaning") from "pragmatic competence" (knowledge of conditions and manner of appropriate use), but sometimes he has used the bare term "competence" to refer either just to "the speaker-hearer's knowledge of his language," or to his "knowledge and understanding." The confusion should dissipate once one realizes that "I-language" is a technical term in the theory of language: it indicates a state of the mind–brain; whereas "competence" is an informal term introduced to avoid irrelevant debate about the notion "knowledge of language."[111] Much of the confusion that has existed is due in part to philosophical preconceptions about what constitutes knowledge,[112] in part to the fact that before the refinement of terminology brought in with the locution "I-language" in the mid 1980s, "competence" served as the corresponding technical term. Now only the informal interpretation survives.

Rather than the two dichotomies hinted at in the heading to this section, our language faculty consists of an I-language (informally referred to as our competence) and a range of performance systems, including a parser. The study of I-language, the focus of research for the last half century, is gradually beginning to approximate in sophistication to study in the hard sciences; discussion of the performance systems is still largely at a pre-theoretic stage of development and only informally characterized. The notion E-language is empty of content and correspondingly unnecessary. I return in chapter 4 to the I-language/E-language distinction, but before that, we need to consider briefly how we came to be made like this.

Evolution and innateness

The complexity of humans, as of all organisms, is a function of evolution, resulting in the genetic determination of a subset of our physical properties.[113] We are predetermined to grow arms rather than wings, and to develop simple rather than compound eyes.[114] One of Chomsky's more striking observations is that there is no reason to suppose that the genetic determination of our mental systems is any different in principle from the genetic determination of these complex physical systems. Much of human nature, including the language faculty and aspects of our moral sense, are putatively innate.[115] Of all Chomsky's radical suggestions over the last half century, it is this that has aroused the most controversy.

Nobody doubts that our eye-color is innate, determined by our genetic make-up. Similarly, nobody doubts that our ability to read is not innate, but must be learned. Assuming that genetic determination and learning jointly exhaust the possible sources of our various attributes and abilities, the choice in these cases is clear. When we turn to more complex domains, the choice is not so straightforward. The most vexed such domain is that of the language faculty. From the fact that frogs and spiders never learn a human language it is clear that, at some crude level, we must be endowed with a predisposition to learning language that these other organisms lack. In contrast, the blatant fact that languages differ from each other, sometimes in quite surprising ways, shows that some aspects of our linguistic knowledge must be learned. No one is genetically predisposed to learn English rather than Amharic; no one is born knowing that the French for "pig" is *cochon* (or, of course, that the English for "pig" is *pig*). Every individual has to learn whether he or she has been born into a community whose members speak a language which (like English) has a word order in which the subject precedes the verb and the object follows it (as in *Frogs eat flies*) or a language which (like Hixkaryana,[116] spoken in Amazonia) has the reverse word order in which the same message would be conveyed by a sentence with the word order *Flies eat frogs*.

So it seems that part of our linguistic knowledge is innate and part is learned. But even this is a somewhat misleading way of putting things, because "innate" and "learned" are not technical scientific terms but belong to the pre-theoretical stage of investigation. Internal to any theory about humans, whether it be of their motor organization, sexual maturation, vision, or language, there must be a balance between genetic and environmental components. But no particular "structure" or piece of "behavior" will be either "learned" or "innate," because notions like "structure" or "behavior pattern" are themselves informal, pre-theoretic concepts, which will be replaced by technical terms in a developing theory, and such technical terms have only a tenuous relationship to their informal equivalents. With this caveat, it is clear that one of Chomsky's achievements is not only to have made, but also to have justified, the claim that far more of our linguistic knowledge is innately determined than had previously been envisaged. The claim is usually expressed in terms of properties of the "initial state" of the language-learning organism. What attributes do we have to ascribe to a newborn human infant (as opposed to a spider, frog, ape, or computer) to account for its ability, and the others' inability, to acquire language: to end up in the "steady state" which characterizes the normal adult speaker of a language? It is clearly possible to give explicit characterizations of the initial state and the steady state; it does not follow that we can meaningfully point to some aspect of the steady state and say that "that bit was innate" or "that bit was learned," as any property will be the result of an interaction between what was specified in the genome and what is in the environment.

Language acquisition

To understand this interplay between the genetic and the environmental in the acquisition of one's first language, it is necessary to look at precisely what it is the mature speaker has command of. A comparison with vision on the one hand, and origami on the other, may be helpful. Human (and other) infants are born with a certain visual ability, which becomes more sophisticated as they mature. Intuitively, the development of the ability to see stereoscopically is a matter not of learning but of the maturational unfolding of a genetically determined program. In contrast, when someone develops the ability to fold a piece of paper into the shape of a peacock, we have no qualms at describing this as resulting from a learning process, and we would be correspondingly surprised to be told it was due to the unfolding of a predetermined genetic program. We have the intuition that these two processes, in each of which an individual passes from being unable to do something to being able to do it, are radically different. But care is needed. It may not be appropriate to say that we learn to see stereoscopically, but it is demonstrably necessary that we have to have some environmental input: apes raised in darkness do not develop a functional visual system. Conversely, while it is true that there is substantial environmental influence in the learning of paper folding, it is also clear that the manual dexterity involved is to a considerable extent the product of the maturational unfolding of innate capacities. It is not that paper folding is learned and visual development is innate, both are both, but to different degrees. Likewise in language, we expect to find a balance between genetic and environmental factors in language acquisition.

Poverty of the stimulus[117]

There are many kinds of evidence that can be adduced to justify the view that becoming able to see in 3-D and learning origami result from a different balance of genetic and environmental factors. First, except in admittedly pathological cases, everyone comes to see in 3-D, but very few make paper peacocks. The universality of the development of stereoscopic vision clearly sets it aside from the specialist development of paper-folding abilities. Even where environmental conditions preclude the normal development of vision, there is no disagreement that the structure of the visual system is genetically determined to a greater extent than origami. Second, the age at which these abilities emerge is strikingly different. There is a "critical period"[118] for visual development, just as there is for the growth of language, but not for learned skills like paper folding, which can be acquired any time in life once the requisite manual dexterity has developed. Infants a few months old never learn origami and, conversely, people who are congenitally blind but develop some light sensitivity in later life, never learn to see properly at all, and *a fortiori* not in 3-D.[119] Moreover, the linguistic knowledge that people end up with is strikingly similar across the community, whereas individual differences in paper-folding ability are comparatively great. We may not all use our knowledge of language with comparable fluency, but the orator and the tongue-tied typically agree on their judgments of the well-formedness of sentences, just as the dextrous and the maladroit agree on what is a nice paper peacock. Third, the evidence on which individuals acquire their knowledge of language is not obviously adequate to account for the depth, variety, and intricacy of that knowledge.

Language learning provides an example of the "poverty of the stimulus" where we end up knowing more than we have learned. Bertrand Russell phrased the general question rhetorically in a form which Chomsky is fond of quoting: "How comes it that human beings, whose contacts with the world are brief and personal and limited, are nevertheless able to know as much as they do know?"[120] In the domain of language this can be illustrated by the convergence of intuitions about sentences speakers have never encountered before. I have traded on this convergence in the discussion of *John speaks fluently English*, assuming, I hope correctly, that you would agree with my judgment. Such examples raise several issues. First, it is important to emphasize that the claim is not that *John speaks fluently English* is incomprehensible, obscure, or even just stylistically infelicitous. It's simply ungrammatical. As someone who knows English, you are aware of this immediately and without doubt or hesitation. Second, the sentence is not particularly long or complicated – it contains only four common words – and is of no philosophical import: it makes no controversial claims about the existence of unicorns or the moral superiority of dolphins. Third, it is unlikely that everyone who shares the reaction that the sentence is "bad" has been explicitly taught that this is the case. Such knowledge is just part of what it means to know English. A common reaction at this juncture is to point out that, while the sentence as such may not have been taught, the sequence of "Noun Verb Adverb Noun" is inferably un-English because it doesn't occur. This raises interesting issues in language acquisition to which we return in chapter 3, but is immediately countered by the observation that our intuitions stretch to much more complex examples than these, as seen in the case of parasitic gaps, such as *This is the man John hired without speaking to*, discussed earlier.

Examples such as these are never taught in the classroom and are vanishingly rare in normal texts or conversation. If this is true (and it is of course a factual claim) then we are left with the problem of explaining how it is we come by the intuitions we have. Chomsky's answer is that we have this knowledge as a joint function of having acquired the lexical items of English and of having embedded them in a framework provided by Universal Grammar (UG):[121] the set of linguistic principles we are endowed with at birth in virtue of being human. For this argument to be remotely convincing, it must be that cases comparable to those cited here occur frequently. A glance at any textbook shows that half a century of research in generative syntax has uncovered innumerable such examples, and has simultaneously removed the plausible alternative explanation that we are taught these things. If correct, this demonstrates that we must ascribe a large part of the knowledge we end up with to the initial state, to UG rather than to the effect of the linguistic input we are directly exposed to. In brief, it is innate.

Word meaning

Evidence for innateness, for properties of the initial state of the child acquiring its first language, can be drawn equally, if somewhat more surprisingly, from the development of the vocabulary: word meaning too is largely innate.[122] As usual there are sane and insane interpretations of this claim. We are not born knowing the meaning and implications of the vocabulary of quantum mechanics, but the knowledge we achieve of huge numbers of words in a very short space of time is grossly underdetermined by the evidence to which we are exposed.[123] The argument is a classical case of poverty of the stimulus. For somewhat more than five years children acquire roughly one new word every hour they are awake, and the knowledge acquired is intricate and often unexpectedly detailed.[124]

Take *near* or *house* for instance.[125] Using these words presupposes no specialist scientific sophistication, they are known by essentially every speaker of the language, and yet our knowledge about them is surprisingly complex. If you paint your house brown you are understood (in the absence of further information) to have painted its exterior rather than its interior surface brown, an observation that generalizes to boxes, igloos, mountains, and even impossible objects such as spherical cubes. That is, if you paint a spherical cube brown it is again its exterior surface that is newly colored. It seems that the properties of our language are such that we treat entities like houses as though they were exterior surfaces. But this only scratches the surface of our knowledge. We can coherently say that we have painted our house brown "on the inside," that is, treating the house as an interior surface. But other usage makes it clear that a house is not always conceptualized as a surface. If it were just a surface (exterior or interior) then you could be near the house whether you were inside or outside it. But that is patently untrue. If John is inside the house and Mary is outside it, and they are moreover equidistant from the wall separating them, we cannot say of John that he is near the house, though Mary may (or may not) be near it, depending on what the contextual determinants of nearness are at the relevant time.

The mention of context might suggest that the knowledge being tapped in examples of this kind is encyclopaedic, rather than linguistic. That is, when you "paint a house brown," all you need from the language faculty is that there is some brown paint in a relevant relation to a house, and the details are filled in on the basis of our knowledge of the world. Knowledge of the world may be a factor in the interpretation, but the uniformity of people's reactions to impossible situations (like painting a spherical cube), and the fact that children are probably exposed more frequently to painting inside than outside buildings makes it clear that the linguistic contribution is paramount. If this description of the facts is even remotely correct, it prompts the question of how such knowledge can arise in the child with such speed and uniformity. The answer again is that the organism must be inherently, that is innately, structured in ways which determine in large part the course and nature of such development.

Universals

If arguments from the poverty of the stimulus are correct, they make further interesting predictions. The claim is that our intuitions are due in part to universal principles.[126] If so, the effect of such principles should be apparent not just in educated speakers of English, but in all speakers of all languages. One of the more remarkable achievements of the generative paradigm is precisely to have corroborated this prediction. We now have evidence from around the world that exactly the same constraints are operative in every language, wherever it is spoken. It is initially surprising that the peculiarity of a (perfectly comprehensible but ill-formed) sentence like *Which person did you wonder whether John hit?* should be mirrored in the comparable peculiarity of its translation into Chinese or Hungarian. It is less surprising when one considers that Chinese and Hungarian children start out just like English children, and the chances of any of them being given explicit instruction about such sentences is fairly remote. Perhaps more surprising is the further implication that, as Chomsky puts it, "evidence about Japanese bears directly on the assumptions concerning the initial state for English."[127] If all children start the same, and if analyzing the acquisition and knowledge of language that people have can cast light on the initial state of their own language, it follows that analyses of every language are of relevance to every other language.

As I have presented it, the evidence for our linguistic knowledge being (partly) innate should be uncontroversial. The opposition to the claim has diminished since Chomsky first made it, but it is still not universally accepted, and objections of various different kinds have been suggested.[128] I look at these objections in chapter 4 to see to what extent they are valid, but before that, it is necessary to look a little more closely at the notion "universal."

The term "universals" allows of many different interpretations, several of which have been used within linguistics. At the most superficial level, but still not without interest, it reminds us that all human languages exploit the same vocabulary of elements: consonants and vowels, nouns, verbs and clauses, and so on. There is some variation from language to language: all languages have consonants, only some have fricatives (like "f" and "v" in English); all of them use nouns and verbs, only some of them have articles and adjectives, or classifiers and complementizers. Linguistic theory must then provide a means for describing all of these in the form of a universal inventory of possible elements: the inventory is universal in the sense that it is rich enough to allow for the universe of languages, not that each language exploits every possibility.[129] The claim is interesting to the extent that the list is finite and small: we know in advance of inspection that no language is going to exploit square verbs or red nouns, or a new part of speech referring to heavy things. Such examples are absurd, but the underlying principle is more interesting: everything the infant needs to find out about the language it is exposed to is already innately specified: all it needs to do is make the right choices from the items listed.

A simple example to show this is the existence of "anaphoric" relations between an item like *him* or *himself* and its antecedent – the item it refers back to.[130] In the pair of sentences *John likes him* and *John likes himself*, the word *him* cannot, but the word *himself* must, refer to John. All languages show pronominal anaphora, and most languages have the kind of contrast illustrated here. However, there are at least three ways in which there can be some variation from language to language. In English, a sentence like *John told Bill about himself* is ambiguous: the item *himself* can be taken to refer either to *John* or to *Bill*. Its German counterpart *Hans hat dem Bill etwas über sich gesagt* has only an interpretation in which *sich* (the equivalent of *himself*) refers to *Hans*. In German, reflexives can refer only to subjects – *Hans* is a subject, but *Bill* is not, hence there is only one interpretation; in English reflexives can refer to subjects or objects. A second possible difference is provided by examples like *John said that Bill should stop injuring himself*. Here *himself* can refer only to *Bill* and not to *John*, so the sentence is unambiguous. Its Japanese counterpart: *John-wa Bill-wa zibun-o kizutukeru-no-o yameru-bekida-to itta* is ambiguous, with *zibun* ("self") able to refer either to *John* or to *Bill*: in English the antecedent of a reflexive has to be "local," in Japanese it can be further away.[131] Lastly, in English, there is a distinction between *himself* and *herself*, *myself* and *yourself*: distinctions of person, number, and gender. In Hindi, all of them are rendered by the same form, *apne* ("self"). These three differences virtually exhaust the major variations among languages with respect to anaphoric dependencies. What is universal is the notion "anaphor," an entity that depends crucially for its interpretation on some antecedent, and the requirement that the anaphor and its antecedent be in a particular structural configuration. What can vary is whether that antecedent has to be a subject, what particular (local or non-local) configuration it has to be in, and whether there are further subdivisions like distinctions of gender and number which are characteristic of other parts of the grammar. There is a sense then in which all of this is universal and putatively innate: the theory, embodied in UG, specifies each and every possibility that languages can exploit, and the child just has to choose which ones it is confronted with. We have a clear case of the interaction between genetic and environmental factors.

In discussing these examples I have made crucial reference to what is impossible as well as what is possible in various languages. Presented with an arbitrary example, we can make an immediate judgment as to whether it is a sentence of our native language or not. It is hard enough to write a grammar that reflects our judgments of well-formedness; it is much harder to replicate the ability we have to characterize sequences as ill-formed. One of Chomsky's contributions has been to highlight this ability, and then go on to explain these judgments on general theoretical grounds. Two points are worth reiterating: first, accounting for such intuitions is radically at variance with any view of language which treats it as a set of utterances, be these actual or possible; second, a corollary of providing a theoretical explanation is that it claims that the facts reflect universal properties of human language and therefore that comparable facts should be identifiable in every language one looks at.

Natural language and the language of thought

Language is a tool for thought. (Chomsky, 1992b: 49)

We all know at least one language, and it is clear that part of that knowledge is innate, part is learned. But what is this complex system for? There are two obvious answers: communication and thought. I shall deal with communication later (see chapter 4); let us look here at the relation between language and thought. Does thinking take place through a language-like medium, via some alternative system such as imagery, or through some combination of these? If it takes place through some language-like medium, then we need to establish whether that medium is the same as natural language or different. That is, do we think in the language we speak – English, French, Vietnamese or whatever – or do we think in something distinct: a "language of thought"? If we think in something distinct from our natural language, what is the relation between the natural language and the language of thought?

These are deep and vexed questions on which it is hard to find consensus. It is also the case that Chomsky is skeptical about the possibility of discovering anything very solid in this area at all.[132] However, a certain amount seems clear and is moreover intimately tied in with Chomsky's general position.

Fodor has argued that English (as a typical natural language) cannot be the language of thought, as preverbal infants and even animals have some demonstrated ability to indulge in rational activity that can be most accurately characterized as thinking.[133] In fact, the conclusion is too strong: his argument could be taken as showing merely that English was not the only medium of thought, and that learning one's first language consisted in replacing an innately specified language of thought by one's native language. The properties of this innate language of thought could then be shared in part with the properties of whatever system animals are endowed with.

There have in fact been several suggestions that the medium of thought is natural language.[134] More accurately, the suggestion is that thinking exploits language shorn of the properties of the sound system. In Chomsky's framework – to be elaborated in the next chapter – that would involve using some extension of Logical Form. This cannot be quite right, as natural languages have properties that are irrelevant or even inimical to thought. For instance, all languages allow phenomena like ellipsis that have no equivalents in the language of thought, and that would in fact be unhelpful because of the problem of retrieving from memory propositions expressed with them. If I tell you that "Chomsky detests hypocrisy and Herman does too," you need to register this in memory in part as the thought that "Herman detests hypocrisy."[135] That is, the proposition rendered effectively and efficiently, but incompletely, by the English sentence using *does too*, has to be fleshed out by the addition of extra material. The process is trivially easy in the case of elliptical examples of this kind, so that the implications for the nature of the formal properties of the system of thought are not usually noticed. Natural languages use devices like ellipsis that we have no reason to ascribe to the language of thought. Similarly, the language of thought deploys devices that do not occur in natural language.

It is reasonably clear that we can include images of friends, evocations of sensations, or abstract swathes of color in our thoughts. It is not that the thought that "roses are red" is itself red, any more than the sentence "roses are red" has to be written in red ink or uttered after drinking a pink gin. Rather, one may bring to mind a scene including roses whose (red) color is explicit without this being verbalized. These imagistic evocations play the same kind of role as lexical items: they are embedded in a thought whose structure may be the same as that of a natural language sentence, but the vocabulary exploited – nouns as opposed to images – may be partly distinct.

Apart from such relatively minor differences, it looks plausible to claim that the structure of sentences is overwhelmingly similar to the structure of thoughts, taking it for granted that thoughts have structure.[136] Just as the English sentence "roses are red" is structurally related in different ways to "delphiniums are blue," "roses were red," and "roses are pink," so is the thought that "roses are red" related to a number of other thoughts: that "(some) flowers are colored," that "roses have physically definable properties," and so on. The validity of the conclusion that "flowers are colored" from the fact that "roses are red" is parasitic on the relation between logic and language, where logic is taken in the traditional sense of describing the "laws of thought," in Boole's felicitous phrase.[137] The structure of formal logical languages is dramatically simplified compared to the exuberance characteristic of natural languages, but that simplification is itself only expressible in natural language.

Thinking involves the use either of language or of a system with huge similarity to language. In this respect, language is the mirror of the mind. Moreover, the evidence for the compartmentalization of the mind we have been discussing is overwhelmingly linguistic. Our knowledge of many aspects of mental structure, from theory of mind to moral judgment, from the identification of visual illusions to the recognition of faces, is gleaned from verbal output. It is not the case, however, that the language faculty is a model for the other compartments of mind. The vocabulary and principles of visual perception or of smell have nothing necessarily in common with those of language. Language is the mirror of the mind; it is not a model of the mind.[138]

Summary

We are not like frogs. The differences are manifold, but the most interesting is that we have language and frogs don't, and having a language enables us to get insight into the mind. What we have seen in this chapter is that a major part of Chomsky's achievement is to have opened up language for inspection, and by so doing has opened a mirror onto the human mind.

By demonstrating that our knowledge of language can be studied by normal scientific investigation as a part of the natural world, Chomsky has brought linguistics into the scientific mainstream. At the same time he has cast light on other facets of the human mind, suggesting analyses and providing evidence for a modular view of our abilities. To do this has necessitated overturning previous views of language and mind, it has involved creative innovation in making explicit the difference between knowledge and the use of that knowledge, and it has given rise to the best evidence since Descartes for the innateness of a specific human ability. Other components of the mind do not share most of the interesting and subtle properties of language that we turn to next, but "it is not unreasonable to suppose that the study of . . . human language, may serve as a suggestive model for inquiry into other domains of human competence."[139]

2　The linguistic foundation

> By studying the properties of natural languages . . . we may hope to gain some
> understanding of the specific characteristics of human intelligence.
>
> (Chomsky, 1975a: 4–5)

Introduction

Chomsky's arguments for the relevance of language to issues in philosophy and
psychology derive their force from the strength of their linguistic foundation.
The perception that he has formulated and solved a range of descriptive and
explanatory problems in the formal study of language ensures that his other ideas
are taken seriously. This attitude makes sense: his arguments for innateness
and rationalism, for instance, rest crucially on the validity of his views on
language. By rationalism is meant the idea, best represented in the work of his
intellectual ancestor Descartes,[1] that reason has precedence over the senses in
the acquisition of knowledge, and that much of this knowledge must be innate.
Chomsky has provided the best evidence in existence for the innateness of some
aspects of our knowledge of language, and hence for Cartesian rationalism. In
contrast, no such direct relation holds between his linguistics and his politics.
As we shall see in detail in chapter 5, there are connections between the strands
of his different activities, but the intellectual justification for his political work
does not rest on his syntactic insights in the way his philosophical work does,
and he frequently emphasizes that there is at best a tenuous relation between
his two careers.

It is of course unsurprising that people who know and admire one strand of
his output should be sympathetic to the other. Chomsky himself was drawn into
linguistics in part because of his interest in and sympathy for Zellig Harris's
political views.[2] Like many linguists, I became interested in his political ideas
because of prior exposure to his linguistics, and I have more than once interviewed potential students for linguistics courses who had been made curious
about the field because of their admiration for his political dissent. However, to
be able to evaluate his philosophical and psychological contribution it is necessary to have some understanding of the linguistic background, while no such

background knowledge is necessary to evaluate his political contribution. What follows in this chapter is an (intermittently historical) overview of certain central notions in his linguistics. It is not possible here either to give a comprehensive history of recent linguistics or to provide a general introduction to generative grammar (the secondary literature is now vast enough to make such an undertaking superfluous anyway),[3] but it is intended to give sufficient information and insight to make his ideas accessible enough to allow for some appreciation of his achievements, and provide the basis for an informed assessment of the validity of the conclusions based on them.

Knowledge of language

Linguistics is the study of our knowledge of language: what it is, and how we acquire and use it. This study is pursued via the construction of grammars; that is, hypotheses about this knowledge and, secondarily, how we come by that knowledge and use it to think or to communicate. Knowledge of language is not monolithic, but is divided into our knowledge of vocabulary on the one hand, and our knowledge of how to combine that vocabulary into sentences on the other. Someone who speaks and understands English has a great wealth of information stored in his or her head. Some of this knowledge is easily accessible and uncontentious: that *frog* is a word of English, that it begins with the same sounds as *frost* and rhymes with *dog*, that it means a kind of anuran amphibian, and so on. This kind of knowledge of the vocabulary belongs to the study of the (mental) lexicon, an area which has, over the years gradually emerged from obscurity to occupy center stage.

The lexicon

A list of "exceptions." (Chomsky, 1995b: 235)

In the early days of generative grammar[4] the lexicon was given minimal attention: lexical items were just introduced by means of the same rules that defined linguistic structure. Neither Chomsky's monumental *Logical Structure of Linguistic Theory* (1955/75) nor *Syntactic Structures* (1957), from which the Chomskyan revolution is traditionally dated, refers to the lexicon as such at all. Fifty years later, the lexicon is of central importance and is even described as being potentially the locus of all variation between languages, so that apart from differences in the lexicon, "there is only one human language."[5]

To a first approximation the lexicon can be thought of as equivalent to a dictionary: a list of all the words in the language. However, there are crucial differences: the mental lexicon contains some information which is typically absent from traditional dictionaries, and lacks some information which is typically present. You know that *ask* and *wonder*[6] are both verbs, and that both can occur in sentences like *I asked what time it was* and *I wondered what time it was*. You also know that it is acceptable to say *I asked the time*, but that *I wondered the time* is impossible – it is not a sentence of English. Given that the sentences are otherwise identical, this difference must be a property of the two verbs concerned, so this information is encoded somehow in the mental lexicon, even though it is not made explicit in most standard dictionaries. Conversely, such dictionaries will tell you that *ask* is related to Old Frisian *askia*, and Old High German *eiscon*, something that is not an essential part of your knowledge as an English speaker. The form of words the "mental lexicon" is used precisely to emphasize this difference between the knowledge that an individual has stored in his or her head, as opposed to the knowledge of a community of scholars stored between the covers of a book.

Like a dictionary the lexicon actually includes far more than a list of words: idioms, like *to bury the hatchet*; clichés, like *it's a hard life*; productive affixes like *non-*, as in *non-occurring* or *non-transparent*, will also feature. To cover this wider domain, the lexicon is usually said to consist of an unordered list of "lexical items" rather than just words. Each lexical item is then characterized by a set of properties, referred to as features, specifying all and only the idiosyncratic, unpredictable information associated with it. That is, there should be no mention in the lexicon of information which follows from deeper generalizations, either about the language being described, or about language in general. As an example, consider the correlation of pronunciation with grammatical category. The word *import* can be either a noun or a verb (as in *Imports are going up again* and *John imports jute*, respectively), and its pronunciation is systematically different in the two cases, with stress on the first syllable for the noun and on the last syllable for the verb.[7] Despite this difference in pronunciation, it is unnecessary (and hence undesirable) to encode it in the lexicon, because it is part of a wider generalization about the relation between stress and part of speech: *torment, present, compact,* and *pervert* all work the same way: for instance, the same stress contrast shows up in *The devils will subject you to endless torment* and *The devils will torment you endlessly*. In brief, the stress is predictable and, as the lexicon should "exclud[e] whatever is predictable,"[8] the phonological representation of these words (that is, the specification of their pronunciation) is simplified to omit such information. As a result, there is a difference between the phonological form (or spelling) of the lexical entry for some item and its pronunciation (or phonetic representation).[9]

This emphasis on economy of representation, on avoiding redundancy, is a joint inheritance from structuralism and the hard sciences, and has been characteristic of all Chomsky's work in linguistics over the decades.[10] A slightly different kind of example is provided by a comparison of English and French.

In English, words can begin with *f* or *v* or *fr*, but not with *vr*; in French, all four possibilities exist. From this it is argued that, although English has a contrast between *f* and *v* (*fat* and *vat* mean different things), the requirement of economy means that the initial consonant of *frog* doesn't need to be spelt out in the lexicon as *f* rather than *v*, since *vr* is not a possible initial sequence in English. Similar arguments are exploited in the representation of meaning. The information that a frog is an amphibian makes it unnecessary to specify that it is an animal: all amphibians are animals, so once you have specified that a frog is an amphibian it is unnecessary to say further that it is also an animal. What it is necessary to specify, of course, is the sound–meaning correspondence, i.e. that *frog* has the various meanings it does, only one of which corresponds to the French *grenouille*. Of most interest, because most complex and most tightly integrated with its behavior in sentences, is the syntactic information inherent to particular words. *Frog* is a noun, more particularly a count noun, so you can say *two frogs*, though you can't say *two froths*, and it is a common noun – you can say *the frog*, though you can't say *the Fred*, and so on.[11]

In addition to inherent features of this kind, it is necessary to specify "selectional" features for each item. The verb *polish* selects a particular category, a following Noun Phrase such as *the silver*, rather than a Prepositional Phrase such as *in a minute* (the sentence *John polished the silver* is fine, but *John polished in a minute* is unacceptable). It is possible that such category selection may not need to be specified in the lexicon, if it is predictable from other, semantic, properties of the verb concerned. *Polish* is logically a two-place predicate: that is, one which selects two semantic arguments, an Agent who does the polishing, and a Patient which is polished. Patients are always Noun Phrases, so this information can be omitted from the individual lexical entry of *polish*. Notions such as Agent and Patient, known as "thematic roles" or "theta roles," are central to the semantic specification of lexical items, differentiating such examples as *undergo* and *undertake* in *John underwent the surgery reluctantly* and *John undertook the surgery reluctantly*, where the relations between *John* and the verb are crucially different.[12] In a fuller account, the properties of the lexicon would be spelt out at much greater length, but other aspects of information which have to be included in individual lexical entries can easily be inferred from the discussion of structural information that follows.

Knowledge of structure

Much of our knowledge is not so easily open to introspection as the vocabulary, and needs considerable teasing out before it becomes apparent. Chomsky has a remarkable facility for devising examples which reveal the subtlety of our command of language. A judicious selection, followed by a brief indication of why they are of interest, appears in (1–7):[13]

(1)   Is the man who is tall in the room?
(2)   Flying planes can be dangerous
(3) a.   John is easy to please
    b.   John is eager to please
(4) a.   I persuaded the specialist to examine John
    b.   I expected the specialist to examine John
(5)   When did John decide which car to fix?
(6) a.   John is too stubborn to talk to
    b.   John is too stubborn to talk to Bill
(7)   I painted my house brown

Example (1), *Is the man who is tall in the room?*, is used to illustrate the pervasive and fundamental property of structure dependence.[14] Consider the task of working out how to form questions from statements. Given a pair of sentences of the kind in (8):

(8) a.   The man is tall
    b.   Is the man tall?

a range of logically possible solutions is available. You could try moving the third word to the front; this works with (8a), but with *John is tall* it would give the impossible *tall John is?*. You could try moving the first auxiliary verb to the front (auxiliaries are things like *is, can*, and *might*; in the present example *is* is the auxiliary), but with *The man who is tall is in the room* this would give the ungrammatical result *Is the man who tall is in the room?*. Mentioning the auxiliary is all right, but what is needed is a rule which refers not to mathematical notions like first and third, but exclusively to *structural* notions like "subject" and "auxiliary." To form a question in English you move the auxiliary immediately following the subject to the front of the sentence. The subject of *The man is tall* is *The man*; the subject of *The man who is tall is in the room* is *The man who is tall*, not just *The man*. The example is trivial, but the moral is vital: all rules in all languages are structure dependent in this way. Despite the logical simplicity of a formulation like "Move the third word" or "Invert the sequence xyz to give zyx" – a simplicity that should appeal to any self-respecting Martian – no rule in any human language uses such formulations. Rules of grammar can't count.[15]

Knowledge of structural relations

Example (2), *Flying planes can be dangerous*, is ambiguous; that is, it has two different meanings, corresponding either to *Flying planes is dangerous* or to *Flying planes are dangerous*. This ambiguity shows that the relation between form and meaning is not as straightforward as one might have hoped. Lexical ambiguity is well known and can be dealt with by listing separately in the lexicon all the meanings of a word. For instance, *frog* can mean not only the amphibian, but also the frog of a horse's foot or the frog on an officer's uniform (assuming that these other meanings are part of the individual's knowledge). But syntactic ambiguity of the kind in (2) is not amenable to a solution by listing senses of words, as the words involved are the same in the two interpretations. The next obvious strategy of listing all the ambiguous sentences is inherently impossible, as the set of such sentences is infinite. It follows that in our production and understanding of examples like this we must be deploying different grammatical rules as well as knowledge of vocabulary.

The examples in (3), *John is easy to please* and *John is eager to please*, show in a different way that sentences do not wear their analyses on their sleeves. (3a) can be paraphrased by *It is easy to please John*, where *John* is the object of *please*; but in (3b) no such paraphrase is possible, and the interpretation is rather that John is eager to please some unspecified person. The pair of sentences in (4), *I persuaded the specialist to examine John* and *I expected the specialist to examine John*, similarly shows that superficial similarity is not an unambiguous guide to structure. That (4a) is *not* parallel to (4b) emerges from the contrast between *I persuaded the specialist that he should examine John* and the impossible *I expected the specialist that he should examine John*. As was the case with *ask* and *wonder*, we need an interaction between the lexicon and the syntax to enable us to explain what is going on.

Linguists thrive on ambiguity, using it – as in the case of *Flying planes can be dangerous* – as a first indication of hidden structural differences. In contrast, (5), *When did John decide which car to fix?*, illustrates a surprising lack of ambiguity. *John decided to fix the car on Saturday* is ambiguous: he may have decided on Saturday to fix the car some time or other, or he may have decided some time or other to fix the car on Saturday. The corresponding question *When did John decide to fix the car?* has exactly the same ambiguity. Given such examples, one would expect (5) to have the same two meanings, but it doesn't; it allows only the interpretation where *when* is construed with *decide* and not with *fix*: that is, when did he make his decision? It may take you a few moments' reflection to persuade yourself that the facts are really as I have described them. What is surprising is that, after reflection, speakers virtually all do agree, despite the fact that sentences like these are not the usual subject of school instruction.

The contrasting examples in (6), *John is too stubborn to talk to* and *John is too stubborn to talk to Bill*, illustrate a different failure of analogy and a different form of complexity. Rather like (3) (*John is easy to please* and *John is eager to please*) they illustrate a contrast between John as subject of *talk* (in *John is too stubborn to talk to Bill*), and as object of *to* (in *John is too stubborn to talk to*), but what is striking is the lack of parallelism in the interpretation of these two superficially similar sentences. Chomsky uses these examples to show that traditional ideas of analogy are not useful in accounting for our knowledge of syntax. The difference between *John ate* and *John ate an apple* is simply that the former lacks the object which is visible in the latter. Accordingly, we interpret *John ate* as meaning that John ate something or other. If this analogy were valid, we would expect it to generalize to the pair in (6), but it does not: *John is too stubborn to talk to* can't be interpreted as meaning *John is too stubborn to talk to someone or other*.

Finally (7), *I painted my house brown*, shows that our knowledge of language extends to the semantic and pragmatic domains in unexpected ways. As we saw in the previous chapter, we all know without thinking that in the usual case it is the exterior of the house that becomes brown, even though there is no ban on painting (and indeed saying) that one has painted the interior of one's house that color.

Any linguistic theory must be able to describe, and will seek to explain, these and innumerable other observations; observations which are, moreover, based on extremely short and simple sentences: all of the examples I have cited have fewer than ten words.

The formal background   A major contribution of the generative enterprise has been the discovery of vast numbers of new facts, a few of which have been illustrated above. How can we account for these facts? To begin, it is worth emphasizing, especially in view of the claim that linguistic theory seeks explanation rather than mere description, that before Chomsky's melding of mathematics and linguistics, it was impossible even to describe many of these phenomena. As a graduate student working on the grammar of a little-known West African language,[16] I was continually confronted by data which I couldn't describe, let alone explain. The situation for today's student is at once both better and worse: better in that there are unlimited descriptive tools to hand for the description of a wealth of weird and wonderful constructions; worse in that he or she is confronted with problems of much greater sophistication and is expected to be conversant with more, and more abstract, techniques. Rules of grammar do not exploit arithmetic notions like "third word" or linear inversion, but they do have properties which can be best described in terms of the branch of mathematics known as recursive function theory, an area within which Chomsky, especially in collaboration with Marco Schützenberger, made significant contributions.[17] Chomsky's exploitation of mathematics to develop new techniques of description – especially the theories of Phrase Structure and Transformational Grammar, the use of syntactic features, the application of indexing – made it possible to bring these facts under control. These technical innovations could then be used even by those who had no sympathy with the philosophical implications of Chomsky's work. Many working linguists who had no interest in his philosophical claims, or were deeply suspicious of them, nonetheless recognized the merits of his formal descriptive apparatus, and were prepared to exploit it in a spirit of philosophical instrumentalism.

Levels of representation[18]

A grammar has to relate meanings to pronunciations, semantics to sounds. In the jargon this is usually referred to as relating LF (Logical Form) to PF (Phonetic Form). Ambiguity shows that this relation is often indirect, so we need to have recourse to structural – syntactic – analysis as well. The basis for the relation is provided by the lexicon, which gives a phonological, a semantic, and a syntactic characterization of every item in the vocabulary. To accommodate our knowledge of sentence structure, what is traditionally referred to as grammar, we need descriptions of different kinds. From the earliest work in generative grammar a crucial notion has been "level of representation," where different levels of representation are postulated to capture generalizations of different kinds about sentences.[19]

To capture generalizations about pronunciation and the sound structure of sentences, the grammar exploits the level of representation called Phonetic Form (PF). To capture generalizations about meaning and the logical properties of sentences it exploits the level of semantic representation called Logical Form (LF).[20] This means that the ambiguous sentences discussed earlier will have the same phonetic form but different logical forms. Distinct sentences that mean the same thing, like *All the children came* and *The children all came*, will have the same logical form but different phonetic forms. Similarly, the partial similarity (and partial difference) between quantifiers[21] such as *every* and *each* is described by assuming distinct semantic specifications for them in the lexicon. This accounts directly for the contrast between *Each child came* and *Every child came*, and indirectly for that between *The children each came* and the impossible *The children every came*. In order to give an adequate description of these semantically conditioned differences of syntactic behavior, it is necessary to have a level of LF at which the precise meaning of every expression is specified in terms of the meanings of its parts – "compositionally," as the jargon has it.

Apart from variations in technical terminology, so much has always been commonplace. What was striking about Chomsky's work from the beginning was the sophistication – and complexity – of his *syntactic* representations. In particular, he argued at length for the necessity of having more than one level of representation within the syntax, postulating the famous distinction between deep structure and surface structure.[22] This terminological contrast didn't feature explicitly in the earliest work, but it is implicit both there and in any framework which exploits the notion of (transformational) derivation. To understand what is involved we need to look at the various rule types that are used in a grammar.

Constituents and rules

Sentences consist of words: not just strings of words but structured sequences of words. An example like (9):

(9)   Harry stirred the stew

is standardly analyzed as having the simplified structure in (10) indicated by the brackets:

(10)   [[Harry] [[stirred] [the stew]]]

That is, [the stew] is a unit or constituent (intuitively this just means that *the* is more closely associated with *stew* than with *stirred*), [stirred the stew] is a constituent, and the whole sentence [Harry stirred the stew] is a constituent. Additionally, every individual word is a constituent. In contrast, neither [Harry stirred] nor [stirred the] is a constituent. In addition to being constituents, these bracketed sequences are of different types or categories: [the stew] is a Noun Phrase (NP), consisting of a Noun (N) preceded by a Determiner (Det);[23] [stirred the stew] is a Verb Phrase (VP), consisting of a Verb (V) followed by a Noun Phrase; the whole string is a Sentence (S), and so on. This additional information is standardly indicated by labeling the brackets with subscripts, as in (11), or by means of a tree diagram (which contains exactly the same information), as in (12):[24]

(11)   [$_S$[$_N$ Harry] [$_{VP}$ [$_V$ stirred] [$_{NP}$ [$_{Det}$ the] [$_N$ stew]]]]

(12)

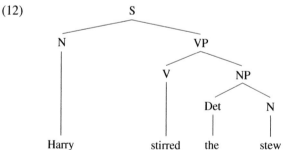

Trees of this kind were generated by means of Phrase Structure rules (PS rules) of the sort seen in (13):

(13) a. S → N VP
     b. VP → V NP
     c. NP → Det N

This formalism just means that a Sentence may consist of (indicated by the arrow, $\rightarrow$) a Noun followed by a Verb Phrase; a Verb Phrase may consist of a Verb followed by a Noun Phrase, and so on. A less impoverished grammar might contain dozens or even hundreds of such rules. It is not possible to give precise figures, as (apart from the fact that no grammar written ever came even near to completeness) the number of rules is dependent in large part on the type of abbreviatory conventions that are envisaged. For some years a great amount of effort was expended in extending and refining such rule sets for English and a variety of other languages, so that they accounted for ("generated") a vast number of different kinds of construction. As we saw in the previous chapter, we can produce and understand any of an *infinite* number of sentences, not just a vast number. The grammar replicates this ability by being recursive: that is, in addition to the rules in (13), it includes rules like those in (14), which reintroduce on the right of the arrow categories which already appear on the left.

(14) a.   VP $\rightarrow$ V S
     b.   NP $\rightarrow$ NP PP

This recursiveness captures the property usually referred to as "discrete infinity":[25] the fact that sentences consist of whole numbers of words (never five and a half words, for instance), and that the number of such words is unlimited. The first of these rules, (14a), allows sentences to occur embedded inside bigger sentences, so we have examples like *Mary thinks [Harry stirred the stew]* or *I suspect [Mary thinks [Harry stirred the stew]]*, and so on indefinitely; and the second, (14b), similarly allows Noun Phrases to be constituents of larger Noun Phrases, giving examples like *The girl with a blue bonnet* or *The girl in the car with a blue bonnet*. These extremely simple additions simultaneously allow an initial account of the ambiguity of the last example: if the car has the blue bonnet (American readers should substitute *hood* for *bonnet*) we have the structure in (15a); if it is the girl who has the blue bonnet, we have (15b):[26]

(15) a.

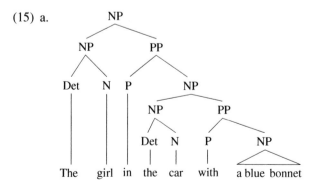

b.

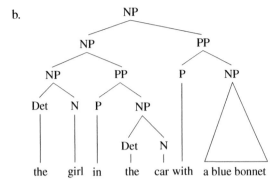

Deep structure

Phrase Structure grammars of this kind were Chomsky's formalization of traditional Immediate Constituent analysis:[27] a formalization that represented a considerable technical advance on previous analyses in making possible a rigorous *syntactic representation* of sentences. But simultaneously with this formalization, Chomsky presented arguments to the effect that Phrase Structure grammar was in principle inadequate to describe some constructions in language. The technicalities of this demonstration are of only historical interest, but the consequential introduction of transformations was, and is, of great importance. Before turning to this issue, it is worth mentioning that the inadequacy of Phrase Structure grammars resides not (or not mainly) in their putative inability to generate particular sentences of English or some other language, but in the unrevealing nature of their description: in particular, they failed to capture differences between pairs of sentences such as those in (3), and they failed to express the relatedness of pairs of sentences such as those in (8).

As an example of why transformations were argued to be necessary (and hence why we need deep structure), consider the following scenario. Suppose you misheard someone utter the example in (9), *Harry stirred the stew.* A natural response might be the question in (16), uttered with suitably startled or incredulous intonation:

(16)   Harry stirred what?

Such echo-questions preserve the word order and structure of the original statement, and could without difficulty be accommodated by means of fairly minimal extensions to a Phrase Structure grammar. However, ordinary WH-questions (those which include a WH-word like *what, who, which, when, how,* and so on) show a radically different word order and structure:

(17)   What did Harry stir?

It is not impossible to generate examples like (17) by adding to the Phrase Structure rules, but the result is inelegant and raises a number of further problems. For instance, it is clear that *what* in (17) is the direct object of *stir* just as it is in (16), and that it remains the direct object however far it is separated from its governing verb, as is shown by "unbounded dependency" examples like (18):[28]

(18) a. What did Mary want Harry to stir?
     b. What did you think Mary wanted Harry to stir?

Building on insights of his teacher Zellig Harris,[29] Chomsky's solution to these problems was to introduce rules of a completely different kind: transformations. Whereas Phrase Structure rules make explicit the internal structure of one particular phrase or sentence, transformations change one whole structure into another. A sentence like (17) would then be generated in two stages: Phrase Structure rules would produce a tree similar to that in (12), and then a new, transformational, rule would change that whole tree into another one, as shown in (19):

(19)

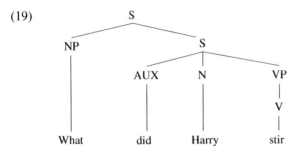

There are many problematic details about what precisely the effect of the transformation should be and how it is achieved. I have provided no account here of how the extra "S" got there or of how the auxiliary verb *did* appeared as if by magic. These were interesting and fruitful problems, but the technicalities are (now) irrelevant. What is important – and still a matter of controversy – is that there are now *two* levels of representation within the syntax. In order to capture particular generalizations in as simple a fashion as possible – for instance, that the notion "direct object" can be associated with the position immediately after the verb; even when it is not pronounced in that position – the theory is made more complicated. Instead of trying to account for everything at a single level, the theory now disposes of two levels, each of which is designed to capture different sorts of generalization. Descriptive adequacy is purchased at the price of theoretical complication.[30] Intuitively, transformations are a little like variations on a musical theme, or Picasso's repeated metamorphoses of a particular picture such as Grünewald's *Crucifixion*. Unlike these metamorphoses, however, transformations are formally explicit, providing rigorous descriptions of the structural properties of sentences, and allowing no vagueness of interpretation.

It is important to note that there is nothing sacrosanct about transformations: they are an ingenious descriptive device, which facilitated the description of what were widely accepted to be significant general properties of languages. Their justification is their explanatory success. In particular there is nothing especially significant about the names or properties of the levels postulated. The trees generated by Phrase Structure rules were, by definition, deep structures, and the trees produced by transformations operating on these deep structures were, again by definition, surface structures. "Deep" and "surface" are simply labels attached to formal constructs of the theory, and have no correlation with philosophical profundity or psychological priority. The common misperception that deep structures were deep in a different sense was probably due to the fact that at one stage, deep structure was deemed to be necessary and sufficient for the determination of the meaning of a sentence,[31] and meaning, of course, is what philosophers and indeed everyone else are pre-eminently interested in. The claim that deep structure determined meaning soon had to be dropped, but the allure of the terminology, and of the idea, took much longer to dissolve.

Description versus explanation

Prior to Chomsky's development of transformational grammar there were many constructions in natural language that it was simply impossible to describe adequately. There wasn't even an appropriate notation for dealing with the unbounded dependency exemplified in (18), for example. The new theory won many converts simply because it provided ways of describing facts that had previously resisted analysis; because these analyses often uncovered the existence of new facts that fell together with those just described, and because in many cases the new descriptive machinery brought together sets of data which had hitherto seemed unrelated. But this success was bought at a cost. Beginning with Bob Lees's dissertation,[32] syntactic analysis in the 1960s became startlingly complex, with an explosion of new rules, both Phrase Structure and transformational, which grew increasingly baroque. There was a certain intellectual satisfaction to be gained from mastering and manipulating the new machinery, but one nagging problem came more and more to dominate discussion: how could children acquire this complex edifice of rules? Not only did grammars now consist of hundreds of rules of different types, many of these rules were ordered with respect to each other. That is, in order to generate only grammatical sentences and no ungrammatical ones, it was necessary to stipulate that rule A precede rule B. Consider a maximally simple example. At this time imperative sentences like that in (20) were derived from simple statements like that in (21) by deleting the subject *you* transformationally:

(20)   Stir the stew
(21)   You stir the stew

Similarly, reflexive sentences like that in (22) were derived from structures like that in (23), where there were two (coreferential) occurrences of the same item, by changing the second *John* into *himself*:[33]

(22)   John hurt himself
(23)   John hurt John

To generate a sentence like (24) on these assumptions:

(24)   Wash yourself

it was necessary to go through two stages, as shown in (25):

(25)   You wash you → You wash yourself → Wash yourself

with the reflexive transformation applying before the imperative transformation. If one attempts to apply the rules in the opposite order, as in (26):

(26)   You wash you → Wash you

one gets stuck with the ungrammatical sequence *Wash you* (linguists traditionally mark ungrammatical forms with a prefixed asterisk). With only two rules to order with respect to each other there are just two different orderings, but with three rules there are six, with four rules twenty-four, with ten rules there are half a million.[34] Chomsky's own Master's thesis demonstrated a depth of rule ordering for Modern Hebrew morphophonemics of twenty-five . . .[35] The problem should be obvious: on top of the mammoth task of learning all the rules, the child acquiring its first language also had to work through an astronomically large number of possible orderings of those rules. The new grammatical theory provided great descriptive potential at the cost of making language acquisition, and indeed knowledge of language itself, apparently inexplicable. As Chomsky put it in an early article with George Miller, "we cannot seriously propose that a child learns the values of 10^9 parameters in a childhood lasting only 10^8 seconds."[36] The tension between description and explanation, often expressed as the need to achieve explanatory adequacy rather than just descriptive adequacy, has dominated linguistics ever since, with repeated attempts being made to reduce the number and power of the descriptive devices required. Crucially, however, this reduction has to take place without sacrificing the ability to analyze sentences, and without raising new problems for the child, or the linguist.[37]

From rules to principles

The first step in the attempt to increase the explanatory power of grammars was the development of universal principles, which could be attributed to linguistic theory and thereby removed from the grammars of individual languages and people.[38] A movement in this direction had been taken as early as 1962 in Chomsky's paper to the International Congress of Linguists, where he proposed the "A over A condition."[39] This principle had the effect of limiting the application of rules to a small subset of the logical possibilities. If a category (such as Noun Phrase) included as part of its structure another instance of the same category (i.e. another Noun Phrase) then any rule that mentioned "Noun Phrase" had to be construed as referring to the more inclusive instance. For example, we saw in (16) and (17) above that *what* can function like the Noun Phrase *the stew* as the direct object of a verb. Objects may be more complex in structure than this example, as can be seen in (27), where the brackets show that the direct object consists in each case of a Noun Phrase with a further Noun Phrase (or Noun Phrases) within it:

(27) a. Harry stirred [NP[NPthe stew] and [NPthe pudding]]
     b. Harry stirred [NP[NPthe stew] that tasted of [NPturnips]]

Just as *what* could replace *the stew* in (9) and (17), it can replace [the stew and the pudding] or [the stew that tasted of turnips], as shown in the question/answer pairs in (28):

(28)   Q.   What did Harry stir?
         A1.   The stew and the pudding
         A2.   The stew that tasted of turnips

But strikingly, it is not possible to question the subparts of these Noun Phrases, even though they are themselves Noun Phrases, as can be seen by the impossibility of the examples in (29):

(29) a. *What did Harry stir the stew and – ?
     b. *What did Harry stir – and the pudding?
     c. *What did Harry stir the stew that tasted of – ?

These examples may seem unimportant, but their significance resides in the fact that they illustrate a general property of language, not just an idiosyncrasy of one rule of English. All rules in all languages obey the A over A condition, as you can test by trying to translate the examples in (29) into your favorite language. That is, all languages treat the larger constituent as an "island" from which nothing can escape.[40] This universality turns what had been a descriptive problem into an explanatory solution. The implication is that when children are working out what the rules of their first language are, they can ignore a whole host of alternatives which are logically possible but linguistically excluded by universal principle. The generality of the principle suggests that it is part of the mental architecture the child brings to bear on the language-learning task, and is not something it has to learn.

As well as simplifying the grammars of individual languages by appealing to universal principles, the tension between description and explanation was resolved in part by factoring out commonalties among rules. Consider an analogy: the chemical elements look at first sight like an unstructured list but, as Mendeleyev famously discovered, they show a regular recurrence of properties when they are arranged in a particular order known as the periodic table. This gives rise to natural classes of elements such as transition metals, lanthanides, and so on. In the same way, different transformations were observed to share common properties, suggesting that they too constituted natural classes. This insight, first spelt out in "On WH-movement,"[41] led to a dramatic reduction in the number of transformations. As can be seen in (30), the rules involved in questions (30a), relative clauses (30b), clefts (30c), and pseudo-clefts (30d) can all move an object from the position next to its governing verb – shown by a dash – and all share a variety of other properties:

(30) a. What did Harry stir – ?
     b. The stew which Harry stirred – was full of turnips
     c. It was the stew that Harry stirred –[42]
     d. What Harry stirred – was the stew

Once these commonalties have been noticed and formalized, the set of rules mentioned here can be reduced to the single generalization "Move-WH."[43] Of course, WH-phrases (that is, phrases containing a WH-word) are not the only things that can be moved. There is a variety of constructions, such as passive, in which Noun Phrases move, but whose other properties are somewhat different. While WH-movement is unbounded, as shown in example (18), NP-movement is usually taken to be bounded; that is, any element which is moved has to stay within the same clause.[44] Accordingly, (31b), the passive of (31a), is grammatical, but (32b), the passive of (32a), is impossible, because *John* has moved too far: out of its clause of origin.

(31) a. Mary kissed John
     b. John was kissed by Mary
(32) a. It is evident that Mary loves John
     b. *John is evident that is loved by Mary

In fact this difference in "boundedness" seems to be only a superficial property of the different rules. All movement, whether bounded or (apparently) unbounded has to be "local": that is, it takes place within the confines of a single clause. This implies that elements that appear to move unboundedly must actually move in a number of steps rather than at one fell swoop. Such movement is called "cyclic" or "successive-cyclic," the idea being that the same rule applies repeatedly in "successive cycles" comprising larger and larger domains. Consider an example, parallel to those in (18), such as (33):

(33)   What might Mary think [Harry stirred – ?]

where *what* has moved from the position indicated by the dash to the front of the sentence.[45] There are two plausible ways in which this could happen: either *what* could move in a single jump or it could move in two steps, first to the front of the embedded clause, marked by the square brackets, then to the front of the whole sentence. The two possibilities (ignoring the complexity occasioned by the position of *might* and *Mary*) are illustrated in (34) and (35):

(34)   [Mary might think [Harry stirred what?]]→
        [What might Mary think [Harry stirred – ?]]

(35)   [Mary might think [Harry stirred what?]] →
        [Mary might think [what Harry stirred – ?]] →
        [What might Mary think [– Harry stirred – ?]]

In (34), *what* has moved straight to the front of the sentence; in (35) it has moved in two stages: first to the front of the embedded clause, and then to the front of the whole sentence. Put like this the choice between the analyses looks obvious: (34) is simpler and so should be preferred over (35). Interestingly, however, there is good evidence that (35) is in fact correct. The simplest such evidence comes not from English but from a variety of other languages including Spanish, Afrikaans, and Scottish Gaelic.[46] Spanish allows a freedom of word order, absent from English, such that in suitable pragmatic contexts, the subject can appear optionally after the verb phrase, so we can have either of the examples in (36):

(36) a.   Maria contestó la pregunta   – Maria answered the question
     b.   Contestó la pregunta Maria   – Maria answered the question

In WH-questions, this "subject inversion" is obligatory,[47] so that (37a) is acceptable, but (37b) is simply ungrammatical:

(37) a.   Qué contestó Maria?   – What did Maria answer?
     b.   *Qué Maria contestó?

The interesting case is then one where we have "unbounded" movement in a complex sentence, as in (38):

(38) a. Juan pensaba que Maria contestó la pregunta
 Juan thought that Maria answered the question
 b. Qué pensaba Juan que contestó Maria?
 What did John think that Mary answered?
 c. *Qué pensaba Juan que Maria contestó?

How do we account for the parallel ungrammaticality of (37b) and (38c)? Such examples indicate that inversion is obligatory in any clause containing a WH-word (here *qué*) in its initial position. But that suggests that the WH-word in the embedded clause has passed through the initial position on its way to the front of the whole sentence, entailing that (35) rather than the apparently simpler (34) is correct.

Apparent boundedness is not the only difference between NP-movement and WH-movement, but these other differences too turned out to be predictable, so in due course it became possible to reduce all movement rules to a single generalization: the principle that you can "Move-α" (where "α" [Greek alpha] stands for any kind of constituent). This principle, which just says that movement is one possibility allowed by linguistic theory, could now be extracted from the grammar of any particular language and ascribed to the language faculty.

This has two striking results: first, the reduction in the number of rules makes the child's acquisitional task dramatically easier; in particular, there may now be so few rules that problems of rule ordering no longer even arise, and all the language learner has to do is discover what precisely α refers to in the language he or she is exposed to. Second, the notion "construction" (things like passive, relative, question) can be eliminated. The rules of the grammar now characterize as well-formed, whole clusters of phenomena: for instance, all those sentences with a moved WH-word. Accordingly, talk of any particular construction is unnecessary, as it is subsumed under a general discussion of "all those things with property X," where property X, for instance, might be "contains a WH-word." It is possible to make a stronger claim: talking of constructions is not just unnecessary, it is wrong. Many sentences have properties that belong to more than one construction type: for instance, *John was expected to leave* is an example of both passive and what is called "raising."[48] To be forced to ask which of these constructions it actually is is unhelpful. Constructions are now just an epiphenomenon: side-effects of more abstract and general principles.

The elimination of PS rules

At the same time as this simplification of the transformational component was taking place, Phrase Structure rules too were being removed.[49] This was effected in two different ways. On the one hand, it had been clear for some time that grammars as conceived in the late 1960s and early 1970s manifested a certain redundancy in that information that was present in the PS rules was repeated, and in fact repeated many times, in the lexicon. For instance, two-place predicates like *bring*, or the verb *polish* that we looked at above, have to be used transitively: that is, they must be followed by an object; whereas one-place predicates like *dither* or *stumble* are intransitive: that is, they cannot be followed by an object but must occur alone or accompanied by a prepositional phrase. Accordingly, we have the contrasting judgments shown in (39) and (40):

(39) a. John brought the wine
     b. *John brought
     c. *The wine brought

(40) a. The government dithered (about disarmament)
     b. *The government dithered disarmament

Such information has to be stipulated in the lexicon as it is not predictable, and this is done by saying, for instance, that the verb *bring* must be followed by a Noun Phrase. But that a verb may be followed by a Noun Phrase is precisely the information provided by the rule in (13b), VP → V NP. As the distributional possibilities of individual verbs are in part idiosyncratic (though largely predictable from their meanings), such information must be left in their lexical entries, and should therefore be removed from the PS rules. That is, the Phrase Structure rule is redundant and can be eliminated.

Three points need stressing: first, not *all* PS rules can be eliminated so easily, and the task of getting rid of them itself resulted in interesting and radical revisions to the theory.[50] Second, it is still necessary to combine or "merge" lexical items from the lexicon to form larger constituents, such as *the wine* from *the* and *wine*, and *brought the wine* from *brought* and *the wine*. Third, it is remarkable that redundancy of the kind illustrated here should be such a good indication of the need for theoretical revision. It is a commonplace of the hard sciences that theories of any elegance must abide by criteria of parsimony, symmetry, non-redundancy, and so on. Part of Chomsky's program has been to show that precisely those same criteria are operative in linguistic theory construction. For a biological system this is more surprising than for a physical system, and it is a considerable achievement to have shown, several times, that this assimilation of linguistics to the natural sciences is both possible and fruitful.

X-bar theory

The second strand in the elimination of Phrase Structure rules is another excursion into generalization: the development of X-bar theory.[51] Verb Phrases contain Verbs, Noun Phrases contain Nouns, Adjective Phrases are headed by Adjectives. The obvious generalization is that X Phrases contain Xs as their "heads," so there is no need to stipulate in individual grammars that this is the case. Moreover, what can follow X tends to be the same irrespective of whether X is N, V or A. Just as verbs can be transitive, intransitive or followed by a clausal complement, as in (41), so can Nouns and Adjectives, as in (42) and (43) respectively:[52]

(41) a. John <u>mended</u> the car   [Transitive verb]
     b. John <u>vanished</u>   [Intransitive verb]
     c. John <u>thinks</u> that frogs are   [Clausal complement verb]
         mammals

(42) a. John is a <u>student</u> of linguistics   [Transitive noun]
     b. John is a <u>hero</u>   [Intransitive noun]
     c. John regrets the <u>fact</u> that frogs   [Clausal complement noun]
         are amphibians

(43) a. John is <u>fond</u> of Mary   [Transitive adjective]
     b. John is <u>comatose</u>   [Intransitive adjective]
     c. John is <u>sure</u> that frogs are   [Clausal complement adjective]
         vertebrates

Again the moral is obvious: there is no need to repeat the range of possibilities separately for each category; rather, that information can be stated once for all in an abstract schema, called the X-bar schema, which covers all categories equally. The way to eliminating the plethora of Phrase Structure rules was now open, and with the later generalization of X-bar theory from categories like Noun, Verb, and Adjective to include all categories –[53] Determiners (like *the*), Complementizers (like *that* in *I know that penguins are fattening*) and so on – the theory has again made possible the simplification of individual grammars, and has lessened the putative learning load for the child.

The guiding intuition behind theoretical development at this stage was the desirability of distributing the responsibility of accounting for knowledge of language among a number of autonomous systems, each of which is maximally simple, but the effect of whose interaction is the accurate characterization of our intuitions in all their complexity. It was freely conceded that a host of facts was still left unaccounted for, but assigning responsibility for the analysis of the set of possible structural relations to X-bar theory, and the general property of movement to Move-α, made possible an extremely simple statement of a wide range of syntactic phenomena. This transition from rules to principles, which reflected the transfer of emphasis from description to explanation, was characterized by a modularization of the grammar reminiscent of the modularity of the mind.

Where previously each construction had been seen as necessitating a rule or set of rules dedicated to its description, it was now the case that a limited number of modules, in conjunction with statements about individual entries from the lexicon, would conspire to produce the range of effects observed. The theory at this stage of its existence was widely known as Government and Binding theory, because of the central importance of two of the notions it exploited.[54] It should be noted, even so, that Chomsky dislikes the terminology precisely because it refers merely to two technical notions which may or may not be important for linguistic description in the long run: "The real approach was the principles and parameters approach that may or may not involve government and binding."[55] Before embarking on a discussion of Principles and Parameters, it is necessary to provide an overview of the Government and Binding framework. Even though government has indeed now disappeared from Chomsky's own work in the Minimalist Program,[56] all current generative grammar presupposes some familiarity with both the concept "government" itself, and with its associated modules.

Government and Binding theory

In addition to X-bar theory and Move-α, there were several separate components dedicated to capturing particular kinds of generalization. Let us look briefly at each in turn, paying most attention to those which are still exploited in current work.

Binding theory

Binding theory accounts for relations among anaphors like *himself*, pronominals like *him*, so-called referring expressions like *John*, and their possible antecedents in sentences such as those in (44):[57]

(44) a. John$_i$ likes him$_j$
      b. John$_i$ likes himself$_i$
      c. Bill$_i$ thinks [John$_j$ likes him$_i$]
      d. Bill$_i$ thinks [John$_j$ likes himself$_j$]
      e. He$_i$ likes John$_j$

In general, pronouns and anaphors have opposite distribution: in (44a) *him* cannot refer to *John*, as indicated by the *different* subscripts, whereas in (44b) *himself must* refer to *John*, as indicated by the identical subscripts; in (44c) *him* can refer to *Bill* but not to *John*, whereas *himself* in (44d) can only refer to *John*; in (44e), just as in (44a), the noun and the pronoun have to refer to different people. After twenty-five years' work the core generalization was extracted that anaphors had to be bound in some local domain, whilst pronouns had to be free (that is, not bound) in that same domain, and referring expressions like *John* had to be free everywhere. "Bound" is a technical term that means "co-indexed with" (i.e. marked with the same subscript) and lower down in the kind of tree shown in (12). There are, of course, many residual problems: for instance the treatment of so-called picture-noun reflexives like that in (45) requires additional complications to the theory:[58]

(45)   John's$_i$ campaign required that pictures of himself$_i$ be placed all over town

but this basic insight makes possible a simple treatment of more complex sentences like those in (46) and (47):

(46) a. John$_i$ expects to visit him$_j$
     b. I wonder who John$_i$ expects to visit him$_i$

As expected, *him* in (46a) can only refer to some unnamed person in the context and cannot refer to *John* (hence they have different subscripts), but once this identical sequence is embedded inside a more complex structure as in (46b), coreference *is* possible, again as indicated by the subscripts. These striking examples have been used by Chomsky not only to argue for the formal elegance of this version of the theory but to demonstrate the implausibility of traditional notions of learning (see chapter 3), the undesirability of the requirement that knowledge be conscious (see chapter 4), and so on. Further examples (whose full analysis would require more elaboration of other parts of the theory) reveal yet more unexpected patterns:

(47) a. The knowledge that John$_i$ might fail bothered him$_j$
     b. The possibility that John$_i$ might fail bothered him$_i$
     c. The realization that John$_i$ might fail bothered him$_{i/j}$

In (47a) *him* cannot (normally) be construed as referring to *John*, whereas in (47b) *him* typically can be taken to refer to *John* (though as before it is possible for it to refer to some unnamed person in the context). This surprising difference correlates with the difference between the felicity of the expression *our knowledge that so and so* and the infelicity of the expression *our possibility that so and so*. In (47c) both referential possibilities are open, as is indicated by the alternative subscripts, with the different interpretations dependent on who is realizing that John might fail. These judgments are both subtle and somewhat variable from individual to individual. Accordingly it takes some considerable effort of introspection to confirm whether one shares the particular intuitions given here. The existence of systematic differences of such interpretive subtlety gives an unambiguous indication of the richness of our linguistic knowledge and the power of current theory to begin to account for it. Given the attention paid to binding theory over the years, it is somewhat chastening to discover that recent theoretical advances have made it unclear precisely how it fits in with the other mechanisms of grammar that are currently appealed to. Whatever its ultimate fate, there is general agreement that some theory of binding is still indispensable.

Locality

I described the core insight of binding theory as being that anaphors had to be bound in some local domain. In (44d) for instance, *Bill$_i$ thinks [John$_j$ likes himself$_j$]*, the reflexive element *himself* can refer to the local noun, *John*, which is in the same clause, but not to the non-local one, *Bill*. The reason for the lack of ambiguity in example (5), *When did John decide which car to fix?*, is likewise a matter of locality: *when* can only be construed with the local verb *decide*, and not the non-local *fix*. A third locality constraint, simply listed at that time as a separate subtheory of the grammar, was known as bounding or subjacency, and set a bound on how far elements can move. More accurately, the constraint determined how many bounding nodes, such as NP, a moved constituent could cross, and explained the contrast between the examples in (48):[59]

(48) a. A rise in the price of oil was announced
       b. A rise was announced in the price of oil
       c. *A rise in the price was announced of oil

(48a) was assumed to have the simplified structure shown in (49):

(49) $_{NP}$[$_{NP}$[A rise] $_{PP}$[in $_{NP}$[$_{NP}$[the price]] $_{PP}$[of $_{NP}$[oil]]]] was announced

To produce (48b) the Prepositional Phrase *in the price of oil* is moved to the end of the sentence, crossing the outermost NP bracket. To produce (48c) it is likewise necessary to move the Prepositional Phrase *of oil* to the end of the sentence, but this movement would cross two NP nodes (the outermost one and also the one delimiting [*the price of oil*]), and this is prohibited by subjacency. It is important to note that, although the phrase *of oil* doesn't appear to move any further than the phrase *in the price of oil*, it has to emerge from a more deeply embedded position, and it is that which violates the bounding condition. It might appear that this analysis, with its mention of "two NP nodes," is at variance with the earlier claim that rules of the grammar cannot count. In fact, all that is needed is the notion of adjacent element: the reference to one and two is just a convenient shorthand. Although I have listed various examples together under "locality," it was many years before the theory developed to a stage where these examples could be given a unified treatment, and issues of locality are still topics of current debate, as we shall see below.[60]

Theta theory

Theta theory accounts for the argument structure associated with particular predicates of the kind we saw with *bring* and *dither* earlier.[61] Some of these differences are semantically predictable, in that the syntactic properties derive from the meaning of the verbs involved, so the difference between the pairs of examples in (50) is a simple function of the number of entities involved in the activity. If you accompany someone there must be at least two people involved, so (50b) is anomalous. Similarly, laughing needs to involve only one person, so (50d) is odd. This is not to say that two people cannot laugh, but one of them cannot laugh the other. One can also construct more complex examples like (50e), but the contrast in acceptability between (50d) and (50e) is completely clear-cut, and the generalization that the meaning of the verbs determines their syntactic distribution holds to a first approximation.

(50) a. John accompanied Mary
     b. *John accompanied
     c. John laughed
     d. *John laughed Mary
     e. John laughed Mary off the stage

The core construct of theta theory, which enables it to account for these facts, is the theta criterion, which says that "Each argument bears one and only one theta-role, and each theta-role is assigned to one and only one argument."[62] In (50a) and (50c) the criterion is satisfied, and the examples are acceptable; but in (50b) *accompany* has a theta role which has been left unassigned, and in (50d) *laugh* appears to have two arguments but can assign a theta role to only one of them, hence their unacceptability. The unexpected acceptability of (50e) is attributable to *Mary* receiving a theta role from *off the stage*.

So far it might appear that theta theory simply recapitulates the kind of (subcategorizational) information represented above in terms of transitivity and intransitivity, but in fact it does much more. First, it provides an explicit foothold for a basic minimum of semantic information. It does this by specifying not only the number of arguments associated with a verb: that *laugh* only takes one argument and that *accompany* needs two, a subject and an object, but also what the properties of those subjects and objects are. Both *undertake* and *undergo* require a subject and an object, but as we saw in the discussion of the lexicon, the semantic interpretation of the two is radically different, as shown in (51):

(51) a. John undertook the surgery reluctantly
     b. John underwent the surgery reluctantly

This contrast is described by saying that *undertake* has an agent as its subject, whereas *undergo* has a patient as its subject (though not all examples are so appropriately labeled).

The second function of theta theory is to provide an explanation for asymmetries in the distribution of so-called expletive elements: items like *it* and *there*, which appear to have a syntactic role but little or no semantic content. Consider in this respect the contrast in (52):

(52) a. John tried to learn Afrikaans quickly
     b. John seemed to learn Afrikaans quickly
     c. It seemed that John learned Afrikaans quickly
     d. *It tried that John learned Afrikaans quickly

Whereas *try* is a two-place predicate – it requires a subject (*John*) and a complement clause, *seem* is a one-place predicate – it requires only a complement clause. Its subject position is therefore thematically (and semantically) empty. English, unlike Italian and other pro-drop languages,[63] however, requires a subject to be present, and this role is taken by the expletive *it*. Such expletives (or dummies as they are also known) can appear only in semantically empty positions. The subject of *try* is not semantically empty in this way, hence the unacceptability of (52d), and the fact that (52a) is interpreted as saying that *John* is the agent of both the trying and of the (putative) learning, whilst (52b) does not suggest that *John* is the agent of seeming. This analysis raises a different problem, however. If *John* is the agent of both *try* and *learn* in (52a), it looks as if the theta criterion is being violated: there is one argument with two theta roles, even if both roles are the same. The solution in this case is to postulate an invisible argument, called PRO (an "abstract PROnominal element"),[64] to bear the theta role involved, so that there is no violation of the theta criterion. Independent evidence for such an empty category will appear shortly.

There has never been agreement about how many theta roles it is necessary to assume, nor what their precise semantic properties are, but they continue to be appealed to in current versions of the Minimalist Program, even though the theta criterion itself has been dispensed with.[65]

Case theory and government

Case theory accounts for the contrast between *he* and *him*, in *he saw him*, and the dependence of such forms on differences of finiteness, as illustrated in (53):

(53) a. I believe him to be a werewolf
     b. I believe he is a werewolf

In each of these examples *he/him* is the subject of the clause *be a werewolf*, but it has to appear in the oblique (accusative) form *him* when the verb (*be*)

is non-finite (that is, not marked for tense), and in the nominative form *he*
when the verb (*is*) is finite. Such morphological differences are of marginal
importance in English, and in many languages – Chinese, for instance – they
are completely absent. But in recent theory, the kind of contrast seen in (53) is
only the outward manifestation of a much more pervasive system of abstract
case (usually written "Case"), a system which is operative in all languages and
whose effects go way beyond the simple difference illustrated here. The central
claim of case theory, embodied in the Case Filter, is that every Noun Phrase in
a sentence has to be assigned Case in order for that sentence to be well-formed.
The absence of Case on any Noun Phrase then causes the sentence to be filtered
out or marked as ungrammatical.

Adopting a notion from traditional grammar, Case is said to be assigned under
"Government." Nominative Case is assigned by a finite verb to its subject;[66]
Oblique Case is assigned by verbs and prepositions to their objects, so you say
He gave it to me, rather than *He gave it to I*. Other configurations, in contrast,
do not allow government. The contrast in acceptability between the sentences
in (54) is then attributed to the fact that in (54a) *her* is assigned Case by *for*,
but in (54b) *seems* does not govern *her* and there is nothing else to assign Case
to it, so the sentence violates the Case Filter:

(54) a. For her to go there seems unthinkable
     b. *Her to go there seems unthinkable

We now have enough theoretical apparatus to illustrate some of the beauty
of Government and Binding theory, which lay in how complex facts emerged
from the interplay of several simple subtheories or modules. For instance, the
well-formedness of a sentence like (55a), in contrast with the unacceptable
examples in (55b–e), emerges from the interaction of several of the principles
we have been discussing:[67]

(55) a. Bill expected John to hurt himself
     b. *Bill expected John to ambition himself
     c. *Bill expected Mary to hurt himself
     d. *Bill expected there to hurt himself
     e. *Bill expected I to hurt myself

The acceptability of (55a) is a function of the interaction of X-bar theory,
defining the possible configurations in which the lexical items can occur (cf.
(55b) with a noun instead of a verb); of binding theory, guaranteeing that only
John and not *Bill* can be the antecedent of *himself* (cf. (55c) where the presence
of a feminine noun makes the agreement possibility obvious); of theta theory,
specifying the argument structure of the verbs *expect* and *hurt* (cf. (55d) where
the expletive *there* cannot be an argument); and of case theory, ensuring that *John*
is suitably licensed by the verb *expected* (cf. (55e) where the pronoun *I* makes

the Case assignment transparent). "Licensing" is a currently fashionable term referring to the need for all items that appear in a sentence to be licit, as though words needed a license to appear in a particular position.

The special licensing ability of *expect* is a lexical property of English, not found in related languages, and allows it to case mark *John* across a clause boundary. The phenomenon raises a problem in that Case was assigned under government, and the simplest definitions of government predicted that (55a), and in fact (53a), should be ungrammatical. Such examples have been analyzed in many different ways, but the poverty of the English morphological case system makes it hard to provide analyses which do generalize appropriately. In the previous chapter I alluded to the possibility of using cross-linguistic data to solve such a problem, and I used Spanish data to cast light on the analysis of English earlier in this chapter. In elegant work from the early 1980s, Peter Cole and Gabriella Hermon did exactly the same thing, showing that only one of the putative solutions to the problem mentioned here could account both for English and also for the Ecuadorian language Quechua. The positions they contrasted were a "raising" analysis and a "non-raising" analysis.[68] In the raising analysis, *him* in (53a) and *John* in (55a) are "raised" from being the subject of the embedded clause to be the object of the verb in the main clause. In the non-raising analysis, no such process took place. They then showed convincingly that only the raising analysis could be made to work for Quechua. If both analyses work for language A, but only one analysis works for language B, then that latter analysis is assumed to be the correct one for both languages. It is logically possible that two languages might require different analyses, but if one analysis can be generalized to both, then theoretical parsimony demands that it be chosen for both.

Since then the theory has moved on, and some of the core concepts have changed quite fundamentally. For instance, the raising analysis mentioned here is incompatible with the description of case marking across a clause boundary and, despite the central role of government over many years, recent (Minimalist) developments of the theory have seen its demise. The technicalities of the description are no longer vital; what is important is the requirement that the theory be able to account for the data, and do so in a way that generalizes to other languages; ultimately to all languages.

Example (55a) illustrates the interaction of several of the modules of the grammar but it exhibits no (overt) movement. However, in the closely related (56):

(56)   John was expected by Bill to hurt himself

we see evidence of the movement of *John* from its position as direct object of *expect* and, more interestingly, we can find evidence of the empty categories alluded to above.[69] The postulation of empty categories has seemed to many to be an affront to common sense, but they are central to Chomskyan linguistics, and it is important to understand why, despite appearances, they are there.

Empty categories

According to Cranmer, "Naturall reason abhorreth *vacuum*," and much the same odium seems to attach to claims that sentences should contain empty elements. Certainly, the idea that there should be phonologically empty words has either outraged or bewildered many members of the linguistic community. In fact, the development of a theory of empty categories has been important in allowing linguists to capture interesting generalizations, to simplify the structure of grammars, and ultimately to provide evidence about the innate endowment that the child brings to the task of first language acquisition.

Traditional descriptions of language frequently refer to "understood" elements, which are not visible (or audible), but whose presence it is convenient to assume.[70] This tradition was adopted and formalized in the transformational treatment of the subject of imperatives, and in the postulation of PRO mentioned earlier. More recently, it has been widely extended, with interesting implications for the levels of representation necessary in the grammar. Consider the pair of sentences in (57):

(57) a.   John wants Bill to go
     b.   John wants to go

It is intuitively obvious that in (57a) Bill is to go and in (57b) that John is to go. Making that intuition grammatically explicit can be effected by assuming, as in fact theta theory requires, that in each case *go* has a subject, even though that subject is invisible in (57b). The structure of (57b) is then something like (58):

(58)   John wants [ec] to go

where "ec" stands for an "empty category," construed as referring to the same person that *John* does, as is explicit in the synonymous *John wants himself to go*.

An empty category is in general one that has syntactic properties but is not pronounced. With sentences as simple as these the gain from assuming empty categories is scarcely overwhelming, but in more complex cases, one can begin to see how benefits accrue. For instance, there is a famous argument involving alternative possible pronunciations of the sequence *want to*. In many dialects of English, one can pronounce (59):

(59)   I want to go

either as spelt, or in the reduced form indicated by the popular spelling in (60), and generally referred to as the result of a process of "*wanna* contraction":[71]

(60)   I wanna go

The range of environments in which this process can take place has to be specified with some care. In particular, there is an interesting contrast between (61) and (62):

(61)   Teddy is the man I want to succeed
(62)   Teddy is the man I wanna succeed

(61) is ambiguous: it can mean either "I hope Teddy succeeds," where *succeed* is intransitive and means "have success," or "I hope to succeed Teddy," where *succeed* is transitive, and means "follow." (62) in contrast is unambiguous: it can mean only "I hope to succeed Teddy." Why should this be? On the assumption that empty categories are syntactic entities that can appear in sentence structure, (61) has two analyses, one corresponding to each of the two interpretations given, and shown – much simplified – in (63):

(63)   a.   Teddy is the man I want to succeed [ec]
        b.   Teddy is the man I want [ec] to succeed

At this point it becomes clear why (62) has only one interpretation. *Wanna* contraction only applies if *want* and *to* are next to each other. In (63a) they are, so (62) has an interpretation identical to that of (63a); in (63b) they are not adjacent, the contraction cannot take place, and so (62) cannot have the interpretation associated with (63b). Although the empty category is not pronounced itself, it has both syntactic properties and an effect on the pronunciation of the surrounding material.

However, there is a problem. The empty categories indicated in (63) arise in each case from the removal of the constituent *the man* from its original position. But the earlier discussion of PRO suggests that (63a) should really have not just one, but two, empty categories, so the analyses shown in (63) should be replaced with those shown in (64):

(64)   a.   Teddy is the man I want [PRO] to succeed [ec]
        b.   Teddy is the man I want [ec] to succeed

The correct statement about *wanna* contraction is then that it is blocked by one kind of empty category, known as a *trace*, but not by PRO.[72] The conclusion may seem undesirably complex in that it involves drawing a distinction between two different invisible entities. It is true that the account would be simpler if there were only one kind of empty category (and PRO may be eliminable in current theories) but if one postulates two different grammatical entities, one expects them to have different properties, and there is no objection in principle to the analysis.

People often object at this point that for them (as in fact for me) *wanna* contraction is impossible (or "substandard") so the argument based upon it is vitiated. This is misguided. The most that such an objection demonstrates is that the dialect of the people concerned fails to provide evidence *for* the position; it does not thereby provide evidence *against* the hypothesis. Fingerprints on a door handle may be evidence of an intruder's guilt; the absence of fingerprints is not evidence of his or her innocence. Evidence for one's hypotheses can be drawn from any language, and even the relatively impoverished dialect that I speak does provide comparable evidence once one looks a little further, as we now will.

Wanna contraction is not the only kind of contraction. For me, and perhaps most speakers of most varieties of English, a sentence like (65a) typically allows the alternative pronunciation shown in (65b), where *I am* contracts to *I'm*:

(65) a. I am the greatest
     b. I'm the greatest

Again, stating the precise conditions under which such contraction is possible is not straightforward: (66b) is simply ungrammatical:

(66) a. John is planning to come at the same time as I am
     b. *John is planning to come at the same time as I'm

(66a) is interpreted as meaning "John is planning to come at the same time as I am *planning to come*." The italicized words are redundant and so are typically not pronounced, even though they are understood, and have a syntactic existence in the form of an empty category. Again this suggests an explanation for the impossibility of (66b): contraction cannot take place adjacent to an empty category; *am* is adjacent to an empty category, left by the omission of *planning to come*, so (66b) is excluded.

Another initially mysterious contrast, illustrated in (67), succumbs to the same explanation:

(67) a. Tell me whether the party's tomorrow
     b. Tell me where the party is tomorrow
     c. *Tell me where the party's tomorrow

Why is (67c) ungrammatical? An answer is suggested by a consideration of the kind of echo-question seen in (16), *Harry stirred what?*, and further illustrated in (68):

(68) a. The party's *where* tomorrow?
     b. The party's *when* tomorrow?

In these examples *where* and *when* appear in the same position as the ordinary locative or temporal phrases that they question, as seen in (69):

(69) a. The party's in the hangar tomorrow
     b. The party's at 11 o'clock tomorrow

The next stage of the argument should be clear: the structure of (67b) is as shown in (70):

(70)   Tell me where the party is [ec] tomorrow

with an empty category marking the place from which *where* has moved, and blocking the contraction of *is* to *'s*.

This explanation rests on the assumption, hinted at before, that when something moves, it leaves behind an empty category, a *trace* of its former abode. Simplicity and theoretical consistency then demand that all movement be treated uniformly, and in the trace theory of movement rules, this assumption is explicitly implemented, so that the structure of (17), given in the tree shown in (19), will in fact include an empty category, as indicated in (71):

(71) $What_i$ did Harry stir $[ec]_i$

The subscripts make explicit the parallelism with binding theory, and guarantee that the trace is associated with the correct moved constituent: this is not a problem in sentences as simple as this one, but becomes important where several items have moved. Moreover, empty categories cannot be tossed into the structure of the sentence just anywhere: a universal condition called the Empty Category Principle (ECP)[73] insists that all empty categories be properly governed, and the empty category and its antecedent (e.g. $what_i$ and $[ec]_i$ in (71)) together constitute a "chain." Again it is necessary that the various different principles of the grammar be compatible with each other, and hence conspire to characterize sentences as (relatively) well-formed or ill-formed. Once a certain degree of complexity is reached, even consistency is a stringent demand, but postulating empty categories is wholly consistent with the rest of the theory, and in fact has been widely construed as having a further dramatic implication: it is supposed to undermine the justification for transformations and, in turn, for the fundamental idea that sentences are generated *derivationally*. Instead of chains arising as a result of (transformational) movement, they could be introduced directly into a representation without requiring any such movement.

The status of transformations

One of the major justifications for having two distinct levels of representation, deep structure and surface structure, linked by transformations, was that it allowed the capturing of different generalizations at different levels. The displacement of constituents from their canonical position in WH-questions and passives motivated the claim that there was a distinct level of deep structure at which items really did occupy their original position. Given an example like *Blair has been elected*, everyone agrees that the position after *elected*, which would normally be filled by an object, is phonetically empty, and that what fills it semantically is somewhere else.[74] Such displacement phenomena can be treated by postulating either more than one position or a single position with special properties. Chomsky refers to these two alternatives as "transformational" and "non-transformational" respectively.[75] At this point, the terminology becomes a little misleading. The "transformational" alternative itself comes in several different versions, depending on the relative emphasis laid on representations and derivations, where derivations are effected pre-eminently by transformations.[76] For some, such as Michael Brody, the notion of derivation is unnecessary. He argues persuasively that you can have representations without derivations, but not derivations without representations, so a purely representational theory is more restrictive than a derivational one.[77] If the postulation of chains in a representational theory is simply a notational variant of postulating movement in a derivational theory, then parsimony in the form of Ockham's razor demands that one do without derivations.[78] If the two theories make empirically distinct claims, the disagreement can be decided one way or the other, but the argument for derivation would have to be very strong to motivate giving up the more restrictive representational theory. If the claim of restrictiveness is correct, it is in principle not possible to find data that could be handled only representationally and not derivationally.

The arguments for the various positions are subtle and complex, and although empirical evidence favoring derivationality has been frequently suggested, there is still no consensus on its cogency. The problem is that accounting for any data always involves appealing to the interaction of a number of different assumptions and principles, with the result that the argument can be potentially undermined by subverting any one of them. Conceptually, it is not difficult to think of a situation which would militate in favor of a derivational approach: if it could be shown that it is necessary to refer to properties of intermediate steps in a derivation, rather than just the representation at LF, this would constitute strong evidence of the need for the derivation. A notional example is the "successive-cyclic" treatment of WH-movement illustrated in (35) and (38) above, where a WH-word appears at one stage in the derivation in a position where it does not occur at LF. The argument, however, is inconclusive as it is not difficult to recast the analysis in such a fashion that the relevant property is encoded in the LF representation itself instead.

Brody's theory has no recourse to transformations in the derivational sense of the term, but it does exploit more than one syntactically defined position, and so is "transformational" in the sense mentioned above. For others, derivations are pervasive, with all grammatical conditions pertaining to them rather than to representations, so such theories are transformational in both senses. Chomsky himself adopts a mixed position in which "structures are formed derivationally but the interfaces [with sound and meaning, NS] are interpreted representationally."[79] He further emphasizes the difficulty of differentiating the positions, and claims that to the extent that it is possible to find empirical differences, they favor his mixed approach. For him, transformations still have something like the coverage they had in the mid 1950s;[80] what has changed is that the complexity of the transformations has been factored out into principles of Universal Grammar, so that what is left is very simple.

This point bears elaboration. Chomsky has frequently pointed out that notions of simplicity are not transparent.[81] Depending on what other devices are exploited, a theory which does not use transformations may be simpler than one that does. Other things being equal, such a theory is then to be preferred; but other things may not be equal. The fundamental problem of linguistic theory is to explain the possibility of language acquisition. It does this by specifying what form the grammar of a human language can take. The best theory is then the one that gives this characterization as restrictively as possible, in a manner which is accessible to the child, where restrictiveness and accessibility are both important. If the postulation of transformations does this most effectively – and it is clearly necessary to provide evidence for any such claim – then a theory with transformations is to be preferred.[82] Whatever the final verdict on derivationalism versus representationalism or other possible alternatives,[83] Chomsky's own work consistently presupposes a derivational approach, a presupposition which motivates many of the theoretical innovations of the Minimalist Program that are sketched out below.

Principles and parameters

Even if it is possible to replace idiosyncratic rules by general principles, it is still necessary to account for the fact that languages are often quite strikingly different one from the other. As we saw in the first chapter, where English has the word order S(ubject) V(erb) O(bject), Japanese has the order SOV, and all the logically possible orders occur somewhere in the world's languages. Rather than write a different set of rules for each possibility, these differences are now attributed to what is called "parametric variation."[84] In Chomsky's original version of this notion, variation was associated with universal principles which specified in advance a narrowly delimited set of all the possible variants. For instance, as we saw in the discussion of X-bar theory, there is a linguistic principle to the effect that all constructions have "heads": V is the head of VP, N is the head of NP and so on. There is some freedom of choice, however, in that the head may occur either before or after its complement. The major difference between (English) SVO and (Japanese) SOV word order then results from the different choice of value for this "Head-first/Head-last" parameter. Using a different analogy, Chomsky sometimes talks of parameters as being like a bank of switches that may be set in either of two positions.[85] Japanese and typologically similar languages like Turkish and Hindi choose one position, English and typologically similar languages like French and Chinese choose the other.

The major advantage of the Principles and Parameters framework lies in its potential for solving "Plato's problem":[86] how children can acquire their first language with such remarkable speed and efficiency. In line with developments in other domains, especially immunology,[87] this is seen as a task of *selection* rather than a task of instruction: the full range of linguistic possibilities comes pre-specified (they "belong to the genotype"[88]) and the child's task is just to choose the right ones. The idea is that everything is already laid out in the child's mind and language acquisition consists simply in selecting particular choices "off the peg." This conception is radical; is it really feasible?

There are between five thousand and ten thousand languages spoken in the world today,[89] a number which is clearly only a small fraction of the possible human languages – past, present, and future – that the child has to select from. Assume then that the child has to select among a million languages, give or take a few thousand. If all choices are binary, this can be done on the basis of "twenty questions" ($2^{20} = 1,048,576$).[90] The language faculty comes pre-specified with a check-list of possibilities, and the child's task in "learning" its first language is to decide on the basis of the incoming data which system it is being exposed to. Every time it gets a definitive answer to a particular question this halves the conceptual search space in which it is operating, and it can dismiss a whole range of alternative possibilities. For instance, the verb is the head of the verb phrase containing it, so all the child needs to do to determine that it is learning an English-type language is to identify which is the verb and which is the object in an utterance like *Eat this*. This is itself no mean achievement, but assuming that the child can so identify *eat* and *this* and associate appropriate meanings with them, then the rest of the structural knowledge comes for free. The universal principle of X-bar theory tells it that all verbs project into verb phrases, but leaves open whether that verb phrase has the structure [V + NP] or [NP + V]. Appropriately decoding *Eat this*, the child knows that it is the former of these possibilities.

More importantly, the Principles and Parameters system has a *cascade* effect: by setting the parameter like this, the child simultaneously knows that it is learning a language in which nouns and adjectives precede their complements as well, as seen in (42) and (43). That is, this knowledge comes without needing to be learnt; indeed, without the need for any overt input of the specific type concerned. Again, we have a dramatic simplification in the learning task confronting the child. It will only need to learn the order of nouns and adjectives with respect to their complements in the rare case where this order differs from that found with verbs. Although at first blush this may seem a vacuous claim – the child only needs to learn what it needs to learn – it is important to note two things: first, in the usual, so-called "unmarked" case the child has to learn only one fact and everything else follows.[91] Second, where there is additional complexity in the input to the child, this predicts that it is precisely in that area that the child will make mistakes.

A close analogy to this process is provided by the "epigenetic landscape" traversed in cell differentiation.[92] As the human egg develops it gives rise to about 350 different cell types, produced by different genes being switched on and off at appropriate times. A choice early in development can have far-reaching effects, effects which may not be evident at the choice-point itself. The pattern of development in the embryo is beginning to be understood in some detail. The pattern of development in language is, at the preliminary stage we have so far reached, surprisingly similar.

There is an obvious problem with this scenario: the child's search space is only decreased if the answers it comes up with are correct. There are not only striking differences (e.g. of word order) from language to language, but most languages allow internal variation: it is possible to say not only *I sometimes eat caterpillars*, but also *Sometimes I eat caterpillars* and *I eat caterpillars sometimes* (though not **I eat sometimes caterpillars*). What the child is to do when the data are not deterministic, i.e. do not allow him or her to settle unambiguously on one or another grammatical choice, is a topic of intense current investigation, and one which is leading to a change in the understanding of parametric variation itself.[93]

Lexical and functional categories

The lexical items of any language are divided into two classes, usually referred to as lexical and functional categories;[94] a designation which is somewhat misleading, as both kinds of category have to be listed in the lexicon. The lexical categories consist of Nouns, Verbs, and Adjectives; the functional categories consist of the rest: Determiners, Auxiliary verbs, Complementizers, Tense and Inflectional elements that license the appearance of the underlined elements in examples like *Frogs croak* and *My frog croaks*, and various others. (Prepositions are a problem: they appear to belong in both groups.[95]) Lexical categories are also known as contentives: they have meaning or content which is independent of the sentences they occur in, whereas functional categories typically have no descriptive content. There is no difficulty in explaining what *tree* or *walk* means, by referring to trees or to walking; it is not so easy to explain what *the* or *if* means.

That languages may differ with respect to full lexical items is a commonplace: everyone is familiar on the one hand with the universality of words for natural kinds, such as *mother* (or *mère* or *Mutter*), and on the other with the occasional problems of translation provided by concepts like "Schadenfreude," "taboo," and "koan" that typically result in borrowing. That differences among languages might be restricted to the lexicon is somewhat less apparent; indeed, given the grammatical differences apparent to anyone learning a second language, blatantly false. Forgetting about phonological (and of course orthographic) contrasts, it may nonetheless be possible to reduce all grammatical differences to the properties of functional categories, and only those.

A simple example is provided by the different properties of complementizers and auxiliary verbs in different languages. In the discussion of questions earlier in this chapter I glossed over the issue of where the WH-word *what* is moved to in examples like *What did Harry stir*? Rather than the structure (19), repeated here, an analysis of the kind shown in (72) would be argued for:

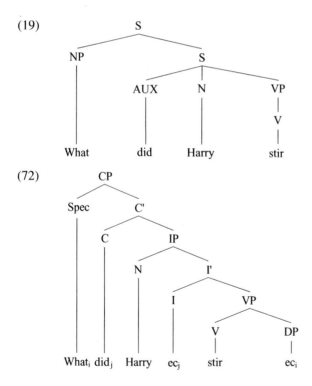

(19)

(72)

Most of the technical details are irrelevant, but a few points need some explanation. First, all sentences are argued to include a complementizer position, so the highest node in the tree is CP (short for Complementizer Phrase).[96] Second, the subscripts and empty categories show that *What* has moved from the direct object position after the Verb to a position known as the Specifier of the CP. Third, the auxiliary verb *did* is not now dominated by AUX but, again as shown by the subscripts and empty category, it has moved from the I position (short for Inflection) to be under the immediate domination of C. Lastly, the label S has been replaced by IP (short for Inflection Phrase) to reflect the fact that all sentences need some inflection to show finiteness.[97]

Two questions arise: why do these movements take place and how does English differ from other languages? The answer to both questions can be shown to reduce to properties of the functional categories I and C. In English, interrogative C is "strong," whereas in French it is "weak." As a result, English has I to C movement – C is strong enough to attract auxiliaries to it like a magnet, but as the French C is weak, no attraction can take place, there is no movement, and we have the contrast in (73):

(73) a.   John has come – Has John come?
     b.   Jean est venu – *Est Jean venu?

Similarly, in English, I is claimed to be weak, but it is strong in German; hence in German, I can attract main verbs in questions, and not just auxiliary verbs, as in English, so we have the further contrast in (74):

(74) a.   John eats bananas – *Eats John bananas?
     b.   Hans isst Bananen – Isst Hans Bananen?

There is further variation when we look at other languages. In Japanese and Chinese, for instance, the equivalents of examples like *What did Harry stir?* appear as *Harry stirred what?*, with the WH-word remaining *in situ*, as in the English echo-question in (16).[98] Despite the difference in word order, however, the interpretation of such sentences is exactly the same in Chinese, Japanese, and English, leading to the suggestion that their structure is identical at LF. The only difference between the two examples would then be whether the WH-word has moved overtly (or visibly), as in English, or covertly (or invisibly), as in Chinese.

The initial view of parametric variation associated parameters with principles of Universal Grammar; this more recent treatment associates them with individual lexical items of different languages.[99] At first sight, this may seem an unfortunate retreat from a position of great elegance and predictive power. It seems intuitively better to have variation associated with universal principles rather than idiosyncratic lexical items. The intuition does not stand up to further scrutiny. What is required is that the set of possibilities be narrow in range and easily attained by the first language learner. This can be achieved by the new system, which simultaneously makes interesting claims and predictions elsewhere. These are, first, that languages need not be wholly consistent with respect to a particular parametric choice: one lexical item may choose one value, and a second lexical item may choose a different value. Second, and most important, variation between languages may now be restricted exclusively to differences in the lexicon. More narrowly still, variation may be restricted to that subset of the lexicon which involves *functional categories*, and perhaps just to the binary choice between strong and weak. The (simplified) tree in (72) may seem counter-intuitive and baroque, but the complexity has rich rewards: it makes explicit the relatedness of apparently dissimilar sentences; it simplifies the child's learning of its first language, as most of the complications are part of Universal Grammar and do not need to be learnt; and it allows a simple and straightforward account of the differences between languages.

Minimalism

One of the more striking manifestations of Chomsky's intellectual vigor is revealed in his repeated revision of his own inventions. Although the core of his ideas and their philosophical and psychological implications have remained largely unchanged for over half a century (*The Morphophonemics of Modern Hebrew*, which contains a number of ideas that have pervaded his work ever since, was first drafted in 1949), the technical implementation of those ideas is subjected to constant change. The latest manifestation of this revolution in the revolution is provided by Minimalism,[100] probably the most radical of the periodic upheavals in Chomsky's thinking, and one which he considers "maybe the most interesting thing I've thought of."[101] The closest, if unlikely, parallel comes from the "relentlessly revolutionary" artistic development of Picasso, who evoked admiration, bemusement, and incomprehension in equal measure. For those who appreciated the paintings of the Blue and Pink periods, Cubism seemed like an assault; for those who grew to appreciate cubist pictures, the excursions into surrealism and welded sculpture were baffling. But even those who don't like it agree that *Les Demoiselles d'Avignon* changed art for ever, and those who banned his work during the war appreciated the awesome power of *Guernica*. Chomsky has several times overthrown the system he has developed, confusing many, alienating some, inspiring a few. In each case the motivation is to deepen understanding, even if that means an apparent sacrifice of previous insights.

The modular theory described earlier in this chapter was known as "Government and Binding," after two of the central concepts involved in the theory. It included the well-established, even traditional, distinction between the levels of representation known as d-structure and s-structure, renamed from earlier versions of the theory because of the confusion caused by non-technical notions of depth and superficiality. Yet in Minimalism, basically an attempt to start again from scratch after forty years' constant research, "government," which played the "central role"[102] for almost twenty years, has disappeared, the distinction between d(eep) and s(urface) structure has not only been abolished, but *neither* of these levels of representation has survived, and even the theory of Phrase Structure has been largely eliminated.[103] There are now just two levels of representation in the grammar, Phonetic Form (PF) and Logical Form (LF), and people are beginning to talk of "the end of syntax."[104] It's actually the beginning, and we are just getting to a stage when "we can at least formulate [interesting] questions."[105]

To give the flavor of the Minimalist Program – the locution is significant, since it is not yet a proper theory of the language faculty, more a policy statement about what conditions such a theory should, ideally, meet – let us look first at the structure of the grammar and then at a particular kind of example and see what sort of question has motivated its analysis over the years.

It is the essence of good science to adopt only those theoretical constructs which it is impossible to do without, either because they are conceptually necessary, or because they are empirically unavoidable. In linguistics the former category must include the lexicon and, if the role of a grammar is to link sound and meaning, the two surviving levels of representation, PF and LF. It is impossible to do without these levels, which constitute the interfaces with articulation and perception (PF) on the one hand, and with the conceptual ("central") system (LF) on the other. There is moreover a requirement of "legibility" – the representations at PF and LF must be legible by other motor and cognitive components of the mind – for instance, to ensure that hearers can decode the sentences they are exposed to, and integrate their contents into long-term memory. As Chomsky puts it: "If language is to be usable at all . . . the expressions generated by L must be accessible to other systems . . . that enter into thought and action."[106] There must in addition be some internal structure to the grammar, as the two kinds of representation, LF and PF, have to be appropriately linked. This is accomplished by positing a common derivation up to a stage called "Spellout," which marks the point where a syntactic object is sent off for phonetic interpretation in one direction and logical interpretation in another. The implication of this is that movement operations which take place after spellout will remain "invisible," giving rise to the contrast mentioned above between the overt and covert movement of WH-phrases. The structure of the grammar is then as in (75):

(75)   LEXICON
                   |
        Merge, Agree & Move
                   |
            SPELLOUT

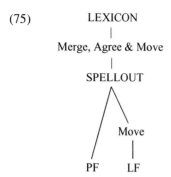

         PF   LF

Several empirical issues about this organization arise: for instance, the point "spellout" is itself claimed not to be a level of representation, as no linguistic generalizations are stated there; and, more generally, it is left open how much of the machinery of the language faculty is entirely idiosyncratic and how much is a function of the need to satisfy legibility conditions. Given the remarkable complexity of the syntax of human languages, and especially given Chomsky's repeated argumentation that we have a genetically determined language faculty which sets us off from the rest of creation, one might expect that the properties of that language faculty would be correspondingly rich and opaque. It is accordingly something of a surprise to read that the aim of Minimalism is to show that "what is empirically unavoidable is imposed by 'design specifications' of external systems,"[107] so that all constraints on grammatical processes are motivated by either perceptual or conceptual considerations. Binding theory for instance, described here as a module of the grammar, is now suspected to be just "an external interpretive system":[108] that is, a set of conditions imposed from outside the grammar proper. Similarly, the reason for the ubiquitous existence of movement, which is clearly not conceptually necessary, may be that it is a response to requirements of communication: putting old information before new, for instance.[109]

This view throws open the whole of linguistics to reconsideration, necessitating a reanalysis of all components. As always, it is necessary to separate the conceptual claims from the technical implementation of these claims in a formal system. Within the former of these, it is also important to keep apart that which is conceptually uncontroversial – essentially the appeal to Ockham's razor – even if the working out of that position gives rise to radical controversy, and the bold, apparently bizarre, speculation that language is a "perfect solution" to the problem of linking representations of sound and meaning.

Accordingly, we will look first at notions of "economy," then continue with the ontology of categories and processes (such as Merge and Agree) that Minimalism requires; we will then briefly examine some of the details of the technical implementation, and look at the extent to which language is "perfect". This last strand in the argument will also have implications for any account of the evolution of language as, if "language is an optimal solution to legibility conditions,"[110] its evolution in such a puzzlingly brief period is less problematic. That is, if the language faculty is as simple as is biologically and physically possible, this suggests a corresponding reduction in the complexity of any evolutionary account of its emergence.

Economy[111]

A central component of the Minimalist Program[112] is an attempt to put flesh on old ideas about "economy": the claim that some principle of least effort is characteristic of the language faculty. There are several different notions of economy, which it is necessary to disentangle. Let us look at one phonological, one pragmatic, and then at the syntax.

Consider the phonological process of assimilation, whereby different elements have (or adopt) the same value for some property. For instance in English the /n/ at the end of *ten* is typically pronounced [m] before /p/ and /b/, as in *ten pears* or *ten bears*. This assimilation is clearly a manifestation of inertia. It is easier for the organs of articulation to stay in the same position than to change from one position to another. In careful speech it is nonetheless possible to pronounce *ten pears* with the original /n/ preserved, so one might want to attribute the phenomenon to performance rather than competence. This would be simplistic, however. First, not all languages manifest the same assimilations, so it is a matter for the *grammar* of each language to specify what is possible and what is not. Second, it is not possible to have a sequence of /n/ followed by /p/ or /b/ *within* a word either: that is, there is a constraint on possible combinations in the lexicon, which precisely mirrors the function of the rule of assimilation.[113] This suggests that, even if its original (historical) motivation was ease of articulation and a matter of performance, it is now a matter of the grammar itself.

A second, pragmatic, kind of economy can be illustrated from the function of certain grammatical connectives. Words like *moreover, anyway, after all*[114] do not add to the content of the sentences containing them, but rather give indications as to how those sentences should be interpreted as relating to each other in terms of the logical structure of the argument in progress. Thus the difference between (76) and (77):

(76)   Chomsky has changed the way we think of ourselves. After all, he's a genius

(77)   Chomsky has changed the way we think of ourselves. So, he's a genius

lies not in their content, but in the relation between the two propositions each one signals. In (76), the clause *he's a genius*, introduced by *after all*, is given as an explanation of the fact that he has been able to change the way we think; in (77), where the same clause is introduced by *so*, it is given as a conclusion that can be safely drawn. In addition, the clause introduced by *after all* is further assumed to be already known to the hearer, whereas there is no such implication with *so*. The motivation for using these words is clearly to facilitate processing: they economize on the hearer's effort in interpreting the incoming signal. Equally, such words differ from language to language (their correct translation is a perennial interpreter's nightmare) and knowledge of them constitutes part of the native speaker's competence.

The core notion of economy as it pertains to the syntax can be most simply illustrated by reference to sentences involving WH-movement of the kind we have looked at repeatedly. Such movement is pervasive in English but it is not unconstrained. Although we can have all of the sentences in (78), example (79) is impossible:

(78) a. I think John saw a buffalo
     b. What do you think John saw?
     c. Who do you think saw a buffalo?
     d. Who do you think saw what?
(79)   *What do you think who saw?

In a question with one WH-word (*who*, or *what*), that item is typically attracted to the front of the sentence as in (78b,c) to occupy the Specifier position in the CP. When two constituents are questioned, as in (78d), only one of the WH-words occurs at the front of the clause (*who*), and the other remains where it was (*what*). The question is: why can't *what* move to the front of the clause in (79), why is (79) ungrammatical? A possible answer is that (79) is less economical than (78d) in the sense that while both sentences contain exactly the same words, *who* starts out closer to the Specifier of CP than *what* does. Where either of two elements could move, the "Shortest Movement" condition determines that only the one which has less distance to travel is permitted to move.[115] The example is oversimplified, but it generalizes to other sentence types, indicating that some such principle of economy is on the right track. One such case is provided by the example of I to C movement, which shifts an auxiliary in *yes/no* questions like that in (80):

(80) a. John might have come
     b. Might John have come?
     c. *Have John might come?

where only the closest, first, auxiliary verb can move to the C position at the front of the sentence. It should be emphasized that all analyses and explanations in terms of economy raise problems of one kind or another, but the predictions they make are so rich that they are worth pursuing.

Another economical plank in the Minimalist platform is the idea that there are no superfluous symbols: every item in a sentence has to have a reason for being there. In the form of the principle of Full Interpretation (the requirement that all elements be properly licensed at both LF and PF)[116] this predates Minimalism, and has a number of useful effects. The first is to prevent the appearance of excrescent constituents, as in (81):[117]

(81) a.   I was in England last year [the man]
      b.   John was here yesterday [walked]

where the bracketed sequences have no conceptual role to play, they are not licensed by any category and so cause the derivation to "crash," that is they make the sentences containing them ungrammatical.[118] More interestingly, this principle ensures that only phonetically interpretable features survive at PF, and only logically interpretable features survive at LF. That is, features which are irrelevant to pronunciation, such as "transitive," must be eliminated before they can reach PF; and features which are irrelevant to meaning, such as "aspirated," must be eliminated before they can reach LF. It follows that expletive elements like *it* and *there*, which have no semantic content – they are uninterpretable – must be deleted by LF.[119] If this principle is incorporated into linguistic theory, it can account indirectly for the near equivalence of the examples in (82):

(82) a.   There's a unicorn in the garden
      b.   A unicorn is in the garden

and it can correctly exclude from natural languages the possibility of having the free variables characteristic of logical languages.[120] The role of interpretability in this sense is now central to current syntax.

The elements of Minimalism

As we have already seen, the minimalist ontology[121] must include a lexicon and a computational system (usually referred to as "C_{HL}," the Computational system for Human Language). The lexicon consists of Lexical Items of two kinds, substantive and functional, each composed of sets of features, such as the difference between [strong] and [weak] referred to earlier. The computational component, C_{HL}, has three subparts: Merge, Agree, and Move. Merge constructs larger constituents out of individual lexical items; Agree establishes relations between a lexical item and some other feature in its domain to yield traditional agreement (of the kind seen in the contrast between *this girl sings* and *these girls sing*) and case checking (ensuring the correct differentiation of *he* and *him* in (53)). Finally Move, which is a combination of Merge and Agree, identifies part of a tree that has already been formed by Merge, makes a copy of that part, and then merges it with another part of the tree, giving rise to larger and larger constituents. Given the preoccupation with theoretical parsimony, it is worth pointing out that, as can be seen from this description, Move is not a primitive relation in the way that Merge and Agree are, and it is accordingly often known as "internal Merge."[122] In principle, Merge might be the only operation needed – as is the case for artificial languages such as the logical calculi which have no agreement or movement but, as a matter of empirical fact, natural languages need the other two as well. Merge then is "indispensable in some form," and although such conceptual necessity does not obtain so obviously for Agree, Chomsky speculates that it too might ultimately be accounted for in terms of "the design conditions for human language."[123] Internal Merge has a somewhat different status: for many years Chomsky had assumed that movement – equivalently, the existence of transformations – constituted an "imperfection" in human language, but in his most recent work he argues rather that "displacement is not an 'imperfection' of language; its absence would be an imperfection."[124] This follows from the observation that, once Merge and Agree are postulated, it would complicate the theory to prohibit their iterated operation to give rise to displacement.

If we now turn to how this minimalist ontology is implemented, we need to ask three questions: What gets merged when? What can agree with what? What can move where? To answer the questions we need to introduce some of the new technical terminology of current work, in particular, "probes," "goals," and especially "phases." Some of these innovations are mainly terminological, others are more substantive. We will look at a central example of each: probes and goals, and phases. The latter in particular represents a substantive innovation, and we need to see what empirical predictions are made, as these will both validate (or invalidate) the technical details, and support the conceptual developments.

Probes and goals   Agreement patterns in language come in various, sometimes unexpected, forms. We saw with the examples in (55) that a reflexive pronoun has to agree in person, number, and gender with its antecedent: *Napoleon admired himself* is fine, but *Napoleon admired herself/ myself/ourselves* are all ungrammatical. Other examples are less transparent: why in the French examples in (83) is there no agreement between the feminine plural *les tables* and *repeint*, whilst there is between (the equally feminine plural) *les* and *repeintes*? And how is it possible to account for the agreement between *are* and the distantly following *several prizes* in (84a) parallel to (84b)?[125]

(83) a. Paul a repeint les tables   – Paul has repainted the tables
     b. *Paul a repeintes les tables
     c. Paul les a repeintes   – Paul has repainted them

(84) a. There are thought likely to be awarded several prizes
     b. Several prizes are thought likely to be awarded

The basic idea is that the phenomena of agreement can be attributed to the effect of a Probe and a Goal, where this process is intimately linked to the elimination of uninterpretable features.[126] Consider again examples like *this girl sings* and *these girls sing*, in which the subject agrees with the verb in number (singular versus plural). The feature "singular" on *this girl* is interpretable, whereas the same feature on *sings* is uninterpretable. That is, the difference between the subjects *girl* and *girls* is meaningful, but the difference between the verbs *sing* and *sings* is redundant or meaningless, being predictable from the feature of the subject. If this is the correct way of looking at the agreement relation, then the uninterpretable feature on *sings* must be eliminated before it reaches LF. This is effected by assuming that it probes for a nominal goal with which it can agree, and on finding one, its own uninterpretable feature is deleted. The technical details are formidably complicated,[127] but the system allows for the unification of a number of apparently disparate phenomena and also has computational implications. In this context it is important to remember that the theory being developed deals with humans, not computers or angels, and that the competence theory we elaborate needs to mesh with theories of performance. For instance, we need to look at the role of parsing and the desirability of avoiding the exponential explosion that threatens to sabotage any device confronted with the complexity of human languages. Here it is encouraging to note that the fact that Merge is binary – that is, only pairs of items rather than larger numbers can be merged in any one operation – follows from making the probe's search for a goal maximally efficient.[128] There has been discussion of such "binarity" for forty years, dating back to Chomsky's attempt with George Miller to devise models of language use which would be computationally tractable, but only now are we beginning to understand it.[129] Similarly, we can make some progress on the nature of "look-ahead" in processing a sentence: how we manage to arrive at the correct interpretation of a sentence which is temporarily ambiguous. The latest stage in the development of an appropriate approach is seen in the introduction of "phases."

Phases   The notion of computational tractability raises the important issue of whether processing considerations should even be relevant for a cognitive system. A competence grammar, the I-language, is a system of knowledge, and although it has to be accessible to performance systems, it is not obvious that performance considerations should impinge on the fundamental properties of such a system itself. Nonetheless, to the extent that properties of the systems converge, so will it be easier to guarantee this accessibility. If it is correct to describe the language faculty as consisting of a lexicon and a computational system, both comprising parts of our linguistic knowledge, then we can view "computation" as being used in two slightly different ways: what one might think of as off-line and on-line (competence and performance respectively). Accessibility to the I-language by performance systems is then enhanced if computation in the static (competence) sense is minimized. As is often the case with matters pertaining to the primitives of the theory, there is no unambiguous answer, but a number of considerations suggest that, at least within a derivational system, computational complexity does matter. A relatively clear domain where this is true is provided by locality: local relations are easier to compute than distant ones, in part because they require less memory for storage. Accordingly, let us assume that *all* computation is local. If it is, then we need some means of implementing this requirement in the grammar.

The basic idea is that "a syntactic derivation takes place in small chunks, called phases,"[130] where each phase consists of a subpart of the array of items selected from the lexicon, which are placed in "active memory"[131] and where "phases should be as small as possible, to minimize memory."[132] Accordingly, as soon as a phase is complete, it is sent off to be interpreted at PF and LF and is thereafter immune to further syntactic operations. In effect, the phase acts as a unit in subsequent computation, reducing the processing load on the system. This is technically implemented by reference to what is known as the "Phase Impenetrability Condition" (PIC), which stipulates that no (external) probe can look inside a completed phase.

Let us look at a previous example – the treatment of WH-movement, as in "What might Mary think [Harry stirred – ?]" (=33). We concluded earlier that *what* had to move first to the front of the embedded clause and only subsequently to the front of the whole sentence: that is, there is successive-cyclic movement. The PIC ensures that the only way WH-movement can take place is precisely in such small steps. In other words, the introduction of the notion phase is a way of *deriving* cyclicity in the grammar:[133] we no longer have to stipulate it arbitrarily. Similarly, phases have the added advantages of potentially explaining (some) island phenomena such as the effects of the A over A condition discussed earlier.

For the introduction of phases to be convincing, it is crucial to have some independent idea of what determines the constitution of a phase. The intuitive answer is that phases are "complete structural complexes," either they are propositionally complete, so CP is a phase, or they are thematically complete, so VP is a phase. Both these definitions satisfy the ultimate desideratum that they have a "natural characterization" in terms of conditions at the interfaces: that "they should be semantically and phonologically coherent and independent."[134]

As usual, there is potential doubt about the direction of explanation. David Adger suggests that "the notion of phase can be derived from the general structure of derivations, essentially by enforcing derivations to have short memories: they forget about material in embedded phases."[135] Given the dispute about representationalism discussed briefly above, one might alternatively argue that the notion derivation could be parasitic on the notion "phase," using any positive results from the appeal to phases to motivate a derivational rather than a purely representational approach. It is too soon to tell, though it is clear that the notions are intimately related.

Perfect syntax

Pursuing the central ideas of Minimalism, Chomsky sometimes talks of syntax as approximating to a "perfect system": an optimal solution to the basic problem of relating sound and meaning.[136] It is putatively optimal in the sense that it manifests properties of simplicity, naturalness, symmetry, elegance, and economy: properties which are initially unexpected of evolved biological structures such as language. In "Beyond explanatory adequacy" he quotes Galileo as saying that "nature is perfect"[137] and, viewing language as a natural object, observes that language is more like a snowflake than the spine or the giraffe's neck. The idea is that the beautiful hexagonal symmetry of the snowflake is a simple function of mathematical laws operating in specific physical conditions, whereas the human spine, poorly "designed" from an engineering point of view, reflects the tinkering of evolution.[138] If this observation is true it has two immediate implications: first, that the strategy of treating language like one treats the objects of the natural sciences such as chemistry is – surprisingly – correct; second, that all the apparently complex and idiosyncratic features of syntax should follow from properties of the interfaces, in line with the ideal scenario sketched out earlier.[139] Chomsky gives several suggestive parallels from the history of science, where the assumption that a "pretty law" holds has led to experiments which confirm the validity of the generalization despite superficially messy data.[140] In the case of language, the basic system is supposedly perfect and it is only requirements of the perceptual or articulatory systems that give rise to the apparent oddities of syntax. This striking hypothesis may of course turn out to be false, as Chomsky says: "You can't change reality, you can only ask: does reality happen to meet these surprising conditions?"[141] So far the signs are encouraging that we can go "beyond explanatory adequacy" in this way: that is, we can begin to explain why the initial state of the language faculty – the cognitive machinery we bring to bear on the task of first language acquisition – has the form it does. We can do so by adverting to "general properties of organic systems":[142] the necessary memory limitations of finite organisms, the speed of processing of the auditory cortex, and the requirements of communication. We can even at last embed the biological discussion in a physical context reminiscent of the work of D'Arcy Thompson and Alan Turing.[143] For the first time, the study of language really is beginning to fall within the purview of the natural sciences.

A historical progression

In the early days of generative grammar the central problem was the construction of a grammar that could assign appropriate structures to sentences.[144] A grammar was a set (of sets) of rules, and the question why particular sequences, such as those in (85), were grammatical or ungrammatical, ambiguous or univocal, was simply a result of the structural analysis they were given by the postulated rules of the grammar.

(85) a. Harry stirred the stew carefully
     b. *Harry stirred carefully the stew

At the next stage the question became *why* were the rules so formulated that they had this particular effect? Despite their apparent complexity, formulating rules at this time was always too easy: one could just as well formulate "antirules" that had precisely the opposite effect. Various answers were provided: typically, there are general (universal) conditions to which rules of grammar have to conform. For instance, they are ordered, accounting for the difference between *wash you and wash yourself, or they obey some principle such as the "A over A condition," hence accounting for the examples in (29), like *What did Harry stir the stew and?*. This in turn prompted the question why the A over A condition should be operative. The answer that it is "universal," characteristic of the grammars of all languages, led to the immediate next question as to why that should be so. This time the answer was that it was a special case of something more general: subjacency. The reason why some kinds of movement were impossible – why *Your brother, to whom I wonder which stories they tell* is ungrammatical in English, while its equivalent in Italian is fine – was attributed to a universal, but parametrized, principle.[145] But subjacency in turn needs explanation. Now the answer is that it is a kind of locality principle: grammatical operations are constrained to apply in some local domain.[146] The response to the question "why should locality principles obtain?" is confronted in the Minimalist Program in terms of least effort: an economy principle. If one continues to ask "why," like any intelligent three-year-old, the answers become more speculative, but advances are still possible. The latest response is in terms of more general properties of humans (and other creatures), and relates to such notions as "elementary considerations of efficient computation," or the limitations of short-term memory, implemented in the theory in terms of the Phase Impenetrability Condition which "sharply restricts search and memory."[147]

At this stage various other questions and objections arise. One potential criticism is that ideas of "least effort" have been around for a long time, so what's so new? The observation is true but irrelevant. As with Newton and the apple tree, it's what you do with the observation that matters. Another question is why any of these logically unnecessary principles should hold. Here the answer is one that has been given repeatedly over the decades: innateness, an issue we return to at length in chapter 4, but one which immediately suggests an answer in terms of evolution.

Evolution

One implication of innateness is that part of the answer to our questioning is evolution,[148] with a further important part played by the physical context in which that evolution has taken place. Some writers have suggested that Chomsky denies that language could have evolved, ascribing a quasi-mystical or religious position to him.[149] As Lyle Jenkins establishes in meticulous detail, this is simply false. There is no doubt that human language evolved, and Chomsky has made reference to its evolution on many occasions. He has been careful to emphasize that we can say with confidence little more than that language did evolve, and that the details of its evolution remain unknown. More surprisingly, he observes that the fact of its evolution should lead us to expect that language might be in some respects "unusable": there is no reason to expect the system to be "well adapted to its functions."[150] We saw some examples of unusable sentences in the discussion of parsing in chapter 1 (a subject to which we return in the next chapter). Nonetheless, in recent work with Marc Hauser and Tecumseh Fitch, he has put forward a detailed proposal regarding precisely which aspects of the language faculty have parallels in other creatures, and are therefore clearly not a special adaptation of *homo*, and which are unique to humans, and hence have presumably evolved relatively recently, though not necessarily in the interests of communication.[151]

The core of the proposal is a distinction between the faculty of language in a "narrow" sense (FLN), and the faculty of language in a "broad" sense (FLB), where FLB includes FLN as a proper subpart. They embed this idea in a yet wider framework, giving rise to the characterization in (86):

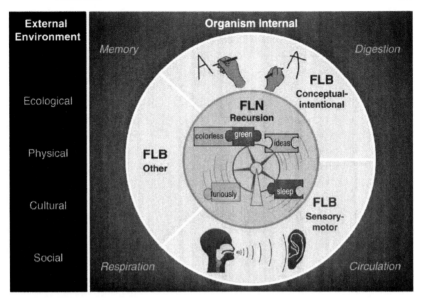

(86) Schematic representation of the faculty of language (Hauser et al., 2002: 1570)

The language faculty is shown as a property internal to a specific organism, a human being, with links to various aspects of the external environment on the one hand, and to the rest of the organism on the other. Some of these internal relations, for instance memory, are intimately tied to the language faculty; others, like respiration, are simply necessary prerequisites for the faculty to be able to operate. FLB then encompasses all aspects of our communicative abilities, including as a proper subpart FLN, the generative device which links sound and meaning.

They then develop three alternative hypotheses: first, that FLB is strictly homologous to animal communication; second, that FLB is uniquely human; and third, that only FLN is uniquely human; and where, more specifically, "FLN" is restricted to recursion and the mappings to the interfaces. They proceed by discussing a wealth of evidence suggesting that "many aspects of FLB are shared with other vertebrates." On the articulatory-perceptual side, this includes vocal imitation, aural discrimination, the neurophysiology of action–perception systems, the biomechanics of sound production, categorical perception, and so on. On the conceptual–intentional side it includes theory of mind, the capacity to acquire conceptual representations, imitation as part of an intentional system, and perhaps more. Nonetheless they conclude that discrete infinity, "the core recursive aspect of FLN currently appears to lack any analog in animal communication," and hence that their third "tentative, testable hypothesis" is correct. Questions of course remain; in particular, how this recursive property, which is also characteristic of the natural numbers, might itself have evolved; whether it evolved for reasons other than communication – for number or navigation, for instance; the extent to which FLN is adaptational, and so on. The provisional conclusion is that "the interface systems – sensory-motor and conceptual-intentional – are given, and the innovation that yielded the faculty of language was the evolution of the computational system that links them." If that is the only part of our language faculty that is unique to us, and the only part to be evolutionarily recent, its surprising simplicity – its "perfection" – would not be as implausible as at first sight appears.[152] The most problematic issue, which remains open, is whether this scenario is plausibly consistent with the prior existence of a conceptual–intentional system, a Language of Thought, which did not already have the property of discrete infinity. Whatever the answer to this question, the surprising conclusion of this venture into the evolution of the language faculty is that the domain of linguistics and the "specific characteristics of human intelligence" that we might expect linguistics to cast light on (see the epigraph to this chapter) may turn out to be narrower than previously thought. This does not diminish their interest nor the complexity of their investigation, but it makes it even more important to embed the study of language in human psychology more generally. Our linguistics must be "psychologically real."

3   Psychological reality

> Psychological reality – that is, truth of a certain theory.
>
> (Chomsky, 1980a: 191)

We have grammars in our heads.[1] That's why we can produce and understand unlimited numbers of sentences; why language can interact with other things inside our heads, like memory and vision and moral judgment; why people who suffer damage to their heads often lose their language in whole or in part; why PET scans show increased blood flow in particular bits of our brains when we carry out linguistic tasks under experimental conditions. The list is almost endless. But are the grammars (or I-languages) in our respective heads "psychologically real" as well as neurophysiologically real? The question has seemed unnecessarily vexed and has attracted a mass of largely unfruitful debate. Why should there be a problem? Most people, including psychologists and philosophers, are happy with the idea that we have something in our heads which accounts for these phenomena. What they balk at is the complexity and opacity of the linguist's account of what we have in our heads. It is unexceptionable to suggest that we have a rule specifying that verbs precede their objects in English, because we can see immediately what the effect of contradicting that rule is: silly sentences like *John onions eats* instead of the correct *John eats onions*. It is not so obvious that the correct analysis of *John was too clever to catch* should contain three empty categories of the kind we saw in the previous chapter.[2] You may by now be convinced that the evidence for such empty categories is pretty good, but postulating three of them in a six-word sentence still strikes many as excessive, just as the physicist's claim that the universe has ten (or eleven or twenty-six) dimensions seems unnecessarily baroque. The response is to temporize and deny that such complexity is really necessary. Some linguists may like to talk about this plethora of empty categories, for instance, but they are not psychologically real: they aren't really there in our heads like representations of nouns and verbs are. This reaction is either patronizing (when the linguists grow up they'll see the error of their ways) or uncomprehending, or both. To claim that the grammar you have hypothesized in order to explain a range of different facts is psychologically real is simply to

97

claim that it's correct. This is not to claim that linguists are specially privileged in being ultimately correct, of course: no one believes that we have the final truth about any of these matters. Nor is it a claim about how language is neurophysiologically implemented in the brain. Exciting though recent advances in our understanding of the brain's structure and function may be, we are still entirely ignorant about what neural differences there might be between speakers of English and Japanese or Swahili, or between talented orators and the habitually tongue-tied.[3] Rather it is a claim that the theory is correct or true in the same way that a theory of physics or biology or chemistry is true: it's the best we have come up with, and has not so far been refuted. In other words, claiming psychological reality for the I-language is not an additional claim, it is simply an indication that we are talking about properties of human beings and their minds rather than of formal systems. A close analogy is provided by Shimon Ullman's "rigidity principle" in vision.[4] Presented with the task of inferring structure from motion, our visual system works on the assumption that what is seen is a rigid body in movement rather than a static entity which is changing its shape. The design of the human system ensures that "remarkably sparse stimulation can lead to rich perception."[5] In vision as in language our innate endowment is such that minimal input can give rise to great richness of knowledge. Arguments from the poverty of the stimulus are comparable in the two domains.

Exactly the same issue has been raised repeatedly in physics:[6] from worries about the reality of atoms to doubts about the status of the extra dimensions of space and time that physicists keep postulating. A recent example is provided by the suggestion that there is a second dimension of time, described as having "many of the hallmarks of an abstract mathematical device rather than a real physical entity."[7] But as Cumrun Vafa, the author of this idea, points out, it has repeatedly turned out that entities which start life as theoretical conveniences, quarks for example, end up being accepted as existing in the physical world. A striking example is provided by the postulation of electron spin, which was described by the Nobel laureate Wolfgang Pauli as "very clever, but of course it has nothing to do with reality."[8] Electron spin is now being exploited in current computers. You don't get much more real than that.

The claim of psychological reality in linguistics is simple, but it raises a range of interesting issues, of which the most urgent are what the causal role of the internalized grammar might be, and how knowledge about this grammar can be integrated with other aspects of our understanding. After introducing the common demand that science should concern itself only with objective, observable phenomena, I look at the tension this can lead to in psychology, and discuss the role of intuitions as evidence. This paves the way for an overview of three of the main areas in which psychology and generative linguistics have shared concerns and interests: language processing, language acquisition by the child, and language loss in cases of pathology. The chapter ends with a glance at connectionist alternatives to the representationalist framework presupposed up till now.

Causality and observability

All theories seek to explain, and ultimately all explanation involves causation or causal mechanisms on the one hand, and the unification of different aspects of our knowledge on the other.[9] Explanation must be distinguished from prediction. Ancient astronomers were able to predict eclipses of the moon even when they believed in a geocentric universe; but their explanation of those eclipses was, to our way of thinking, flawed. In contrast, I think I understand why we have eclipses of the moon, but I can't predict them. I probably could, if I carried out the requisite observations and calculations, but the accuracy of *his* predictions still did not enable Ptolemy to provide the correct explanation. It is not that prediction is unimportant; it is crucial if we want to make our theory testable, as it is only by laying itself open to potential falsification that any enterprise achieves scientific status. But prediction and explanation are independent notions.

Consider a different example, which simultaneously illustrates the need for integration or unification of different parts of our knowledge. To explain why a helium-filled balloon moves *forward* in a car as it accelerates, we need to refer to the pressure gradient among the molecules of air in the car caused by the back window striking nearby molecules. This pressure difference is sufficient to overcome the inertia of the helium but not of objects denser than air, so the balloon moves forward. At a unificatory level we can assimilate this phenomenon to the theory of gravitation via Einstein's *principle of equivalence*, which treats acceleration and gravitation as different manifestations of the same thing.

As in physics, so in linguistics. To explain why *John is coming at the same time as I am* is acceptable whereas *John is coming at the same time as I'm* is unacceptable (see page 75 above), it is necessary to refer to abstract properties of the I-language that we know, including such notions as constituency, structure dependence, and empty categories, and show how they interact to predict the judgment claimed. To explain why on some occasion we might say *John is coming at the same time as I am* to convey the message that he won't be able to escort you to the ball, we need to integrate that linguistic analysis into a theory of performance involving notions of context, relevance, and implicature:[10] unifying our grammatical and our pragmatic theories. In each case there is an explicit assumption that the constructs of the respective theories (pressure, constituent, inertia, implicature, and so on) are causally implicated in the explanation. If they weren't, either they would be irrelevant to the explanation, or the explanation would be to that extent inadequate.

Insistence that explanation deal with causal mechanisms can give rise to a certain tension when it is combined with observability. Causes are rarely directly observable, but scientists are supposed to be objective, and justify their theories on the basis of observable phenomena. The nineteenth-century controversy between Louis Pasteur and Felix Pouchet about spontaneous generation was settled observationally.[11] People used to believe that mice were produced spontaneously from cheese and rags left in dark cupboards, but when careful experiments were carried out to see if life really could emerge from non-living material, it ultimately became clear that not even bacteria could develop like that. Interestingly, Pasteur ignored those of his own experimental results which apparently showed the spontaneous generation he was attacking. He was so convinced that his own view was correct that he simply assumed that the experiment was flawed in some way. A similar interplay between theory and observation can be seen in the reaction to Einstein's theory of relativity. Its final acceptance was sealed by the confirmation of its prediction that light would be *seen* to be gravitationally deflected during the eclipse of 1919, but younger physicists accepted the theory without evidence, even in the face of counter-evidence, because it made sense of the world. Most strikingly, Einstein himself believed that "pure mathematical construction enables us to discover the concepts and the laws connecting them, which give us the key to the understanding of the phenomena of nature."[12] Experimental evidence is a useful bonus as long as it goes the right way. If it goes the wrong way, the assumption is that the experiment was badly devised or carried out. This is made explicit in Einstein's correspondence with Max Born, where the focus of discussion is whether it is worth checking particular experiments to see where the (presumed) errors were. Despite the fact that Pasteur's and Einstein's successes were not as simple or as clear-cut as history remembers them – the crucial observations were neither uncontroversial nor always heeded – they exemplify the general view that science deals in observables. More accurately they exemplify the fact that the *evidence* for the theoretical constructs which are causally effective must be observable, but the distinction between data and evidence is one that has been often neglected.

When the requirement of observability is transferred to psychology, it can result in a form of behaviorism which denies any validity to mental constructs: in particular it denies any causal role to mental events ("the ghost in the machine"[13]), as these are, essentially by definition, unobservable. The founding father of behaviorism, John B. Watson, argued that "a scientific psychology should just concern itself with what is 'objective,' and 'observable,'"[14] and B. F. Skinner, following in his footsteps, deliberately limited himself to the study of observable "input–output" relations. A light flashes (input) and a rat presses a bar (output) in order to receive a pellet of food;[15] you hold up a pencil, say "Please say 'pencil'" and the subject says 'pencil.' Behaviorism of this kind was still the dominant paradigm, and provided an influential, if not exclusive, background to psychology in the 1950s when Chomsky was developing his first theories of language. His review of Skinner's major book, *Verbal Behavior*,[16] perhaps the most devastating review ever written, not only sounded the death-knell for behaviorism, but also laid the foundation for current mentalist linguistics and cognitive science more generally. The crucial advance in this transition is that mentalism pays due attention to the "built-in structure"[17] which both makes first language learning possible, and underlies all of our linguistic and cognitive abilities. In principle, then, it provides a basis for explaining how our knowledge of language arises.

Psychological reality and the nature of evidence

It is a common fallacy that there are two different kinds of explanation, linguistic and psychological, each pertinent to one discipline or the other. It is rather the case that explanation in either a psychological or in a linguistic theory may draw on evidence of either a linguistic or of a psychological nature. The constituency of a particular sentence can be corroborated (or cast into doubt) by reference to the predictions it makes about other sentences: that is, by purely linguistic data; or by reference for instance to the results of psychological experiments in which one has to identify the location of "clicks" arranged to occur in different positions in the sentence.[18] The two forms of evidence are equally valid, though the depth and complexity of the purely linguistic kind is in general greater than the psychological.[19]

A theory is psychologically real, then, if it makes claims of a psychological kind and is true. However, the linguist is often confronted not just by one unique account of particular data, but by a range of competing analyses, where it is not always obvious whether alternative descriptions are really different or are merely "notational variants"[20] of each other. If the constructs we postulate have causal powers then notational variants will be (causally) indistinguishable, but genuine alternatives will ultimately make different empirical predictions. For instance, the use of brackets rather than tree diagrams in syntax cannot cause anything: they are simply different ways of representing the same thing. That is, it makes no difference whether you represent *John eats onions* as a labeled bracketing as in (1):

(1)   [$_S$ [$_N$ John] [$_{VP}$ [$_V$ eats] [$_N$ onions]]],

or as a tree diagram as in (2):

(2)

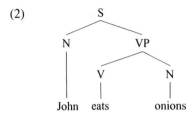

These are notational variants containing exactly the same information and are descriptively and causally equivalent.

By contrast, a grammar which represented the same sentence as in (3):

(3)   [$_S$ [$_N$ John] [$_V$ eats] [$_N$ onions]]

that is, without a VP, could still describe the same set of possible sentences, but also predicts specific empirical differences. For instance, the analysis in (1) claims that *eats onions* is a constituent, while that in (3) claims that it is not. Constituents can do things that non-constituents cannot, like being replaced by pro-forms; so (1) predicts the possibility of *John eats onions and Mary does so too*, and the corresponding oddity of *John eats onions and Mary does so cheese*. This last example is of dubious acceptability because the natural interpretation of *does so* is to mean *eats onions*, as in the preceding example, so we end up understanding it as meaning *John eats onions and Mary eats onions cheese*. This borders on gibberish, so we try to interpret it rather differently, perhaps as "John *eats* onions and Mary does something equally interesting to cheese." The crucial point is that (3) is not just a notational variant of (1), it embodies a different theory of our knowledge. The theory is wrong, but because people are expert at making some kind of sense of virtually everything they hear, the conclusion that it is wrong needs much further justification. This is another case where our competence and performance interact in complex ways. Our interpretive abilities are so good that it is not immediately obvious that the decreased acceptability of such odd examples is to be attributed to the grammar rather than to performance systems: hence that (1) rather than (3) is correct. There is also the further implication that such expressions are not just "ungrammatical" and to be excluded from consideration, but must be generated by the I-language with their particular peculiar characteristics.

This simple example can serve to emphasize the contrast between an entity of the I-language (such as VP or an empty category) and the hypothesis the linguist makes about that entity: his or her theory of VPs or empty categories.[21] The different grammars responsible for (1) and (3) can describe the same set of sentences, including the one under discussion, but they define different I-languages, so the sentences are given different structures. Linguists then account for a speaker's intuitions about this and a whole range of other sentences by attributing to him or her a mentally represented, that is a psychologically real, VP. The hypothesis may, of course, be wrong, but that speakers have *something* in their heads is undeniable.

The theories from which such hypotheses derive are meant to explain a wide range of data and, conversely, particular data may constitute evidence for one theory or another; but *which* data are to be explained is itself not self-evident. One of Chomsky's contributions has been to re-emphasize (especially for the philosophical community) that the lay notion of language as a social and political construct is not an appropriate domain for theory construction. A more fruitful domain is the psychological notion of language as the knowledge of individuals. This is not given *a priori*: the justification for defining the domain and indulging in whatever idealizations one does is to be found in the results that accrue. Displaying and explaining the knowledge of native speakers is a task of paramount importance because the efforts we have expended in concentrating on this area have been rewarded by corresponding insights. But such knowledge is not available to direct inspection, so finding and evaluating the evidence adduced for a theory that purports to characterize that knowledge is far from straightforward.

Intuitions

> Linguistic analysis cannot be carried out without the use of . . . intuition.
> (Chomsky, 1955/75: 87)

The simplest and most accessible evidence comes in the form of the intuitions of native speakers about the well-formedness of sentences of their language, and their rejection of ill-formed sequences: intuitions that I exploited throughout the last chapter. Such appeal to intuitions is anathema to some psychologists and traditional linguists. Scientific objectivity is taken to preclude the possibility of intuitions being reliable, so any theory built upon them must be inherently flawed.

The objection is based upon a misunderstanding of the difference between the native speaker's intuitions about the sentences of his or her language and analytic intuitions (or prejudices born of experience) about what is the best scientific account of a range of data. Only the former, which have the same status as perceptual judgments of the kind found with ambiguous figures like the duck–rabbit, are relevant for linguistic theorizing. The latter may be useful in prompting one to look for evidence in a particular direction, they do not constitute that evidence. All native speakers have such intuitions, only linguists have the prejudices. A further common objection is that intuitions are unreliable because they differ from speaker to speaker, making a scientific consensus about the "facts" impossible.[22] But such variation is expected in a domain which treats individuals, and can be used as a source of evidence for two further claims. First, the existence of such variation makes it difficult if not impossible to defend a view of a language as a set of publicly available well-formed formulae; second, the fact that intuitions are variable or unclear is itself in need of explanation, and the precise nature of the disagreement may provide evidence for a structural distinction. For instance, everyone agrees that *Sometimes John beats his wife* and *John beats his wife sometimes* are acceptable and roughly equivalent in meaning. *John beats sometimes his wife*, however, meets with no such agreement. Some speakers dismiss it out of hand as impossible, others try to embed it in a structure like *John beats sometimes his wife, sometimes his father, sometimes his uncle – he's always beating someone*, where it sounds more natural; yet others simply accept it as being on a par with the other examples. This lack of agreement can be used as evidence for the different grammatical status of the positions in the sentence in which the adverb may appear, as opposed to those in which it may not. This is still a long way from having an adequate analysis of those positions, but whatever analytic conclusion one arrives at will have followed in part from the disagreement.[23] It is as though one were gleaning evidence from different languages, where no one expects complete agreement. Of course, the situation becomes parlous if a particular analysis presupposes intuitive judgments that are not found in any speaker of any language.

The most extreme case is where an argument is crucially built upon one particular type of example. The demise of the example would then undercut the argument and the theoretical position based upon it. A simple instance is provided by Jaakko Hintikka and Gabriel Sandu's analysis of quantification.[24] They argue that their Game theory can, but Government Binding theory cannot, account for the binding relations in sentences like (4) and (5):

(4)   Tom and Dick admired each other's gift to him
(5)   *Tom and Dick admired each other's gift to themselves

where (4) has the interpretation given in (4′), and (5) is ungrammatical:

(4′)   Tom admired Dick's gift to Tom, and Dick admired Tom's gift to Dick

For me and all those whom I have consulted, (4) cannot have the interpretation in (4′): the sentence is well-formed, but only on a reading where *him* is distinct from each of *Tom* and *Dick*. By contrast, (5) is fully acceptable despite its complexity. *Prima facie* this looks like a classic case of shooting oneself in the foot. An explicit prediction is made and the evidence seems to go in exactly the wrong direction. However, it is appropriate to point out that the authors making the claim are working in what is for them a second language. It may be that the argument can be reconstructed on the basis of data from languages other than English, though I must admit to a certain skepticism. Whatever the possibilities in this direction, it is clear from this cautionary tale that the role of native-speaker intuitions is crucial, as they determine what the theory needs to describe. It is also worth emphasizing that the fact that a language provides no evidence for a particular claim is *not* evidence against that claim. If one is interested in the properties of tone characteristic of languages like Chinese, or of the click sounds characteristic of languages like Xhosa, it is unlikely that English will provide much evidence.[25] One would be rightly skeptical of linguists who supported their claims about tone or clicks on exclusively English data, but it could nonetheless be the case that those claims were true and, if data were adduced from the relevant languages, seen to be true.

A less tendentious case of intuitional disagreement is provided by the classic example of the presumed paraphrase relation between actives and passives. In early generative grammar, *John loves Mary* and *Mary is loved by John* were supposed to be derived from the same structure and, by hypothesis, to have the same meaning up to stylistic variation. Although Chomsky had already constructed problematic examples, Jerry Katz and Paul Postal argued that, while pairs of active–passive sentences might be used on different, contextually determined, occasions, if one of the two were true the other would have to be true too: an important consideration at a period when the analysis of meaning was parasitic on the analysis of truth.[26] This position, which was a central plank in the "standard theory" of the mid 1960s,[27] was undermined by examples like *Everyone in this room speaks two languages* and *Two languages are spoken by everyone in this room*. It was argued that these differed systematically in that the former allowed that the two languages be different for each person (English and Chinese for me, French and German for you, and so on), whereas the latter entailed that the languages were the same (e.g. English and Chinese for everyone). If this difference is genuine then it follows either that actives and passives are not related to each other in the way claimed, or that the relationship is not meaning preserving. In either case a radical revision of the theory would be necessary. Although it is never the case that theories are falsified by mere data, as opposed to analyses of those data, it looked as if one of the main claims of the theory was impugned, with dire effects for the whole edifice:[28] and all depended on the intuitions of the speakers of the language about pairs of simple sentences.

The theory ultimately moved on and the importance of the issue waned. For these particular examples the consensus emerged (among some at least) that both sentences allow of both interpretations, but that they are preferred in different situations; for other examples like *Many arrows didn't hit the target* and *The target wasn't hit by many arrows* the putative paraphrase relation remained unclear.[29] As a result, the claim of the relatedness of actives and passives was maintained, and any differences were attributed to the interacting effects of interpretation taking place at surface structure as well as at deep structure.[30]

In the whole debate the role of intuitions was crucial, and remains so for a variety of other types of sentence. A comparable case is provided by examples where there is also a clear dialectal difference. For me, *All the children haven't come* has the interpretation that some of the children have come and that some of them have not. It can*not* have the interpretation that *none* of the children has come.[31] Many speakers share the intuition that the former interpretation is more natural, but they also allow the second one as well. The matter is of considerable importance as some theories predict that both possibilities should exist, others make no such prediction. If we are to use linguistic data to decide between competing theories, it is crucial that we know what those data are. More particularly, we need to know what the data for each individual's I-language are, not for some average or mixture, because such averages are not psychological entities.[32] The theory we devise must, of course, be able to accommodate all speakers, but as individuals, not as communities.

When intuitional data are not decisive, it is necessary to have recourse to alternative forms of evidence. In fact, one always looks for evidence in as many places as ingenuity allows: from language change, from language acquisition, from psychological tests of sentence production and comprehension, from neurological investigation of normal and pathological cases, and so on. What it is crucial to emphasize is that none of these kinds of evidence is inherently superior to any other, though *causal convergence* among the different kinds – that is, where various kinds of evidence seem to conspire to give the same verdict – can be overwhelmingly convincing, as when for instance cladistics and molecular biology (occasionally) give the same results for evolutionary relatedness.[33]

One major disagreement between linguists and psychologists is that the latter frequently assign greater importance to experimental results than to any other kind of evidence.[34] Intuitions are considered too ephemeral, intangible, and subjective to be usable, except when they are under experimental control. Accordingly psycholinguists exploit the same techniques that are adduced in the description of any other cognitive faculty: producing and interpreting utterances in a variety of situations, tracking eye movements while subjects view linguistic stimuli, playing different signals in each ear, and measuring response latencies. I alluded above to a simple example using click location to corroborate the postulation of particular syntactic boundaries. Experimental subjects are played tape recordings of sentences which contain clicks at various positions in their structure. Subjects tend systematically to report hearing clicks displaced from their actual position to positions which correspond to major syntactic boundaries, suggesting that speakers are influenced by an intuitive notion of structure equivalent to that postulated by linguists.[35] The results are intriguing, and can provide support for claims about constituent structure. It should be noted, however, that this support is not stronger than that provided by linguistic analysis, and is in fact far less well motivated than such evidence in terms of its interconnection with other theoretical constructs. Its importance lies in its convergence with the more extensively justified claims of the syntacticians. One could even go further: suppose that listeners displaced the clicks not to the edge of the constituent but to the middle – to *John eats* [click] *onions* rather than to *John* [click] *eats onions*. The conclusion could still have been drawn that this supports the NP–VP analysis on the Gestalt principle that the integrity of an entity is preserved by displacing clicks to its mid point. Crucially, the linguistic analysis is presupposed to be correct for such simple cases, and the experiments are redesigned until they give the right results for them. Once this has been achieved, the experiments can be applied to cases where the linguistic analysis is unclear, in the hope that they can constitute a tool to provide appropriate independent evidence for those cases. In the case of click experiments, the results in these unclear cases were ambiguous, and the tool was abandoned: no one does click experiments any more.

Similar observations pertain to the use of response latencies: the length of time it takes a subject to respond to a particular stimulus. Consider causal verbs.[36] There is an uncontroversial contrast in the meaning of pairs of sentences like *Mary saw the cat* and *Mary killed the cat*. The latter is causative, describing a situation in which Mary caused the cat to die, whereas the former has no such causal interpretation. It was intermittently suggested (by linguists and psychologists) that this interpretive difference was a reflection of a syntactic difference: *Mary killed the cat* was supposed to be syntactically complex, containing an abstract predicate CAUSE, absent from the sentence with *see*. Roughly, *Mary killed the cat* has the meaning and the structure of *Mary caused the cat to die*; but *Mary saw the cat* is just that, with no comparable internal complexity. One of the tests of this hypothesis was to see if, under experimental conditions, subjects took longer to understand the more complex sentence than the simple one, on the assumption that the presumed syntactic complexity would be reflected in a difference in processing time. The results showed no difference and so provided no support for the hypothesis. The absence of support does not, of course, amount to refutation, but it does suggest that on this occasion there is no reason to diverge from the simplest possible syntax. In whichever direction evidence of this kind points, it remains true that the strongest evidence *at the moment* is that of internal linguistic analysis, simply because the deductive structure of linguistic theories is now dramatically deeper than that of theories in any of the related domains. This is not a matter of principle: as other branches of psychology develop theories of equal sophistication, we can hope that the evidence they provide will be of comparable depth. At the moment, however, the chain of argument leading to, say, the linguistic claim that we deploy a VP in our internal grammars, is based on a wide array of analyses from a variety of sources, all of which cohere to produce a particular analysis, and all of which must be compatible with all the other subdomains of syntactic analysis (case theory, binding theory, locality, and so on), whereas the prediction of the click experiments was relatively shallow, and could stand or fall on its own.

One particular way in which it is possible to diversify the linguistic evidential base is by having recourse to other languages, as we saw with the Spanish and Quechua examples in the last chapter. Another example is provided by the analysis of serial verb constructions: sentences like *John ran and bought a paper* or *Which paper did John run and buy?* where the underlined verbs constitute the "series" involved.[37] These sentences provide a wealth of descriptive and theoretical puzzles: why can one not say *The paper was run and bought?*; what is the precise difference between such examples and those including *both*, as in *John both ran and bought a paper?* But to answer these questions requires evidence from languages which have a wider range of such constructions than does English. In searching for explanations in this area, Annabel Cormack and I have appealed to data from Nupe, from Japanese, from dialects of Norwegian, and so on. There are two points to make: first, the logic of the argumentation is that, as we saw before, given two putative analyses both of which work for one language, but only one of which works for the other, then that one must be correct for both languages.[38] The second point, which is a corollary of the first, is that only reference to a wide range of languages will allow one to explore, ultimately to exhaust, the space of possible variation among languages and make feasible a theory whose range is indeed the class of possible human languages. In turn, this argument is valid only on the assumption that languages are indeed cut from the same cloth: an assumption that fifty years' work has now made virtually unassailable. In the year that saw the publication of Chomsky's *Syntactic Structures* (1957), Martin Joos was able to write that languages could "differ from each other without limit and in unpredictable ways."[39] No one believes that any more: a major achievement of the Chomskyan paradigm.

I have emphasized the division between linguistics and psychology but, given that Chomsky views linguistics as part of psychology,[40] it is important to stress the harmony as well. While Chomsky's review of Skinner's *Verbal Behavior* demolished behaviorist psychology, his new syntactic paradigm struck a responsive chord among psychologists of language.[41] In particular, his work with George Miller was influential in persuading the psychological community that (transformational) generative grammar was a theory which could directly explain a range of facts about human sentence processing.[42] In retrospect, some of these expectations were naïve, and Chomsky himself always insisted on the indirect nature of the relation between his competence grammatical theory and any model of performance which included such a theory. However, indirectness of the relation does not deny the causality of the relation; it implies only that the causal mechanisms must be less directly implemented than had been assumed. Indeed, there is usually a correlation between the indirectness of these relations and the richness of the deductive structure of the theory concerned.

Consider Darwin's bumble-bees. In *The Origin of Species*, Darwin observes that bumble-bees ("humble-bees" for him) are the only kind of bee that can fertilize red clover, so that if bumble-bees became rare or extinct, clover would become correspondingly rare. But the number of bumble-bees in any area depends in part on the numbers of field-mice (which destroy their honeycombs); and the number of field-mice is in turn dependent on the number of cats (which eat them); and cats of course congregate in villages and towns. "Hence it is quite credible that the presence of a feline animal in large numbers in a district might determine, through the intervention first of mice and then of bees, the frequency of certain flowers in that district!"[43]

Transformations may not have the immediate appeal of bumble-bees, but their causal role in explaining linguistic phenomena is probably greater. At least this perception certainly underlay the use by the psycholinguistic community of Chomsky's competence theory. Its exploitation can be seen in three distinct areas: Language Processing, Language Acquisition, and Language Pathology. I have argued that much work in linguistics relies crucially on our being able to appeal explicitly to the intuitions of the native speaker, but in these three domains knowledge of language can be empirically tested without such direct appeal, making the results more immediately palatable to an experimentally oriented community. There is a fourth domain, historical linguistics, of which this is also true, but it lends itself less happily to psychological investigation because of the difficulty that one is dealing with data drawn from a large number of speakers, often over a prolonged period, so that it is impossible to assume that you are tapping the construct of a single mind. Even though the question of psychological reality is problematic here, and I shall have no more to say about the history of languages, it is worth emphasizing that interesting and persuasive work in the Chomskyan framework is being carried out in the historical study of languages too.[44]

Language processing

It is customary to divide language processing into language production – what goes on when we speak – and language perception – what goes on when we hear and understand others speaking. Some aspects of language production, in particular the choice of what to say, are probably mysteries for human beings: issues which for the foreseeable future are beyond our comprehension. Even ignoring this difficulty, most results of any significance have come from language understanding, as the study of language production has lagged behind the study of perception. Recent advances in imaging technology, which allow us to observe the brain's activity as specific tasks are carried out, are beginning to make language production amenable to investigation, but even in this domain most research on language processing involves comprehension rather than production.[45] In general, most insight has been gained from the study of sentence understanding, though this topic raises serious issues about the relation between the grammar and the mechanisms that exploit the grammar, in particular the parser.

The derivational theory of complexity

The clearest example of both the enthusiasm and the subsequent disillusionment of the psychological community vis-à-vis generative grammar is provided by the Derivational Theory of Complexity and its perceived failure. When transformations were first used in the generation of sentences, their most obvious role was in deriving passives, questions, and negatives from the structure underlying statements. At an early stage in the history of the theory, all the sentences in (6) shared a common deep structure (that is, they were generated by the same Phrase Structure rules of the kind illustrated in chapter 2) and were differentiated by the application of one or more of the transformations whose names are given to the right:

(6) a.	The Seventh Fleet shelled Haiphong	[NO TRANSFORMATION APPLIED]
b.	Haiphong was shelled by the Seventh Fleet	[PASSIVE]
c.	The Seventh Fleet did not shell Haiphong	[NEGATIVE]
d.	Did the Seventh Fleet shell Haiphong?	[QUESTION]
e.	Was Haiphong shelled by the Seventh Fleet?	[PASSIVE QUESTION]
f.	Haiphong was not shelled by the Seventh Fleet	[PASSIVE NEGATIVE]
g.	Didn't the Seventh Fleet shell Haiphong?	[NEGATIVE QUESTION]
h.	Wasn't Haiphong shelled by the Seventh Fleet?	[PASSIVE NEGATIVE QUESTION]

This suggested the simple hypothesis that these transformationally more complex sentence types should be correspondingly harder to process; in particular, a negative or a passive sentence should take longer to process than its corresponding positive or active congener.[46] There ensued a spate of experiments designed to test subjects' performance on all the possible combinations of passives, negatives, questions, and so on, suitably controlled for sentence length, frequency of the lexical items concerned, and all the other details beloved of experimental psychologists. Initial results were encouraging: passives took longer to process than actives; passive questions took longer still; and negative passive questions took longest of all. The conclusion was immediate and dramatic: transformations were "psychologically real," and transformational grammar was vindicated. Chomsky described the results as "a beautiful example of the way creative experimental studies can interweave with theoretical work in the study of language and of mental processes."[47]

However, when a wider variety of structures was tested, there turned out to be no simple correlation between complexity (as reflected in processing time) and the number of transformations involved in the derivation of the respective sentences. The sentences in (7) were thought to differ from each other only in that one has undergone a transformation which the other has not, but no difference in processing difficulty was detectable; and in (8) the shorter, more easily processable, sentences were transformationally more complex than their longer congeners.[48]

(7) a. John picked up the box
    b. John picked the box up
(8) a. Kennedy was assassinated by someone
    b. Kennedy was assassinated
    c. The man who was sitting in the corner ordered a drink
    d. The man sitting in the corner ordered a drink

To add to the psychologists' misery, the theory kept changing: transformations at first could, and then could not, "change meaning"; the demarcation between obligatory and optional rules was unstable; and the role of transformations in the eponymous theory was gradually but inexorably reduced, leading to bemusement or downright hostility on the part of those trying to apply and test the theory.[49] The resulting disenchantment with linguistic theory in general and generative grammar in particular was understandable but naïve. First, there was a surprising and irrational expectation that it was not only likely but also desirable that generative linguists should suffer from intellectual stagnation, and so leave the field in its pristine form for others to play in. Second, the disillusionment reflected a failure to distinguish language and thought: processing a negative utterance may take longer than processing a positive utterance for a variety of different reasons. At the very least one needs to distinguish the possibility that negatives involve a more complex *grammatical* representation from the possibility that they are more complex *conceptually*, and that it is relating the negative utterance to some representation in the language of thought that takes extra time. Third, and most importantly, it revealed a failure to distinguish adequately between grammars and parsers (ultimately, between competence and performance), between our knowledge of language and the mechanisms that use that knowledge.[50] The issue has been consistently problematic, with repeated claims that it is unnecessary to postulate both grammars and parsers, and that if one or the other can be jettisoned, we could perhaps do without the grammar. If true, this might be seen as undermining a considerable proportion of the generative edifice, so it is important to look at what parsers do.

Grammars and parsers

Grammars are representations of what we know; parsers are the mental devices which we use to exploit that knowledge in understanding (and perhaps producing) utterances. There are also computationally implemented parsers; that is, mechanical devices that can be used to process sentences and perhaps model the abilities of human beings, but I am restricting attention here to what we have in our heads. Some of the more successful machine parsers pay little attention to the insights of grammarians, achieving their success by brute force, analyzing millions of alternative possibilities every second. Just as chess-playing computers do not win their matches the way humans win theirs,[51] these parsers do not analyze sentences the way we do, and if one is interested in understanding the human mind, the details of the programs such computers use are of little concern in either case.

Parsers in this human interpretation are standardly taken to incorporate the I-language as well as perceptual strategies, memory structures, and perhaps other devices.[52] A parser takes an input signal and assigns it a perceptual characterization that is related systematically, but in largely unknown ways, to a structural description generated by the grammar. This in turn is related, again in largely unknown ways, to a mental representation in the language of thought. In brief, a parser maps sounds into thoughts by using the grammar.

A good example of how parsers and grammars interact is provided by the (parsing) principle of "minimal attachment."[53] Some sentences, like those in (9), present what are known as "local ambiguities":

(9) a.   Rita knew the answer to the problem by heart
    b.   Rita knew the answer to the problem was wrong

Until the word *by* or *was* is reached, the structure of such sentences is ambiguous between a reading in which *the answer to the problem* can be construed as the object of the verb *know*, or as the subject of the embedded sentence *the answer to the problem was wrong*. At a stage when they have been exposed only to the sequence *Rita knew the answer to the problem*, hearers and readers typically do not leave the structure indeterminate, but leap to the conclusion that the former analysis, indicated in (10a), rather than the latter, indicated in (10b), is correct:

(10) a.   Rita knew [NP the answer to the problem . . .
    b.   Rita knew [S[NP the answer to the problem . . .

Sentences which are ambiguous are accounted for by making the grammar provide two (or more) different analyses for them, so both the analyses in (10) are made available by the grammar, and the parser automatically opts for that analysis which minimizes complexity. (10a) is simpler in that it consists of a proper subset of the elements present in (10b), so the NP *the answer to the problem* is attached as the sister of the verb *know*, rather than as the daughter of the S which is the sister of the verb. The principle by which the parser does this is parasitic on the grammar: it refers to grammatical concepts and constructs; and is independently motivated by results from a range of experimental studies: records of eye movement, of response time, of misinterpretations, and so on.

After nearly half a century of research in generative grammar, itself founded on millennia of traditional language study, we know a huge amount about grammar and the grammars of particular languages. There is still a great deal of theoretical disagreement among professional linguists, and it is probably true to say that those working in a Chomskyan framework are a minority, but it is uncontroversial that there has been dramatic progress, much of it due to Chomsky's influence. By contrast, despite a few suggestive results of the kind associated with the principle of minimal attachment, we are still relatively ignorant about parsers. There is disagreement about what levels of grammatical representation (if any) parsers can refer to, whether they should be rule-based or principle-based,[54] whether they should operate top-down or bottom-up, from left to right or right to left, whether they should be allowed to compute several representations at once or only one at a time, whether they can back-track, and so on. The grammatical analysis of a sentence like (9a), *Rita knew the answer to the problem by heart*, is reasonably straightforward; how the parser should treat it is less clear. One could either start with the (top-down) assumption that what is being parsed is a sentence and predict its constituency, or wait for individual words and compute their relations (bottom-up); one could take each item as it comes (left to right), or wait till the end of the sentence and work backwards (right to left). In either case an obvious alternative is to devise some compromise between the various possibilities, working top-down and bottom-up simultaneously, for instance, but making such compromises explicit (and implementing them on a computer) is not simple. It's not even clear whether parsers should be the same for all languages, except insofar as different parameter settings define differences of superficial structure, or whether there should be a simple fit between grammars and parsers at all.[55]

An interesting response to this situation is the attempt to resurrect earlier claims that the grammar and the parser are one and the same thing: that there is no need for a grammar separate from the operations of the parser.[56] It would follow from this that the Derivational Theory of Complexity could be reinstated: if there is no grammar as such, but there *are* parsing processes to deal with each different kind of construction – passives, questions, and so on – then it would be not unexpected that the time taken up by these operations would increase cumulatively.

At first blush, the enterprise would seem to be misconceived. First, denying the difference between the grammar and the parser involves an apparent denial of the competence–performance distinction: the distinction between knowledge and its deployment. As Chomsky says: "I don't see how it's possible to deny the competence–performance distinction . . . It's a conceptual distinction. There's no evidence for or against the distinction between cognitive states and actions."[57] Second, it makes the unfortunate claim that ungrammatical but easily comprehensible examples like *John speaks fluently English* are not ungrammatical at all, but have their questionable status as a result of not being successfully parsed, and so are allied with garden-path and center-embedded sentences. This seems at best to sacrifice an interesting distinction, at worst to render linguistics contentless. However, it has been forcefully argued that this reaction is simplistic. In interesting work Colin Phillips has argued for the more subtle claim that the crucial difference is whether one views grammars as cognitive systems that operate in real time or not. The traditional Chomskyan position is that grammars are "timeless," whereas parsers (and producers) operate in real time. If one gives up this claim, and adopts the position that "grammatical knowledge is . . . a real-time system for constructing sentences," then it becomes possible to unify the grammar, the parser, and the producer.[58] It is important to note that this is not to deny the difference between grammaticality and parsability, but to claim that the same system may either be used in real time or not. The crucial point seems to be what additional mechanisms, such as memory and attention, are involved in "using" the grammar in these different ways. Chomsky's point about the difference between cognitive states and actions remains valid; the properties of the cognitive system itself remain open to empirical investigation. In this respect it is striking that Chomsky's current system talks explicitly of the possibility that "computational complexity matters for a cognitive system," noting that "it is not clear why [this] thesis should be true," but expressing the suspicion that it "might be correct."[59] If it *is* correct, then unification is correspondingly more plausible.[60]

Assuming nonetheless that the grammar and the parser need to be distinct, it is still not self-evident which should be responsible for particular phenomena. An interesting example is provided by the principle of subjacency mentioned in the previous chapter, which accounts for the impossibility of sentences like *A rise in the price was announced of oil*. Robert Berwick and Amy Weinberg tried to deduce such locality effects, which are prevalent in the grammars of all languages, from the properties of the human parser.[61] The idea was that the theory of grammar didn't need to contain a locality principle like subjacency, because its effects could all be attributed to properties of the parser. As the parser can only scan a limited amount of material at a time, relations between elements that exceeded that "window," non-local relations in other words, would fall outside its scope and fail to be processed. Theoretical parsimony, which rejects multiple accounts of the same phenomenon, then demands that the grammar say nothing about subjacency. However, the logic of their argument suggests that the direction of explanation could equally well go the other way:[62] that is, that the relevant property of the parser could be deduced from the properties of the grammar. That the direction of explanation *should* go this way is supported by the observation that the same grammatical principle can explain aspects of first language acquisition, whereas it is not clear how a parsing principle could do that. There are other problems for parsers as a replacement for the language faculty.

Parsing problems

What has generally been common to all work in sentence processing is the assumption that we need to account for the speed and facility with which people interpret sentences, where such interpretation necessarily involves the parser. In a surprising, and initially puzzling, observation, Chomsky contradicts the traditional truism that parsing is "quick and easy," and suggests in contrast that languages are in part "unusable."[63] What could this mean? As we saw in the discussion of (Fodorian) modularity, understanding the sentences of one's language is usually claimed to be "fast" and "mandatory." The meanings of ordinary sentences are usually grasped essentially instantaneously. Even when confronted with examples of arbitrary obscurity or implausibility we have no choice but to understand them, and understand them as obscure and implausible. Consider the following quotation: "Chomskian grammar . . . proceeds to much greater phenomenological depths with its scheme of 'deep structures' which via a set of rules generate, i.e. 'bring to the surface,' the sentences or 'phonetic events' which we actually speak and hear."[64] George Steiner's account of generative grammar is misguided and ill-informed, but its constituent clauses are easily parsed and understood; and understood to be wrong. More interestingly, we seem to parse with complete facility examples that are on reflection found to be both incoherent and ungrammatical: a famous example is the "seductively natural" (11):[65]

(11)   *More people have visited Russia than I have.

Despite this apparent contradiction of his claim, Chomsky has some persuasive examples to show that, in a number of cases, even this first (parsing) stage in interpretation is blocked. Some sentences containing empty categories, as in (12), or which display center-embedding or "garden paths," as in (13) and (14), are resistant to ordinary decoding of the kind the parser is supposed to deal with automatically:[66]

(12)   John is too stubborn to expect anyone to talk to
(13)   Articles linguists psychologists respect write are hard to understand
(14)   I convinced her mother hated me

Each of these examples provides evidence that parsing is not as straightforward as it is usually made out to be. To understand (12) it is necessary to run through various possibilities in one's head before arriving at the conclusion that it is fundamentally different from the longer, but less difficult, *John is too stubborn to expect anyone to talk to Bill*; (13) tends to leave people totally baffled, even though it has the same basic structure as perfectly acceptable examples like *The book those linguists I met wrote is incomprehensible*; and (14), despite its brevity, lures one almost inexorably to construe *her mother* as a constituent, blocking the acceptable reading more obviously manifest in the parallel *I convinced him mother hated me*. As we saw in chapter 1, garden-path sentences exhibit "local ambiguities": at a particular stage of processing, the sentence allows more than one interpretation, only one of which is grammatically possible by the time one has reached the end of the sentence. In (14) it is possible to construe *her* either as the object of *convince* or as the possessive modifier of *mother*. When one has heard or read *I convinced her mother . . .* , it is the latter interpretation which is usually computed, leaving no role for *hated*, and resulting in confusion. It is possible to devise strategies to circumvent the problems raised by such examples; indeed, much of the literature on so-called "perceptual strategies" is a response to problems of this kind. Such strategies are distinct from the rules or principles of the grammar, and raise interesting questions about cognitive penetrability (that is, whether the internal workings of the grammar are accessible to the central system[67]), but their immediate relevance is that they make clear that it is necessary to differentiate constructs of the grammar and mechanisms of the "parser."[68] This is explicit in Bradley Pritchett's attempt to explain why and how the full range of garden-path phenomena have the effects they do. He has developed a theory of the parser which is systematically parasitic on the properties of a Chomskyan grammar. Parsing involves "the application of grammatical principles locally at every point during the processing," and whether a particular sentence which displays some local ambiguity will be a garden path or not: that is, whether it will subvert the parser, depends on which grammatical principle is at issue.[69] The example in (14) is confusing because it is claimed to violate case theory. At a stage when *her* has been analyzed and *mother* is being processed, unless *mother* is construed as being part of the same constituent as *her*, it lacks Case and so violates a principle of the grammar. When the reader or listener then attempts to integrate *hates* into the interpretation of the sentence, there is a further problem: *hates* assigns a theta role to its subject but there is no subject to assign it to, so he or she is forced to reinterpret the sequence *her mother* as two constituents. This in turn involves thematic reanalysis – changing the theta role assignment – a computationally complex process, which causes stress to the parser. By contrast, the example with *him* instead of *her* involves a local violation of case theory when *mother* is reached, but there is never any need for thematic reanalysis, as *hates* will assign both case and a theta role to *mother*. The technical details are complex and controversial, but the implications are straightforward: the grammar and the parser must be distinct, and the relation between them can give rise to confusion as well as clarity. Fortunately, the latter is more usual.

All garden-path sentences involve local disambiguation – the resolution of a temporarily indeterminate meaning – and thereby impose an unwanted burden on the person parsing them, as he or she has to entertain two analyses simultaneously or in quick succession. It is clear that such a process is "uneconomical" in the sense that it requires the deployment of resources beyond the conceptual minimum: two or more analyses are needed instead of a single optimal one. Language understanding is normally so effortless that the complexity of the system we manipulate is often forgotten. This usual effortlessness in the face of complexity suggests that our linguistic system is designed so that it usually maximizes the economy of its processes. Much recent work has been devoted to attempts to specify how this notion of "economy" might be more precisely defined.

Economy

> simplicity is increased by . . . reduction of the length of derivations. (Chomsky, 1951: 52)

Economy can be a matter of competence or of performance, though the performance notion is intuitively somewhat easier to grasp.[70] For example, in his seminal discussion of vision, David Marr suggests that in any domain where "performance is fluent" it will be necessary to invoke a "principle of least commitment":[71] a principle that stops you doing things you'll later regret and so have to undo. In the context of parsing, this idea translates into a demand that back-tracking, where you go back and start processing a sentence again, should be minimized or excluded.[72] Parsing is part of performance, and considerations of "least effort," as Chomsky expresses it, sound as if they have to pertain to performance, especially when he writes that economy conditions "require[s] that the least costly derivation be *used*."[73] But Chomsky's economy principles are unambiguously matters of competence, in that they pertain to representations and derivations internal to the language faculty and exclude relations beyond the interfaces. In earlier versions of the theory they applied to relations among d-structure, s-structure and LF.[74] With the demise of the first two, they now pertain to the stages in the construction of representations at LF and PF, and crucially do not go beyond these to systems of interpretation or production. It is the grammar-internal characterization of individual sentences that has to be economical. As an example of economy considerations of a purely grammatical kind, consider the standard account of the difference between the French and English examples in (15) and (16):

(15) a. John often kisses Mary
     b. *John kisses often Mary

(16) a. Jean embrasse souvent Marie
     b. *Jean souvent embrasse Marie

The semantic interpretation of these sentences is the same; that is, in relevant respects they have the same meaning. Accordingly, it is assumed that they must have the same representation at LF, that level of the grammar at which meaning relations are captured. Producing this representation involves the movement of the verb (*kisses/embrasse*) to an abstract structural position, in order for the agreement between the subject and the verb to be checked.[75] The obvious difference in word order between the two languages is then attributed to the "visibility" of that movement. In French, the movement of the verb has an *overt* effect – it takes place before spellout, whereas in English it is *covert* or invisible – it takes place after spellout, so the adverb *often* can intervene between the verb and its subject. In English, the impossibility of (15b) follows from the assumption that covert, invisible movement is more economical than visible movement, an assumption embodied in the principle of "procrastination": leave movement as late as possible; specifically, until after spellout.[76] Generating (15b) would then constitute a violation of "procrastination." Clearly, the same account cannot be operative in French. Here, overt movement of the verb does not violate "procrastinate" because the morphological systems of French and English are different in the relevant respect. French verbal features are "strong" (in the sense introduced in the last chapter) and, because strong features are visible at PF, they need to be eliminated before PF by being checked. Checking can only occur after movement, so this movement must take place before spellout and hence is visible. English verbal features are "weak," and as weak features are invisible to the phonology, they do not need to be eliminated until LF, hence movement need not take place until then. The crucial difference between the languages then reduces to a parametric difference between weak and strong features. At the moment this remains a stipulation: something for which we have no explanation, but it is important to note two things. First, given the assumption of a contrast between weak and strong, and the existence of independently motivated principles, the facts fall out with minimal fuss. Second, the economy principle "procrastinate" is entirely internal to the language module. It is a principle of competence not of performance, as it involves simply the properties of representations which are neutral as between speaker and hearer, and have no necessary implications for parsing.

Even if this analysis is capable of describing the facts, it may be objected that the need to stipulate a difference between weak and strong features is no better than stipulating that in English certain adverbs may precede the verb and in French they may not. This objection would be valid if the examples cited were the only ones for which the weak/strong distinction worked, but it applies to a range of different construction types in English and other languages; that is, a single stipulation (weak versus strong) brings coherence to a number of different phenomena, whereas a stipulation in terms of adverbial placement does not generalize. More generally, we saw in chapter 2 that economy, in the guise of "shortest move," accounted for the contrasting acceptability of examples like *Have John will left?* and *Will John have left?*. In fact, this economy principle generalizes to account also for the impossibility of examples like *John is likely for it to seem to have left* and *What did you persuade who to buy[ec]?*.[77] That is, the postulation of economy within the grammar allows for the beginnings of an explanation rather than just a description.

The unexplained contrast between strong and weak features remains a challenge to future research, but it is already possible to see the insight it could bring to the problem of how the child can learn its first language with apparently effortless speed and success. If all that is necessary for the acquisition of grammar is the selection of a particular value, strong or weak, for a small number of features, we can begin to understand a process that had previously looked mysterious. First language acquisition is the second area where Chomsky's ideas have been adopted and adapted by the psycholinguistic community, and it is that to which we turn next.

Language acquisition (Plato's problem)

Teaching versus learning

A language is a corpus of teachable things. (Ryle, 1961: 5)

The eminent philosopher Dagfinn Føllesdal reports that "my parents taught me the semantics of 'it is raining' by rewarding me for saying 'it is raining' when, in their opinion, it was raining."[78] Most people's childhood is rather different, and it is now generally accepted by all who have thought about the subject that parents do not actively "teach" children their first language. The reasons are simple: no parent has the necessary explicit knowledge to do so, and children anyway acquire their knowledge of their first language long before they are in a position to understand the relevant instruction even if the parents could provide it. How would *you* set about teaching your three-year-old relative clauses? Some aspects of one's language *are* explicitly taught in school: the spelling conventions of the written representation of language; some forms of technical vocabulary; the shibboleths of socially stigmatized patterns like avoiding *It's me*. But it is noteworthy that these are all marginal. Many people in the world are illiterate, but the illiterate still have knowledge of their language. Every speaker has mastery of a range of technical vocabularies: for football, music, or biochemistry; and whether these are acquired by informal interaction or by explicit teaching is of little import. Such technical terms are anyway an inessential part of the whole of one's vocabulary: ignorance of the difference between a *bogey* and a *birdie* would not exclude one from membership in the linguistic community, even if it debarred one from membership in the golf club. Stigmatized patterns are simply manifestations of social awareness about a minute portion of the resources of one's language; and as Chomsky put it sardonically with regard to *Pygmalion*, learning these has little to do with language acquisition and rather more with "the acquisition of a certain system of cultural snobbery."[79]

Learning versus growing

Explicit teaching is at best of only peripheral importance in the acquisition of one's first language. It is less widely accepted that "learning" is also an inappropriate notion to use, but Chomsky has periodically made the striking claim that it is largely irrelevant to language acquisition: "in certain fundamental respects we do not really learn language; rather, grammar grows in the mind."[80]

There are two major implications of such a claim. First, whatever the processes of "learning" may be, they are not characteristic of language acquisition, so this should progress less like standard examples of learning and more like the development in the child of stereoscopic vision, or in the embryo of a simple rather than a compound eye. Second, such development should be maturationally (endogenously) controlled, passing through a critical period and manifesting identical stages of development in all individuals irrespective of the idiosyncratic differences among the languages being acquired, and the environments in which that acquisition takes place. Let us look at each of these points in turn, embedding the discussion in Chomsky's "parameter setting" theory of language acquisition.[81]

Parameter setting

Learning of the sort that takes place in school or the psychologist's laboratory typically involves association, induction, conditioning, hypothesis formation and testing, generalization, and so on. None of these seems to be centrally involved in (first) language acquisition, which takes place before the child is capable of exploiting these procedures in other domains. Moreover, the pattern of errors (and non-errors) found in children makes traditional "learning" implausible as the basis for acquisition. There are some areas where analogy, hypothesis formation, and generalization do seem to play a (restricted) role: morphology is the obvious example. It is well known that children (over-)generalize patterns of phonology and morphology, so that they produce examples like *three sheeps comed* instead of the adult *three sheep came*. Such examples are evidence that the child is developing its own rule-based grammar, rather than acquiring language purely imitatively: parents do not usually provide models for the exact forms the child comes up with. It is remarkable that such errors are *not* characteristic of other domains of acquisition, in particular, syntax. Although the analogy should be just as obvious to an adult or to a Martian scientist, children do not make errors of a kind which would lead them to give (18) an interpretation in which *who* and *he* refer to the same person, on the model of the example in (17) where, as shown by the subscripts, this *is* a possible reading:[82]

(17)   Who$_i$ thinks he$_i$ is intelligent?
(18)   Who$_i$ does he$_{j/*i}$ think is intelligent?

These examples are parallel in relevant respects to the *stubborn* sentences we looked at earlier. If language acquisition proceeded on the basis of analogy, such failures of interpretation would be mysterious. If acquisition, specifically the acquisition of syntax, is a matter of setting switches, of choosing among a set of pre-specified possibilities, as is claimed by the Principles and Parameters program, then such examples become comprehensible: analogy works only for non-parametric choices. Notice that this form of argumentation exploits two unusual (and controversial) points: the *non*-occurrence of some phenomenon, and the existence of an alternative, radically new, theory of acquisition. The first is itself rather surprising and raises further problems. It is difficult to find corroboration for the claim that something will not be found, except not to find it. If it *were* found, of course, the theory from which the non-occurrence followed would be refuted, apparently satisfying an elementary requirement of testability. Unfortunately, as Chomsky has emphasized elsewhere, theories are not refuted by data but only by analyses.[83] Suppose, implausibly, that some one individual (adult or child) constructed the "impossible" analogy in (18). It would still be necessary to establish that this was in fact part of that person's competence and not simply a performance mistake. This is not an easy task: people will often assent to the suggestion that a sentence is well- or ill-formed, simply because they find it easy or difficult to understand but, as has repeatedly been emphasized, comprehensibility is not the whole story.

An interesting example exploiting the claim about the non-occurrence of particular error types has been provided in work by Ad Neeleman and Fred Weerman. The basic word-order difference between English and Dutch, with English having Verb–Object order and Dutch having Object–Verb order, is easy to acquire and is indeed acquired early. If this acquisition is effected by the setting of a particular parameter, rather than being the result of just learning the construction, then their parametric theory predicts that Dutch children will produce utterances with adverbs intervening between the Object and the Verb, but that English children will never produce utterances with an adverb intervening between the Verb and the Object.[84] Their predictions appear to be borne out. Dutch children do produce examples like (19):

(19)   ik wil de yoghurt even   pakken
         I want the yoghurt quickly get
         "I want to get yoghurt quickly"

where the adverb *even* intervenes between the Object *de yoghurt* and the Verb *pakken*; and English children produce sentences with adverbs after the Object, like that in (20):

(20)   didn't have a nap today

where the adverb *today* follows *a nap*, but they never produce examples like the made-up one in (21):

(21)   didn't have today a nap

where the adverb intervenes between the Verb *have* and the Object. That is, the non-existent (21) is an example of an "impossible mistake." To say children never produce such examples is of course not provable, but it is testable, and the authors ransacked the largest international corpus of child data in checking their predictions, and happily found no counter-examples.[85]

The second, equally important strand in the argument, the availability of a new theory, can be illustrated by elaborating an analogy with the immune system.[86] It was long thought that the development of antibodies by the immune system was a kind of learning process, triggered by exposure of the organism to some noxious influence. If the body was invaded by the bacteria responsible for diphtheria or tetanus, for example, the immune system would be thereby prompted to spring into action and produce antibodies to combat them. This common-sense assumption was supported by considerations of economy and novelty: it was *a priori* implausible that the huge number of antibodies available to combat disease could have been specified in advance, and it later became apparent that antibodies were developed in response to artificial substances that could never have been present in the evolutionary record. Nonetheless, over the last half century this position has been abandoned in favor of the now universally accepted view that antibody formation is a "selective" and not an "instructive" process. "Innate repertoires turn out to be truly immense," so that there is always a "pre-existing antibody of high affinity" available to combat invaders.[87] It transpires that "learning," in any sense of the word, is unnecessary to explain the body's immune response system. The parallel with language acquisition is strikingly close. From a position where language learning (even if not teaching) was self-evidently the correct way of conceptualizing the child's development of its first language, we now have a position where the favored conceptualization is in terms of the switch-setting metaphor of Principles and Parameters theory: a selection process.

If this view is correct, and if the discussion in chapter 2 to the effect that parametric variation is limited to the set of functional categories is right, we can turn to the prediction that language acquisition should be largely endogenously driven rather than being just a reaction to external stimuli. The development of other biological systems is subject to maturational control, often taking place in a particular window of opportunity referred to as the critical period. It is interesting that there is mounting evidence both that first language acquisition takes place only during a critical period, more accurately a number of critical periods, and that the actual development of language is best viewed in maturational terms.[88]

The critical period hypothesis

The critical period hypothesis claims that there is a genetically determined "window of opportunity" for language acquisition. If the child does not learn its first language during this period then it will never attain full native-like mastery of any language. It was first suggested in full coherence by Eric Lenneberg, who drew an explicit analogy with the imprinting of birds, specifically goslings.[89] As soon as they hatch out, baby goslings attach themselves to the first moving thing they see, and follow it around thereafter on the (usually safe) assumption that it is a mother goose. To be successful, such "imprinting" has to take place within the first few minutes after hatching. First language acquisition has a much longer time span at its disposal, but the principle is the same: it must take place at the very latest before puberty.

Evidence for the hypothesis comes from a number of different directions. The most obvious is the contrast between the end state achieved in first and second language acquisition, where the second language is acquired after the age of about nine or ten years.[90] It is striking that any child learns the language of its environment faultlessly in the space of a few years. By contrast, people transferred to a different environment in adulthood have notorious difficulty in acquiring a second language with the same degree of fluency and with the same intuitions as the native speakers. This is true largely irrespective of the motivation and degree of exposure of the speakers concerned. There are to be sure a few talented individuals who appear to be able to achieve native-like ability, but they are rare, whereas every child except in cases of pathology achieves perfect mastery of its first language, and indeed of a second or third language if its exposure to them comes early enough. If there is indeed a window of opportunity, beginning at birth and extending for the first decade of life, this situation is immediately explained.

A second strand of evidence comes from certain pathological cases. It is generally agreed that speech function is lateralized, such that in normal right-handed people the language faculty is located in the left hemisphere.[91] Aphasia (loss of language caused by brain damage) is then typically associated with damage to the left hemisphere, while comparable insults to the right hemisphere leave the victim linguistically unaffected.[92] In some intractable cases of epileptic seizures, the only treatment is hemispherectomy (strictly speaking, hemidecortication), the surgical removal of part of the brain. Recovery from such an operation, in particular the recovery or development of linguistic ability, is correlated with age. If the operation is carried out in infancy, recovery is often good, but operations carried out later have a less successful outcome, and by puberty recovery of linguistic ability is extremely rare.[93] There is some variation from individual to individual, suggesting that the critical period is not rigidly demarcated, or that there is more than one such period, but the correlation is significant and the critical period hypothesis provides an explanation of that fact.

Further evidence for the working of a critical period comes from the differential linguistic development of Down's syndrome children with varying severity of the condition. Down's syndrome children are typically very slow in learning and using language, though in some cases mastery of language falls within normal limits.[94] In severe cases they never develop proper mastery of the syntax of their native language: even though their lexical development may continue throughout life, their syntactic development appears to be cut short at around the age of puberty. It looks again as if language development falls into two different categories: lexical development, which is relatively unconstrained by maturational factors (though even here it seems that the phenomenal vocabulary growth of about one new word per hour over a period of years is never continued post-pubertally),[95] and aspects of syntactic development, which are parametrically determined. It is this syntactic progress which is cut off at the end of the critical period. If puberty represents the absolute end-point of the critical period, this observation is immediately explained.

Further suggestive evidence is found in the differential acquisition of Sign Language by the deaf at different ages. Here the argument is slightly more complex. In an elegant paper Rachel Mayberry showed that "subjects who acquired American Sign Language as a second language after childhood outperformed those who acquired it as a first language at exactly the same age."[96] At first blush it would appear that this *second* language superiority was counter-evidence to claims about the privileged status of first language acquisition. However, Mayberry's subjects were unusual in the following respect. Roughly nine out of ten deaf children are born to hearing parents, while about one in ten are born to deaf parents. It is this latter group which is linguistically privileged, in that they are exposed to normal (signed) linguistic input from the very beginning (signed languages are languages like any others – just conveyed in a different medium), whereas those born to hearing parents risk getting no usable linguistic input at all. Mayberry's finding pertained to a comparison of two groups: first, people who had acquired a spoken language, had then gone deaf and so had had to learn ASL as a second language in adulthood; second, people who had been congenitally deaf, and had had no signed input, and so had grown up essentially language-less. For these people ASL was their first language, but it was being acquired after the critical period. In such a situation, the prior existence of some (spoken) language base, even if it was no longer directly usable, was apparently sufficient to trigger the development of the language faculty to a higher degree than first language acquisition carried out after the critical period. That is, if first language acquisition is to be "perfect," it must take place within this "window of opportunity."

One last strand of evidence comes from the sad cases known as wolf children: children who have been abandoned or isolated in infancy and brought up in conditions where they have been deprived of normal linguistic input. The most famous and most chilling case of such a child is Genie.[97] Genie's mother was partially sighted; her father was psychotic. From the age of about two to thirteen years, Genie was kept incarcerated, harnessed to a potty by day and caged at night; half-starved, frequently beaten for making any noise, growled and barked at by her father and brother, and essentially never spoken to. When she was fortuitously discovered, she gave evidence of knowing a few words such as *rattle, bunny,* and *red,* but she appeared to have no syntax at all. She did respond to gestures, and appeared cognitively somewhat less deprived than her linguistic performance would lead one to expect. She was taken into care and exposed to intensive language (and other) input, leading to the possibility of testing the predictions of the critical period hypothesis. After encouraging initial progress, Genie was the victim of mismanagement to a degree bordering on cruelty, but she does provide us with some evidence. In the few years immediately following her rescue, her development was remarkable, and her vocabulary in particular grew dramatically in size, including subtle discriminations of form and color. However, despite the fact that she showed some ability to create novel utterances, her syntax *never* developed, suggesting that the stimuli she was exposed to had come too late – outside the critical period – to trigger normal language maturation. The case is not entirely clear-cut, because it is impossible to know whether the trauma she had suffered or her mental state when she was first locked up were such that she would never have been able to develop language anyway. Given that we know of many cases where normal language develops even in the presence of gross impairment in other cognitive domains, it seems most plausible that her failure to master ordinary syntax was indeed due to her deprivation in the critical period. What is striking is that she lacked precisely those attributes of language which are, by hypothesis, the fruit of the maturational unfolding of the genetic program in terms of the fixing of parameters. The acquisition of vocabulary is not so tightly constrained, as witness the fact that we go on adding to our vocabulary throughout our life, but the acquisition of the core syntactic properties of language, a core which is specified genetically up to parametric variation, is restricted to this critical period.[98]

Why should there be a critical period? In the case of imprinting, the benefits are clear. Goslings need to identify Mummy as soon as possible in order to survive, and once she is identified it is crucial that they not imprint on subsequent moving things: that is, the imprinting mechanism must be switched off once its work has been done. In language you need to fix your parameters as early as possible so that you can deploy the system in its full complexity without continual changes. In general, there is no need to "learn" things that come pre-packaged in modules, they are available virtually instantaneously provided the relevant triggering experience is provided.[99] "Instantaneously" is a relative term and even with a large innate component there is still a lot more to internalize in language than in recognizing a conspecific goose, so even syntax takes a year or two to get established.

This leaves unanswered the vexed question of why languages differ at all. The Minimalist Program suggests that the "equations" linking sound and meaning allow of several equally good solutions. There are "conditions imposed by the general architecture of the mind/brain," but these conditions can be met in various ways.[100] The choice among them is then either arbitrary or a response to external pressures arising from the need to facilitate language processing or to allow for different pragmatic functions, such as what the relative prominence of different constituents of the sentence should be. A more focused answer to the problem is a matter for future research.[101]

Maturation

A corollary of the genetic hypothesis is that the development of language should be roughly the same across all children, irrespective of the language they are exposed to, not only in terms of its occurrence within a critical period (or periods), but also in terms of the appearance of identical patterns across different

languages. One particular (controversial) example of this commonalty is provided by what is known as the maturation of functional categories.[102] This
means that children go through a stage in their language acquisition in which
functional categories are absent, and that these then mature, or come "on-line,"
at a particular stage, when the children are roughly two years old.

This hypothesis accounts for a range of phenomena in the language of very
young children, in particular the remarkable similarity of their productive syntax
around the age of two. The existence of many constructions in adult language
is dependent on the presence of categories or principles which are claimed to
mature at a particular stage of development. Accordingly, such constructions
are absent prior to the emergence in the child's grammar of those categories or
principles. As discussed in chapter 2, most, perhaps all, parametric differences
are dependent on the operation of functional categories. If functional categories
are absent, because they have not yet matured, then there should be no parametric
differences between the very early stages of different languages: between early
child Italian or Greek, English or French, Irish or Chinese.

Let us investigate the claim by reference to one particular parametric difference. The world's languages are often described as falling into two classes:
null-subject languages like Greek and Spanish, in which subject pronouns can
be freely omitted, and non-null-subject languages like English and French, in
which subject pronouns are obligatory.[103] This contrast gives rise to examples
like that in (22), contrasting Spanish with English:

(22)   baila bien   He *or* she dances well

where *baila* means "dances" and *bien* means "well." In Spanish it is acceptable,
indeed normal, to say simply the equivalent of "dances well" for "he or she
dances well," whereas in English it is obligatory to retain one of the pronouns
he or *she*. By contrast, little children seem to make all languages null-subject,
giving rise to the similarities seen in (23–26) from respectively Greek, English,
French, and Italian:[104]

(23) a. kani padhl   She's making a puzzle
         (literally: "makes puzzle," where *kani* is third person singular)
     b. thelis tili   I want cheese
         (literally: "want cheese," where *thelis* is **second** person singular)

(24) a. want Daddy   I want Daddy
     b. eating cereal   I'm eating cereal

(25) a. veut lait   He wants some milk
         (literally: "wants milk," where *veut* is third person singular)
     b. est pas gros   It's not big
         (literally: "is not big," where *est* is third person singular)

(26) a. tanti ocattoli porta   She's bringing lots of toys
         (literally: "many toys brings," where *porta* is third person singular)
     b. pendo chetta   I'm taking this
         (literally: "take this," where *pendo* is first person singular)

This similarity is striking, but could perhaps be accounted for by a simpler story appealing to the saving gained by leaving out the subject, especially when the context in which the sentences are uttered usually makes it clear what that subject must be. The Greek examples show that it is the context that tells us who the subject is, and that this is not shown by the agreement, as children often get the agreement wrong. In this case (23b) the child used the second person, when she intended to refer to herself.

However, such an alternative account won't explain the development of Irish. The structure of the Verb Phrase (VP), as provided by Universal Grammar,[105] allows for the appearance of subjects and objects on one side or the other of the verb: either Verb–Object or Object–Verb. If there is a subject present as well, this gives rise to four possible word orders: SVO, SOV, VOS, OVS – that is, all and only the word orders in which the Verb and the Object are next to each other. In the absence of functional categories, there is no possibility of producing the other two logically possible word orders VSO and OSV, where the subject intervenes between the Verb and the Object. These word orders are produced by moving (or "raising") the Verb to a higher position in the tree, but raising cannot operate without functional projections, as only functional categories provide "landing sites" for a moved element to be attracted to. Accordingly, this analysis predicts that, universally, VSO word order is impossible in early child language, even where the ambient adult language has precisely that as its normal word order. Irish, which normally has VSO word order, is an example of such a language. As can be seen from the examples in (27) from a child learning Irish as its first language, it converts the input into an SVO sequence, which is in accordance with the constraints of its still immature system. As Ianthi Tsimpli put it: "the role of the input, however crucial, cannot override restrictions regulated by the nature of early grammars."[106]

(27) a. Aoife ithe bruitin   Aoife is eating potatoes
         (literally: "Aoife eating potatoes")
     b. Dadai amuigh baint pratai   Daddy's gone out to get potatoes
         (literally: "Daddy out getting potatoes")

This is a remarkable finding: even though the input to the child contains examples of the canonical VSO type, the child's own productions are constrained by the absence of functional categories to be of a different type. These examples and their interpretation are not, of course, without problems. The most severe is that, although it is a VSO language, Irish characteristically uses initial auxiliary verbs, giving the (simplified) sequence "Aux S V O." Simple omission of the auxiliary by the child would then give rise to the word order SVO that *is* typical of the adult language.[107] Given the importance of the prediction being made, it is an urgent task for the future to test it on other VSO languages, preferably ones that do not use initial auxiliaries as freely as Irish. Whatever the outcome of such investigations the putative evidence for the maturation of functional categories, and consequently for the genetic determination of (part of) the developing grammar, is striking.

Language pathology

The clearest "non-intuitional" evidence for properties of the language faculty comes from cases where language either fails to develop properly because of some genetic defect, or is sabotaged by illness or trauma.[108] Because of the specific dissociations that occur, such cases seem to provide strong support for the kind of (sub-)modular structure of the grammar argued for in the previous chapter. I will look at three specific examples: the case of a child born without part of its brain, the polyglot *savant* mentioned previously and, more problematically, subjects with Specific Language Impairment.

Agenesis of the corpus callosum

In looking at evidence for the critical period hypothesis, I cited the example of recovery from hemispherectomy, a drastic procedure carried out to alleviate the effects of intractable epilepsy. An alternative, and equally drastic, treatment either to control severe cases of epilepsy or to stop the spread of malignant tumors, is commisurotomy, severing the patient's corpus callosum, that part of the brain that connects the two hemispheres and allows communication between them.[109] As we saw earlier, despite a certain amount of variability, the language faculty is normally predominantly located in the left cerebral hemisphere, whereas a variety of other functions are usually resident in the right hemisphere. Integration of the different functions is in part the responsibility of the corpus callosum, and the surgical procedure "splitting the brain" gives rise to a range of strange dissociations. For instance, if subjects are allowed to feel a pencil with the left hand (so the tactile information goes mainly to the right hemisphere), they can give evidence that they have correctly identified the pencil, but are unable to report the fact verbally, as verbal behavior is the province of the inaccessible left hemisphere.

Occasionally "split brains" of this kind occur congenitally, i.e. as an accident of birth. Heike Tappe reports the case of a child who was born without a corpus callosum. Her syntactic development was qualitatively similar to that of normal children of the same age, suggesting that syntactic competence (concentrated in the left hemisphere) requires no cross-hemispheric communication. By contrast, the development of her semantic and encyclopaedic knowledge, in particular the acquisition and processing of word-naming abilities seemed to depend on inter-hemispheric communication, and was correspondingly defective.[110] As discussed earlier, Chomsky's theory claims that there is a basic distinction in the language faculty between the lexicon and the "computational system."[111] The case described by Tappe now provides evidence that this distinction is underpinned by an architectural difference of the human brain, because not only does mastery of the different linguistic components dissociate, but we also have neuro-anatomical evidence serving to give an initial idea of how that dissociation might come about. It is not expected that there will ever be a one-to-one correlation between neurological and linguistic categories; it *is* expected that gross linguistic distinctions will find some kind of definable neurological reflex of the kind seen here.

The *polyglot* savant

The difference between the lexicon and the computational system that was introduced in the last chapter and highlighted in the previous section is actually more complex than has been suggested. In our work on the polyglot *savant* Christopher, Ianthi Tsimpli and I proposed that it was necessary to make a more subtle distinction in the structure and location of the lexicon.[112] In particular we argued that the lexicon should be split so that "conceptual" properties of lexical items were separated off from purely "linguistic" properties. Lexical entries are standardly taken to consist of triples of syntactic, phonological, and semantic features, and simultaneously to provide a link to encyclopaedic information: so *tiger* is a noun, it is pronounced with an initial /t/; it means TIGER and, in addition, we know that tigers are typically stripy. As a refinement of this traditional position, we postulated an autonomous component containing all and only information about functional categories such as complementizer, determiner, tense, and so on. This suggestion was partly motivated by two asymmetries in Christopher's talent. His ability to master second and subsequent languages is dramatic but incomplete. In particular, his ability to learn new words and their complex morphological properties is impressively good but, presumably as a function of the end of the critical period, he is consistently unable to integrate this knowledge into the rest of the language faculty in order to achieve mastery of the syntactic implications of this complex morphology. For instance, he quickly and easily learned the morphological paradigms of verbs in several languages, and used this knowledge appropriately to identify the referent of missing subjects in pro-drop languages. Yet he was systematically unable to use this morphological knowledge as a way in to learning the syntactic fact that such languages typically also allow the subject to occur postposed after the verb.[113] That is, in null-subject languages like Spanish, you can say not only *baila* to mean "He *or* she dances," but also *baila Juan* to mean "John dances." Christopher always rejected such examples with an inverted subject as ungrammatical. Although his English syntax is like that of any other native speaker, the syntax of his second languages is defective, in large part to the extent that their syntactic patterns deviate from those of the English base he starts from. In this case he could cope with the simple omission of the subject, but he was unable to generalize his mastery of this structure to other syntactically related ones. It looks therefore as if part of his lexicon in foreign languages is intact, indeed enhanced, whereas part is defective: a conclusion that should come as no surprise in a framework where linguistic knowledge is crucially distinct from non-linguistic knowledge, and is compartmentalized along the lines indicated. Christopher's unusual talents and disabilities provide further evidence for the fractionation and dissociation of abilities which normally go together, and provide further evidence for the kind of framework Chomsky has argued for over the years. Learning new lexical items and their inflectional endings is not subject to a critical period of any kind, but mastering the intricacies of parametric variation and the syntactic patterns dependent on them can take place only in this one window of opportunity.[114] Despite his talent, by the time Christopher acquired his second languages, he had missed this opportunity.

Specific language impairment (SLI)

Although language pathology is the area which gives the clearest indication of how and where language is represented in the brain, it is important not to be seduced into thinking that there is some simple relationship between constructs of the language faculty and neuro-anatomical configurations. Indeed, there is no claim in the area which is not contested. Gradually, however, some consensus is emerging as more and more case studies are taken into consideration. Some of the clearest results have been provided by a detailed study of one particular family, the K family, and by the more general study of the disability they seem to suffer from.[115]

    If Chomsky is right that language is largely genetically determined, that our language faculty is to a considerable extent innate, then we should expect to find cases of aphasia associated with an abnormality in a particular gene or genes. The K family seems to exemplify precisely such a case of a language disorder caused by "autosomal dominant transmission": that is, where the condition is passed down from generation to generation irrespective of the sex of the affected family members. The evidence needed to support such a claim is of necessity complex, as we need to show both the existence of a language deficit (rather than a more general cognitive deficit), and that it is genetically determined.

Fortunately, the epidemiological evidence for a genetic aetiology is clear, as should be apparent from the "family tree" given in (28):[116]

(28)   Incidence of SLI in the K family

```
                 ♀=(♂)                        1st generation

   ♀    (♂)    ♀    ♂    ♀                     2nd generation

  (♀)   (♂)   (♀)  (♂)   ♂                     3rd generation

   ♂    (♀)   (♀)  (♀)  (♂)

  (♀)              ♀    ♀   (♂)

   ♂               ♀    ♀   (♀)

                   ♂        ♂

                           (♂)

                            ♀

                           (♂)

                            ♀
```

♀ and ♂ are the standard signs for female and male, underlining indicates that the person concerned suffers from a language problem, while parentheses indicate unaffected members of the family. In the first generation, the mother was affected but her husband had normal language. They had five children (the second generation): three girls, all of whom are affected, and two boys, one of whom is and one of whom is not affected. In the third generation there are twenty-four children: eleven affected (five boys and six girls) and thirteen unaffected. Assuming (uncontroversially) that the characterization as "affected" and "unaffected" is accurate, no one would doubt with this set of figures that the cause of the problem is genetic, and more recently the gene whose mutation appears to cause the problem, FOXP2, has been identified. The crucial question then is whether the problem afflicting the family is indeed a language deficit.

Although they have little or no difficulty with vocabulary, and their non-verbal abilities are normal, the affected family members have problems with plurals, with tense, with gender, with aspect: with all those parts of grammar where abstract morphological features are exploited.[117] Let us concentrate just on tense. In this domain they confuse *watch* and *watched*; they produce spontaneous speech including examples like *She remembered when she hurts herself the other day*; they mistakenly self-correct themselves, producing sequences like: *We did it // we do it last month*; their diaries contain entries like: *Monday 17th October: On Saturday I got up and I wash myself and I get dress and I eat my breakfast and I watched TV all day and I went to bed. On Sunday I got up and* . . . The list could be continued but, strikingly, they have no problems with the use and understanding of temporal adverbs like *yesterday, today,* and *tomorrow*, suggesting that "the impaired subjects had no trouble with the concept of temporal reference . . . but were insensitive to the grammatical requirement that tense be marked on the verb." Myrna Gopnik reaches the conclusion that "grammatical rule-processing and lexical memorization are two psychologically, linguistically and neurologically distinct processes, one of which can be impaired relative to the other."[118] If correct, this provides more support for the Chomskyan paradigm, both at a general level regarding innateness, and in the detail of his claims about linguistic organization.

The analysis is (of course) controversial:[119] the language of most of the affected family members is very markedly abnormal, and there have been attempts to attribute their difficulties to processing deficits or to general cognitive problems, rather than to grammatical factors. However, the evidence for a dissociationist interpretation of the facts is becoming more persuasive, and other cases of SLI make the case stronger still. Heather van der Lely has investigated the array of disabilities shown by SLI children, concentrating on one particularly striking individual.[120] This boy, "AZ," is of above average intelligence, yet he shows systematic inability to manipulate those aspects of syntax which are usually taken to be core examples of the language faculty: simple recursion, tense marking, distinctions between pronouns and reflexives, and so on. Dissociation of abilities of this kind is direct evidence of their autonomy and indirect evidence of their genetic determination. The issue is still open, but the evidence is looking good.

Connectionism: the behaviorists strike back

All the preceding discussion has presupposed that the mind can be usefully viewed as a mechanism that carries out computations over representations of some kind. The rules and principles of linguistic analysis all tacitly accept that it makes sense to talk of "words," "sentences," and "constructions." The generalizations of psychology and the philosophy of mind are all dependent on the assumption that cognition involves the manipulation of mental representations. The last twenty-five years has seen the emergence (or re-emergence) of a radically different approach to the study of the mind. Known alternatively as "Connectionism," "Neural networks" or "Parallel Distributed Processing," this approach denies the need for symbolic representations at all.[121] All the complexities of human thought and language can emerge from interactions among a set of processing units which can take on different activation values.

A connectionist network consists of a set of nodes that collect inputs from a variety of sources (both inside and outside the system), and transmit inputs to other nodes, thereby activating them in turn. The connections may be unidirectional or bidirectional, and are differently weighted so that the next node along may be either inhibited or excited. "Learning" results from training a network by repeatedly exposing it to vast numbers of examples of the pattern to be acquired. Moreover, there is no need to postulate any kind of initial domain-specific structure to the network. The linguists' and psychologists' appeal to modularity, especially any form of genetically determined modularity, is superfluous. The complex structure of the modular mind is an emergent property dependent solely on the input, especially the number of times a particular stimulus features in that input. In other words, the statistical frequency of the input tokens is vital to a network's learning success, a property which enables it to capture our sensitivity to such things as word-frequency effects. One simple example (among many) of such frequency effects is that people typically take longer to respond to rare words like *suricate* (a kind of meerkat) even when they know them, than they do to respond to common ones like *elephant*, a fact that networks simulate automatically.

The structure of networks is explicitly reminiscent of the neural architecture of the brain and, crucially, they exploit no symbols. As Georges Rey puts it: "there is no causally efficacious constituent structure to the mental representations that play a role in the processing."[122] In brief, we can do without the complexity inherent in the use of the symbols so beloved of linguists, psychologists, and philosophers, and we need lose no interesting generalizations as a result, as networks are extremely proficient at replicating the pattern-recognition abilities which are a necessary part of human cognition. The fact that we may not know *how* networks achieve their results, or that we may feel disquiet that it takes a quarter of a million repetitions to train one to recognize *Boys like girls* as well-formed is irrelevant.

If one could really account for the full range of human mental abilities without needing to appeal to symbols and operations on those symbols, it would be theoretically parsimonious and desirable to do so, but a certain skepticism is called for. It is not implausible that connectionism could function as the implementation for theories of mind and language. That is, it is clearly necessary to relate symbolic theories of the kind we have been presupposing to the physiological and physical processes that embody them in the brain. For some aspects of such implementation, connectionism is well-suited. It is quite a different matter, however, to claim that connectionist neural networks can *replace* those symbol-manipulating theories, and that it is unnecessary to postulate any initial genetically determined structure.

The claim is, however, widespread, and appears to rest on a rather strange notion of language. For many connectionists, as for behaviorists, language is merely a skill and, as Jeffrey Elman and his connectionist colleagues stress in a leading statement, "any arbitrary skill can achieve 'automaticity' if it is practised often enough."[123] That this view is not just an aberration can be seen from the rest of their discussion: we are told that "Grammars are complex behavioral solutions to the problem of mapping structured meanings onto a linear string of sounds," and that "the line between learning and maturation is not obvious in any behavioral domain. Language is no exception in this regard."[124] There are several issues: the knowledge of language which underlies our intuitions of ill-formedness is not what is normally meant by "skill," and it is not simply a matter of behavior, as we can retain our knowledge in the absence (temporary or permanent) of the ability to make it manifest, as when we are knocked unconscious, for instance. It is true that it is hard to draw the line between learning and maturation, because some phenomena appear on the borderline between the two, but this doesn't imply that there is no distinction to be made. In vision, the contrast between developing stereoscopic vision and learning to identify different kinds of moth is clear; in language the contrast between acquiring the principles of binding theory and learning the vocabulary of biochemistry is similarly not in dispute. The fact that we may not be sure which side of the learning line face recognition or the mastery of word order should come is simply an invitation to research.

If we compare our knowledge and use of language with domains where the activity may be appropriately labeled a "skill," for instance, expertise at chess or tennis, it is clear that the abilities are different in kind. Pattern recognition is of great importance in all these areas, but it alone cannot solve all our linguistic and psychological problems. It is true that what connectionism is best at is recognizing patterns. The trouble is that it can recognize too many: including ones that humans appear not to be able to. Elman gives the example of the array in (29), where the task is to predict on the basis of the sequence on the left, whether a 1 or a 0 will occur in the right-hand column:[125]

(29)   1 0 1 1 0 1   1
          0 0 0 0 0 0   1
          0 0 1 1 0 0   1
          0 1 0 1 1 0   0
          1 1 1 0 1 1   0
          0 0 0 1 1 1   0

and asks what the network will do with (30):

(30)   0 1 1 1 0 1   ?

He suggests various possible hypotheses one might test: that the display is symmetrical about the center, that it manifests even parity, or that 1 occurs in fifth position. All of these are counting algorithms and, as we saw before, grammars can't count: rather, all linguistic operations are structure dependent. We have then two competing kinds of account – connectionist and symbolic – for comparable data, so the obvious question is who is right? In our work on the polyglot *savant*, Christopher, Ianthi Tsimpli and I carried out an experiment that answers this question.[126]

We taught Christopher and a number of controls an invented language we called "Epun" which, while like ordinary human languages in most other respects, had a number of impossible, structure-independent, rules. Our hypothesis was that, because of his generally poor cognitive abilities, Christopher would be unable to learn these patterns, but that normal (undergraduate) controls would be able to bring their general intelligence to bear and work out the relevant rule by treating it as an intellectual problem-solving exercise. What we confronted them with was the task of learning a structure-independent rule of emphasis formation: add -*nog* to the end of the third word of the sentence, where the concept "third word" clearly necessitates counting. For example, ignoring the different lexicon of Epun, the emphatic equivalent of "The man went yesterday" would be "The man went-*nog* yesterday." As predicted, Christopher was totally unable to work out this rule: he can count sufficiently well to cope with the notion "third word," but the process was so linguistically alien that he never mastered it. More interestingly, neither did the undergraduates. Despite the controls' putative greater intelligence, the linguistic format of the experiment appeared to inhibit them from making the appropriate structure-independent generalization, even though they could work out comparable problems in a non-linguistic environment with ease.

This result is important because connectionist networks have no difficulty in learning such a structure-independent regularity. But if they are aiming to replicate the behavior of human beings then they should *not* be able to do so. It is possible to tweak a network so that it would be unable to learn structure-independent operations, correctly replicating the behavior of human subjects, but such manipulation requires building in the "innate" structure that networks were designed to avoid and which is anathema to (most) connectionists.[127] The problem is acute because humans *are* capable of identifying such patterns in the context of a puzzle, but not apparently in the context of language learning. Demarcating such domains is precisely what any version of the modularity hypothesis is designed to do. It seems that modularity and structure dependence are the prerequisites to, not the outcome of, language acquisition.

Connectionism is not only let down because of its failure on structure dependence. It is striking that the linguistic areas in which it has had some (questionable) success are phonology and morphology; it has nothing of any interest to say about syntax, semantics or the language faculty more generally. As Chomsky put it somewhat caustically "In the case of language, the evidence for connectionist models is, for the moment, about zero," and the evidence for the validity of such models in characterizing other (central) properties of mind is no better.[128]

Does connectionism have anything to offer the linguist? It has one useful role to play: spelling out precisely what constitutes a good poverty-of-the-stimulus argument. Linguists tend to adduce such arguments blithely, and rather too easily, in defence of innateness claims. What connectionist networks can do is show the extent to which such claims are really justified. In chapter 1, I used our mastery of "parasitic gap" constructions as an argument from the poverty of the stimulus for universal properties of language, arguing that the input contained too few instances of such sentences for it to be plausible that we could infer their rather complex properties on the basis of normal induction. I am reasonably confident that this is true, but neither I nor anyone else has collected the relevant data and attempted to devise a network that could reproduce the judgments of a human being after comparable exposure. Connectionists could usefully do this, and perhaps undermine part of the Chomskyan edifice at the same time, though even if they could define for us what constitutes such an argument, they would still be a long way from demonstrating that connectionism could be a replacement for a representationalist, modular theory.[129]

So, we do have grammars in our heads, and the rules that make up those grammars are "psychologically real." These simple assumptions, defended by Chomsky and his followers in fifty years' work, make it possible to provide principled explanations not only for purely linguistic patterns, but also for results in three main areas of psychological investigation: language processing, language acquisition, and language pathology.

4   Philosophical realism: commitments and controversies

> We construct explanatory theories as best we can, taking as *real* whatever is postulated in the best theories we can devise (because there is no other relevant notion of "real"), seeking unification with studies of other aspects of the world.
> (Chomsky, 1996a: 35)

Language is central to every aspect of our lives: intellectual, social, and cultural. So any insight that linguistics can provide should be welcomed by disciplines that rely on an understanding of language: philosophy, psychology, computer science, literature, the study of individual languages, anthropology, and others too numerous to mention. Yet the reaction to Chomskyan linguistics has sometimes been suspicious, hostile or even antagonistic, and the domain where there has been most resistance is philosophy. In the eyes of (many) linguists Chomsky's arguments are cogent and convincing.[1] Why don't the philosophers agree? In this chapter I want to look at Chomsky's philosophical commitments and the overall coherence of his linguistic theory, and try to explain some of the bases for the disagreements and misunderstandings. I have used the headings "commitments" and "controversies," but the commitments are controversial, and the controversies reflect commitments, so the boundary between the two is by no means clear-cut.

Commitments

Chomsky has argued powerfully for realism, naturalism, and mentalism: three strands in his thinking that converge in his internalist concentration on I-language as opposed to E-language. In turn, these commitments have a range of implications for issues as varied as the mind–body problem, the theory of innate ideas, the "private language" debate, the problem of reference, the nature of knowledge, and reduction versus unification in the philosophy of science.

Realism

The first strand in Chomsky's thinking is a commitment to realism;[2] that is, the constructs and entities in the theories he develops deal with real features

138

of the world, just as the constructs of chemistry or biology do. It is easiest to see the import of this claim by comparing it with alternative "non-realist" interpretations of linguistic theory which he argues against. This is particularly important, as "realism" covers a multitude of possible positions, and most of the people referred to in this section could claim to be realists under some interpretation of the term.

Many philosophers and linguists adhere to a form of instrumentalism, by which linguistic theories are simply calculating devices, which make no truth claims.[3] Someone may exploit the technical apparatus of generative grammar, including all its subtheories, simply because it enables them to give a succinct description of the data. They make no claim that these devices are in any way represented in the heads of speakers; they are simply tools. Chomsky discusses several close analogies in the history of science, including Newton's theory of gravity, Boltzmann's molecular theory of gases, and the case of the distinguished French chemist Berthelot who, as Minister of Education, blocked the teaching of atomic theory because it was a "mere hypothesis," not a description of reality.[4] Chomsky's realism is categorical. If anything in generative theory was a candidate for instrumental status it would presumably be empty categories, but he talks, for instance, of the "direct evidence that the trace t, though not pronounced, is actually present in the mental representation of the sentence."[5]

Instrumentalism is close in certain respects to nominalism, which attempts to minimize the number of theoretical entities it is necessary to postulate, denying any reality to anything except the elementary particles of physics. Such a position, associated in the case of the philosophy of language mainly with Quine, leads to a kind of double standard in which the "special sciences," which include psychology and linguistics, are always at a disadvantage vis-à-vis physics. For Quine "natural science" consists exclusively of "theories of quarks and the like."[6] What is included by "the like" is left vague, but it certainly does not include nouns and verbs, let alone empty categories. I return to the reductionist presuppositions implicit in this position at the end of the chapter.

A third view of linguistics with reductionist overtones construes it as dealing with Platonic objects: abstract entities in a mathematical world. As such, these entities cannot interact with things in the world, they can have no causal powers, and have no necessary relation to the minds or brains of individuals. Platonism of this kind is tantamount to claiming that linguistics is not an empirical discipline:[7] it has no more to do with facts in the real world than does logic or mathematics, or my favorite art book, which draws a distinction among various kinds of dragon: *ao*, "a dragon with horns," *ying*, "a dragon with wings," and, intriguingly, *chi*, "a legendary hornless dragon."[8] I assume that this is not an empirical claim. Chomsky is committed to the empirical nature of linguistics.

I-language revisited

At the heart of Chomsky's linguistics is the notion of I-language, a term which replaces one of the uses of the term "grammar" in his early work.[9] "Grammar" was used ambiguously to designate both what we have in our heads, and the linguist's theory of what we have in our "mind–brain."[10] In Chomsky's current usage "grammar" still refers to the linguist's theory, but the object of that theory is now referred to as "I-language," where "I" is a mnemonic for Internal, Individual, and Intensional.

"Internal" means that the domain that the linguist is studying is internal to the mind–brain of particular speakers and hearers, rather than expressing a relation between the mind and the outside world. In earlier work Chomsky observes that "every speaker of a language has mastered and internalized a generative grammar that expresses his knowledge of his language."[11] This mode of expression is potentially misleading in that it suggests that something external is incorporated ("internalized") into the organism during the process of first language acquisition. Some exposure to external stimuli is obviously necessary to trigger language acquisition, but the resulting system is one which has no direct connection with the external world. As will be seen below, this is particularly relevant to issues of reference and the putative word–world relationship.

The second mnemonic, "individual," follows naturally from internalism. If linguistics is about I-language, and I-language is about mental representations and the relations among them, rather than about those representations and their relation to the external world, then I-language must be internal to the mind–brain of particular people; assuming, presumably uncontroversially, that mental events (ultimately brain states) are themselves individual rather than collective.

The third "I," "intensional" (NB not the same as "intentional"),[12] has two different implications. First, it suggests that the internal system of rules and principles that constitutes our grammar operates in terms of procedures whose formal properties are important. Both you and a pocket calculator can compute 6 times 17 to get 102, but you almost certainly don't do it the same way. The procedures you use are extensionally equivalent, but they are intensionally different. In looking at knowledge of language, linguists want to find out how humans work, what procedures are actually used in the computation. The fact that the same result could be arrived at by some other device, operating in radically different ways is irrelevant. Second, it suggests that the grammar will give an interpretation of some kind, sometimes rich, sometimes impoverished, to every event it is exposed to. When you know a language you can provide interpretations not only for well-formed sentences of the kind we have looked at repeatedly but also for sentence fragments, isolated words, and even sentences that are ill-formed or ungrammatical. We know that an example of the kind *I speak fluently French* is ungrammatical, but we also know what anyone who uttered it intended to convey: we give an interpretation despite the ill-formedness. The linguistic system represented in the mind–brain gives some account of everything submitted to it: good sentences, bad sentences, sentences in other languages, ums and ahs, coughs; perhaps – Chomsky suggests – even to non-linguistic events like a squeaking door.[13]

Representation and computation

Chomsky's commitment to the internalism of I-language is based on and supported by a massively detailed account of its structure and workings. At the heart of this account is a computationalist view that postulates the existence of different kinds of representation and argues that cognition consists in carrying out computations over them.[14] The appeal of a computational view of language, and of cognition more generally, is threefold. A computer running a particular program is a device which has unbounded competence (its output is potentially unlimited); it constitutes a system which allows abstract elements to arise from a physical base and interact causally with the world; and, most importantly, it provides a physical implementation of a system whose operations can consistently relate one well-formed formula to another, thus promising in principle a characterization of valid inference. Chomsky has always avoided computer analogies as misleading, especially because of the arbitrary nature of the software–hardware distinction.[15] However, provided that we don't forget that we are not ourselves computers, the analogy can reinforce the importance of the computational character of our mind.

As with his realism, Chomsky's representationalism and computationalism are both construed literally. He talks of "what is actually represented in the mind of an individual," and writes that "the brain uses such notations as . . . ," where the dots are tentatively filled in with a labeled bracket of the sort discussed in earlier chapters.[16] He further makes the general claim that the mental systems allow "something akin to deduction as part of their computational character," a position which presupposes both representation and computation, and one which accords well with other aspects of human cognition.[17] For instance, it is directly compatible with models of inferencing which likewise postulate computations over formal representations.[18]

It needs to be emphasized that Chomsky's computationalist commitment entails that the linguistic symbols which feature in descriptions of our knowledge of language, entities like Noun, Verb, Complementizer, and the hierarchical tree structures into which they enter, have causal properties in the sense that they underlie any explanation of the linguistic knowledge and intuitions of native speakers.[19] Thus, the fact that I interpret the *him* in *Bill thinks John likes him* as referring either to *Bill* or to some third person, but not to *John*, is caused by the rules and representations in my head. Different representations would cause me to make different judgments. It is also important to note that his representationalism does not entail the existence of something outside the head which is "represented": a representation is just a "postulated mental entity" that does not need to be understood relationally as a "representation of" something existing independently in the world.[20]

A major strand in the argumentation for the Computationalist–Representationalist position derives from the fact that it allows significant generalizations in a way that non-representational theories do not.[21] It is not contentious that our knowledge is implemented in neural terms of some kind, though that is still more an act of faith than anything else,[22] but it is no more likely that the neurological level will allow significant generalizations about language than that particle theory will allow appropriate generalizations about glaciation, economics or embryology. That is, all the generalizations that linguists have produced over the centuries presuppose a system of linguistic representations with computations defined over them. The best argument for representationalist theories is then their explanatory success, and the marked lack of comparable success by their non-representationalist rivals.

Naturalism

> the reach of naturalistic inquiry may be quite limited. (Chomsky, 1994e: 194)

> We will always learn more about human life and human personality from novels than from scientific psychology. (Chomsky, 1988b: 159)

As the epigraphs to this section suggest, Chomsky does not believe that much of what makes us human is amenable to scientific investigation. But an exception where there has been great, and in part surprising, progress is in the study of language. This success has been built on the assumption that linguistics is an empirical discipline, like any of the so-called "special sciences" such as geology, biology, or bacteriology. That is, linguistics is conducted according to the methodology of the natural sciences, a methodology that is most fully developed in and characteristic of physics, though it need not follow that linguistics is reducible to physics or any other of the "hard" sciences.

Chomsky's linguistic naturalism has been the object of sustained attack, most notably by the distinguished philosopher Willard van Orman Quine. In general, Quine adopts a naturalist stance, so it is somewhat surprising that he appears to place different requirements on theories in psychology and in physics.[23] All theories are underdetermined by the data: in any of the natural sciences, there are in principle many possible theories compatible with all the evidence available. It may of course be excruciatingly hard to come up with even one theory that covers *any* of the data satisfactorily, but if one does, many will. Explanations in psychology (and *a fortiori* linguistics), however, are held by Quine to have additional problems of "indeterminacy" that physics, the only science whose hypotheses are "genuine," is immune to. As a result, putative explanations in linguistics are denied any validity.

Quine's position rests crucially on the (mistaken) assumption that properties of formal languages carry over unchanged to human languages: an assumption based on a construal of human language as E-language in the sense discussed in chapter 1, rather than Chomsky's notion of I-language. The pivot of Quine's argument is that grammars, viewed as sets of rules, are effectively indistinguishable one from the other if they generate the same set of sentences. The idea that one set of rules might be correct and another set incorrect when they are "extensionally equivalent" in this way is supposed to make no sense. "There is no fact of the matter" in such cases.[24] This opinion is in turn based on the assumption that rules are purely descriptive of behavioral patterns and cannot be causally involved in that behavior: they "fit" but do not "guide" the speaker. To illustrate his point, Quine chooses the abstract example of a string ABC, which might be described as having either the structure [AB][C] or the structure [A][BC].[25] As long as the rules of the grammar generate [ABC], he claims that it makes no difference which of these analyses is chosen. This is empirically false, so let's look at two real examples showing why.[26] First, consider the case of examples like *Harry stirred the stew* or *Mary cut the cake*, analyzed in chapter 2. It is equally easy to generate these sentences and indefinitely many like them either with the structure in (1) shown earlier:

(1)

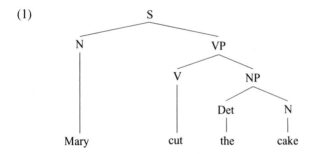

or with a similar structure missing the VP, as given in (2):

(2)

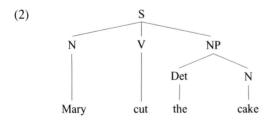

The structures are "weakly equivalent" in the sense that both accommodate the same sentences,[27] but the first makes a number of predictions that the second does not: the sequence *cut the cake* is a constituent[28] in (1) but not in (2) and so is expected, correctly, to reappear in other examples like (3) and (4):

(3)   Mary intended to [cut the cake], and [cut the cake] she duly did
(4)   What should I do next? [Cut the cake]

Such examples have no intrinsic philosophical interest whatsoever, but they can be used to provide evidence in an empirical domain for one analysis over another. That is, the assumption that sentences include a VP in their structure makes possible an economical and parsimonious description of a wide range of related examples. Moreover, that these examples *are* related is claimed to be a fact about the mental organization of speakers of the language. Only the analysis in (1) can capture this relationship, so only the analysis in (1) is correct.

A second example makes it clear that Quine's abstract example was particularly unfortunate, as *both* analyses are correct, but they are correct for different examples and the analyses correlate with quite different meanings. Listening to the radio I recently heard a news report about the arrest of a "black cab driver." I interpreted this as having the structure [black][cab driver], and was mildly irritated that the reporter should consider the race of the driver relevant. It soon became clear that what had been intended was [black cab][driver] – the driver of one of London's black cabs, and I still had no inkling what race he or she was. The example is revealing, as different phrases require one or the other analysis in order to be interpreted rationally: a *magnetic soap holder* and a *speckled trout cooker* are structurally ambiguous, like *black cab driver*, but only one interpretation of each is likely to be appropriate in the world in which we live.

For the philosopher, syntax may be of little interest: Richard Montague put it clearly and succinctly when he wrote "I fail to see any great interest in syntax except as a preliminary to semantics."[29] With the logical syntax of the calculus there is no difference between [AB][C] and [A][BC], and if what matters are the meanings conveyed by language, there is no need to attribute much significance to syntax. For the linguist, who knows how much more complicated syntax is than outsiders think, it is more interesting. Its interest resides in part in that it reflects semantic differences, but equally importantly in that it is characteristic of a specifically human ability of a complexity sufficiently great to underpin a rich theory. Crucially, the analyses provided by that theory make empirical predictions and may be right or wrong. There *is* a fact of the matter.

Mentalism

"Mentalism" is an unnecessarily vexed term. Chomsky is a mentalist in the sense that he is attempting to understand the workings of the human mind within the framework of the natural sciences. An electrical engineer does not agonize over the correct demarcation of the "electrical," nor a chemical physicist over the definition of the "chemical." Similarly, Chomsky is not concerned to make metaphysical claims by saying that language is a "mental" phenomenon. Rather, he is merely expressing a pre-theoretic interest in a particular domain. "Contemporary mentalism . . . is a step toward assimilating psychology and linguistics within the physical sciences."[30] This is not to deny that there are philosophical problems attached to any such demarcation, but these problems are largely irrelevant to the practice of linguistics. Linguistic theory does, however, have implications for philosophy, and Chomsky has some radical observations about the mental which any metaphysical discussion needs to accommodate. The first of these is best illustrated by the problem (if such it is) of "tacit knowledge"; the second, by the putative incoherence of the "mind–body problem."

Tacit knowledge[31]

I know that penguins live in the Antarctic. Moreover, I know that I know this: I can reflect on the fact, tell other people about it, and compliment myself on my general knowledge. Such accessibility to consciousness is standardly taken to be criterial for something to count as knowledge. If something is not consciously available, at least in principle, then on this view it does not count as knowledge. My knowledge of English is only in part like this. I know that *penguin* is a word of English, that it denotes a kind of flightless bird, that it begins with a /p/. All this is consciously accessible and part of my knowledge of English comparable to my general encyclopaedic knowledge. I also know much more than this; for instance that *Penguins eat voraciously fish* is wrong. Again, this is consciously accessible, propositional knowledge about part of my language. But, in virtue of being a speaker of English, I also "know" the rules of the grammar that determine that this sentence is wrong. And what these rules might be is not available to my conscious introspection. As a linguist, I may suspect that the oddity of the sentence is a function of the principle "Procrastinate," but that is certainly not the kind of knowledge that is consciously available to normal human beings, and it is not what determines that in conversation I say *Penguins eat fish voraciously* rather than the incorrect alternative.[32] It was for this reason that I put "know" in inverted commas. Our language is mentally represented and constitutes a kind of "tacit knowledge," where "tacit" simply means that it is not in general accessible to consciousness. But since Kant, the received philosophical view has been that if something is unconscious, it *ipso facto* cannot really count as "knowledge."

Discussing rules of language in this spirit, Quine affirms that "behavior is not *guided* by the rule unless the behaver knows the rule and can state it";[33] Searle asserts that "the speaker should be in principle capable of an awareness of how the rules enter into his behaviour";[34] Dummett, Nagel, and others make comparable demands.[35] What is striking about all these claims is the paucity of reasons given for the requirement of conscious accessibility, or even discussion of what it means.

There are two issues: a terminological one concerning the latitude we permit in the use of the particular lexical item *know*, and a substantive, philosophical one concerning the nature of knowledge of language vis-à-vis other kinds of knowledge. Chomsky's early use of the term "knowledge" elicited philosophical anathema, so he had recourse to the neologism "cognize" to replace "know" in the particular domain of knowledge of language.[36] More interestingly, he attacked and undermined the claim that consciousness was a necessary condition for knowledge either in the case of language or more generally. That there are differences of accessibility to consciousness is simply a reflection of our ignorance rather than a principled indication of significant differences in status. What is important is that the principles which guide our behavior are mentally represented and causally efficacious. To demand conscious awareness of those principles – in vision, moral judgment or language – is unnecessary, hence irrational, unless some independent reason for making the demand is provided. The most common reason for the requirement that rules be accessible to consciousness is that this is suggested, even if not entailed, by the use of language for communication. But here it seems that the argument is predicated on a fallacy of "perfect communication," to which we will return.

The mind–body problem

Since Descartes, philosophers have been preoccupied with how the mental can affect the physical, how something which is by definition insubstantial can cause changes in spatially located entities: in other words, how the mind can move the body. Descartes himself appealed to causal powers in the pineal gland, begging the question of whether this gland was itself mental or material. As we have seen, Chomsky's linguistics is avowedly mentalist and the mental representations postulated have causal properties. It might therefore appear that he is confronted with the same metaphysical problem that concerned Descartes. Chomsky has cut the Gordian knot by emphasizing a more fundamental difficulty: the mind–body problem cannot even be formulated. It cannot be formulated, not because we have too limited an understanding of the mind, but because we don't have criteria for what constitutes a body. In a typically radical attempt at clarification he points out that, with Newton's insights about the demise of contact mechanics, the Cartesian notion of body was refuted and nothing since has replaced it. Newton "exorcized the machine; the ghost remained intact," and in the absence of a coherent notion of "body," the traditional mind–body problem has no conceptual status, and no special problems of causality arise.[37] As Chomsky puts it, the "basic contention of Priestley and other 18th century figures seems uncontroversial: thought and language are properties of organized matter – in this case, mostly the brain."[38] It is striking that a major philosophical issue is dismissed at a stroke. Modern science since Newton has made no serious effort to define "body," so there cannot be a mind–body problem, and it cannot therefore have any implications for language, or anything else.

Controversies

Chomsky's linguistics has consistently raised philosophical hackles. His ideas are at variance with conventional wisdom about the nature of human language itself, and about the relation of language to the world, to the community, and to the individual. Simultaneously he has used linguistics to defend positions on innateness and human nature which were considered to be either defunct or indefensible. The ramifications of his theory are rich, diverse, tightly integrated, and subtle. They are also incompatible with the preconceptions of the majority of those who have thought about the subject.

Language and the world

The first, and most fundamental, area of disagreement resides in how to conceive the relationship of language to the world. There are two distinct issues: the first involves the status of linguistics as a discipline; the second involves the word–world relationship. I look at the first of these here, and return to the second later.

Language as mathematics   For a number of philosophers, the study of language is treated as a branch of mathematics rather than an aspect of psychology. Languages are taken to be Platonic objects existing independently of the humans who speak them, and possessing mathematical properties which could not be expressed if attention were limited to the subparts of such languages accessible to human mental structure. For the study of artificial languages such as the predicate calculus, this is a viable assumption; it is less plausible when applied to natural, humanly spoken, languages. A classic statement of the position is provided by Montague, who opens one of his most famous papers with the categorical statement: "I reject the contention that an important theoretical difference exists between formal and natural languages." Unfortunately, in the absence of a criterion for measuring important theoretical differences, this claim is meaningless. Montague was aiming to develop a theory of truth, and it is rather obvious that he seriously underestimated the complexity of the syntax of natural language, and misconstrued the aims of the generative grammarians whom he criticized. The demand that they, or anyone, provide a "rigorous definition, complete in all details . . . of some reasonably rich fragment of English" is a bizarre goal to set oneself in the natural sciences, as can be seen by replacing "English" with "biology" or "chemistry."[39] Moreover, the linguist's preoccupation with explanation rather than description, allied with the fact that natural languages are replete with idiosyncratic irregularities, means that it is not a goal that most of those interested in I-language would even set themselves. As we saw in the first chapter complete coverage is neither attainable nor even desirable. More recently, Katz has repeatedly claimed that language is an abstract object in Plato's sense, and that failing to take account of the mathematical properties of languages leads to a failure to capture significant linguistic generalizations and, more seriously, to the incoherence of the philosophical underpinnings of Chomsky's paradigm.[40]

Before evaluating this claim, we need to distinguish it from a separate issue concerning the axiomatization or logical formalization of the linguistic analyses provided by working linguists. For Chomsky the interest and importance of analyses of language reside in the implications they have for philosophical and psychological issues. This is clearly not incompatible with a mathematical axiomatization of those analyses. Indeed, Chomsky's early work was renowned for its mathematical rigor and he made some contribution to the nascent discipline of mathematical linguistics, in particular the analysis of (formal) languages in terms of what is now known as the "Chomsky hierarchy."[41] But formal languages share few properties with natural language, and results of any empirical interest were minimal.[42] In recent years, the emphasis on formalization has been considerably reduced, leading some to suggest that generative theory has become woolly and untestable.[43] Chomsky's common-sense response is to say that he does "not see any point in formalizing for the sake of formalizing. You can always do that."[44] The answer is cogent, provided that the unformalized analyses and principles are sufficiently explicit to make it possible to test the predictions they generate. This is itself not always straightforward, as principles of any degree of complexity and deductive depth are likely to be interpretable in a range of different ways, depending on co-varying assumptions. In the current state of knowledge, formalization is often unrewarding, as formal systems which are complete and consistent are too impoverished adequately to express the generalizations made, and require the making of arbitrary decisions about matters that are not properly understood. Formalization is like careful experimentation: it is to be undertaken when there is a specific purpose in view, or a particular hypothesis to test; it is not done for its own sake.

Whether one studies linguistics as part of mathematics or part of psychology is a question of taste (or definition), but there are substantive issues. First, are the different domains compatible, or does capturing the significant generalizations of one entail missing those of the other?[45] Second, if there are incompatibilities, and if there is any validity to the mathematical analysis of natural languages as Platonic objects, does this refute the Chomskyan position?

Katz's answer is straightforward: he claims that the properties of the psychological constructs postulated by linguists entail that they *must* be treated as abstract objects, and Chomsky's failure to acknowledge this results in the whole of his framework being called into question. The reason for this rather dramatic conclusion is that as abstract objects by hypothesis have no causal powers, and Chomsky's theory deals with causal entities, there is an unbridgeable gap between the phenomena to be explained and the devices postulated to explain them.[46]

There are two reasons why one could conclude that the objection is not cogent. First, we have seen that Chomsky is committed to representationalism, and although abstract objects themselves may not have causal powers, representations of abstract objects by an organism may indeed have causal powers. Second, Chomsky's notion of I-language anyway renders it immune to Katz's claims. Part of Katz's discussion revolves around the mathematical properties of the set of sentences that constitute a natural language: is this set denumerably infinite or is it non-denumerably infinite?[47] As Alexander George has documented, the argument that languages are non-denumerably infinite is flawed.[48] But even if it was not, there would be no serious implication for Chomsky's position, because the argument presupposes a view of (E-)language that he has explicitly repudiated: language for him is I-language, a state of the mind–brain, and not a set of sentences. His claim is stronger than Katz and others seem to realize: the issue of denumerability is irrelevant, because the conception of a language as consisting of a set of sentences is incoherent in the absence of some indication of how that set is generated, and this is feasible only in terms of procedures which are parasitic on I-language. Katz is aware of the I-language/E-language distinction, but he appears to ascribe comparable status to both,[49] writing that "although theories of the speaker's knowledge of a language are no doubt psychological theories, there is no reason to think theories of the languge [sic] known are also psychological theories." Indeed, but what he misses is that, for Chomsky, there is no such entity as "the language known" distinct from the speaker's knowledge of it, so there is no possible theory of it. Accordingly, Katz's conclusion that sentences are abstract objects and "Chomsky's generativism as well as his psychologism have to be given up" fails to go through. Katz's critique appears to rest on the mistaken assumption that because a finitely represented device, the I-language, has an infinite range, it must itself be infinite: he writes of "expressions [being] mental/neural objects."[50] The conclusion seems unwarranted; it is the means of generating expressions which is a mental/neural object, not the formulae generated. We can carry out any of an infinite number of operations in various domains – moral, social, ethical, visual, cognitive – without it being necessary to postulate an infinity of abstract objects for each one. Language deploys a dedicated syntax, characterized by specific principles which can, where relevant, be mathematically specified, but the possibility of mathematical specification itself has no implications for the intrinsic properties of natural language, as mathematical systems have no properties of their own, except those we stipulate.

There is an added twist in that Katz describes his own position as realist and Chomsky's as anti-realist. This is a confusing terminological point: realism, equivalently Platonism, for Katz entails that the entities postulated exist independently of the human mind. For Chomsky an I-language cannot exist independently of the human mind because it is a property of the mind–brain. Chomsky's position is nonetheless realist, on the minimal assumption that the mind–brain is part of nature and subject to empirical investigation, just as other aspects of nature can be investigated by geologists or biologists.

Language and the community

Language is used for thinking, but it is a commonplace of the philosophical literature that the essential purpose of language is communication.[51] This is often taken to be so self-evident that it needs no justification and is just assumed, as in Davidson's off-hand remark "Language, that is, communication with others."[52] It is further assumed that communication is made possible because speakers and hearers have in their heads the same theory of meaning "determining the truth-conditions of sentences of the language."[53]

Public language   The conception of language as being equivalent to, or pre-eminently designed for, communication lends support to the view that languages are public constructs, codes associated with a particular community or country that people learn and use with greater or less correctness, efficiency, and elegance.[54] Different languages have properties that make them easier or harder to master for speakers of other languages: tones (like Chinese), complex morphology (like Greek), a rich technical vocabulary (like English), and so on, but all of them contain words and phrases that refer to entities in the outside world, like trees, modems, and perhaps quarks. On such a view it makes sense to talk of someone having partial or incorrect knowledge of a public language. In the context of first language acquisition, the implication of this would be that the child is exposed to a body of data (words and sentences of English, Chinese or Swahili) and learns the language accordingly. More particularly, the child would be exposed to only a subset of the total data and so would end up knowing only a subset of the language. As a corollary, some people have a better knowledge of the language than others, and can give authoritative judgments on matters of dispute or in areas of special expertise. Moreover, the data the child is exposed to would provide overt evidence of all the structural properties of the language, both universal and particular, that are relevant to its acquisition, so that there would be no need to look beyond them for explanations of the adult speaker's ultimate ability.

There is an initial element of plausibility in such a public language scenario, especially insofar as it pertains to vocabulary. It is obvious that no one knows the entire vocabulary of English as recorded in a major dictionary, and it is equally clear that in this domain all speakers tend to bow to authority.[55] If I am unsure of the meaning of *photon* or *funky*, I can look them up, or ask a physicist or a student, and if I trust the authority, I am likely to modify my use of language accordingly. On closer examination, however, this plausibility evaporates: it only works for some of the vocabulary – people are very resistant to modifying their use of words like "hopefully" in accordance with the demands of the pedagogues – and it doesn't work for anything more than a minute fraction of the grammar of the language. We are not explicitly taught how to use reflexive pronouns, for instance, and it is not self-evident that everyone who makes the complex acceptability judgments documented in chapter 2 has had exposure to comparable overt input. In any case, understanding language in the individual must take logical precedence over any understanding of language in the community, as the latter is parasitic on the former: individuals utter sentences, communities do not. While it is usual to talk of "the English language" as spoken in different continents and in different centuries, there could be no mental or psychological reality to an entity so dispersed in space and time. The popular usage is convenient, but disguises the fact that language in this sense does not correspond to a scientific domain. Crucially, there are no laws or principles that hold of "English," "Chinese" or "Dutch" as social or national constructs, any more than there are principles that hold of the Dutch visual system; but there are (grammatical) principles that hold of the linguistic knowledge of each individual.

It was for reasons of this kind that Chomsky redirected the focus of linguistic investigation to the individual mind rather than the collectivity of society, developing the notion of I-language, in contradistinction to the external and extensional force of E-language. The justification for the distinction lies ultimately in a judgment about what is an appropriate domain for theory construction. Once one grants that individuals have *knowledge* of language, as evidenced in their ability to produce and understand any of an indefinitely large number of sentences on the appropriate occasion, to make intuitive judgments of well- and ill-formedness about sentences and phrases, or even to make mistakes, it makes sense to try to formalize that knowledge explicitly, to see what kinds of generalization govern it, to distinguish it from other kinds of ability, and so on. However difficult such an enterprise may be, it is coherent. Just as we have theories of human vision or moral judgment, we can envision having theories of human knowledge of language. It will be part of any such theory to determine whether the boundaries of such a domain are well-defined. It might turn out that the best theory of knowledge of language is one that treats it as a special case of encyclopaedic knowledge, or of mathematical knowledge, or of brain functioning more generally. Our earlier discussion of modularity and dissociation makes these possible scenarios implausible, but all are in principle rationally defensible. In contrast, the task of providing a theory of public language has proved intractable, and has done so because there is no such domain. We can talk about E-language as we can talk about unicorns, but there are few treatises on the anatomy of the unicorn, and equally few theories of E-language; and for the same underlying reason – neither exists.

The view that language is public and can be in essence equated with communication is underpinned by a presupposition that both – language and communication – are manifestations of a single code. The traditional idea underlying the so-called code model of communication is that a thought is encoded by one person into a signal in a language system, this signal is propagated through some medium – air in the case of the spoken (or signed) word, paper in the case of writing – and is then decoded into an essentially identical thought by a listener or reader: language "operates as a code for thought" in Dummett's phrase.[56] Since the work of Paul Grice, and more particularly Dan Sperber and Deirdre Wilson,[57] this code model has been replaced by an inferential model which takes a language code as a point of departure, but which sees communication as crucially involving not just decoding but inference as well.[58]

The contrast between coded and inferred information corresponds to the distinction in linguistics between semantics and pragmatics, to which we turn next. Before doing so, it is relevant to emphasize the terminological point that for linguists generally, semantics refers to a domain internal to the I-language, and deals with relations among mental representations, whereas for philosophers, semantics usually refers to the alleged relation between mental (or public) representations and mind-independent entities in the world.[59]

Semantics and pragmatics   The idea that the success of communication is entirely dependent on the linguistic code arises from a failure to recognize the role of an inferential system of pragmatics, distinct from the decoding provided by the syntax and semantics. That is, the grammar only provides clues as to the content of the message that the speaker is trying to communicate to the listener. These clues are exploited by the pragmatics to construct a representation which owes many of its properties to the context created *ad hoc* to allow interpretation to take place. Consider a simple example. Suppose I tell you that *Fred can see you now*. You must work out who I am referring to by the name *Fred* (reference assignment);[60] whether he has just finished with his previous visitor or has recovered from eye surgery (disambiguation); whether the utterance is to be construed as reason for walking into the next room, going upstairs, running away, adjusting your tie, or some combination of these and other possibilities (implicature). This will be done on the basis of inferences to the best explanation, depending on what you know about me and the ambient circumstances, what you assume I (think I) know about you and your interests, and so on indefinitely. Most of this is not coded in the few words of the given utterance, but is inferred. Communication of this kind is parasitic on language (though non-verbal communication is common enough), but the message coded in the language gives you only hints about what I have in mind.[61]

That language makes an important contribution to communication has never been denied, least of all by Chomsky, but little specific about the structure of language follows from this fact. Language is not "designed for communication," because, strictly speaking, natural objects are not "designed for" anything. On an informal interpretation of "design," it is worth distinguishing the evolution of the language of thought and its interface with LF on the one hand, and the evolution of the articulatory–perceptual system and its interface with PF on the other.[62] The needs of communication clearly motivated the latter development, but were a factor of minimal importance in the former. Whether facilitating communication played any significant role in the evolution of the mapping between LF and PF is moot. It may be true that redundancy, for instance, which seems to pervade language, facilitates communication and is therefore motivated by it; but none of the properties of language that are of philosophical or psychological interest (its creativity, its recursive power, its putative innateness) are in any way dependent on such redundancy. If language is in many respects not designed for communication, it is no surprise that it is not optimally usable; that parsability is not guaranteed, and so on.[63] More particularly, if even the most intricate sentence provides only clues as to the message being communicated from one person to another, the assumption that speaker and hearer have to give this message an identical structure in a shared public language is false.

Chomsky has had little to say about the role of pragmatics or about theories of communication more generally.[64] This is unsurprising, as they are tangential to his ideas about language. Language is a code linking representations of sound and meaning. If communication were to be accounted for in terms of a simple extension of that code, then the apparently intractable problems of the code model in dealing with communication might risk carrying over to analyses of language where it is precisely the code which is at issue.

A theory which draws a principled distinction between semantics and pragmatics claims that the linguistic meaning of an utterance is not equivalent to the thought conveyed, but is a set of structured clues as to what this might be. Such a theory undercuts Dummett's view (which he himself characterized as "absurd") that if communication is not perfectly determined by the language then it must rest on faith.[65] But communication is never guaranteed and what the hearer takes to have been communicated can only be an inference to the most plausible explanation. By addressing an utterance to someone, a speaker does guarantee that he or she is trying to say something which it will be worth the addressee's while to attend to, and that interpreting the utterance will involve no gratuitous effort on the addressee's part.[66] If you are mistaken about your interlocutor's knowledge or beliefs, you may fail to communicate what you intended, you may fail to communicate at all. Even if you are not mistaken, you will still only bring your hearer to an approximation of the cognitive state you are in yourself, as your utterance will be interpreted against a background set of assumptions that cannot be shared in their totality.

This position denies one of the premises in the externalist view: that unless the external world determines the content of the thoughts of a speaker "it is an utter mystery how that agent's thoughts can be publicly available to another."[67] Such thoughts are *never* available "deterministically": that is, in a way that ensures identity between the mental representations of the speaker and the hearer. The partial success of everyday intercourse still needs explaining, and Chomsky suggests that the assumption that one's interlocutor is in relevant respects identical to oneself, is sufficient basis for the "more-or-less affair" of communication.[68] Such an assumption, which presupposes an inferential view, is uncontroversial when it comes to the sound system of language: Chomsky's pronunciation of English differs systematically from mine, but this has minimal effect on our ability to understand each other, and no philosophical implications whatever. No one has made the case that things are different on the meaning side.

Once one abandons the preconception that communication is solely the result of decoding and adopts the view that it is rather the effect of inference, the indirect criticism of Chomsky's position becomes irrelevant. The fallacy of perfect communication may also be at the root of the traditional insistence that knowledge of language be (potentially) conscious. We may be conscious of the propositional content of what we say and who we are saying it to; academic discourse in particular is overwhelmingly self-conscious in this way. It does not follow, however, that we are conscious, even potentially conscious, of the mental procedures which underlie those conscious processes, nor even of the content of the individual words (words like *individual*) that we use to convey the propositions. Consider the kind of disambiguation alluded to in discussing the example *Fred can see you now*. The inferential (relevance-theoretic) account of the way we do this involves an interesting claim about human mentation. Right or wrong, it is a hypothesis about mental processes which are typically not available to consciousness, any more than the mental processes involved in the way we interpret a glance or a smile are available. It is important to distinguish the results of the processing, which are (partly) consciously accessible, from the way we do it, which is not.

Authority   Unlike our knowledge of mathematics or of penguins, our linguistic knowledge is largely unconscious or tacit; it is acquired without the need for formal instruction; and it is deployed without the need for reflection. If you hear that *John thinks Peter betrayed himself* you know that the one betrayed is Peter, and that if John had been intended, the speaker would have had to say *him* rather than *himself*. Any notion of external authority in regard to this knowledge is beside the point. We are usually ready to accept authoritative statements concerning our encyclopaedic knowledge – e.g. penguins do not live in the Arctic, or that *idiosyncrasy* is spelt with an *s* and not a *c* – but we are loth to accept correction to our grammar, except in a tiny subset of cases where superficial phenomena, like the splitting of infinitives, have been stigmatized for reasons that are not always easy to defend on strictly linguistic grounds. For instance, if you tell me that *I deplore your behaving like this* is not a proper sentence of English, I shall feel free to ignore you. It may not be grammatical for *you*, but that is not criterial for *my* grammar, even if we are deemed to speak the same language. The implication is that the rules of grammar that comprise our competence are like the rules of visual perception that enable us to judge distance, and not like the rules of the Highway Code that, in Britain, instruct us to drive on the left.

Appeals to authority are sometimes appropriate. It may be the case that I am prepared to defer to you in an area where you have more expertise than me: perhaps you can tell a yawl from a ketch and I cannot. Alternatively, I may insist that I am right, when you use *arthritis* to refer to a pain in your waist and, as a doctor, I know that the accepted usage precludes that possibility.[69] More usually, where there are differences between speakers, as when you use *mitigate* the way I use *militate*, I make allowances accordingly, mentally interpreting what you say in a way that is not characteristic of my own usage, just as when I correctly interpret pronunciations from a different dialect. But none of these possibilities has the implication that there is an abstract reality in which *yawl*, *ketch* or *arthritis* have their meanings or their pronunciations essentially. All those examples where authority is plausibly involved crucially appeal to differences in encyclopaedic knowledge. Once noted, such differences may influence our usage, but this does not imply that we are thereby acceding to some rigid word–world relation.

Much of our use of language is similarly encyclopaedically modulated. When playing with little children, I'm likely to talk of *bunnies*, when talking to my friends, the same animals would be called *rabbits*, and with my colleagues in the biology department I might refer to *lagomorphs*. Linguistic theory provides no account of what determines the choice of a particular form in a particular situation: the only role of the language faculty is to satisfy the requirement that lexical entries have access to the encyclopaedic information associated with individual words.

Examples of this kind make it clear that the rules we follow have not been agreed upon by social convention, but are psychological (mental) constructs.[70] That is, the study of linguistic competence is part of psychology rather than part of sociology, philosophy or mathematics. In order to explain our ability to produce and understand novel utterances, we impute tacit knowledge of linguistic rules to the speaker and hearer, and some of these rules may differ from person to person. As with any scientific endeavor, the detailed formulation and formalization of such rules will change as we improve our understanding of the human mind, but the nature of the claim – that we are dealing with mental constructs – is established. Hence we are dealing not with social constructs but with individuals.

Language and the individual

The idiosyncrasy of linguistic knowledge   Despite our ability to communicate, and despite general (rather surprising) unanimity about the well-formedness of particular sentences, no two speakers of English are identical in their linguistic knowledge. Everyone tends to agree about the interpretation and relative acceptability of the examples in (5): sentences (5a) and (5b) are grammatically and semantically identical, and mean something similar to the structurally distinct but equally well-formed (5c). In contrast (5d) is surprisingly different from (5c) – it is unacceptable – even though its putative meaning is clear, and even though it has been formed on obvious analogy with it:

(5) a.   It is likely that El Niño governs our climate
     b.   It is probable that El Niño governs our climate
     c.   El Niño is likely to govern our climate
     d.   *El Niño is probable to govern our climate

But opinions typically differ with the pair of examples in (6):

(6) a.   That asteroid will probably hit us
     b.   That asteroid will likely hit us

where (6a) is acceptable for everyone but (6b) is acceptable for some, and unacceptable for others (such as me).[71] It is not that I have never heard examples like (6b), nor that I don't understand what someone who utters it means. It is simply not part of my language. In this case the difference is a dialectal one: (6b) is more characteristic of American than of British English; in other cases the difference may be generational, or entirely idiosyncratic. For me, (7) is perfect, and means roughly the same as (8):

(7)   I promised John to go
(8)   I promised John I would go

For my (equally English-speaking) sons, only (8) is possible and (7) is ungrammatical. Again, it is not a matter of comprehension, but of individual differences in the internalized grammar. Such differences are easy enough to describe and are linguistically of considerable importance in that variation among extremely closely related dialects allows us to investigate one particular syntactic phenomenon while holding everything else constant. But they raise a problem for someone who wishes to know what is characteristic of "English," as it makes sensible questions unanswerable: does the grammar of English have rule x or rule y? Are (6b) and (7) sentences of English or not? One possible conclusion is that language is irremediably vague and ill-defined, and hence not a proper area for theory construction at all.[72] As we have seen, there are independent reasons for thinking that this conclusion is true for traditional notions of "public language," but it is fortunately false of the logically prior domain of I-language.

Variation and "private language"   Idiosyncratic differences of the kind described here are expected in a theory which focuses on individual, internally represented, knowledge. Every individual's experience is different, and even members of the same family are exposed to different phenomena and, more importantly, interpret those phenomena differently and hence construct marginally different grammars.[73] Over a period of generations, especially in circumstances of isolation or separation, such differences aggregate and give rise to different dialects and, ultimately, different languages. In the short term, requirements of communication prevent the divergence from being too great, and there is anyway no problem of principle in accommodating variational data within the theory. If required, it is always possible to write marginally different grammars for two individuals: each of my sons, for instance. What is important is that both grammars are cut according to the same cloth: their rules instantiate the same principles, exploit the same theoretical vocabulary, display the same constraints, and overlap sufficiently to characterize mutually intelligible systems. It is not an objection that the theory fails to explain (all aspects of) the variation: the controversy arising from Chomsky's idealization to homogeneity of the linguistic community discussed in chapter 1 was simply misconceived. Writing different grammars containing slightly different rules describes variational differences adequately. What determines the development of individual differences in my children is an interesting question about what constitutes a possible diachronic (historical) change: a question which is largely unanswered but whose answer will almost certainly presuppose a descriptive account within the framework of a theory of the kind exploited here. It is certain that the answer will not demand giving up the idealization to homogeneity. If this idealization were really untenable, it would have to be the case either that the brains of human children are not adequately endowed to acquire their first language unless the input contains contradictory information, or that their brains are appropriately endowed, but that first language acquisition proceeds without using that endowment. Neither position seems plausible.

Individual variation is not only pervasive, it is *prima facie* evidence for the possibility of a "private language," of the kind that Wittgenstein denied.[74] For Wittgenstein and his followers language is "intrinsically social" and "public availability is a constitutive aspect of language."[75] It follows that a private language, that is, a language which is essentially the property of a single individual, rather than something shared by a community of individuals, is impossible. Such a language could not guarantee successful communication with anyone else, because whatever rules were being followed would not be publicly available and shared. Two issues are important: the notion of rule following and the notion of guarantee. We have already seen that communicative success is only partial, and that this part is due to processes of inference as well as to the operation of the grammar. There are accordingly no guarantees that one's intended meaning will get across; still less that its implications will be correctly interpreted. The issue of rule following is less straightforward.

Rules of language   There may be few problems in ascribing rule following to oneself, but a potential difficulty does arise with regard to the ascription of rule following to someone else, in particular, in deciding whether they are following the same rule as oneself.[76] Here though, it is relatively straightforward to adduce empirical evidence to decide the matter. Consider again the child who over-generalizes, saying *It's mine teddy* instead of *It's my teddy*. We have no difficulty in understanding what is said, what is intended, and how it differs from what we would have said ourselves. The regularity of the child's behavior is evidence that it is rule-governed and not random, it is simply using a rule (linguistically formulable) that is distinct from the one we use. Comparable remarks carry over to other instances of variation of the kind we have already seen.

The teddy-bear example is of direct relevance to Saul Kripke's interpretation of Wittgenstein as providing problems for Chomsky's views on our having knowledge of and using rules of language. Kripke makes the assumption that to attribute rule following correctly to people, it is necessary that they interact with other members of a community (who are alike in the relevant respects), and the case of Robinson Crusoe, who interacts with no one, is then taken to raise difficulties for any such notion of rule following, and by implication for Chomsky.[77] Now the child is clearly a member of our community, and indeed communicates successfully with the rest of us, but it does so using a somewhat different language, so the Wittgensteinian requirement that there be "general agreement in the community responses" is too strong a demand. Similarly in the case of Crusoe, Kripke suggests that we may finesse the problem of whether he too can be correctly described as following rules by "taking him in to our community," and assimilating him to our own "form of life," on the Cartesian assumption that he has a mind like us. So far, so good, but Kripke then entertains the possibility that Wittgenstein might deny us the right to take Crusoe into our community in this way.[78] But the only justification for such a denial is either based on an idea of guarantee that we have seen to be indefensible, or is simply a stratagem to defend the hypothesis that there is no private language from possible refutation. To take Crusoe into the human community is essentially to say that he shares UG, which is distinct from ascribing to him rules of grammar which could only develop contingently through interaction with members of a community. That is, the Kripkensteinian[79] ploy of considering one person "in isolation" is not a problem for Chomsky's ideas on language as crucially involving rule following.[80] It is a fact of our existence that we do not develop in isolation. Whether we are talking about the ascription of possible points of view via a theory of other minds, or the interpretation of a particular utterance on the basis of linguistic decoding and pragmatic inference, we do so in a context which denies the possibility of isolation. If a Robinson Crusoe or a Genie[81] does develop in isolation, he or she will contingently fail – despite their possession of UG – to develop any specific rules of language and hence any shared rules, but this does not impugn in any way the potential provided by that innate endowment.[82]

The appeal to UG also allows us to overcome the possible tension occasioned by adverting to rules, when recent versions of grammar have largely given up rules in favor of universal principles. Linguistic behavior is rule-governed, but in general the rules involved can be automatically induced from the interaction of specific lexical items of the language with universal principles. The rules that are followed are in large part predictable from general linguistic theory, and so do not need to be spelt out in individual grammars.

The Wittgensteinian argument about the impossibility of a private language fails to go through because it ignores the distinction between linguistic and pragmatic (inferential) processes, and because it is a fallacy that a community is needed to justify the notion of rule. If the Wittgensteinian argument was sound it should generalize to the justification of phonetic rules, say the rules of aspiration of plosives, but no one believes that minor idiosyncratic (but regular and hence rule-governed) differences of pronunciation have any philosophical import. Further, the consistency of an individual's linguistic judgments and the unhesitating conviction with which they are usually made indicate that only an explanation in terms of rule following is rational. The fact that such judgmental ability is common across the species, and that linguistic variation is endemic in all human speech communities, suggests that the private nature of these rules is no bar to communication and hence no argument for public language. In sum, the notion of common public language is not only unnecessary but, as Chomsky puts it, "completely foreign to the empirical study of language."[83]

Skepticism and rule following   In his attack on the view of Wittgenstein and others that there is no private language,[84] Chomsky adopts a dual strategy of empirical argumentation on the basis of linguistic data, allied with a radical rejection of the relevance of the skeptical position: a rejection which takes us back to the demands for certainty mentioned earlier. A major justification for the existence of public language has traditionally been that it removes one plank from the skeptic's attack on the existence of other minds. For example, Akeel Bilgrami suggests that the "publicness constraint" is required to avoid skepticism about other minds.[85] This seems fallacious, as it suggests that if there were a public language then that would be a defence against skepticism. But there are no defenses against skepticism, so Chomsky's rejection of a public language leaves him no worse off in this regard than anyone else: "There is no answer to Wittgenstein's skeptic *and there need be none.*"[86] Complete skepticism (the view that it is in principle impossible to have knowledge of anything) is never refutable but, like Descartes, Chomsky combats skeptical problems by a form of (modest) foundationalism.[87] On this view, there is no possibility, and hence no need, for certainty. The only strategy to adopt is to have recourse to the "best theory,"[88] that set of ideas which will give the richest explanatory results: in other words, the index of truth in science is success. The skeptical position itself is without interest, as it leads to no new insights or understanding, it simply side-steps *all* arguments, not just critical or contrary arguments. You cannot know or prove that you are not now dreaming, but the fruits of assuming that you are would be minimal, and at least in scientific work "skeptical arguments can be dismissed."[89]

Chomsky's skepticism about skepticism follows from his view of the nature of knowledge and the irrelevance of traditional conceptions of truth. Knowledge is standardly defined as "justified true belief," that is, it presupposes an external notion of truth and an ill-defined concept of justification.[90] One of Chomsky's philosophical contributions is plausibly to have extended the concept of what falls under "knowledge" to knowledge of language. If this extension is granted, it is clear that both justification and the certainty associated with real knowledge are irrelevant. The reason why an individual follows a particular rule on a particular occasion is simply because he or she is so constituted.[91] As a joint function of genetic determination and exposure to a particular environment, one construes *John* and *him* as referring to different people in *John saw him* but as referring (potentially) to the same person in *John wonders who saw him.* The situation is no different from the fact that we see a particular configuration and sequence of visual stimuli as a rotating cube rather than a plane changing in size and shape: it is a property of our (genetically determined and contextually triggered) visual system. Asking for philosophically valid grounds for such an interpretation is unrealistic and unnecessary. A philosophical reaction might be that this is simply a cop-out, an evasion of the interesting issue. But this is to miss the point of what Chomsky is trying to do: he is not attempting to solve the problem of skepticism, or to identify criteria for knowledge in general; he is developing a theory of one kind of human knowledge – knowledge of language. His response to the objection that knowledge of language is not knowledge in the real sense was long ago to deploy a special technical vocabulary to allow epistemological problems to be addressed "without irrelevant sidetracks": "competence" was introduced to characterize "unconscious knowledge," and "cognize" was used to replace "know" in contexts where conscious accessibility to that knowledge was in question.[92] But these concessions are merely terminological: all the philosophical consequences that are of interest can be derived from the technical concepts, such as I-language, that he defines. In particular, there is no rational objection to explaining our judgments of the well-formedness of previously unencountered sentences in terms of rule following (with all its philosophical implications), and indeed no viable alternative has ever been suggested. Chomsky demurs at my characterizing his demystification of philosophical usage as a "contribution." "I don't see why it's a 'contribution' to suggest that we use the term 'knowledge' in the ordinary way . . . Why not use the terms as in ordinary usage, rather than philosophical doctrine, at least until some theory is put forth that allows us to move to a more explanatory plane."[93] Perhaps, but it is important to emphasize that only within the framework of some explicit theory does it make sense to deviate from common-sense notions of knowledge, and to note that there are principled limitations to what we can know. The existence of such limitations deserves a little elaboration.

Chomsky's observation that there are necessary bounds on our knowledge in general, and our science-forming capacity in particular, has led him to the striking observation that our abilities necessarily impose limitations on us: if you are designed to be able to do x, you may *ipso facto* be incapable of doing y.[94] Bats can do things we cannot and *vice versa*, so our inability to use echolocation to find our way around is not an unfortunate limitation but a function of our other talents, some of which, for instance our language faculty, would have to be sacrificed if we could echolocate.[95] Bats have evolved so that their larynxes can produce pulses at frequencies up to 200,000 hertz, their ears can detect the resulting echoes and their brains can appropriately analyze them. Our sensory system has evolved somewhat differently, but with comparable specialization for various aspects of the transmission and reception of language. Part of being human, a large part in fact, consists in our having language of this kind; another aspect of being human is that we do not have unbounded abilities in other domains. We could not have evolved in all possible directions. It follows from such limitations that some intellectual issues are likely to remain in principle forever beyond human understanding: "mysteries" rather than "problems" in Chomsky's terms.[96] Bats can echolocate with wonderful facility, but understanding the physics of echolocation is presumably beyond them. We can manage the latter and not the former. Similarly, we can exercise free will consciously and creatively, but it may nonetheless be true that we will never have a theoretical understanding of how we do it, as it is probable that "human science-forming capacities simply do not extend to . . . any domain involving the exercise of will."[97]

The nature of our mental make-up, what is potentially knowledge for us and what is not, and the relation of such knowledge to truth and the world brings us to another major area of controversy: the status of semantics.

Problems of semantics

The question of truth, conformity to an external reality, does not enter.
(Chomsky, 1980a: 27)

The domain of semantics is habitually divided into two parts: sense and reference, where "sense" expresses the difference in meaning between expressions such as *the morning star* and *the evening star*, and "reference" picks out the entities in the world to which they correspond – in this case the same entity.[98] Relations of sense can be treated internally: the different lexical entries of *evening* and *morning* in our mentally represented grammars are enough to capture the contrast; but relations of reference cannot in principle be so treated, because they go outside the head by definition. Chomsky's work can be interpreted as an ongoing attempt to achieve explanation in the syntactic domain, perhaps in the domain of sense, but as claiming that external relations of reference are outside its scope. Accordingly, criticism of his program for not achieving what he believes is in principle impossible of achievement is pointless. The disappointment is understandable, but nevertheless misguided, as the internalist perspective that Chomsky has developed over the last few decades has clarified the issues involved even in the treatment of those problems it has not really solved.

Intentionality   Part of the disillusion with the Chomskyan paradigm within the philosophical community arises then from his perceived failure to solve those problems which mainly preoccupy philosophers. Despite a markedly greater interest in meaning, the philosophy of language has traditionally shared its attention between semantics and syntax. The problem of describing the syntactic or combinatorial properties of languages, both natural and artificial, has to a considerable extent been solved by the work of Chomsky and his followers. For example, philosophers work with disambiguated languages, because logical consequence and valid inference can only be defined as relations among unambiguous sentences. The sophistication of current work in syntax means that the divide between logicians and linguists can be partially bridged, as ways are found to relate the multiply ambiguous syntactic structures of sentences of English to suitably explicit and unambiguous logical forms. In this area there is no longer serious disagreement.

By contrast, the problem of semantics, in particular the treatment of intentionality, which has been the other major focus of the philosophy of language, has been left relatively untouched by Chomsky's work.[99] The study of intentionality – that property in virtue of which mental processes are about the outside world – may be partly a mystery rather than a problem: that is, it may "lie beyond the reach of our minds."[100] For Chomsky, language is necessarily internal, and the relation of that internal construct to things outside is not obviously amenable to study within any plausible empirical discipline. Because of this internalist commitment, Chomsky suggests in his discussion of the language faculty that "It is possible that natural language has only syntax and pragmatics," and that there is no semantics – "all of this is pure syntax."[101] This does not mean of course that he denies that we manipulate relations of sense, for instance the entailment relation between *John persuaded Bill to go* and *Bill intended to go*; rather, he is claiming that such relations are at heart syntactic, and that no separate level of representation within the grammar is needed to account for them. More importantly, it is supplemented by the observation that "it is not assumed that language is used to represent the world."[102]

Because there are different interpretations of the word "semantics," the claim that there is no semantics needs a little elaboration. If a grammar is a means of linking sound and meaning, and semantics is defined as the study of meaning then, as Chomsky says, "putting aside phonology, virtually everything I've done in the field since LSLT falls within semantics."[103] The interpretation that Chomsky intends to reject is not this one but the traditional technical sense of semantics, referring to a pairing between words and mind-independent things in the world. On this interpretation he says there is good reason to believe that no semantics for natural language exists, any more than there exists a phonetics for natural language connecting phonological representations to sounds in the world. Semantics, even "formal semantics," is strictly internalist.[104]

Truth   If the idea that language is pre-eminently designed for communication is widespread, the idea that words refer to things, and sentences refer to states of affairs, in the world is even more deeply entrenched among modern philosophers. There is a widely held assumption that meaning can be usefully described in terms of truth, that is, the meaning of a sentence is given by its truth conditions: the set of conditions whose fulfilment would guarantee the truth of the sentence. At first blush this idea is eminently sensible: if someone asks whether the assertion that *Scandinavians are dolichocephalic* is true, then a prerequisite to being able to answer the question is knowing what the word means ("long-headed"). That is, to say that *Scandinavians are dolicho-cephalic* is true is equivalent to saying that *Scandinavians are long-headed* is true, or *Scandinavians are dolichocephalic* means that Scandinavians are long-headed. In such cases truth and meaning seem to be inter-convertible in a reasonably simple way, but only because I have chosen an example which allows of a straightforward linguistic definition. It is perhaps possible to extend such a truth-based analysis to the treatment of natural-kind terms like *cat*, *gold*, and *water*, on the assumption that their meaning is determined by "causal connection" to their referents.[105] By this is meant that a word such as *cat* picks out cats, rather than dogs or clouds, because there is a causal chain linking utterances of the word to examples of the animal. But saying that "*cat* picks out cats" is hardly calculated to promote greater understanding of the nature of meaning. The lay response to such claims – basically asking "well, how does that help?" seems entirely appropriate. There are anyway serious problems with this position, such as cases of mistaken identity, or Chomsky's examples of the need to take the speaker's view into account. Whether something is deemed to be a *desk* or *a hard bed for a dwarf*, whether a cup of liquid is described as *tea* or *polluted water* is dependent on our perceptions, not just on physical facts about the world.[106] If your water source is contaminated by having had tea thrown in it, what emerges from the tap may be chemically indistinguishable from tea you have deliberately prepared. It is nonetheless correctly described as (contaminated) *water*, whereas what you have made is correctly described as *tea*. The external reality is largely irrelevant to the linguistic description.

A theory of sense based on truth conditions takes us crucially outside the language faculty.[107] I take it that the claim that there is a language faculty with a particular syntax, including the levels of representation of LF and PF, is established. The details, of course, will always be a matter of controversy, because linguistics is empirical and undergoing constant revision. It should be similarly uncontroversial that we need a (pragmatic) theory of interpretation: that is, communication involves more than coding and decoding within the language system.[108] Granting the need for syntax and pragmatics, perhaps nothing else is required; indeed, adding anything else would be pernicious. The claim of "no semantics" is then to be glossed as saying that all linguistically significant generalizations can be captured either within the grammar as defined, or by the pragmatics; and being forced to ask such questions as "Is this really tea?" is counter-productive. It is still the case that lexical items have semantic properties: the differences between *think* and *believe*, *buy* and *sell*, *cat* and *dog*, are all (in part) semantic, but they do not motivate a level of semantic representation which is distinct from those syntactic levels or from pragmatic interpretations which lie outside the grammar.

There are both terminological and empirical issues involved here. There has to be some theoretical account of our knowledge of language and our ability to deploy that knowledge. If this is taken to involve semantics by definition, then we obviously need a semantic theory. But this is just terminological imperialism. If a condition of being taken seriously is that I use such and such terminology, I'm happy to use it. But this obscures the empirical fact that there is a range of data independently accounted for under the theory of syntax, and another range of data independently accounted for by a theory of (pragmatic) interpretation. Once these two domains have had their say, there is nothing left to account for that semantics can coherently deal with. This is not intended to slight the very considerable achievements of semanticists. I am assuming that traditional semantic notions such as ambiguity, compositionality (the fact that the meaning of a sentence is predictable from the meaning of its parts and the syntactic structure uniting them)[109] and the myriad complexities of quantification are all syntactically or lexically expressed, and that their syntactic properties can accordingly underlie any explanation of our semantic intuitions. From a strictly linguistic point of view, semantic representation would be just a further level of syntax.

Chomsky's skepticism about semantics is not then in conflict with his realism. Linguistics makes truth claims: claims about sound and meaning, claims about UG, claims about the factuality of I-language; but a theory of I-language contains no level of semantic representation, and can capture philosophically relevant truths without one.[110] This can be illustrated from one further area where Chomsky holds a position on truth which is controversial and anti-Quinean: his adherence to the analytic/synthetic distinction.[111] Analytic sentences are those which are true in virtue of their meaning, synthetic sentences are those which are true in virtue of facts about the world. There has been considerable debate as to whether there are any analytic truths and, following Quine, many, if not most, philosophers have concluded that there are none. The reason is that it is difficult to determine whether classic examples of the genre, such as *All cats are animals* are necessarily true or not: suppose all cats turn out on closer inspection to be Martian robots, are they then "animals"? Chomsky suggests that the focus of the debate has been misplaced. Once one considers more complex examples it becomes clear that there are good cases of analyticity. He provides examples of the kind *If John persuaded Bill to go to college, then Bill decided or intended to go to college* . . . , and *If John killed Bill, then Bill is dead.* Whatever one learns about the facts of the world, these remain (analytically) true, and crucially different from examples such as *If John persuaded Bill to go to college, then he is a fool*, which may be synthetically true.[112] These are facts about conceptual structure, which are reflected in the properties of the language faculty. They are facts, moreover, which are not controversial, and which have an explanation in terms of the linguist's account of the semantic properties of the words concerned and the structural properties of the sentences containing them.

Problems of reference   We began the discussion of semantics with the evening star, let us end it closer to home. One of Chomsky's favorite examples in his discussion of reference is *London*.[113] At first sight it seems straightforward to say that *London* refers to the city which is the capital of the UK. But Chomsky draws a distinction between our use of the word to refer to London – something which is unproblematic – and the unjustified further claim that, because we can use the word to refer, the word itself refers to some real entity in the world. London might be destroyed and rebuilt elsewhere, but it would still be London; I can refer to the same entity by using terms like *the city where I work, the capital of England,* or indefinitely many others; or I can use the word *London* with no referential intention at all as when I say in exasperation *Look, either you work in London or you don't work in London, there are no other logical possibilities*. To say in these circumstances that the word *London* itself refers to the real-world entity London solves no problems and is unnecessary. To repeat, this does not deny that humans use language to refer, or that they exploit the language faculty in doing so, but referring goes outside the language faculty as well. Chomsky has not offered a solution to the problem of reference, but he has contributed original analyses of the use of part of our vocabulary – words like *London* and *house* – and has used them to put a traditional problem in a different perspective.

This change of orientation reflects a deep disagreement about the nature of meaning. The philosophical tradition is wedded to the assumption, usually associated with the name of the nineteenth-century philosopher Gottlob Frege,[114] that it is possible to assign truth conditions to every possible (assertoric) utterance. The alternative view is that semantic relations are nothing to do with things in the world but are relations between mental representations: they are entirely inside the head. To support his position, Chomsky provides a striking analogy: he argues that the assumption that *London* picks out a specific entity in the world is as inappropriate as postulating a real-world entity of nearness which is possessed to a greater or lesser extent by pairs of various objects. Whether London is *near* Birmingham is not something which is determined by facts in the real world, but by our perspective on those facts. In the context of European cartography London and Birmingham are *near*; in the context of the Ramblers' Association, they are not.[115] No one has suggested that nearness should be assigned the status of an externally valid absolute, but Chomsky's point is that externalist philosophical assumptions about language – in particular, that there are common meanings expressed in a public language – are equivalent to doing just that.

Innateness[116]

Chomsky's views on meaning are controversial, but the part of his work for which he is most famous, infamous according to some, and the one for which he has been most vociferously criticized, is his argument that a substantial part of the faculty of language is genetically determined: it "is some kind of expression of the genes."[117] The simplest formulation of this claim, which recalls the rationalism of Descartes, and explicitly juxtaposes this with the empiricism of Quine, is that "Language is innate."[118] The claim is so radical, and so counter-intuitive in the face of the existence of close on 10,000 different languages in the world, that it is necessary to summarize and evaluate the evidence for the claim and try to undermine the various kinds of counter-evidence that have been presented. At various times Chomsky has presented many different kinds of evidence in favor of the claim that language is in large part genetically determined. These include the speed and age-dependence of acquisition; convergence among grammars, analogies to vision and other modular abilities, species-specificity, the "over-determination" of language acquisition in deaf or blind, or deaf–blind children, but above all (as we saw in chapter 1) the existence of universals on the one hand and poverty-of-the-stimulus arguments on the other.[119]

Poverty of the stimulus   The core of all poverty-of-the-stimulus arguments is that you end up knowing more than you have been taught, more even than you could have learned, because the input is too impoverished to provide the information that underpins the knowledge or ability you uncontroversially have. Chomsky is fond of using the example that the developing embryo does not choose to grow arms rather than wings, or to have brown eyes rather than blue ones: these alternatives are decided for it by its genetic make-up. Language is supposed to be comparable. Similarly, a child does not learn, and is certainly not taught, how to achieve puberty at the age of twelve or so. This too is genetically determined, even though the contribution of the environment is more obvious in this case: malnutrition delays menarche. Again language is supposed to be comparable. To acquire a language the mind needs a linguistic input, just as to attain puberty the body needs a nutritional input but, as we have seen, the richness of the knowledge the child ends up with goes far beyond that input.

Universals   Although there are innumerable languages in the world, it is striking that they are all equally complex (or simple) and that a child learns whatever language it is exposed to. There is no preference for any language or any kind of language – tonal, inflectional, or whatever – and in the space of a few years, all children achieve mastery of the system they are immersed in.

The implication of this observation is that all languages must be sufficiently similar to permit acquisition by any appropriate organism: basically a human baby. Not all babies learn to play chess or hunt penguins or play the didgeridoo, but except in cases of pathology they all master their first language. Indeed, failure to master one's first language is taken to reflect a pathological condition; failing to master algebra or the piccolo has no such implication.

Against this background it is expected that, as we saw in some detail in chapter 2, languages should share common properties, thereby providing evidence for a universalist rather than relativist position. These universals of language determine the form of the language that children acquire: indeed, so much of the language is pre-determined that acquisition in the usual sense is unnecessary; the language just develops on the basis of some triggering input. If there are indeed universals of the kind we have looked at, they are in need of explanation. The simplest such explanation is that universal properties of language are innate, and hence a "nativist" stance is supported.[120]

It follows from nativism that evidence for learning is hard to come by in the linguistic domain. This somewhat surprising observation means simply that the standard notion of learning is not one that fits the acquisition of language.[121] As we saw in the discussion of parameter setting in chapter 3, learning is normally taken to include hypothesis formation and testing; processes of assimilation and accommodation; conditioning, abstraction and induction. But none of these seem to be relevant in first language acquisition. One might object that evidence for such things is overwhelming: just consider children's over-generalizations of the kind that we discussed earlier (*three sheeps comed* and so on). There are two crucial rejoinders. First, that these may indeed show some measure of hypothesis formation, but they do not show hypothesis testing: children are remarkably resistant to correction of the type that would immediately provide evidence that their hypothesis was wrong. Second, there is an even more important response: there are domains in which children do not make mistakes. Whereas the over-generalization seen in *sheeps* and *comed* is frequent, over-generalization in domains which involve the fixing of parameters is vanishingly rare. Children form morphological analogies, but they don't form syntactic ones of the kind *didn't have today a nap* that we looked at in chapter 3. The category of non-occurring mistakes is important.

If language is not learned, how is it acquired? Jerry Fodor made the point a generation ago that "to learn a language you already need to know a language."[122] To learn that a new word such as tabescent has the meaning "wasting away," you need a representational system rich enough to express notions of "progression," and "emaciation," which are constitutive of the new word's meaning.[123] This argument for an innately determined language of thought, suggesting that much of what we know is antecedently given, carries over from the vocabulary to the grammar of the language. More particularly, as we saw earlier, it seems that as in immunology, the process of language acquisition is one of selection rather than instruction.[124] As Chomsky puts it: "in the case of language and conceptual development, it [learning] seems to have little if any place."[125] Grammar just grows.

Objections to innateness explanations   This innatist scenario should by now be plausible. Perhaps it is even inevitable, yet there have been many objections to the claim that language acquisition requires any appeal to innateness at all. Chomsky professes himself puzzled by such objections: "Is the idea supposed to be that there is no (relevant) difference between my granddaughter, her pet kitten, a rock, a chimpanzee? No one can be that crazy. But if there is a relevant difference, then we accept the 'innatist scenario.' So what can possibly be under discussion, except for the nature of the innate endowment?"[126] I find this response convincing, but in the light of the repeated and continuing nature of the objections, it is worth spending some time demonstrating that the standard criticisms are unpersuasive. As a preliminary, it is perhaps necessary to dismiss the radical objection to the claim that there is innate knowledge of language simply because it is incorrect to talk of knowledge of language at all – we simply have "dispositions to verbal behavior," hence postulating innate knowledge is either unnecessary or incoherent.[127] I take it that the preceding discussion has established that it is coherent to talk of knowledge of language and that even if we had mere dispositions to verbal behavior, we would still need to explain how we came by them. Taking this as granted, the first and simplest of the standard objections is that children are exposed to so much input that they have plenty of time to learn grammar without the need for innateness. In brief, there is no poverty of the stimulus. The counter-argument appeals to a refinement of the notion "poverty" involving the absence of "negative data."

It is true that children are exposed to vast quantities of linguistic input, probably running into millions of utterances. Estimates vary, but even if one cedes the most expansive claims, it is still not the case that an anti-innatist argument would go through. This is true for a variety of reasons: first, the "input" may not coincide with the "uptake."[128] The fact that a child has heard a million utterances doesn't mean that it has understood, interpreted, analyzed, and benefited from those utterances. Children are notoriously impervious to correction, repeating the same mistake again and again. In response to this, opponents of innateness may invoke the role of motherese, the reduced form of language typically used by care-givers to the children in their charge, in which the grammar is simplified, utterances are kept short, intonation patterns are exaggerated, and the child's limited abilities are accommodated as far as is possible. The idea is that motherese is tailored to facilitate language acquisition. This raises the problem that simplified language is unlikely to facilitate the learning of a complex system. A language can be generated by all sorts of different grammars, so the more evidence the child receives in the form of different construction types, the smaller the set of grammars it has to choose among. Logically, motherese complicates rather than simplifies the child's task.[129]

There is a potential tension between the claim that motherese is unnecessary for language acquisition, perhaps even pernicious (as it removes one class of evidence from the input data), and a claim made in chapter 1. There I argued that idealization to homogeneity is not only defensible and desirable but, on the assumption that variation is irrelevant to language acquisition, perhaps conceptually necessary. Despite its elimination of some complexities, motherese provides variation of a different kind and it is conceivable that the child acquiring its first language needs such variation in order to be exposed to sufficient data to fix the parameters, or at least would benefit from such variation. Interestingly, there is no evidence that this logical possibility corresponds to reality.

The argument that children are exposed to enough input to guarantee learnability also leaves unexplained why adults placed for years in an environment where it is necessary for them to learn a second language only very rarely approximate the fluency of children. Second language learning is only extremely rarely as successful as first language learning.[130]

Apart from these considerations, there is a further powerful argument for the necessity of invoking some innate structure: the absence of negative evidence.[131] That is, children acquiring their first language are not given (systematic) information about their mistakes. Typically, children are corrected for telling lies or being rude, not for being ungrammatical. Much of Chomsky's linguistic argumentation exploits, and seeks to explain, native-speaker intuitions of the kind we have seen repeatedly in earlier chapters. We know immediately that both the sentences in (9):

(9) a.   John told a story to Bill
    b.   John told Bill a story

are grammatical, but that in (10):

(10) a.   John recounted a story to Bill
    b.   *John recounted Bill a story
    c.   John said something nice to Bill
    d.   *John said Bill something nice

while all are comprehensible, (b) and (d) are simply not part of our language. How do we know? A first answer might be that we know that (10b, d) are impossible because we have never heard them, any more than we have heard (11):

(11)   *Bill a story recounted John

This response might conceivably work for (11) but it cannot work for (10). First, I have frequently heard non-native speakers of English say (10b, d) or comparable sentences, but I am still not tempted to treat them as grammatical, and (when it is socially appropriate) I am still happy to correct their mistake. Second, such a response would fall foul of the obvious fact that we have not previously heard most of the sentences we are ready to accept as part of our language. Even the claim that one should deal in terms of structures, rather than sentences, won't work when one looks a little more closely. As we have seen, one of the most striking aspects of children's language is that they over-generalize. Such over-generalization of a simple rule is not totally unconstrained but is circumscribed to occurring in certain linguistic domains. One area where it occurs frequently is in examples, parallel to those in (11), like those in (12):

(12) a. I said her no
     b. Don't say me that or you'll make me cry
     c. Shall I whisper you something?

The interesting question then is how do children retreat from a grammar in which examples like (12) are well-formed to the adult grammar in which they are ill-formed? Although it appears that they are not consistently corrected – that is, there is no negative evidence systematic enough to account for the con-vergence of intuitions among adult speakers about such sentences – there is one form of indirect negative evidence which may play a role in children's linguistic development, especially around the age of two. This is the reformula-tion by the adults around them of children's incorrect utterances in a corrected, fully grammatical, form. Thus the child's utterance *the plant didn't cried* might be reformulated by the adult as *the plant didn't cry*. Such clues may well be exploited by the child, but it is unlikely that all children receive sufficient infor-mation at all relevant ages to account for the full range of examples of retreat. This transition must, then, be internally controlled, hence based on general and innately given linguistic principles.[132]

A different kind of objection to innateness is provided by Hilary Putnam, who claims that as some abilities are learned and not innate, "Invoking 'innate-ness' only postpones the problem of learning; it does not solve it."[133] This is to misunderstand the claims that Chomsky is making. Certain aspects of our language are not innate but develop on the basis of exposure to relevant input. In a minority of cases this input could constitute the basis for learning of a traditional kind, where even overt teaching may have a role to play. This is irrelevant to the central claim of Chomsky's innatism, namely that the human organism is endowed at birth with a rich structure which is precisely sufficient to make such learning possible. It is striking that Putnam does not raise the com-parable question with regard to the development of the visual system, which also involves the interplay of genetic and environmental factors. Presumably, he makes the tacit assumption that language is cognitive in a way that vision is not, and hence that discussions of language have to meet additional criteria of adequacy: another instance of the methodological dualism that Chomsky has repeatedly rejected.

A variety of researchers from Quine through Halliday to current Connectionists have argued that all you need to acquire language is general intelligence; postulating any innate mechanism specific to language is unnecessary.[134] It is not denied that there is an "innate quality space," to use Quine's term, but this has nothing necessarily to do with language. As Elman and his colleagues put it: "a domain-general pattern recognition device would suffice"; that is, language acquisition is subserved by an undifferentiated network that suffices for everything, including vision, intelligence, face recognition, and so on.[135] There are serious problems with this position. It ignores the kind of dissociation I documented earlier, and as we saw in part in the previous chapter, it completely ignores the differences between pattern recognition in the linguistic domain and in other, e.g. problem-solving, domains, and provides no account for the specificity of processes in these domains. It is, to say the least, not obvious how one can explain the emergence of the rigidity principle in vision, or subjacency in language, in the absence of prior structure; structure, moreover, which is specific to the respective domains. Again, the refusal to treat the development of language as parallel in terms of its genetic determinants to the development of vision is left unmotivated.[136]

A less direct argument against innateness tries to undermine the support it receives from the existence of universals by claiming that these are the result of monogenesis, therefore in no need of innatist explanations.[137] The monogenesis hypothesis claims that all human languages are descended from a single ancestor. While we know that English and German are related to each other in a way that English and Chinese are not, it is suggested that if one goes back far enough in time (say 100,000 years), then maybe all current languages are related, and this relationship is sufficient to explain whatever universals there may be. Hence the existence of universals is not a plausible argument for innateness.

Suppose the claim that all languages are related is true. In order for this to explain the fact that all speakers of all extant languages obey constraints of the same kind, e.g. that all rules are structure-dependent, it must be the case that the effect of this relatedness is still operative in the minds of these speakers. This in turn must rest on one of two assumptions: either the primary linguistic data which the child learning its first language is exposed to are sufficient to determine the form of the grammar the child is acquiring; or the universal properties of language have become encoded in the genes of the children. If arguments for the poverty of the stimulus are correct then the first of these alternatives cannot be adequate. The fact that languages change superficially so much that monogenesis is not obviously true shows that the primary linguistic data change from generation to generation. Moreover, it is striking that on the one hand children create new examples they have never heard, but on the other there are mistakes which, despite inherent plausibility, they never make. The implication is that the explanatory effect of monogenesis itself rests on the assumption that this effect is operative because it has been incorporated into the genome. I conclude that neither this nor any of the other arguments against innateness explanations is plausible. What precisely it is that is innate, and how much of that is exclusively linguistic is the focus of ongoing research; indeed, it is the subject matter of linguistics.[138]

Unification and reduction[139]

Advances in scientific understanding have often involved accounting for one concept in terms of another, more basic, one: the explanation of (a large part of) mathematics in terms of set theory; the treatment of meaning in terms of truth; the explanation of heredity in terms of biochemistry, and so on. As a result, the reduction of one discipline to another is often taken to be the self-evident goal of science, with the reduction of chemistry to physics and the later reduction of biology to chemistry being paradigm examples. What reduction means in this context is that the significant generalizations of one discipline can be expressed in the framework of a more basic discipline, ultimately always physics. The discovery of the electron in the nineteenth century meant that the nature of the chemical bond could be understood in a new light: specifically, in a physical light.[140] The development of molecular biology in the second half of the twentieth century meant that the structure of the cell could similarly be understood in a new light: specifically in the light of biochemistry. In an attempt to replicate such successes, psychologists have tried to reduce their discipline to physiology: rather than saying that a rat depressed a bar in an experiment, a physiological account of the muscular mechanisms involved is provided; instead of talking of hunger, one talks about the activity of the nerve centers in the hypothalamus. Are such alternatives illuminating, or should we concentrate on the kind of unification we saw in chapter 3, rather than attempting a reduction?

To answer this question, we need to note that the success of the reduction of chemistry to physics was only possible when physics itself was radically revised, so "reduction" is an odd description. Moreover, examples of successful reduction, even of this modified kind, are extremely rare, and there is little reason to think that language (or cognition more generally) is likely to succumb to a reductionist approach. No one doubts that human activities, including the use of language, are transacted in accordance with the laws of physics: we do not speak in a vacuum or construe sentences faster than the speed of light. What is at issue is whether the generalizations characteristic of the study of language (or geology or economics) can be couched in the vocabulary of physics: in terms of the interaction of elementary particles for instance. Fodor cites the case of

Gresham's law (bad money drives out good) and emphasizes the impossibility of reducing such a law to physics, because of the implausibility of giving a (physical) characterization of "money" that would cover cowries, cheques, and credit cards. There is no reason for greater optimism in other domains.[141]

David Lewis makes an eloquent case for the reduction of mind to "physical – in particular, neural – states," where these are ultimately cashed out in terms of such notions as mass and charge. He fails, however, to confront the Fodorian problem mentioned in the previous paragraph: namely, that there are generalizations in the special sciences which it is irrational to expect to be subsumed under any physical description. This does not, of course, deny that any particular instantiation of, say, WH-movement in someone's utterance of a sentence (*What did Lewis claim?*, for instance) will satisfy the laws of physics. Presumably even the brain states that are involved in the silent rehearsal of the sentence underlying the utterance obey those same laws, and do so in partly similar ways, making physical generalizations about WH-movement even harder to envisage. The reductionist position is logically tenable, but what is at issue is whether it is remotely realistic to think that Lewis will ever be in a position to honor the promissory notes that he issues: "When we know more we shall know what pattern of neural activity it is" that underlies particular mental states; or "we may reasonably hope that future physics can finish the job."[142] After several centuries in which the completion of physics has been eagerly anticipated, it is hard to be optimistic.

The contrast between reduction and unification can be seen clearly in the case of the tension between connectionist and computationalist–representationalist accounts of cognition and language.[143] Computationalism claims that operations of both a symbolic and a subsymbolic kind are necessary. We need both to manipulate symbols of the kind given to us by the words of our language, and we need to specify some way in which those words are physically realized in a working system: either metal and plastic or flesh and blood. Reductivist, or "eliminativist," connectionists can be construed as denying the need for any symbolic representation. The brain demonstrably contains neurons which transmit electric impulses. Equally demonstrably the brain does not, for instance, contain sad cells or colored cells, or cells filled with nouns. Theoretical parsimony is then taken to demand that a respectable science restricts itself to dealing in those things which are demonstrably there; hence talk of symbols is unjustified, and the complexities of human mentation must emerge from neural interactions. The echoes of behaviorism are resonant. When Shakespeare described Viola in *Twelfth Night* as pining in thought with a green and yellow melancholy, it seems unlikely that he thought the thoughts in her head were actually green and yellow. It is also unlikely that her state of mind could be captured without having recourse to symbols. The traditional view that he was manipulating symbols which represented "green," "yellow" and "melancholy," and that these words were in turn encoded in his and our brains in some subsymbolic way should not be particularly controversial, especially in the absence of coherent reductionist alternatives.

Here as elsewhere, unification is desirable, but only faith or dogmatism leads one to think that the unification will be reductionist in character. As Chomsky points out with regard to correlations between electrical activity in the brain and different kinds of linguistic stimulus, "the findings remain something of a curiosity, because there is no appropriate theory of electrical activity of the brain – no known reason, that is, why one should find these results not others."[144] In contrast, there is now considerable understanding of the computational properties of language, so trying to reduce the known to the relatively unknown seems a rather perverse strategy. Chomsky is committed in principle to unifying his linguistics with some future brain sciences, with pragmatics, with any worked-out theory in a relevant domain. Despite the burgeoning sophistication of current imaging, "which should be particularly valuable in sketching out the general architecture of systems and how they interact," the sophistication of linguistic theory is, at present, so far in advance of that of any of the other disciplines that unification is only on the horizon.[145]

Conclusions

The breadth of Chomsky's interests in linguistics and psychology is already remarkable. In this chapter we have seen that his philosophical system of ideas is equally extensive, and profound.[146] He has worked out a consistent and integrated position which combines realism, naturalism, and mentalism, and he has developed a radical theory of I-language which has served as a basis for challenging many of the received opinions in the discipline. He has undermined traditional thinking on the relation of language to the world, to the community, and to the individual. His conception of grammar, backed up by massive technical analysis, has underpinned arguments in areas as diverse as the private language debate, Cartesian skepticism, the analytic/synthetic distinction, the unification of science and, pre-eminently, the question of innateness and rationalism.

This should be enough, but we shall see in the next chapter that he has a coherent vision which extends to the political domain as well.

5   Language and freedom

Explanation and dissent: the common threads

> . . . working in a science is useful because you somehow learn . . . what
> evidence and argument and rationality are and you come to be able to apply
> these to other domains.[1]
>   (Chomsky, 1988c: 696)

Relentless dissent

The pressure to conform is great. It takes courage to speak or act in contradiction
to the majority of one's fellows. Chomsky's work in all fields can be described
as an unrelenting refusal to follow the herd: a book of interviews with him
is entitled *Chronicles of Dissent* (1992b) and a political biography by R. F.
Barsky has the title *A Life of Dissent* (1997). His dissent is no mere obstinate
rejectionism, as it is combined with a sustained defense of alternatives: scientific
creativity in the case of his linguistics; anarchist humanity in the case of his
politics; the centrality of explanation in both. In his words "the task of a scientific
analysis is to discover the facts and explain them."[2] In this final chapter I look
at the strands linking Chomsky's scientific work to his political activism: his
commitment to rationality, his refusal to take things at face value, his passionate
defense of what he conceives to be right, and his dispassionate analysis of
relevant alternatives. I begin with a glance at the tension between common
sense[3] and scientific explanation, and give a brief overview of his intellectual
background, before turning to a more detailed analysis of the main areas of his
polemical work.

Common sense and theory

It is obvious that two people can speak the same language; that it makes sense to
talk of English from medieval times to the present; that children are taught their
first language, or at least learn it from their parents and peers; that language
is somehow socially defined and is designed for communication. To many, it
is equally obvious that democracy in the free world (while perhaps in crisis) is

morally superior to various forms of fascism and communism; that we operate a free-market economy; that we have a choice in voting Democrat or Republican, Labour or Conservative; that the media are constructively critical of our governments and institutions.

Yet Chomsky has argued that each of these "obvious" propositions is false, and has elaborated detailed alternatives to each of them. His objections emerge naturally from his commitment to the necessity for rationality in science and political analysis alike, and to radical dissent from any position which fails to meet such standards of rationality. His constructive alternatives stem from a vision of human nature which combines penetration with wonder, insight with fanatical hard work.

Not all received wisdom is rejected. In language as in politics, there is the difficult but necessary task of identifying when common-sense observations are to be preserved and made rigorous, and when they are to be rejected as misleading. The scientific enterprise only rarely adopts common-sense categories unchanged: for the layman "plants" and "animals" exhaust the possibilities of living things; for the scientist, the properties of bacteria and blue-green algae necessitate a more complex taxonomy. In this case the lay view is simply under-informed and there is no confrontation between science and common sense: few people have a vested interest in blue-green algae. In other cases, the opinion of experts may be the product of deliberate obfuscation, as with so-called scientific justifications for racism, where lay prejudice is given a veneer of respectability from genetics.[4] In such cases, that which is claimed (self-servingly) to be self-evidently true may be actually false, even self-evidently false: examples include the benevolence of one's government, the learning of one's first language.[5] Conversely, that which is apparently false may turn out on analysis to be true. As "States don't act on moral grounds,"[6] there is no moral difference between the leaders of the countries of the "free" world and those of our enemies; the Palestinians are fighting for a peace that the Israeli government is trying to prevent;[7] that language is innate.

It is important to emphasize the "on analysis" here. One of the major contributions that Chomsky has made is to have clarified the issues involved. It *is* obviously true that various people "speak the same language," but the notion of language involved in this particular locution is not the same notion of language as is relevant to the scientific discussion of our knowledge of language or of how we acquire our first language. Likewise, the "crisis of democracy," frequently interpreted as the pernicious result of external infiltration of (Western) political systems,[8] was actually the title of the first publication of the Trilateral Commission,[9] and addressed the "crisis of ungovernability" which had arisen in the 1960s when "the normally passive general population threatened to participate in the political system."[10]

The problem of seeing when common sense must win and when it must succumb to scientific investigation is pervasive, and rarely soluble without prolonged analysis. We looked earlier at the debate between representational and connectionist models of cognition, a classic case of where current science, in the form of connectionism, repudiates the common-sensical view that we represent the world to ourselves by using language or language-like constructs, and that we act out of the beliefs and desires so represented. Although Chomsky has stated that "We hardly expect the constructions of the science-forming faculty to conform to common-sense understanding,"[11] a position which might lead one to expect him to have a certain sympathy with connectionism, he has argued repeatedly for representationalism. Common sense in this case may still be lacking serious scientific backing, but all the insights that have been achieved over the last fifty years presuppose some form of symbolic representation, and non-symbolic alternatives have solved virtually none of the outstanding problems now well defined by linguistics. The value of any theory is measured in terms of its explanatory success. If the most successful theory accords with common sense, so well and good, but there is no reason to expect such conformity or to make it criterial.

These disparate domains are unified not only by Chomsky's relentless dissent from orthodoxy, but by constant emphasis on explanation. In language and in politics alike Chomsky seeks to understand and explain why things are as they are and, where appropriate, to change them.[12] Although there is a constant emphasis on explanation, it is important to note that the nature of that explanation is radically different in the two domains. Scientific explanation of the kind which is now characteristic of linguistics is the product of theory construction, where explanatory depth is sought rather than descriptive breadth. Such explanation is not possible in politics, certainly not now, perhaps not ever. The chain of inference from observation to conclusion is short and reasonably obvious in politics. Dropping cluster bombs on civilian targets is wrong, so we should try to stop it. One does not need much theory to arrive at that conclusion, and arguments in justification of the practise arouse dissent and contempt. Nonetheless there is a need to explain why it is that people both carry out such activities and try to justify them. To a first approximation the explanation is one of economic advantage, to which everything else is subordinate. Substantiating such a subversive claim is only plausible if the documentation in favor of it is so overwhelming as to be unanswerable:[13] here descriptive breadth is essential. Chomsky has provided the relevant documentation in the form of over fifty books and innumerable articles, with titles as diverse as *At War with Asia* (1971a), *Deterring Democracy* (1991a), *Class Warfare* (1996b), *Profit over People* (1999a), and *Power and Terror* (2003b).

In the study of language, there is scope for more sophisticated argument, and the nature of the evidence is quite different. Chomsky makes the difference explicit in a contrast between what he calls "Plato's problem" and "Orwell's problem."[14] Plato's problem, which is characteristic of many aspects of our cognition, can be stated succinctly as "How can we know so much when the evidence is so slight?" In particular, how is it that we have such intricate knowledge of our native language? How did we acquire such knowledge? Orwell's problem, which is characteristic of our political beliefs, is the converse: "How can we remain so ignorant when the evidence is so overwhelming?" In particular, how is it that we frequently believe the propaganda we are subjected to by the establishment, even when its claims are at variance with common sense and a huge amount of clear evidence? In forming our political beliefs we seem to ignore a plethora of easily available evidence; in the case of our knowledge of language we have intuitions and abilities of a complexity for which the evidence is minimal.

In the light of these differences, it might seem implausible that there should be principles unifying the two domains, but three properties are characteristic of all Chomsky's intellectual work: rationality, modularity, and creativity.[15]

Rationality, modularity, and creativity

Chomsky himself has frequently stated that any intellectual relation between his linguistic and his political work is extremely tenuous, but there are certain common strands which bear teasing out. Much of his political analysis involves the dissection of the linguistic usage of government and the media. Such dissection doesn't require syntactic genius, but it is undoubtedly helped by a sensitivity to language developed over half a century. More interestingly, he sees a parallelism arising from a general conception of human nature in terms of "the underlying and essential human need for freedom from external arbitrary constraints and controls."[16] This plea for freedom resonates most strongly in his political activism, but one needs only to remember Chomsky's critique of Skinner's behaviorist view of language, whose aim was "to provide a way to predict and control verbal behavior by observing and manipulating the physical environment of the speaker" to realize how close the parallel with language is.[17]

Rationality

Chomsky says that he knows of no argument for irrationality: "[Reason] is all we have," and that he tries "consciously to avoid irrational belief."[18] One might think that there could be no argument for irrationality: the notion "argument" presupposes rationality, so what is surprising is that many scholars systematically reject or ignore standard canons of rationality. There are at least three different categories. First, there is the uninteresting class of those who simply substitute emotional rhetoric for argument: many of Chomsky's detractors fall into this category. Second, there are those who assert contradictions, and are hence technically irrational, but who do so for reasons of propaganda, and rely on the reader's gullibility or prejudice to escape detection. This is the category of those "drowning in their own hypocrisy"[19] that Chomsky has concentrated on most, and who will be discussed below. Third are those like the philosophers Michel Foucault and Richard Rorty,[20] who deny the possibility of rationality, claiming instead that all argumentation is subjective and that the appearance of rationality is merely a disguise for vested interests of power, or a property only of our own local culture. If this claim were true, it would contradict Chomsky's rationalist stance; but such relativist and subjectivist positions, while popular and widespread, are ultimately incoherent. The claim that all argument is subjective can itself be subjected to critical (rational) analysis. If it is an objective claim it is contradictory: it would be false if true. If it is a subjective claim then, by hypothesis, it cannot exclude the objective claim that it is false. On either interpretation the thesis is self-defeating.[21] So Foucault's claim (in a debate with Chomsky) that "one doesn't speak in terms of justice but in terms of power," or that truth and knowledge are simply reflections of a "will to power," and his rejection of any culture-independent notion of human nature, are all based on unjustified assumptions which attempt to subvert the possibility of a logical response.[22] Worse, they leave no room for any kind of explanation for human aspirations to freedom and the potential for creativity, attributes which are potentially explicable if human nature can be objectively and rationally investigated.

There are limits to rationality. There is ultimately no response to total skepticism, to the claim that we can know *nothing* for certain except our own existence. But this means only that a working scientist has to give up claims to certainty, not claims to the rationality of the enterprise in which he or she is engaged. This should not be a worry: however great the discovery, no scientist believes that he or she has found the ultimate answers. The best one can hope for is to push explanation a little further and raise new questions of greater depth, where these new questions may show the earlier advances to be interestingly wrong. One might even come to the conclusion that the whole enterprise one is engaged in is spurious. As Chomsky puts it, "we cannot exclude the possibility that a future science of mind may simply dispense with the concept of language in our sense," just as generative linguistics has dispensed with the traditional lay notion of (E-)language.[23]

There are also domains, such as the human emotions, where rationality, though necessary, is inadequate to explain the full range of our experience.[24] It may be true that "something one cannot understand constitutes a painful void,"[25] but this is not a reason for giving up rationality in those areas where understanding is possible. Chomsky has spoken of the difference between "problems" and "mysteries": those phenomena which are within the range of human under-standing, and those which are now and perhaps for ever beyond us.[26] The latter category includes such perennial problems as free will and maybe the emotions; the former includes everything that falls within our science-forming capacity. There is a third domain of common-sense understanding, where we have an intuitive grasp of some area, and where closer examination may lead us to the conclusion either that its scientific investigation is feasible, characterizing it as a "problem", or that it is impossible, putting it at least for now in the class of "mysteries". To understand each of these we need recourse to some model of human cognition. For this some notion of modularity is crucial.

Modularity

In the opening chapter we looked at modularity largely from a traditional Fodorian perspective in which modules correspond to the senses, plus lan-guage, and are equated with input systems that feed the (non-modular) central system.[27] Despite the claims of connectionists, some such picture is generally accepted for the language faculty, for vision, for touch, and so on. Chomsky's view of modularity is more general and more radical: a modularity of the central systems, which is impossible in Fodor's terms. There is increasing evidence that a huge range of our abilities is underlain by specific mental modules: personal-ity discrimination, moral judgment, music, the sense of number, the intuitions of "folk physics," face recognition, theory of mind, and many others. Not only is it the case that "the human brain appears to have a subsystem dedicated to language,"[28] but there appears to be an innate basis for virtually all human activ-ities, so that the human mind is richly structured in the domain of social reality, in scientific reasoning, in the analysis of personality, and in aesthetic and moral judgment. Whether our faculty of moral judgment is strictly modular is an open, perhaps terminological, question, but two things are clear: first that "There is some component of our intellectual system that involves moral judgments";[29] second, that the impoverished input to which the child is exposed in the course of its upbringing is inadequate to account for the generality, depth, and subtlety of moral judgments in the individual, and the commonalties across moral sys-tems in the species. Chomsky argues that "whenever we see a very rich, intricate system developing in a more or less uniform way on the basis of rather restricted stimulus conditions, we have to assume that there is a very powerful, very rich, highly structured innate component that is operating in such a way as to create that highly specific system . . ."[30] No one doubts that the development of our visual system is genetically determined, because the environmental control is self-evidently inadequate to account for it. By parity of argument we should conclude that "there's a biological endowment which in effect requires us to develop a system of moral judgment and a theory of justice."[31] The parallel is made more strikingly in the remark that "David Hume, two hundred and fifty years ago, pointed out that the foundation of morals must be what we nowadays call generative grammar . . . some set of principles that we're capable of applying in novel situations – again, without limit."[32] Whether our moral systems are as homogeneous and as intricate as this implies is a matter of dispute. However, that there can be objective moral standards, of the kind reflected in our vocabulary by the distinction between "kill" and "murder," or "rights" and "duties," seems to be established.[33] Such objectivity and the ubiquity in the world's languages of such terms suggest that they are a reflection of some deep, genetically determined, property of human beings. Chomsky is still insistent that our ignorance is still so great that ethics and morality are not a proper domain for theory construction.[34] Nonetheless, if modularity is motivated in part by the kind of dissociation discussed in chapter 1, then interesting confirmation of the putative modularity of the moral system is provided by some cases of brain damage. Antonio Damasio describes the case of Phineas Gage, who had an iron rod blown through his head by an explosion and who as a result of his appalling injuries lost all normal social control so that his "ethics, in the broad sense of the term, were violated,"[35] even though his intelligence and other faculties were unimpaired.

Malleability and plasticity

Modularity, whether of language, vision or morality, is the result of innate properties of the system; that is, it is to a large extent genetically determined, and constitutes a significant part of what it is to be human. Our genetic endowment is inalienable. Modularity in the moral domain is then incompatible with any view which assumes the unconstrained malleability of the intellect. For Chomsky, humans need to be free to develop in whatever way maximizes the potential of that innate endowment, and to limit our social and moral choices is to violate our nature. An innate moral organ is incompatible with a philosophy which licenses social control. The possibility of malleability of the kind beloved of politicians, capitalist, communist, and fascist alike, could be taken to "eliminate the moral barriers to coercion . . .",[36] a result which is anathema to Chomsky and explains his opposition over the decades to any denial of human freedom. This can be seen in his critique of two strands of Skinner's work: on the one hand, his behaviorist psychology as epitomized in his *Verbal Behavior* (1957), and on the other hand, his novels *Walden Two* (1948) and *Beyond Freedom and Dignity* (1971), which argue for an extreme form of social engineering, and for a society where the "self-destructive" ideals of freedom and dignity are replaced by total technological control.[37] Chomsky's contrary stance is part of a long libertarian tradition, which goes back to Humboldt's assertion that there are "fundamental needs" of inquiry and creativity at the core of human beings, and is in direct line of descent from Bakunin's "instinct for freedom." In Chomsky's words: "intrinsic to human nature is the desire to create under conditions of freedom and lack of constraint."[38]

There is a clear intellectual link between Chomsky's vehement opposition to a view of human malleability which might license political control and his scorn for connectionist views of the human mind–brain. The parallel to malleability is the apparent genetic underdetermination of the human brain, as seen in its "plasticity."[39] By plasticity is meant the fact that in the event of damage to the brain, one region can be co-opted to carry out the function usually effected by a different region. This is then used as an argument against the genetic specification of modular systems, in particular the language system, and in favor of the "equipotentiality" of the neonate brain. The idea is that the claimed innateness of modularity is undermined by the brain's ability to compensate for injury in one area by "redeploying" its forces. If a child suffers damage to the language area (e.g. in the form of a left hemispherectomy) the language function may be taken over by the right hemisphere.[40] It is supposed to follow that modularity cannot be pre-specified, but is an emergent property determined in large part by the environment.[41] But it is not clear that plasticity raises any kind of problem for an innatist modular view. Apart from the fact that a module might be subserved by widely dispersed neural machinery, the very notion of plasticity presupposes that particular regions are, in the absence of pathological conditions, pre-specified for particular (modular) functions. Interestingly, the neurological literature is full of more and more fine-grained analyses of correlations between particular functions and the same area of the brain in individual after individual.[42]

In any modular domain, be it language, morality or whatever, certain possible functions are licensed and certain others are excluded. This is important as it defends the hypothesis of modularity against the attack of vacuity. That is, the connection between Chomsky's moral and scientific views is in part that both of them stem from a general view of the mind which, by making certain (modular) assumptions, excludes the possibility of particular alternatives.[43] Chomsky sometimes characterizes this with his customary ability to surprise by saying that limitations on human ability in various domains are to be expected, perhaps even welcomed, because they are the natural consequence of our abilities in other domains. One area where any progress in coming to theoretical understanding is minimal, and likely to remain so, is in the field of human behavior.[44] That is, the human mind is probably no more capable of inventing a scientific account of some aspects of human behavior than a spider is of inventing a theory of arachnid behavior. The most striking example is provided by our inability to cast light on the notion of free will, an area of central importance to human beings but which is totally opaque to scientific understanding. This ignorance is probably principled: our minds are not constructed in a way that makes this issue (and others) amenable to our intellect. Chomsky even surmises that *all* areas of human ability beyond those like vision and language which are genetically pre-specified are mysteries: we shall never develop a scientific understanding of how and why our aesthetic sense differentiates Mozart and Salieri or Rembrandt and Pollock, any more than the spider will develop an understanding of how and why it builds webs of one configuration rather than another.

Creativity

A conception of our abilities in terms of constrained modularity suggests a connection between the creative use of language and creativity in other domains. As Chomsky puts it: "the study of language can provide some glimmerings of understanding of rule-governed behavior and the possibilities of free and creative action within the framework of a system of rules that in part, at least, reflect intrinsic properties of human mental organization." The crucial concepts are *freedom*, "the essential and defining property of man,"[45] albeit freedom within a framework of constraints, and *perfectibility* in the sense of Rousseau's "faculty of self-perfection":[46] the ability of man to progress indefinitely on a path of self-fulfilment. All organisms are constrained by their inherent properties, but the limitations on the movements of a frog or an amoeba are rather tighter than those on the movements of man, because man has a mind. "To Descartes and his followers ... the only sure sign that another organism has a mind, and hence also lies beyond the bounds of mechanical explanation, is its use of language in the normal, creative human fashion . . ." The freedom which humans can attain is not absolute, but is limited by their nature: "it is no denial of man's capacity for infinite 'self-perfection' to hold that there are intrinsic properties of mind that constrain his development." Chomsky is even more categorical: it is meaningless to talk of creativity unless there are limitations: "without a system of formal constraints there are no creative acts." Only the consciousness of freedom makes possible the aspiration to change and improve the condition of man.[47]

There is a certain tension here in Chomsky's thinking, a tension which probably underlies his dismissal of there being any fruitful tie-up between the different strands of his work. The tension resides in the interpretation of "creativity." On the one hand there is the creative use of language, on the other there is the intellectual and moral creativity of a free individual. But these different forms of creativity are governed by processes and constraints of radically different kinds, though both of them can come together in the case of (the use of) language. We can tease out the vastly complicated details of the structure of sentences of natural languages and of the universal grammatical principles that constrain them, but we are barely able to begin to explain how we choose to deploy those structures in the expression of our thoughts. There is little doubt that both are constrained by the properties of our minds, but whereas one is a problem amenable to scientific analysis, the other seems as remote from detailed understanding as it did two thousand years ago; it is still a mystery. Despite this basic difference between the two domains in which Chomsky works, between the scientific and the political, the parallels that link them seem to me to be systematic and consistent enough to provide some insight into his thought processes. There is no necessary connection between his linguistic and his moral commitments, but the connections are nonetheless more than accidental.

As is implicit in several of the preceding quotations, Chomsky's ideas on human nature are the culmination of a long, libertarian, largely anarchist, tradition. It is to this background that we now turn.

The anarchist background

I'm some kind of anarchist.[48] (Chomsky, 1988c: 744)

"Anarchist" is normally a term of opprobrium, reserved for members of one or another lunatic fringe with a tendency to throw bombs around. This unfortunate connotation is the result of the term's ambiguous derivation from *anarchism*, a system of political ideas combining the best of socialism and liberalism, and *anarchy*, a state of lawlessness and disorder. Chomsky is an anarchist only in the former of these meanings.

His intellectual forebears in this area include Jean-Jacques Rousseau (1712–78), Wilhelm von Humboldt (1767–1835), Pierre-Joseph Proudhon (1809–65), Mikhail Bakunin (1814–76), John Dewey (1859–1952), Bertrand Russell (1872–1970), Anton Pannekoek (1873–1960), and Rudolf Rocker (1873–1958), all of whom share a vision of human society free of oppression from concentration of power: whether that power is in the hands of the church, the state, slave-owners, feudal lords or private corporations. None of these thinkers had a program with which Chomsky (or anyone today) could sympathize *in toto*: Proudhon and Rousseau both thought women inferior, with Proudhon "rat[ing] their intellectual and moral value as one-third of that of men";[49] and Bakunin's "passion for destruction," even if creative, encouraged unremitting violence. Humboldt is the most interesting and probably the one to whom Chomsky feels closest. Like Chomsky, he was a "profound theorist of general linguistics" and a "forceful advocate of libertarian values." His emphasis on the necessity of individual freedom and creativity is strikingly similar to Chomsky's, and only his naïveté vis-à-vis the potential evils of capitalism weakens his position and diminishes his appeal.[50]

In more recent times, the ideas of Rudolf Rocker have both influenced and been congenial to Chomsky. Rocker's major book opens "Anarchism . . . advocate[s] the abolition of economic monopolies and of all political and social coercive institutions within society," and emphasizes that "every type of political power presupposes some particular form of human slavery." In his admiration of the workers' syndicates in Catalonia, his vitriolic attack on all forms of capitalism, and his repeated emphasis on the necessity for freedom, Rocker provides a clear model for much of Chomsky's political writing and activism.[51] The parallels are particularly striking when one learns that Chomsky's first article, written when he was ten, was about the fall of Barcelona in the Spanish Civil War.[52]

Although anarchism as a political movement may seem to be of marginal importance on the world stage, anarchist ideas have enjoyed some limited success and, in the light of events at Seattle, Genoa, and elsewhere, can be seen to have had some influence. The evil effects of governments, where the extent of the evil is roughly commensurate with the power of that government's armed forces, are more widely recognized than hitherto, even by people who would dissociate themselves from the severity of Chomsky's attack. Populist protests against the horror of the Vietnam War awakened many who had previously been apathetic about politics, and persuaded them that they had to be actively engaged in the struggle. While the Vietnam War is long over, comparable campaigns are ubiquitous: the governments of the United States and the United Kingdom have just unleashed another unjustified and unsanctioned attack on Iraq. That this is no isolated aberration is seen from the fact that the United States and its allies have dropped bombs on over twenty countries since the end of the Second World War.[53] The battle against governmental abuse of power needs to be fought constantly, and Chomsky is tireless in his exposure of the latest establishment hypocrisy. In this context it is disquieting to be told that in some respects the government is not the greatest threat to individual freedom.

Chomsky has frequently pointed out that the most serious dangers inhibiting our freedom from "the curse of economic exploitation and political and social enslavement" inhere more in transnational corporations than in state governments,[54] as governments at least have some minimal accountability to an electorate. The major international companies have resources which are frequently greater than those of many states, and they use these resources to maximize profits for their directors and share-holders. In some instances this provides employment and even a reasonable standard of living for the workers in the countries where the companies locate their operations. But as is clear from the repeated movement of production to places where the wages are more and more depressed, there is a perennial risk of exploitative unemployment. Recent examples run the gamut from the manufacture of shoes or cars to the domination of the media by a small number of conglomerates, which try to put smaller rivals out of business. As a result, the income gap between the rich and the poor becomes ever wider, and less defensible. A particularly chilling example is provided by the granting of a patent to the United States Department of Agriculture and a Mississippi seed firm for a technique to sterilize seeds.[55] The idea is that the seeds produced by plants will be sterile, forcing farmers to buy new seeds from seed companies every year, rather than being able to save seed from one year's crop to replant for the next year. A more effective way of simultaneously maximizing profits for industry and poverty for the people would be hard to imagine.

The clearest statement of Chomsky's position in this debate appears in a series of articles entitled "Rollback: the return of predatory capitalism," which appeared in Z Magazine, a radical journal which "aims to assist activist efforts for a better future."[56] Here Chomsky traces the origins of the infamous "Contract with America" (Newt Gingrich's attempt to divert even more funds from the poor to the rich) to the classical capitalist theory of David Ricardo and Robert Malthus, and spells out the appalling consequences for the poor of this new form of class warfare. Both in the United States and Europe, we can see an alliance of the rich and the politically powerful trying to ensure that subsidies go to big business, while benefits to single parents or the disabled are reduced: "free enterprise is socialism for the rich: the public pays the costs and the rich get the profits."[57] This recent critique marks an extension of his traditional (and continuing) preoccupation with American foreign policy to domestic concerns – concerns which have an overwhelming, and overwhelmingly negative effect on the lives of the non-élite majority.

Such criticism is systematically negative, and Chomsky is often criticized for failing to complement his attacks on government and the capitalist establishment with positive suggestions for replacing them. This is only partly fair. He says explicitly that "I hate to give suggestions," because everyone should work things out for themselves and then act, rather than relying slavishly on someone else's authority and simply observing.[58] However, like Humboldt he has "an anarchist vision" in which "social action must be animated by a vision of a future society . . . deriv[ing] from some concept of the nature of man," and it is this vision of a fair society without gross inequalities that he tries to propagate.[59] It may sound utopian, but there have been enough successful examples to make it a rational, if not a realistic, goal: the anarcho-syndicalist movement in Spain before the Civil War; the kibbutzim in the early days of the modern state of Israel;[60] the workers' councils in the former Yugoslavia. It is not an accident that the failure of the first and the last of these was largely the effect of external repression on the part of the establishment. The possible influence of individuals in counter-balancing the might of the state and of multi-national corporations, even the influence of individuals with Chomsky's energy and stamina, may seem minuscule. Most people probably do not share Antonio Gramsci's "optimism of the will,"[61] but there is little reason to think that there is a better alternative to Chomsky's advocacy of collaboration and social activism in the pursuit of achievable ends. "Being alone, you can't do anything . . . But if you join with other people, you can make changes."[62] To further the possibility of bringing about such changes he produces a seemingly endless stream of letters and articles which appear in a bewildering array of publications from the prestigious *Index on Censorship*, to the obscure *Open Eye, Covert Action Quarterly*, and the sadly defunct *Lies of our Time*. The situation may look bleak but it is "an organizer's dream" because the scope for change is so huge.[63] Moreover, even if there is no political program to compare with his work on language, one can share his hope "that the intensive study of one aspect of human psychology – human language – may contribute to a humanistic social science that will serve, as well, as an instrument for social action."[64] One can hope, but the hope will only be realized if it is not used as an excuse for inactivity.

The Encyclopédistes

A second strand in the background of Chomsky's thinking shows that he has a clear affinity with the Encyclopédistes of the eighteenth century. The Encyclopédie, compiled under the direction of Denis Diderot with contributions from Rousseau and Voltaire, was founded on the assumption that the truth speaks for itself. If you present people with the facts they will automatically be persuaded of the truth. The assumption was perhaps naïve, but the Encyclopédie was so critical of traditional institutions and ideologies that it was condemned. Chomsky does not think the process of persuasion is so straightforward, as witness his characterization of "Orwell's problem" above, but his technique is the same, as the availability of the truth is a necessary prerequisite to establishing any kind of decent society. "I don't have faith that the truth will prevail if it becomes known, but we have no alternative to proceeding on that assumption."[65] Accordingly, what he does is "provide . . . [a] service to popular dissident movements and scattered individuals" who are trying to oppose the power of corporate propaganda and indoctrination. It is worth emphasizing again that, in the Western world, this propaganda comes not just from the state, not even mainly from the state, but from the corporate media, the entertainment industry, the public relations industry, and even the universities.[66] As the same élite is active in government, finance, education, and industry it is often hard to disentangle the various interactions between the state and the establishment. Former members of all political parties regularly, and notoriously, take up positions of power, prestige, and profit in the board-rooms of business and the senior common rooms of universities. A particularly clear example of the concentration of influence is provided by the career of Jimmy Carter. He was a founding member of the Trilateral Commission, whose support was of great significance in his successful campaign to become president. He then repaid that support by staffing the top ranks of his administration with other members of the Commission. Comparable remarks pertain even more blatantly to the Bush dynasty currently in power.

The opposition to libertarian movements is powerful and deeply entrenched, but the hope underlying Chomsky's political activism is that ultimately the standards of rationality associated with scientific endeavors (physics, linguistics, and so on), will be generalized to "ideological disciplines such as academic history and political science."[67] The hope may be slim, but there is no alternative, as it is important to remember that for those in power it is rational to attempt by any means at their disposal to preserve the inequalities that benefit them. Like so many other properties we have looked at, morality and rationality dissociate. But it is time to look at some examples of Chomsky's critical analyses.

The critique of (American) foreign policy

Chomsky is most widely known for his excoriation of the foreign policy of his native America. For four decades he has produced a series of devastating attacks on the lies, deception, inhumanity, and murderousness of the policies of the state. Central to this sustained attack is a constant emphasis on the disparity between the actions of the government and the portrayal of those actions by the official propaganda system. Corporate propaganda always emphasizes the superior moral values and benevolence of the home country. When one looks at other countries, it is easy to be dispassionate and see self-serving deception for what it is. It is somewhat harder to accept the same evaluation of one's own country. Indeed, many people are offended by the suggestion that their own country indulges in propaganda at all. "We" disseminate information; it is only "they" who peddle propaganda.[68]

The truth is harder to bear. Amnesty International produces regular reports of human rights abuses, documented by country. One expects to see catalogues of horror from Iran and Iraq, from China and the South American dictatorships. It seems appropriate that (in some years) there should be no entry for countries such as Norway or Finland.[69] It is shocking and unsettling to see several pages devoted to detailed accounts of violations by one's own country, and the immediate instinct is to disbelieve, to find excuses. At first, this is easy: the violations may not be as horrifying or as numerous as in some countries, but soon it becomes clear that this is wishful thinking. The United Kingdom is less powerful and therefore less pernicious, but the documentation of abuses by Amnesty International and by Liberty makes chilling reading: ill-treatment of prisoners, racism, the denial of rights to refugees and asylum seekers, and persistent censorship.[70] Recent examples in the United Kingdom include the abolition of the right to family reunion, the removal of welfare benefits from refugees (overturned in part by the courts), the fining of airlines for allowing refugees with inadequate documentation into the country, the redefinition of many refugees as economic migrants. None of these is catastrophic (except for the individuals immediately concerned), but taken together they result in unnecessary danger and misery for thousands of people.

The United States is both wealthier and more powerful than the United Kingdom. Its responsibilities and potential for doing good or evil are correspondingly greater. One of Chomsky's major contributions has been to provide massive documentation of the American record. The breadth of attack is awesome: it covers the whole world – from South-East Asia to South America, from East Timor to Israel, from pig farming in Haiti to the British Opium Wars of the nineteenth century. There is informed discussion in his books and articles of the situation in Angola, Argentina, Australia, Brazil, Britain, Burundi, Cambodia, Canada, Chile, Colombia, Costa Rica, Cuba, the Dominican Republic, El Salvador, France, Greece, Grenada, Guatemala, Haiti, Honduras, India, Indonesia, Iran, Iraq, Irian Jaya, Israel, Japan, Korea, Laos, Lebanon, Libya, Mexico, Namibia, Nicaragua, Panama, the Philippines, Poland, Saudi Arabia, Somalia, Syria, Thailand, Timor, Tunisia, Turkey, Uruguay, Venezuela, and above all, Vietnam. This list is not exhaustive, yet in every instance he makes reference both to the mainstream literature and to surprising and little-known sources. The Encyclopédistes would be proud of the documentation.

It is important to note that he does not restrict himself to abstract discussion. In February 2002, for instance, he went to Istanbul in support of Fatih Tas who had been arraigned before the courts on a charge of spreading separatist propaganda.[71] What Mr Tas had actually done was publish a Turkish collection of Chomsky's political essays in which he accused Turkey of "brutal repression" of the Kurds. Lawyers for the defence had asked that Chomsky be indicted as co-defendant and, although the prosecutors declined to do so, there is little doubt that his presence was the reason for Mr Tas being acquitted.

In the majority of cases his involvement is motivated by the fact that these countries have in one way or another been subverted by the United States and her allies. His concentration on perceived American evil is not due to ignorance of the evils of other countries, or to hatred of America. Rather, it is because America, as the world's only super-power, has the greatest ability to wreak destruction on its own and other peoples; and because he himself is American, and hence shares the responsibility for what is done in his name.[72] This point is particularly relevant because the greater freedom enjoyed by the privileged in the West brings with it greater responsibility to tell the truth and expose lies (the primary responsibility of intellectuals). Chomsky spells this out in his discussion of the courage of the Soviet newscaster, Vladimir Danchev, who denounced the Russian invasion of Afghanistan from his studio in Moscow.[73] A similar example is provided by the Japanese history professor Saburou Ienaga, who spent thirty-two years conducting a series of law-suits against his own government for censoring school text-books he had written.[74] The point is simple: if we in the West made remarks about Russia or Japan comparable to those made by Danchev or Ienaga, they could be dismissed as foreign hostility; if nationals of the respective countries do it, that defense is unavailable.

Comparable remarks obtain about Chomsky's critique of successive Israeli regimes. Because he is a Jew, he is expected to show loyalty to the Jewish state, and his dispassionate refusal to temper his criticisms has resulted in his being described as "anti-Semitic," or a "self-hating Jew," and has brought down a virulent tirade of opprobrium.[75] Dispassionate appraisal is regularly viewed by those sympathetic to the object of criticism as hostility. If you criticize capitalism, you must be a communist; if you object to Tory or Republican policies, you are automatically assumed to be sympathetic to the views of Socialists or Democrats. For many, it is unthinkable that you could be disinterestedly critical of both sides. As a result of this simplistic political dualism, Chomsky has been described as "outside the pale of intellectual responsibility," and attacked for the "perversity" of his views by public intellectuals and political commentators alike.[76]

Despite the universality of Chomsky's political interests, there are four areas to which he has paid particular attention: South-East Asia, especially Vietnam; Central and South America ("our little region over here" as Henry Stimson put it[77]); Israel and the Middle East; and East Timor. I will look briefly at the first and last of these: the best and least known respectively of his targets. Then, as a bridge to his dissection of domestic policy, I will give a rapid overview of his massive reaction to the events of September 11, 2001.

Vietnam

Down Orwell's memory hole. (Chomsky, 1992b: 66)

Chomsky first came to the attention of the non-academic public by virtue of his position on the war in Vietnam; he has returned to the subject repeatedly over the years and has now published thousands of pages on it.[78] From the mid 1960s he crusaded tirelessly and actively against American involvement in South-East Asia, addressing meetings, taking part in demonstrations, going to prison on several occasions, and writing innumerable articles in favor of withdrawal. In this activity he was never alone. There were other groups and individuals on the same side in the struggle between "hawks" and "doves." But there was also a crucial difference, not just that Chomsky's presentations and arguments were always backed up by monumental documentation, much of it culled from the official archives of the government he was opposing, but that his position was always a moral one. The hawks wanted to use more force and win, even if they had to destroy the country to save it (in the appalling words one officer used); the doves were afraid that the war was not winnable and that therefore the US should get out. Only a tiny minority argued that any involvement in the war was immoral and that the US should get out for that reason. Chomsky headed that minority.

He became the leader of an even smaller minority when he talked about the subsequent sanitization of history. The point he makes most forcefully is that thirty years after American withdrawal from Vietnam and half a century after the first involvement of American troops, there is no reference in official and scholarly histories of the events to the "American invasion of South Vietnam."[79] The most important event in the region's history has been expunged from the record by a sophisticated system of propaganda, documented in great detail in *Rethinking Camelot* (1993b). It is not claimed that everyone who goes along with this obfuscation of the truth is guilty of deliberate distortion or is part of a monstrous cover-up. Most are both totally sincere and unaware of being manipulated. What is most frightening and most in need of being revealed to the general public is how the limits to the debate have been distorted. The government, the media, and even academics depict the situation in terms of a polarization between hawks and doves, when on *moral* grounds both hawks and doves occupy the same end of the spectrum of choice. Chomsky cites one doveish view that "the greatest problem is that bombing huts and villages will kill civilians and push the population still further towards active support for the Vietcong."[80] That it might be inherently immoral and entirely indefensible to bomb huts and villages is not considered relevant; indeed, not even considered. The existence of a publicly sanctioned choice (like the choice between different business-oriented political parties) leads to the mistaken impression that that choice exhausts the set of viable possibilities. Chomsky's aim is to make people aware that the range of choices is dramatically more extensive and includes those made on moral, humanitarian, and libertarian grounds.

East Timor

East Timor, a former Portuguese colony, was invaded by Indonesia in December 1975 with the connivance and military support of the US government.[81] The following years saw an appalling catalogue of horrors and atrocities, resulting in the death of perhaps 10 percent of the population.[82] The scale of bloodshed decreased later but was still horrendous, with Britain providing the bulk of the weapons of destruction. Indonesia was condemned by the United Nations, and all nations were enjoined to desist from providing Indonesia with arms or support. The reaction of the US government, barely reported by the media, was to increase the supply of arms to Indonesia and to subvert the efforts of the United Nations. As the American ambassador to the UN (D. P. Moynihan) wrote in his memoirs: "The Department of State desired that the United Nations prove utterly ineffective in whatever measures it undertook. This task was given to me, and I carried it forward with no inconsiderable success."[83] Comment is superfluous.

The events described are, sadly, not unusual, but they provide an unusually clear illustration of the dual standards prevalent throughout international relations. Aggression by our allies is not aggression; what would be war crimes if perpetrated by others are concealed as aberrations or unfortunate accidents; and even the media, supposedly searching for the truth, neglect to mention unpalatable facts if they reflect badly on us.

Chomsky's work in this area is relevant on two different levels: first, in bringing to people's attention the facts of American, Australian, and British complicity in evil; second, in making people aware of the tacit collaboration of academic and media experts in this evil by failing to report that for which they had more than adequate documentation. As Chomsky writes, "The responsibility of the writer as a *moral agent* is to try to bring the truth about *matters of human significance* to *an audience that can do something about them*."[84] This third strand, stipulating that your audience should be potentially effective, has given rise to considerable vilification for Chomsky personally. He has attacked the roughly simultaneous atrocities of the Indonesians in East Timor and of the Khmer Rouge under Pol Pot in Cambodia, describing both of them as "crimes against humanity,"[85] but devoting vastly more attention to East Timor, providing extensive documentation of Western duplicity and guilt. In his discussion of each of these near genocidal campaigns, he has treated the sources with detached objectivity, pointing out, for instance, that the reports of Cambodian atrocities had been grossly exaggerated, lied about, and in some cases fabricated by the West.[86] The crucial difference between the two cases was that the crimes of the Indonesians implicated many states in the West, whereas those of the Khmer Rouge did not, and if you "ignore or justify the crimes in which [your] own state is implicated, that is criminal," and it is criminal because you could do something about it.[87] As a result Chomsky (and his co-author Ed Herman) were stigmatized as apologists for Pol Pot in a series of attacks characterized by what Milan Rai calls "a high level of dishonesty."[88] The facts are complex, the interpretations often difficult, but pointing out the lies of our leaders is not the same as advocating the cause of the victims of those lies. The significant fact that emerges is that Chomsky has uncovered a huge number of largely suppressed facts and, more significantly, embedded them in a theoretical framework which makes it clear how and why the establishment acts as it does. In an interesting coda to this issue, Chomsky points out that no one has ever objected to the fact that he and Herman also criticized those who exaggerated the crimes of the United States: "on that matter, one is allowed to call for accuracy."[89]

9–11: terrorism and the "war on terror"

> There can't be a War on Terror. It's a logical impossibility. (Chomsky, 2002i: 1; see also Chomsky, 2002g)

The attack on the World Trade Center and the Pentagon in September 2001 is widely seen as having changed the world and as being, in Chomsky's words, a "defining moment" in the annals of terrorism.[90] Two years on, the events are still reverberating around the world and serving as an excuse in numerous countries for the suppression of civil liberties in the interests of the concentration of power in the hands of the élite.[91] Chomsky has published a huge amount on the subject, most notably two books: *9–11* (2001a) and *Power and Terror* (2003b),[92] but literally dozens of other articles and chapters in books as well. His predictable reaction was encapsulated in the opening words of his paper on the aftermath of September 11: "The new millennium has begun with two monstrous crimes: the terrorist attacks of September 11, and the reaction to them, surely taking a far greater toll of innocent lives."[93] It is expected that he should characterize the events as "horrifying atrocities"; perhaps less expected that the reaction to the atrocities should be put in the same moral category.[94]

Chomsky's reaction to the episode and its aftermath epitomizes his attitudes and techniques. There is initial revulsion and horror, followed by an attempt to understand and explain the events, where this understanding involves the usual dispassionate dissection of historical causes with an even-handedness that has led to the accusation that he is an apologist for the terrorists.[95]

The reaction of horrified revulsion needs no explanation. What is surprising and depressing is that the attempt to understand why the events happened – and thereby have some chance of preventing repetitions – should be viewed as anything other than elementary sanity. Such understanding should then bring with it constraints on what might constitute a rational political response to the outrage – adhering to the rule of law or going for immediate violence.[96]

As always, Chomsky's mode of understanding is through historical contextualization, where this involves cutting through official propaganda (or 'spin' as it is euphemistically termed) and analyzing the motives of the various participants. His point of departure is the "moral truism" that you should apply the same standards to yourself as you apply to others, something which is virtually unheard of in the realpolitik that dominates the world.[97] In a sustained discussion of the double standards common in government and the media, he provides his usual dissection of cant, hypocrisy, and the manipulation of the historical record.[98]

Let's begin with the definition of "terror." Just as with "information" and "propaganda" (p. 189 above), there is an asymmetry of usage: our enemies, whether private or "rogue states," indulge in "terror"; we and our allies practise

"humanitarian intervention" to ensure "stability." There is in fact a legal definition of terrorism, one which is used for instance in US army manuals. It is
"the calculated use of violence or the threat of violence to attain goals that are
political, religious or ideological in nature . . . through intimidation, coercion
or instilling fear."[99] But if one accepts this definition (which Chomsky finds
"simple" and "appropriate") it follows that "the US itself is a leading terrorist
state."[100]

Evidence for this rather unorthodox perception comes from innumerable
sources. Perhaps the most blatant is the US reaction to the UN General Assembly
resolution in December 1987 condemning the plague of terrorism and calling
on all nations to act forcefully to overcome it.[101] The resolution passed 153–2,
with the US and Israel voting against. Equally striking is the fact that the US
was condemned by the World Court (the International Court of Justice) for the
"unlawful use of force" – i.e. international terrorism – against Nicaragua.[102]
The reaction to this was to say that the World Court had discredited itself by
making the judgment, and when the Security Council subsequently called on all
states to observe international law, the US vetoed the resolution. These events
elicited minimal comment in the mainstream US press at the time, and have
not of course been seen as relevant during more recent criticism of Iraq for its
failure to comply with UN resolutions.[103]

Such matters may seem abstract or arcane, but the implication of these attitudes, and the level of morality they reflect, is brought forcibly home by a
statement Chomsky (and others) have quoted more than once: (Secretary of
State) Madeleine Albright's remark on national TV that "a half million deaths
of Iraqi children as a result of the sanctions regime . . . were a 'hard choice' for
her administration, but . . . 'we think the price is worth it.' "[104]

It is also noteworthy that putting the events in historical context – even
though this is deemed to be "unpatriotic" – by looking at the incidence of
state-sponsored terror over the last years/ decades/ centuries – shows striking
parallels between this "war on terrorism" and the previous one (in 1985). The
war on terrorism was not declared immediately after September 11, "rather, it
was redeclared, using the same rhetoric as the first declaration twenty years
earlier" when the Reagan administration announced that a war on terrorism
would be central to US foreign policy.[105] Similarly, what was really new about
this particular terrorist attack was not "the scale of the crimes; rather the choice
of innocent victims."[106]

The double standards are "universal" – all colonial and imperialist powers
act the same way.[107] So it is not just a fact about America, it's just that (as
an American) Chomsky feels responsibility for what is done in his name and
hence the need to point out the lies. Whether you look at Japanese atrocities
against the Chinese, Israeli atrocities in Southern Lebanon, British atrocities
in India during the Raj, American attacks on countless countries from North

Korea to Nicaragua, the victims are the colonized and the atrocities take place away from the centers of "civilization." The numbers killed by those civilized countries are orders of magnitude higher than those killed in the 9–11 attacks but, by definition, these do not count as "terrorism," as terrorism is only what our enemies do. When the definition cited above is used to draw the obvious parallels the reaction is outrage or incredulity. This reaction has been repeated for at least thirty-five years, since Chomsky compared the counter-insurgency manuals used by the US army with the counter-insurgency manuals used by the Japanese in the 1930s. The reaction was that he was trying to "justify" the Japanese atrocities by comparing them to the American counter-insurgency operations in Vietnam, the tacit assumption being that whatever the Americans did must be right and just.[108] That both could be equally bad was beyond comprehension.

A similar example is provided by Chomsky's comparison of the events of 9–11 with the American attack in August 1998 on the Sudanese Al-Shifa pharmaceutical plant, probably responsible indirectly for the deaths of tens of thousands of people.[109] The justification for the attack was that the plant was supposedly producing nerve gas for use in possible terrorist attacks. Despite the fact that the US never provided any evidence for this claim, and vetoed the Sudanese suggestion that the United Nations investigate the episode, the comparison elicited outrage. The victims were not deemed to be comparable. Chomsky also draws attention to the fact that there was an explicit tie-up with al-Qaeda: shortly before the attack on Al-Shifa, Sudan had detained two men suspected of bombing American embassies in East Africa and had offered to co-operate with the US over extradition proceedings. The offer was rejected, with probably far-reaching effects, and the tie-up has been systematically air-brushed out of history.[110]

A simple lesson from much of Chomsky's political work is that the rhetoric of those in authority is seldom to be taken at face value. But even if we believed everything we were fed, it seems that our "defense of civilization" after 9–11 is rapidly descending to the same moral level as that of the terrorists. It is ironic that to defend Western values (as the usual cant goes) we have had to incarcerate over 12,000 people, denying them rights guaranteed under the Geneva Convention, and subjecting many of them to ill-treatment bordering on torture. The conditions at Guantanamo Bay are probably more severe than those in Afghanistan, where the Americans' admitted techniques of "stress and duress" are revolting and can result in the death of the victims, as at Bagram air force base.[111]

Are there any crumbs of comfort to be rescued from the catalogue of mendacity, deceit, and hypocrisy? Chomsky quotes the radical pacifist A. J. Muste as saying that "the problem after a war is with the victor. He thinks he has just proved that war and violence pay. Who will now teach him a lesson?"[112] The only crumb I can find is that public awareness of the real situation is greater than it has ever been. As a result of the anti-war movement, there was enormous popular opposition to the 2003 war on Iraq in the months before the assault began. Such opposition *before* the event has "no historical precedent" and this, together with the documentation emerging from the Hutton inquiry in Britain, may make war-mongering by the establishment somewhat harder in future.[113]

The critique of domestic policy

The primary source of evil is inequality. (Rousseau, *Observations*)

Chomsky's anarchist criticisms of governments, in particular his own government, and especially since the publication of *9–11*, are well known. His criticisms of the domestic scene are less well known, and generally less well understood. It is easy to feel moral outrage at the napalming of a Vietnamese village or the murder of Iraqi children; it is less obvious that policies on health insurance, on free trade, on fruit growing in Guatemala, or on pig farming in Haiti are of comparable iniquity.[114] Yet in many ways Chomsky sees the greatest danger for the contemporary scene in capitalism, as epitomized by transnational conglomerates. Governments are responsive to a modicum of control by the ballot box, but capitalism can operate unconstrained: "Private structures are just tyrannies."[115] In fact, it's not governments or capitalism *per se* that are bad but any "concentration of power."[116]

Chomsky's thesis over many years has been that the key to understanding the acts, as opposed to the words, of governments is to look at considerations of self-interest and power. Political power is ultimately based overwhelmingly on economic power, so the actions of governments are best interpreted in the light of their effects on the economy. To this end, government and big business form a mutually beneficial cartel. There are two basic techniques for maintaining the inequality between the rich and the poor to the advantage of the former: internationally, the government coerces subordinate regimes into giving favored treatment to foreign investors; nationally, the government raises taxes which are diverted to the support of industries rather than to the welfare of the general populace. Internationally, the coercion may be direct or indirect, subversion or invasion, but in either case the results, documented at sickening length, are appalling: consider the implications of headings such as "The economic role of terror," or the juxtaposition in a headline of "Indonesia: Mass Extermination, Investors' Paradise."[117] Nationally, there is state support of privilege in the form of tax concessions and massive subsidies to business and industry, while help is withdrawn from the poorest and those most in need, usually in combination with hypocritical rhetoric about the need for self-reliance and an avoidance of dependence on the welfare state. Herman sums it up nicely in his definition of tax reform: "Reducing taxes on business firms and the wealthy to improve their incentives to save, invest and work. These reductions can be offset by reductions in welfare expenditures and benefits to the impoverished and working poor to improve *their* incentives to work."[118]

It is impressive that Chomsky has a vision of the world in which apparently arbitrary and meaningless details make sense because they fit into an overall framework. His command of facts and figures on the international scene is remarkable; his range on the domestic front is no less telling and inclusive. Looking through a few of his books and articles I came across discussions of: advertising, authority and the family, birth control, blasphemy, capitalism, capital punishment, class and class warfare, drugs, the demise of the *Daily Herald*, Darwin and language, religious fundamentalism, Gandhi, greeting cards, gun control, miracles, nuclear power, the Opium Wars, organic food, Queen Elizabeth, racism, sports, Tolstoy's novels, Yeltsin, and Zionism. Any of these would serve for the purposes of illustration, but I will look at just two examples.

Pig farming in Haiti

In the symbolically entitled *Year 501*,[119] Chomsky describes how the US initiated a program to slaughter the entire stock of Haitian pigs. The motivation was fear that swine fever in the neighboring Dominican Republic might threaten the US pig industry. By the time the program began to be implemented, there was no trace of the disease in Haiti, but the pigs were still killed, even though they constituted the basis of the peasant economy. Replacement pigs were provided from Iowa, but only to those peasants who could afford to feed and house them according to US specifications. Unlike the original hardy pigs these ones often succumbed to disease or could survive only on expensive feed. The result was an economic catastrophe for the peasants, but considerable profits for the ruling Haitian clique and, of course, for the US pig industry. In the scale of atrocities this does not count very high; Haiti itself had seen far grimmer effects of US power in the form of occupation by the marines in support of American business, but the episode is symptomatic of the overwhelming importance of economic considerations in the determination of policy, and of the interpretation of unlikely facts as evidence for his thesis by Chomsky.

Haiti is not an isolated example: traditional (and highly successful) modes of rice farming in Liberia were destroyed by the imposed transition to plantation cash crops. The accumulated wisdom of the Kpelle was treated with "irrational disdain" as part of a process which was of great benefit to Western agribusiness and the petrochemical industry, but which tended to ruin indigenous culture, and impoverished the rich genetic pool of rice varieties.[120] In Guatemala, the governments of Arévalo and Arbenz attempted to introduce agrarian reform and expropriate land held by the (American) United Fruit Company.[121] These moves were stigmatized as "communist," the CIA engineered a coup in 1954, and Guatemala entered on a period of gruesome repression which continues, under American protection, decades later, with the loss of life running into tens, if not hundreds, of thousands.

Drug trafficking[122]

Governments in the West, both in America and elsewhere, target drug trafficking as a major problem facing society. In *Deterring Democracy* (1991a) Chomsky puts this in perspective from four different points of view. First, substance abuse is a serious problem, but the substances whose abuse leads to the greatest misery are alcohol and tobacco. In the USA, the estimate of deaths from these drugs was about 400,000 per year, roughly 100 times more than the deaths from the targeted drugs. Indeed, the targeted drugs include marijuana, which has never been identified as the cause of any deaths. The Clinton administration finally began to take apparently stringent measures against the tobacco industry, but the main effect of this was to increase exports to the third world, as had already happened with regard to Thailand and Japan, and which was characterized by the US Surgeon General in the following terms: "when we are pleading with foreign governments to stop the flow of cocaine, it is the height of hypocrisy for the US to export tobacco."[123] The hypocrisy is seen to be blatant when it is realized that these exports are backed by the threat of trade sanctions to force East Asian markets to accept American tobacco and by advertising aimed at "emerging markets."[124] Echoes of the British role in the Opium Wars of the nineteenth century are striking, and a good indication of the consistency of policy: "free trade" is invoked as justification in the one case as in the other. It may be objected that the statistics cited are misleading, in that the relevant figures for victims of substance abuse should pertain not to the entire population, but to the number of users. With something like half the population admitting to experimentation with cannabis, even this corrective would do little to change the balance and, more importantly, would have no implications for the other aspects of the issue.

The second strand to the drug debate is more sinister: fear of drug trafficking is used as a substitute for the communist menace as a pretext for sending financial and military help to client regimes. When Colombia asked the US government to install a radar system to enable them to intercept drug traffickers on its southern border, the request was granted, but the installation was placed where its only function was to monitor Nicaragua and the Sandinistas.[125] The effect on the drugs trade was minimal, the potential for the subversion of another state was considerable.

Thirdly, the drug menace is used as a means of social control. The drug budget is financed in part at the expense of social welfare programs. Increases in homelessness and unemployment lead to despair and a reliance on drugs to make life tolerable, yet most of the drug budget is devoted to law enforcement rather than to educational programs, or to attacking the financial institutions that benefit from the money laundering that the drug trade brings with it. As Chomsky remarks, "the banking industry is not a proper target for the drug war."[126] Similar remarks apply to the chemical companies: 90 percent of the chemicals used to produce cocaine originate from companies in the US, but these companies, involved in the production of pharmaceuticals and fertilizers (not to mention defoliants), are off limits because they are essential for "national security";[127] that is, they are part of the economic establishment, and hence protected.

Fourth, and perhaps most significant, is the evidence that the "free press" systematically swallows and propagates the government line, rather than drawing its readers' attention to the duplicities of the drugs policy. Again this is not surprising, as the free press constitutes part of the same privileged big business that stands to gain from government policy.

This reaction to governmental and business activities may seem paranoid and, if it was limited to a single event, it could justifiably be interpreted as irrational. This is why the massive documentation that Chomsky goes in for is so important. One could believe that one or two examples of establishment skulduggery were aberrations or mistakes. When one has read a hundred such examples the rational skepticism one applies to the propaganda exercises of our enemies or third world dictators begins to take over, and one sees that one's own political and industrial élite are no different from any others. On this morning's radio there was a news item about how prisons (in England) convert those who are not drug users into addicts.[128] Sadly, it fits all too well.

This leads naturally to an area to which Chomsky has devoted much of his political activism: the role, and control, of the media.

The critique of media control

A recent pamphlet has the title *Media Control: the Spectacular Achievements of Propaganda*.[129] In it Chomsky outlines the role of the media in disseminating propaganda throughout the twentieth century. In comparison with his monumental compilations with Ed Herman it is a slight document, and it contains no references, but it encapsulates the bases of his position in an accessible form.[130] The usual view of the press in the West is that it is to a large extent independent, progressive, outspoken, subversive of authority . . . in a word "free." Against this comforting view he and Herman juxtapose their "propaganda model" which suggests that the "purpose of the media is to inculcate and defend the economic, social, and political agenda of privileged groups that dominate the domestic society and the state."[131]

Chomsky and Herman discuss their model in terms of five filters which "narrow the range of news" that becomes accessible to the public, blocking the aspirations of the weak and the poor, and conspiring to guarantee that the media propagate the views of big business under whose control they remain.[132] The first of these filters is the need for huge investment to set up and run newspapers or television channels that can reach any appreciable proportion of the population. Although there are literally thousands of newspapers, only a small minority of these has influence outside a narrow local or specialist domain, and this minority is under the control of a small group of families and corporations. The second filter comes from the power of advertising revenue to promote or cripple a particular paper or channel. In England, the demise of the working-class *Daily Herald* was "in large measure a result of progressive strangulation by lack of advertising support." The third filter arises from the fact that the source of much news is determined by government and corporate organizations, which may have many thousands of employees dedicated to providing appropriate material. A striking example is provided by their documentation of the "public-information outreach" of the US Air Force, which included no fewer than 140 newspapers.[133] The fourth filter is the ability of the government and its subsidiaries to produce what Chomsky and Herman call "flak": any criticism is met by negative responses in the form of letters, phone calls, petitions, and not infrequently, litigation against the critics, for all of which considerable resources are required. The propaganda model was devised fifteen or more years ago, yet all these constraints still hold. There was some hope that the World Wide Web might subvert at least some of the monopolistic tendencies of the mainstream media, until it was handed over to private power in 1995, and even now, the task of ensuring (voluntary) censorship is much harder than it is with the traditional media.[134] The expression "voluntary" may seem odd, but Chomsky has frequently observed that the greatest danger to freedom comes from "self-censorship": the mind-set of the majority is such that external censorship is unnecessary.[135] To become a successful journalist or academic, you have to absorb the values of those in power and jump through the hoops provided by the establishment. Once you have done this, external suppression is no longer needed. In fact, citing Orwell's long suppressed introduction to *Animal* Farm, he elsewhere describes "the whole educational and professional training system [as] a very elaborate filter, which just weeds out people who are too independent."[136] The final filter, the ideology of anti-communism, whereby any opponent of the establishment could be put beyond the pale by being labeled "communist" is no longer operative because of the downfall of the Soviet Union. Instead, opponents of the establishment risk being tarred with any other handy brush – lending support to terrorism or narco-trafficking – so that their influence is correspondingly diminished.

To illustrate the workings of the model I take two of Herman and Chomsky's examples: the press's reaction to different murders, and its coverage of elections in various third world countries. Before doing so, it is perhaps worth mentioning that an appropriate rational reaction to the propaganda model would be to disbelieve it. As I am sympathetic to many of Chomsky's ideas in areas where I have some knowledge, I'm likely to take on trust what he says in areas of which I am ignorant. Life is too short to check all the references he and Herman cite, but I took a hundred at random and spent two days in the library verifying their accuracy. There were some sources which the University College London library doesn't hold, but in those it does I found no misrepresentation. There is still room for different interpretations of the data, but the facts are accurate.[137]

Murder

Some victims are worthy, some are unworthy, depending on one's point of view. Herman and Chomsky use their propaganda model to explain the different reactions of the press to the murder of a Polish priest, Jerzy Popiełuszko, by the Polish police in 1984, and the murder of a hundred priests over a period of sixteen years in Latin America.[138] The crucial difference is that Poland was at that time an enemy, communist, state; the relevant countries of Latin America were entirely within the United States sphere of influence. As predicted, the coverage was uneven, both quantitatively and qualitatively. Popiełuszko's death was highlighted in considerable detail and the case was used as a point of departure for a sustained attack on the government of a police state. In contrast, the murders of victims in South America, including a national figure in the Salvadoran church, Rutilio Grande, were scarcely mentioned, and certainly elicited no outpouring of condemnation. Even the murder in 1980 of Archbishop Oscar Romero, a vocal opponent of the American-backed Salvadoran government, elicited only muted reaction.[139] Herman and Chomsky devote some fifty pages to documenting the differences and following up the implications of the cases. Whatever one's sympathies in the case of the particular examples chosen, it is hard to disagree with the conclusion to another of Chomsky's books that, if we are to protect ourselves from manipulation, "there can be no more urgent task than to come to understand the mechanisms and practices of indoctrination."[140]

Third world elections

Just as the propaganda model predicts the differential treatment of worthy and unworthy victims, so also does it predict that the coverage of elections in the third world will depend crucially on whether the countries involved are our clients or our enemies. In the former case, the elections – whatever happens – will be taken to legitimize the power structure; in the latter case, whatever happens, they will be taken to be meaningless.[141] A paradigm example of the contrast is provided by the elections in 1984 in El Salvador and Nicaragua. Both countries were in turmoil, but El Salvador was a protégé of the United States, whereas Nicaragua was under the Sandinista government that the Reagan administration was attempting to overthrow.

As expected, the media coverage was distorted. In Nicaragua, voting was not obligatory and the election was seen by independent European observers as generally free. In El Salvador, voting was obligatory, and the voters were widely seen as subject to military intimidation. In American press accounts these facts were largely ignored. More generally, reports in the mainstream press emphasized problems of disruption by rebels and dissidents in El Salvador and described the mechanics of the election in detail, ignoring the fact that the disruption was largely the result of terror from the ruling junta. In Nicaragua, the reverse scenario obtained: emphasis was laid on the parlous state of the country and little mention was made of the attempts by the (rather popular) government to ensure a genuinely secret ballot. Again, Herman and Chomsky provide detailed statistical analyses in support of their conclusions. If they are correct, the results are disturbing and unpalatable, even "unthinkable" according to one American friend. Unthinkable or not, the evidence is now available for discussion. Again, as predicted by the model they are proposing, the safest reaction is to ignore what they say, in the hope that their message will die from lack of exposure. It is not an accident that academic discussion of the model is minimal.[142]

The treason of the intellectuals

> What I find terrifying is the detachment and equanimity with which we view and discuss an unbearable tragedy. (Chomsky, 1969a: 294)

In 1927 Julien Benda published a book, *Le Trahison des clercs* (*The Treason of the Intellectuals*), in which he denounced as moral traitors those who betray truth and justice for racial or political considerations. Its theme is close to that of Chomsky's first political essay, entitled "The responsibility of intellectuals," and it is a theme which has been central to his work ever since.[143] That responsibility is twofold: to tell the truth (and, as a corollary, to uncover the lies of those in power) and to modulate one's behavior in terms of the foreseeable consequences of one's actions. There is nothing very profound in these injunctions and, as Rai points out, they are hardly the foundation of a political or ideological theory but, if obeyed, they color the whole of one's life.[144] More to the point, the common failure to obey them leads to a servility to power which amounts to a form of prostitution.

One expects politicians to lie in the perceived interests of their country or party (the English politician William Waldegrave became notorious for saying as much explicitly[145]), and it is something of a truism that "States are not moral agents."[146] One expects better of the intellectual, academic community, and Chomsky deploys some of his most savage venom against those who "murder history" in the interests of their government and their own feelings of moral virtue, not to mention their own prestige and economic advantage.[147]

A characteristic example is provided by his dissection of historian Arthur Schlesinger's claim that "human rights is replacing self-determination as the guiding value in American foreign policy."[148] This was written against a background including the war in Indo-China, the intervention in Indonesia alluded to above, and a series of repressive forays in Guatemala, Chile, and Cuba. The hypocrisy becomes stark when Chomsky continues by quoting a memorandum that Schlesinger had presented to J. F. Kennedy when he was adviser to the president shortly before the abortive Bay of Pigs invasion in 1961. The document reveals details of how "it would be necessary to lie about the Bay of Pigs invasion," of who should tell the lies, of what answers the president should give, and so on *ad nauseam*. The question of the right of the Cubans to self-determination was an irrelevance, yet Schlesinger was a distinguished historian helping not only to mold public opinion but documenting affairs of state for posterity. If even academics lie there is little hope.

The technique of dissection

The vile maxim of the masters of mankind. (Chomsky, 1993b: 9)

Chomsky's major analytic technique is the classic academic's accumulation of massive documentation, relying both on standard references and on sources that are frequently ignored by mainstream commentators and historians. A glance at his bibliographies is startling: a page chosen at random from *Deterring Democracy* cites reports from *Pax Christi* Netherlands; *Colombia Update*; the Guatemala Human Rights Commission; Amnesty International, as well as mainstream sources such as academic books, the *Wall Street Journal*, the *Boston Globe*, and so on. Even with the mainstream press the quotations selected are unsettling: in this case the "Unsettling Specter of Peace" (from the *Wall Street Journal*) with its implication that only conditions of war are favorable to big industry.[149] Together with this esoteric coverage goes a talent for uncovering official statements which are tantamount in many cases to admissions of guilt. For instance, Chomsky has frequently cited NSC68 (National Security Council Memorandum number 68 from 1950) and PPS23 (Policy Planning Study number 23 from 1948), which talk of the need to "overcome the 'excess of tolerance' that allows too much domestic dissent," or "unreal objectives such as human rights," as opposed to the realizable objective of maintaining the situation in which the United States had "about 50% of the world's wealth, but only 6.3% of its population."[150]

This documentation is allied with a use of irony which has become more and more savage over the years. Chomsky has always had a taste for irony in his linguistic work. For instance, in an early discussion of Robert Dixon's claim that *milk* and *white* would be likely to co-occur in British culture, he writes: "The high probability of the phrase 'white milk' in normal British English was a fact unknown to me before reading this."[151] A mildly sardonic attack of that kind is inadequate for the description of political activity. The behavior of government is often so appalling that it evokes an anguished and shocking response which speaks of "superficial atrocities" and "benign bloodbaths," of "mere genocide," and on and on.[152] His technique of dissection can usefully be looked at under a variety of heads.

The exposure of warped perspective

Treason doth never prosper: what's the reason?
For if it prosper, none dare call it treason.
Sir John Harrington (1561–1612), On Treason

I have remarked above on Chomsky's refutation of the standard, perhaps universal, assumption that we are virtuous and our enemies are vicious. The clearest case of a disparity in perspective is provided by the repeatedly documented observation that, depending on the identity of the perpetrator, two apparently identical acts can be viewed as war crimes or as unfortunate errors. In Jim Peck's *Chomsky Reader*, there is documentation of how, in South Vietnam, activities such as destroying dikes to cause starvation, which were deemed illegal at Nuremberg, were admitted brazenly by the Pentagon and the administration.[153] Similarly, the bombardment of Laos in the 1960s and 1970s, the most intensive aerial attack in history, with two tons of high explosive dropped for every man, woman, and child in the country, was described by the *New York Times* as being aimed mainly at "the rebel economy and social fabric."[154] What is most chilling is that, as Chomsky remarks, there was no public reaction to this appalling claim, which "sets American policy at the moral level of Nazi Germany."[155]

The example of warped perspective that Chomsky has most frequently cited, and for which he has been repeatedly attacked, is the contrast between the Western-supported Indonesian rape of East Timor, and the atrocities committed by the Khmer Rouge in Cambodia.[156] For Chomsky, the crucial point is that the West could have affected the situation in East Timor, but instead lent its support to a tyrannous client regime, whereas the atrocities in Cambodia were committed by an official enemy, over whom we had little if any control. The usual stance of any normal person is to attack one's enemies and support one's friends. But this is an amoral, and potentially immoral, stance which should be resisted by the "responsible intellectual": "our country right or wrong" is a fundamentally evil doctrine.[157] A perennial point that Chomsky makes is that inveighing against the official enemy is generally pointless: it will have no material effect. We take minimal notice of enemy propaganda, and can usually ignore it even when it is true. Exposing the lies and attacking the immoral actions of one's own side by contrast *may* have some effect, and is therefore an undertaking worth attempting. Such criticisms may not bring rewards at home, indeed they will often bring hostility and outrage, but it is at least possible that they will be effective.

The most striking instances of warped perspective can be seen, as in Orwell's *1984*, when friends and enemies change their roles. Examples are legion: before the Gulf War Saddam Hussein was supported despite his appalling human rights record, but this record was used as a major justification for the war after Iraq threatened Western oil interests by invading Kuwait;[158] Manuel Noriega, despite his known involvement in the drugs trade, was supported and even kept on the CIA payroll, because he was useful in the war against Nicaragua. He "stole" both the elections of 1984 and 1989 in comparable fashion: on the first occasion he was supported and praised; on the second, he was vilified and the way was prepared for the invasion of December 1989. The reasons for such volte-face are equally striking: in case after case it is because the henchman has asserted his independence from the boss: "It's all quite predictable, as study after study shows. A brutal tyrant crosses the line from admirable friend to 'villain' and 'scum' when he commits the crime of independence."[159]

To finish this section, let me quote another startling but common-sense observation. The Japanese attack on Pearl Harbor has been a symbol of monstrous evil for over sixty years: it is "the day that will live in infamy" to use the standard cliché. There are interesting questions about whether the West knew in advance of the impending attack, but Chomsky observes simply: "one would have to search diligently for a discussion of the proper rank, in the scale of atrocities, of an attack on a naval base in a US colony that had been stolen from its inhabitants by force and guile just 50 years earlier." The previous colonial status of Hawaii and its mode of acquisition are not usually mentioned.[160]

The exposure of suppressed precursor events

One of the most obvious, but frequently most striking, techniques of Chomsky's political writing is the way he draws attention to what is omitted: to "Hamlet without the Prince of Denmark," as he puts it.[161] To begin, consider an event in the Vietnam war.

In August 1964 the US Destroyer *Maddox* was attacked in the Tonkin Gulf by the North Vietnamese. The incident was denounced as an "unprovoked armed attack" and was later used as justification for escalation of the war and the Gulf of Tonkin Resolution. What was suppressed, but was admitted much later in US government papers, was that "The North Vietnamese are reacting defensively to our attacks . . ."[162] In the context, the fact of such attacks does bear mentioning.

The discussion of these events, and the exposure of their suppressed precursors, is part of a systematic attempt on Chomsky's part to prevent the perversion of the historical record on a grander scale: namely, the attempt to heroize Kennedy by suggesting that he was secretly attempting to withdraw from Vietnam and was assassinated for his pains.[163] As a result of Oliver Stone's film *JFK*, this interpretation of history is becoming standard. Chomsky's *Rethinking Camelot* is a book-length attempt to ensure that all the relevant information is taken into account (or is at least available), showing that there is essentially no evidence for the claim that Kennedy ever deviated significantly from the war policies of his predecessors.

Comparable examples could, as always, be multiplied. As always, Chomsky has provided the documentation. The Israeli invasion of Lebanon in 1982 was officially justified in the United States by reference to Lebanese and PLO terrorism, ignoring the repeated attacks by Israel of the previous years.[164] Members of the peace movement in Germany who demonstrated against an extension of Frankfurt airport were vilified in the *New York Times Magazine* for their irrational and Hitlerite belief that the extension was part of a NATO–United States plot. As Chomsky pointed out, the main function of the extension was admitted to be "to increase the military potential of the airport, which is used by United States Air Force units assigned to the North Atlantic Treaty Organization." This was not deemed worthy of mention in the original article.[165]

The exposure of debased language

Semantic hygiene. (Chomsky, 1996a: 218)

The area where Chomsky's professional expertise as a linguist might best be expected to help his political analysis is in the exposure of cant. While it is true that he brings his customary penetration to the subject, it is not significantly different from, for instance, Herman's deadly serious update of Ambrose Bierce.[166] As he emphasizes repeatedly, in areas of this kind you need not technical expertise but common sense and healthy skepticism. Again, however, it is illuminating to cite some examples.

As we have seen, there is a long tradition of using the term "communists" to refer to any regime opposed to Western political or business interests, but the usage is even worse than appears at first sight.[167] Chomsky quotes a State Department report which uses the term explicitly to refer to those who believe that "the government has direct responsibility for the welfare of the people," and a judgment to the effect that the primary threat of communism is the economic transformation of the countries concerned "in ways which reduce their willingness and ability to complement the industrial economies of the West." That is, the underlying rationale is, as usual, economic, and the means used to secure assent to policies which would otherwise look barbaric, involves perverting the language to hoodwink the voting majority. By contrast the "free world" is used to refer to us and our friends, even when they happen to be sadistic dictators of the kind found in several South American republics. One is reminded of the habit of the satellites of the Soviet Union including "democratic" or "free" in their names.

Similar subtlety is used in the distinct terminology used for identical actions by our friends and our enemies. With a panache of which Orwell would have been proud, we designate as "terror" or "terrorism" what our enemies perpetrate, but what we do is "retaliation" or "legitimate pre-emptive strikes to prevent terrorism," or occasionally "counter-terror."[168] In *Pirates and Emperors* (2002a), Chomsky devotes considerable space to the definition and redefinition of "terrorism" as it pertains to the weak and the powerful respectively. We expect there to be one law for the rich and another for the poor; it is slightly more surprising to find that difference enshrined in the choice of vocabulary.

Another favored ploy of even liberal politicians is to coin euphemistic or meaningless neologisms to disguise what is going on. A striking example is Adlai Stevenson's characterization of the self-defence of the Vietnamese as "internal aggression"; while any form of "unwelcome internal political development" is labeled "subversion."[169] By contrast, when our allies indulge in the same behavior, it is called "preventing the spread of violence" or ensuring "stability." Kissinger's doctrine of establishing "stable regimes" in Latin America meant regimes sympathetic to America, not to their own peasants.[170]

South Vietnam, of course, provides the best example of all. If the Soviet Union "invaded" Afghanistan – and "an invader is an invader unless invited in by a government with a claim to legitimacy" as the *Economist* put it[171] – then the US "invaded" Vietnam in 1962 (and escalated the war in 1965). But, as discussed above, it is "inconceivable" that we in the West could be aggressors and could have "invaded" the country: we "defended" the Vietnamese against aggression, even if that aggression was "internal." Once one begins to observe the propaganda carefully, the twisted vocabulary becomes transparent: "peace" and the "peace process" are whatever our side wants and works for; "moderates" are those who do our bidding; a fight to save jobs usually means a fight to save profits and may in fact entail the loss of many jobs.[172] *Caveat lector.*

Moral absolutes and options for the future

I disapprove of what you say, but I will defend to the death your right to say it. (Attributed, apocryphally, to Voltaire)

Freedom of speech is for Chomsky close to an absolute, and he would certainly endorse Voltaire's aphorism, but for good reason he is careful to adopt a more subtle position: "I doubt that there are moral absolutes. Life's too complicated, and moral principles aren't an axiom system."[173] Where freedom of speech exists, the choice of exercising it must be made responsibly, as the effects of your choices are always the most important consideration. Chomsky puts it rather starkly in the words: "Either you're a moral monster or you'll ask the question, What are the consequences of what I do?"[174] Freedom of speech is not always self-evidently an unmixed blessing, and must be used with caution.

The Faurisson affair

The morass of insane rationality. (Chomsky, 1969a: 11)

The trouble with moral imperatives is that they rely ultimately on a non-rational base. To a liberal American or European, it may seem self-evident that freedom of speech should be defended: "I support the right of people to say whatever horrendous things they like," and that any claim to circumscribe such freedom must be argued for: "any form of authority requires justification," in Chomsky's words.[175] These beliefs were at the root of his widely quoted and much criticized defense of the French historian Robert Faurisson, who was convicted of "falsification of history" for denying *inter alia* that the gas chambers existed.[176] Faurisson is a professor of history whose research led him to question the existence of gas chambers in Nazi Germany and to doubt the Holocaust. What apparently preoccupied him was inconsistency in the details of contemporary reports, and he used these putative inconsistencies to question the truth of the events as a whole. Chomsky's own attitude to such works on the Holocaust had been stated years earlier: they are beneath contempt, as is shown by his remark about "the morass of insane rationality" that attends any discussion of the details of such evil, and that by "entering the arena of argument and counter-argument . . . by accepting the legitimacy of debate . . . one has already lost one's humanity."[177] Elsewhere, he says quite categorically that "the conclusions of standard Holocaust studies are taken simply as established fact."[178] Nonetheless, people should be allowed to say or write whatever they wish to. Accordingly he first signed a petition in favor of freedom of speech, specifically on behalf of Faurisson (about whom and whose work he claimed to "know very little"), and then wrote a short memoir on the "distinction between supporting somebody's beliefs and their right to express them."[179] This memoir was published as the preface to Faurisson's *Mémoire en défense contre ceux qui m'accusent de falsifier l'histoire: La question des chambres à gaz.*[180] This defense of freedom of speech unleashed a series of vitriolic diatribes against Chomsky, many of them hysterical in tone. Even some of his supporters were alienated by the upsurge of hostility, and feared that he had seriously damaged his own position. Barsky, who is overwhelmingly sympathetic to Chomsky, says that "the Faurisson affair does tend to throw some of Chomsky's character flaws into relief, most clearly his unwillingness to practice simple appeasement."[181] But this seems exactly wrong. As Chomsky says elsewhere: "You do not compromise a serious principle."[182] If there is a basis for criticizing his actions in the Faurisson affair it is, I think, rather that, as one has a moral responsibility for the foreseeable consequences of one's actions, Chomsky should perhaps have foreseen the negative effect of his actions and refrained from writing the way he did. Perhaps, but on balance perhaps not. Even had he foreseen the furore which would erupt and the degree of alienation that would ensue, the moral doctrine of defending freedom of speech is probably higher. Whatever the decision, a corollary of any absolutist defense of freedom of speech is that you combat perceived distortions of the truth with equally forthright refutations of the lies: speaking out on every possible occasion, so that your position does not lose out by default. In this spirit Chomsky addresses innumerable meetings and writes endless letters, using the kind of massive documentation that has characterized all of his work (political, psychological, philosophical) throughout his career.

Islamic fundamentalism

Comparable dilemmas surface all the time. There has been much discussion of the case of Hizb-ut-Tahrir, a fundamentalist Islamic organization opposed to the state of Israel, to homosexuality, to feminism, and to anything which might oppose (their particular brand of) Islam.[183] Their positions are based on a strongly held belief in the correctness of Islam and the authority of a certain interpretation of the Qur'an. Those beliefs are for them moral absolutes, just as freedom of speech is absolute for others. These different "categorical imperatives" lead inevitably to incompatible outcomes. Once one accepts a particular kind of authority, other choices are necessarily foreclosed. If that authority is divine the loss of choice may seem acceptable, if only to the hierophants.

In deciding what attitude to adopt to a framework of ideas at radical variance with one's own, it is usual to draw a distinction between documentation (including the exposure of lies) and propaganda (including incitement to violence).[184] It is not always easy to distinguish the two, but the difference is sufficiently clear to have been enshrined in law, in that (in England) the former is generally legal, while incitement to violence is illegal. Similarly in the USA freedom of speech has been protected, apart from "incitement to imminent lawless action," ever since a Supreme Court decision of 1969, which drew what Chomsky calls "a reasonable line."[185] Identifying which side of that line a particular example of intolerance comes is not easy, but the moral and legal end-points are clear enough. He is quoted as saying that Marx was correct in "using the resources and in fact the liberal values of the civilization that he was trying to overcome, against it."[186] It follows that Hizb-ut-Tahrir, for example, is right – according to its own lights – in using our (somewhat diluted) toleration of their right to say what they like in an attempt to remove that right from us, and impose Islamic conformism. A characteristic expression of their view can be found in an attack on Salman Rushdie which includes the explicit remark: "we never claim that something called free speech exists in Islam."[187] At this stage we are faced with what Thomas Nagel calls "a battle of world views, which must be fought out at ground level."[188] In a domain where unanimity is not possible, that is, where moral or ethical claims are incapable of achieving universality because of differences of sincerely held belief, there are no rational grounds for accepting – or denying – freedom of speech as an absolute. I think this pessimistic conclusion is too strong, as the divine basis supporting views in conflict with freedom of speech is itself irrational. The same problem may nonetheless arise with less invidious forms of authority of which this is perhaps not true.

Authority

Most of the discussions of such ethical problems are couched in a framework which, implicitly or explicitly, accepts the validity of authority – state authority, religious authority, moral authority – and are attempts to provide support for, or reasons to dissent from, that authority. As an anarchist, Chomsky doesn't accept that right to authority, and part of the basis of his anarchism is precisely revulsion at the idea of subjection to state power, rational or irrational. Paternalist justifications of authority (of the sort that have underpinned the class system of the West for centuries) are anathema, except when they are really paternalist: "I think you can give an argument that you shouldn't let a three-year-old run across the street. That's a form of authority that's justifiable. But there aren't many of them . . ."[189]

Chomsky's radical rejection of authority in all its forms extends to himself. He is often asked by questioners to tell them what to do, whether on matters of personal commitment or political activity. His almost unfailing response is to say: "I don't give advice," to say there's no reason why his "personal reactions . . . should interest anyone."[190] The cult of personality is entirely alien to him. This is not to say that he shows any false modesty: he clearly feels that it would make sense for the burden of political activism, or the task of popularizing linguistics, to be more widely distributed, so he could spend more time on academic work. There are things that he can do in these areas that no one else can, whereas many tasks could perhaps be carried out as effectively by anyone with the time and motivation to take them on. His response could also be viewed as a little ingenuous: people need guidance; life is too short to question every law or challenge every institution, and most of us need role models. To reconcile these observations one needs to distinguish the provision of factual information as a basis for letting people come to decisions, and the idea that someone who provides such information thereby obtains some authority over what should be done with it. The former is a duty, the latter is an unjustifiable additional assumption, though there is little doubt that Chomsky is including himself among "those who hope to act constructively to change [the world] for the better" as he put it.[191] His position is closest to that of Alexander Herzen who observed that "we do not proclaim a new goal, but we expose the old lies."

The positive program

He nonetheless makes it obvious what he thinks people should do in general terms: they should take whatever issue moves and motivates them, get together with like-minded friends and colleagues, whether these are in unions, workers' committees, information systems, political clubs, or whatever, and work by individual activism for whatever cause they feel strongly about. The emphasis on co-operation is pervasive in his political writing as in his discussion of linguistics and academic work more generally. "Poor people and suffering people can only defend themselves against power . . . by working together." Similarly he says "there has not in history ever been any answer other than, Get to work on it."[192] On the academic side, he regularly insists on the co-operative nature of the enterprise that he and his colleagues and students are engaged in, and his own work obviously feeds off the contributions of colleagues around the world. He describes his own political role in the terms I quoted above: "What I'm trying to do is simply provide the kind of service to popular dissident movements and scattered individuals that any person who has the resources, the privilege, the training, etc. should perform."[193] Very similar remarks would apply to his work in linguistics, though the notion of service makes less sense here because of his unique domination of the field.

Practical applications of Chomsky's work are not obvious. Given that he has revolutionized our thinking about language and human nature, it is surprising that there is little spin-off in education. One might expect that his ideas on language acquisition would have implications for second language teaching, that his ideas on the nature of language would reverberate in therapy for aphasic stroke victims. There have been forays into both these and other fields by practitioners influenced by Chomsky, but there is no Chomskyan school of language teaching or speech therapy, just as there is no Chomskyan political party. To ask for either would be to misunderstand the nature of his achievement, which is about understanding and explanation rather than applications and implementation. Implications enough arise from an understanding of his work: language instruction and language therapy are more likely to be effective if they are founded on an accurate description of language but, as with Descartes or Galileo, applications are indirect. Despite this his scientific work has changed the way we see ourselves, and his political work has woken up tens of thousands of people to the realities of power. Most importantly, he has shown us a means of intellectual self-defense.

Conclusion

No-one has ever said it better than Gramsci . . . "you should have pessimism
of the intellect and optimism of the will."   (Chomsky, 1992b: 354)

By any criterion Chomsky's achievement is vast. As the guiding spirit of the
cognitive revolution, he has been instrumental in changing our view not just of
language but of human nature. He has tamed the infinite complexity of language,
and in doing so has given us a new appreciation of what we owe to the hand
of nature and what we owe to the environment. He has done it through insight,
through fanatical hard work and by devoting his efforts to problems rather than
mysteries.[1] The problems have come in different forms: some, like I-language,
are amenable – when suitably dissected – to theoretical discussion; others,
like politics, require not so much a theory as the dispassionate application of
common sense in the scrutiny and presentation of the facts. Solving any of them
requires dedication.

By contrast, there are mysteries where neither of these techniques appears
to work. The creativity of genius, the everyday problem of free will, even
the apparently banal Cartesian problem of what causes our particular use of
language on given occasions, all seem still to lie beyond the reach of our
intellect. Chomsky has had little to say on these areas, where agnosticism is
the only rational position to adopt, but even here he has clarified the issues
by drawing the relevant distinctions and by proposing a framework for the
debate.

In some cases he has also raised the prospect of transferring particular phenomena from the status of "mysteries" to "problems." The most obvious such
area is the evolution of language that, because of the difficulty of getting relevant
evidence, had long seemed inscrutable.[2] For many years Chomsky suggested
that we could say little of interest beyond the truism that language is the result
of evolution, but his recent work with Hauser and Fitch, building on a massive
cross-disciplinary base, has begun to shed light here too. A related example
comes in his latest preoccupation with the question of how "perfect" language

is as a solution to the problem of linking sound and meaning. A few years ago such questions could not even be posed and it is not yet clear whether they can be convincingly answered.

What is clear is that after half a century of research he still has the power to surprise, pushing explanations ever deeper. Chomsky is no ordinary genius.[3]

Envoi

Chomsky has created, and for fifty years has dominated, the field of modern linguistics. Working in this field, he has revealed the amazing complexity of human languages but at the same time has provided striking evidence that there is really only one language, and that it is largely innate. He has demolished the behaviorist framework that guided research in psychology, he has restored the mind to its previous position of Cartesian eminence and he has challenged traditional philosophical thinking on what constitutes human knowledge. In passing, he provided new impetus to mathematical linguistics, and stimulated debate in fields as disparate as education and anthropology, stylistics and immunology. And he has done this while devoting the majority of his time to political activism, engaging in a relentless struggle against the lies of government and the evils of concentrated power. To do this he talks and writes to every conceivable audience – from the House of Representatives to rap-metal bands, from academics in Western universities to prosecuting magistrates in Turkey.[1]

Chomsky doesn't believe in heroes, but it is not surprising that for many he has become one. And there can be little disagreement that he has fulfilled his expressed hope that "I've done something decent with my life."[2]

Notes

INTRODUCTION

1. On there being only one language, see e.g. 1991d: 26.
2. The expression "conscience of the West" is from Smith, 1985: 105.
3. The most illuminating interviews are those with David Barsamian (Chomsky, 1992b, 1994c, 1996b, 1998d, 2001b), Larissa MacFarquhar (2003), and James Peck (1987).
4. The baseball match is from 1994c: 270; boxing from 1994c: 99.
5. The "hermit" quotation is from Barsky, 1997: 34.
6. The remark that subjects should not be personalized is from 1991c: 3.
7. The quotation about his high school is from Peck, 1987: 5–6.
8. For Harris, see 1988c: 261.
9. His Master's thesis is 1951/79.
10. For Carol Chomsky's work, see e.g. C. Chomsky, 1969, 1986. For background about her, see Hughes, 2001.
11. The quotation "work like a maniac" is from 1988c: 741; the "big ego" is from p. 742, and "pre-Galilean" is from p. 418.
12. Berlinski, 1988: 80.
13. Montague's remark is cited in Berlinski, 1988: 140.
14. Postal's remark is cited in MacFarquhar, 2003:77.
15. The vilification is from de Beaugrande, 1991: 441.
16. The "crackpot" and "outside the pale" remarks are cited in 1993e: 85.
17. An account of one of his times in jail is provided by Mailer, 1968: 180.
18. On death threats, see 1994c: 142.
19. For "paranoid," see e.g. Lau, 2001.
20. "willful naïveté" is from Powell, 2002, p. F4.
21. The quotation "try admitting . . ." is from Billen, 2002: 5.
22. The quotation from Carol Chomsky is from Hughes, 2001: 45.
23. The quotation on responsibility is from 1995f: 34.
24. For my own putative expertise, see the references under Smith in the bibliography, and Smith 2002e.
25. One typical example of the adulation Chomsky receives can be seen in the special issue of *Frontline* (New Delhi, December 21, 2001) devoted to him.
26. "Nobody is a hero" is from 1994c: 145. Elsewhere (2002h: 94–95) he describes draft resisters and people struggling in the third world as his heroes.
27. On avoiding questions, see 1988c: 774.
28. For Wittgenstein's influence, see 2003c: 295.
29. The remark about Russell is from 1994c: 144.

30. Ahad Ha-'am is also known as Asher Ginzberg, 1856–1927. The remark about "an excess of rationalism" is from the *Encyclopaedia Britannica*.
31. For William Chomsky, see 1988c: 260; Barsky, 1997: 19; MacFarquhar, 2003: 68.
32. The Darwin quotation is from Burkhardt, 1996: 99.

CHAPTER 1   THE MIRROR OF THE MIND

1. Chomsky discusses frogs (and witches) in 1995a: 21, 1997g. See also Searchinger, 1995, Part 1.
2. My claim about frogs might not be uncontroversial after all: see Lieberman, 2001, and Smith, 2002a.
3. On bonobos and their abilities, see Smith, 2002b, and references therein.
4. See e.g. Dennett, 1996, for a cogent recent discussion of different mental abilities.
5. Hockett, 1942: 3.
6. Hjelmslev, 1961: 11.
7. For Construction Grammar, see Fillmore et al., 1988: 504; Goldberg, 2003.
8. For discussion of word order, see Smith, 1989: ch. 6.
9. It has been claimed that a seventh type is provided by so-called free word-order languages, like Sanskrit or Warlpiri (see Hale, 1982). Logically, one might also expect "blends," languages like German which appear to have different word orders in main and subordinate clauses. There is always evidence in such cases to suggest that one of these orders is basic.
10. For sign languages, see e.g. Sutton-Spence & Woll, 1999, for British Sign Language, or Neidle et al., 2000, for American Sign Language.
11. For Nupe, see Smith, 1967.
12. I-language is discussed extensively below. The term is first used in 1986a: 22, the concept goes back to the beginning of Chomsky's work, where it was referred to with the ambiguous term "grammar."
13. Breaking eggs and breaking legs typically involve differences of volition on the part of the subject, though strictly speaking both examples allow both interpretations.
14. "linguistic disobedience" is from Brodsky, 1987: 136.
15. On Galileo, see 1988c: 242; 2002b, especially chapter 2 "Perspectives on language and mind" (The Galileo lecture), where he refers to Galileo as "the master"; to appear: 3.
16. Boyle's Law says that the pressure of a gas varies inversely with its volume at constant temperature. On ideal gases, see 1988c: 270.
17. "a distortion of reality" (p.c. April 1998); cf. "distortion of the truth" in 2002b: 99. Compare: "'idealization' is a rather misleading term for the effort to gain better understanding of reality," 1998c: 115.
18. The quotation is from 1965: 3; the highlighting of "ideal" is mine.
19. "frees the explorer" is from 1994e/2000a: 90. This article is a sustained attack on the "methodological dualism" that prompts some writers to exclude mental aspects of the world from scientific investigation. Elsewhere (1979: 57), Chomsky says that "Opposition to idealization is simply objection to rationality."
20. On hesitation phenomena, see Goldman-Eisler, 1968.
21. On the critical period, see below and chapter 3.
22. On the idealization to instantaneity, see e.g. 1981c: 224, 1986a: 52.

23. On the use of negation by children, see e.g. Klima & Bellugi, 1966.
24. "Illegitimate idealization" is from 1993a: 11, in his discussion of Adam Smith. For a brief discussion of the possibility that "grammar" might not be an appropriate idealization, see 1979: 189.
25. "'impurity'" is from Duranti, 1997: 74–75.
26. "limited range of data" is from Duranti, 1997: 74, citing Labov, 1972.
27. "the human condition" is from Duranti, 1997: 75.
28. It should be noted that Pierrehumbert et al. (2000: 292) claim that variation facilitates acquisition (but not that it is necessary for acquisition).
29. The quotation on processing mechanisms is from 1980a: 200. Elsewhere (1999i: 393) Chomsky claims that he "never had any particular views of language processing beyond what seems fairly obvious . . .".
30. Fromkin, 1988: 131.
31. On physical laws, see 1994e: 193.
32. On modularity, see 1975a, 1984, 1988c: 239, 1999i, 1999j; Smith, 2003a.
33. On the history of brain damage, see Fromkin, 1997: 8.
34. On lateralization, see Lenneberg, 1967. For the surprisingly rich role of the right hemisphere in language processing, see Beeman & Chiarello, 1997; Chiarello, 2003.
35. On the visual system, see Tovée, 1996: 14.
36. There are interesting examples of synaesthesia where this "little" becomes salient. See Baron-Cohen & Harrison, 1997; Grossenbacher & Lovelace, 2001.
37. See Fodor, 1983.
38. Chomsky also has reservations about other aspects of Fodor's claims, e.g. the speed and mandatoriness of sentence processing. See 1986a: 14, and below. There is useful discussion of the similarities and differences in Fodor, 2000.
39. The quotation about Feynman is from Gleick, 1992: 228.
40. On the accessibility of the visual system to consciousness, see Motluk, 1997. The *locus classicus* for visual ability in the absence of conscious awareness comes from "blindsight"; see Weiskrantz, 1986.
41. On the Titchener illusion, see e.g. Carey, 2001; Franz, 2001. For the centipede, recall Mrs. Craster's rhyme:

> The centipede was happy quite,
> Until the Toad in fun
> Said "Pray which leg goes after which?"
> And worked her mind to such a pitch,
> She lay distracted in the ditch
> Considering how to run.

42. Schacter et al., 1996; see also Motluk, 1996; Gazzaniga, 2002.
43. PET stands for Positron Emission Tomography. The subject is injected with radioactive liquid and the emission of positrons in the brain is monitored to see where activity is greatest.
44. The hippocampus is part of the lateral ventricle of the brain involved, among other things, in memory.
45. For vision, see Marr, 1982.
46. On language as an output system, see e.g. 1986a: 14. For a summary of Fodor's and Chomsky's notions of modularity, see Smith, 2003a.

47. The suggestion about interpreting everything is in 1987b: 37.
48. On the distinctness of language and vision, see 1984: 16.
49. On the language of thought, see Fodor, 1975; Smith, 1983; Carruthers, 1996.
50. On face recognition, see Johnson & Morton, 1991.
51. Autism is a pathological condition, characterized by social withdrawal, self-absorption, problems with language and, occasionally, prodigious talent in one narrow area. Frith, 1989/2003, provides a lucid overview and an explanation of the condition in terms of a theory-of-mind deficit.
52. For the Sally-Anne test, see Baron-Cohen et al., 1985.
53. The developmental relationship between language and theory of mind seems to be intimately bidirectional. Thus there is evidence that the representational expressive power of language – specifically the development of "*that*-clauses" is necessary for the emergence of theory-of-mind abilities and, conversely, that the meta-representational expressive power of theory of mind underpins the linguistic ability to differentiate, for instance, the epistemic and deontic uses of modals illustrated by *You must be unmarried* (Garfield et al., 2001; De Villiers & de Villiers, 1999; Papafragou, 1998, 2002; Smith, 2002c). For the relation of theory of mind and pragmatics, see Wilson, 2003.
54. On double dissociation in general, see Shallice, 1988.
55. On Capgras's Delusion, see Coltheart et al., 1997; Ellis & Lewis, 2001.
56. On language as an "organ," see 1980a: 188, and elsewhere.
57. For Piaget's theory, see e.g. Piaget & Inhelder, 1966. For discussion of the "cognitive prerequisites," see Bellugi et al., 1993. For the classic "debate" between Chomsky and Piaget, see Piattelli-Palmarini, 1980.
58. For recent discussion of double dissociation, see Fromkin, 1997; Smith, 2003a.
59. The physical characterization of William's syndrome comes from Karmiloff-Smith et al., 1995: 198.
60. The quotation on language and intelligence is from Bellugi et al., 1993: 179. It remains the case, of course, that some minimal cognitive ability is prerequisite to the possession of language. See Smith & Tsimpli, 1997.
61. The quotation on "subtle impairments" is from Annette Karmiloff-Smith (p.c. September 2002); see also Thomas & Karmiloff-Smith, in press.
62. For the case of Christopher, see Smith & Tsimpli, 1995, Morgan et al., 2002a, and references therein.
63. Christopher's failure to conserve number was tested by giving him two strings with the same number of beads on each. When the beads on one string were spaced out more widely than those on the other string he said consistently that that string contained more beads. When the beads were pushed together, he reversed his judgment.
64. "Fragments of genius" is the title of Howe, 1989.
65. On stroke victims with a range of dissociations, see Shallice, 1988. A poignant example is provided by Sheila Hale's (2002) account of her husband's loss of language.
66. For SLI, see e.g. van der Lely, 1997a, 1997a, b; Leonard, 1996. The examples come from a highly intelligent boy (with a non-verbal IQ of 119) at the age of fifteen years. See van der Lely, 1997a: 7.
67. On modules and quasi-modules, see Smith & Tsimpli, 1995; Tsimpli & Smith, 1998; Smith et al., 2003.

68. On the nature of mathematical knowledge, see Dehaene, 1997; Spelke & Tsivkin, 2001; Smith, 2002c. Chomsky makes the intriguing speculation that the complex kinship systems of so-called "primitive" societies are "a kind of mathematics" (2002h: 99).
69. On autism and Down's syndrome, see Frith, 1989; Karmiloff-Smith, 1992b; Rondal 1995.
70. This position on modularity is reminiscent of Jackendoff's (1997) "representational modularity."
71. On meta-representation, see Sperber, 1994. In fact meta-representations are much more complex than just "second-order."
72. On learning, see 1980a: 136–140; 1991c: 17; chapter 3 below.
73. On "modularization," see Karmiloff-Smith, 1992a.
74. The *locus classicus* for "competence" and "performance" is 1965, but see also 1963: 326; for introductory discussion, see Smith, 1994a.
75. On recovery from aphasia, see 1988b: 10.
76. On intuitions and *flying planes*, see 1955/75: 62ff.
77. On rules, see 1980a, 1986a, and many other places. For elementary discussion, see Smith, 1989.
78. On infinity and creativity, see 1966a; Winston, 2002:17.
79. The teddy-bear example is from Smith, 1989: 5.
80. On I-language and E-language, see 1986a: 21ff; Anderson & Lightfoot, 2002: 12–17; Baker, 2001.
81. On language as a set of sentences and what's wrong with such a view, see 1957: 13, etc.; for discussion, see Smith & Wilson, 1979: ch. 1; Carr, 2003.
82. Chomsky's view has always been internalist, even when the formal focus of his work led him to concentrate on properties of the output of the grammar.
83. On language as a species property, see 1988b: 2.
84. On language as the focus of interest, see 1957.
85. The quotation on mechanisms is from 1997d: 2.
86. The characterization of a grammar as a device which should generate "all and only" the sequences of some language is based on 1957: 13.
87. The quotation about WFF is p.c. April 1998.; cf. 1996a: 48.
88. For a possible example of a generalization that presupposes the notion E-language, see the discussion of Katz in chapter 4.
89. For recent discussion of the gradient nature of judgments of acceptability (though with the surprising conclusion that these are inimical to Chomsky's position), see Pullum & Scholz, 2003. For gradience more generally, see Aarts, 2004.
90. For parasitic gaps such as *This is the man John hired without speaking to*, see 1982d; Engdahl, 1983.
91. On the relative ill-formedness of parasitic gap constructions, see 1986b: 55–56.
92. On alchemy, see Dobbs, 1991.
93. For the caveat, see 1986a: 151.
94. On the weight of sentences, see Smith, 1989: 14.
95. On understanding theories rather than the world, see 2002b: 100; 1999j: 6.
96. On the I-language or grammar as being neutral between speaker and hearer, see 1965: 9.
97. On parsing and "garden path" sentences, see 1986a: 25. For recent surveys, see Altmann, 1998; Phillips, in press.

98. *cotton clothing* is from Marcus, 1980: 206; *her friends* is based on Pritchett, 1988. See below, chapter 3 for further discussion.

99. For early discussion of "center-embedding," see Miller & Chomsky, 1963. The oysters are adapted from Townsend and Bever, 2001: 30.

100. On ungrammaticality and degrees of grammaticality, see 1955/75, 1961; for discussion, see Smith & Wilson, 1979; Smith, 1989.

101. On look-ahead, see Marcus, 1980.

102. For an example of a parser incorporating minimalist principles, see Weinberg, 1999.

103. The best example of someone who seeks to integrate grammars and parsers is Phillips, to appear.

104. The quotation about parsers is from 1995b: 28.

105. For relevance theory, see Sperber & Wilson, 1986/95; Carston, 2002. Rather than choosing the interpretation which just "fits the context," you take the one which gives you the most reward for the least effort. Sperber & Wilson, 1986/95: 260f.

106. For "implicature," see Grice, 1975; Sperber & Wilson, 1986/95.

107. On "pragmatic competence," see 1980a: 59.

108. For a recent example conflating the competence/performance and I-language/ E-language distinctions, see Duranti, 1997: 15.

109. On the Bloomfieldian position, see 1986a: 19. Chomsky (p.c. April 1998) describes the position as "mysticism."

110. The quotation about spontaneous speech is from Goldman-Eisler, 1968: 31.

111. The quotation about "pragmatic competence" is from 1980a: 224 (cf. 1981b: 18); that on "competence" is from 1965: 4; that about "knowledge and understanding" from 1995b: 14. On competence as an "informal" term, p.c. April 1998.

112. It is striking that the locution "to *know* a language" is unusual in the languages of the world. In many languages, *know* in this sense translates as "hear," or "speak," and "know" is reserved for talking of real knowledge.

113. On innateness, see 1967b; 1975a: ch. 1; and innumerable other references.

114. On growing arms rather than wings, see 1984: 33.

115. On the role of genetic factors in language and language pathology, see Gopnik, 1997; Stromswold, 2001. Early observations on the genetic determination of language, and our ignorance of their details, appear in Chomsky & Miller, 1963, e.g. p. 272.

116. For Hixkaryana, see Derbyshire, 1985.

117. For poverty of the stimulus, see 1991c: 17, and many other places. A useful survey of the complex and controversial issues involved can be found in Ritter, 2002.

118. On critical periods, see 1988b: 159; Smith, 1998.

119. On the development of light sensitivity in later life, see Thompson, 1993.

120. Russell is quoted in 1971b: 78; 1986a: 25; 1987b: 18; 1988b: 3–4. The original is from Russell, 1948.

121. On UG, see 1986a *passim*, 1995b: 4–8, 17–20.

122. The claim that word meaning is largely innate is from 1997d: 3; cf. Fodor, 1975, and chapter 4 below.

123. On innate knowledge of vocabulary, see 1992d: 116.

124. On the rapidity of the acquisition of vocabulary, see 1992d: 113; cf. S. Carey, 1978: 264; Bloom & Markson, 1998.

125. *near* is discussed in 1995a: 19; see also Searchinger, 1995: Part 1. *house* is discussed in 1996a: 21f.

126. Universals have been central to all Chomsky's work from the beginning; see e.g. 1965.

127. The quotation about the relevance of Japanese to English is from 1997d: 2.

128. For skeptical reactions to Chomsky's views on innateness, see Elman et al., 1996; Tomasello, 2003.

129. That universals might not be instantiated in all languages has been clear since Prague structuralism (see e.g. Jakobson, 1941).

130. On reflexives, see chapter 2 below and the references cited there.

131. I am grateful to Fuyo Osawa for providing me with an appropriate Japanese example. Japanese informants differ in their reaction to the interpretation of this sentence.

In the sentence *John-wa Bill-wa zibun-o kizutukeru-no-o yameru-bekida-to itta,* *-wa* marks the subject, *-o* marks the object, *zibun* means "self," *kizutukeru* is "injuring," *yameru* is "stop," *bekida* is "should," *-to* is the complementizer ("that"), and *itta* means "said."

132. On Chomsky's skepticism, see 1993c.

133. Fodor develops his argument at length in his 1975.

134. Suggestions on the language of thought include Smith, 1983; Carruthers, 1996.

135. Ed Herman is co-author with Chomsky of a number of political books.

136. On the structure of thoughts, see e.g. Evans's "Generality Constraint" (1982: 104).

137. The "laws of thought" is the title of Boole, 1854.

138. On Chomsky's skepticism about language as a model of the mind, rather than a mirror of the mind, see 1993c: 34.

139. The final quotation is from 1975a: 5.

CHAPTER 2   THE LINGUISTIC FOUNDATION

1. On Chomsky's debt to Descartes, see e.g. Winston, 2002: 30.

2. For discussion of Chomsky's relations with Harris, see Barsky, 1997. Harris's major linguistic work, which acknowledges Chomsky, is his 1951.

3. For good introductions to Chomsky's linguistic work, see e.g. Adger, 2003; Cook & Newson, 1996; Radford, 1997a, 2004a; Roberts, 1997; Smith, 1989; and at a somewhat more advanced level, Chomsky & Lasnik, 1993.

4. On a point of terminology it is worth emphasizing that "generative" is used in the literature with systematic ambiguity. The more general interpretation of the word is as a near synonym of "explicit," and in this sense essentially all current theories are "generative." The narrower interpretation is as a characterization of work in (transformational) generative grammar in its various manifestations over the years. This is the interpretation that I intend throughout unless an indication of the wider sense is explicitly given.

5. The quotation about "one human language" is from 1995b: 131; cf. also 1993c: 50.

6. The difference between *ask* and *wonder* is implicit in the *Oxford English Dictionary* in that the latter verb lacks one of the entries found for the former.

7. Stress has been central to work in generative grammar from the beginning: see e.g. Chomsky et al., 1956; Chomsky & Halle, 1968.

8. The quotation about "whatever is predictable" is from 1995b: 6.
9. I avoid the term "phonemic" in this discussion because part of the early work in generative phonology was devoted precisely to arguing that such a level was at best "highly dubious": see e.g. 1964: 69, building on Halle, 1959. For extended discussion of (early) generative phonology, see Chomsky, Halle & Lukoff, 1956; Chomsky & Halle, 1964, and especially Chomsky & Halle, 1968. Recent developments can be found in Goldsmith, 1994; Kenstowicz, 1994; Roca & Johnson, 1999. Current phonology is dominated by Optimality Theory (see e.g. Kager, 1999).
10. The emphasis on economy which was characteristic of structuralist and Prague School phonology (see e.g. Harris, 1951) was instrumental rather than realist in orientation.
11. It is possible to say *the Fred* in examples like *This is the Fred I told you about*, where several people called Fred are under discussion, the implied contrast is that between the normal *I saw the boy* and the odd *I saw the Fred*.
12. On selection and theta roles, see e.g. Haegeman, 1994.
13. Example (1) is from 1975a: 31; (2) is from 1955: 228; (3) is from 1964: 34; (4) is from 1965: 22; (5) is modified from 1986b: 11; (6) is from 1986a: 8; (7) is from 1995a: 20.
14. For structure dependence, see e.g. 1971b: 86f., 1988b: 45f.
15. We shall see experimental justification of the claim that rules can't count in chapter 3.
16. The West African language is Nupe; see Smith, 1967.
17. For recursive function theory, see e.g. Post, 1944. Chomsky's mathematical contribution was to do with the subpart of recursive function theory known as "subrecursive hierarchies," the domain where automata theory and formal language theory fall; Schützenberger tied this work into classical analysis. See e.g. Chomsky, 1963; Chomsky & Miller, 1963; Chomsky & Schützenberger, 1963. For the history of mathematical linguistics see Tomalin, 2002. Lyons, 1970: 109, remarks that "Even if it were decided eventually that none of Chomsky's work on generative grammar was of any direct relevance to the description of natural languages, it would still be judged valuable by logicians and mathematicians."
18. For levels of representation, see e.g. 1955/75, 1957, 1995b: 21ff.
19. More accurately, linguistically significant generalizations are captured by the mapping of syntactic structure to PF and LF.
20. Despite belief to the contrary, Chomsky has been preoccupied with questions of meaning from his earliest work: see e.g. 1955a: 18; 1955b. See also his 1972c, 1975a, 1980a, 1993c, 1995a, etc. Semantics in generative grammar boasts a huge literature. Useful recent points of departure include Larson & Segal, 1995, and Heim & Kratzer, 1998.
21. "Quantifiers" are expressions like *some, all, twenty-three*, and so on that determine the quantity of the noun they modify. A detailed discussion of *each* and *every* can be found in Beghelli & Stowell, 1997.
22. For "deep structure," see 1965, especially pp. 16ff., 198ff.
23. In recent work *the stew* would be a DP rather than an NP. The difference is irrelevant for the points being made. Technically, a constituent is any sequence of items that can be traced exhaustively to a single node.
24. Strictly speaking, this tree and the associated PS rules are anachronistic in that *Harry* would have been described as an NP as well as an N, because it shares certain aspects of the behavior of NP.

25. For "discrete infinity," see e.g. 2002b: 48f.; Hauser et al., 2002.
26. The triangles in (15) simply indicate that the internal structure of the constituents is unspecified, as it is not relevant to the discussion.
27. For Immediate Constituent analysis, see Wells, 1947; Robins, 1989.
28. For unbounded dependencies, see 1977a; McCloskey, 1988.
29. Relevant works by Harris are his 1951, 1952, 1957, 1965.
30. On descriptive adequacy, see 1964; Smith, 1989: ch. 11.
31. On the determination of meaning by deep structure, see 1965; Katz & Postal, 1964; for discussion, see Partee, 1971.
32. See Lees, 1960, the published version of the first MIT linguistics Ph.D. thesis. It was largely this thesis (rather than subsequent work by the Generative Semanticists) that prompted Chomsky to develop the lexicalist alternative that appeared as his 1970c.
33. For reflexives and binding theory more generally, see Haegeman, 1994. The situation is more complex than I have described it: see Reinhart & Reuland, 1993; Reuland & Everaert, 2001, among many other references.
34. On rule ordering, see e.g. Pullum, 1979.
35. The Master's thesis is 1951/79. For discussion, see 1955/75: 29.
36. The quotation is from Miller & Chomsky, 1963: 430. The notion of parameter appealed to is not the same as the current notion discussed below. The length of childhood is perhaps a little brief: 10^8 seconds is a little over three years.
37. On descriptive and explanatory adequacy, see 1964, 1965; Smith, 1989, ch. 11. The subject is revisited in a recent paper, to appear.
38. As Chomsky put it later "The gravest defect of the theory of transformational grammar is its enormous latitude and descriptive power" (1972e: 67).
39. The A over A condition first appeared in 1962/64.
40. Translating (29) into some languages may give rise to acceptable results if there is a pronoun in the position of the dash, giving something like: *What did Harry stir the stew and it*. See Ross (1967/86), where the term "island" originated, for detailed discussion.
41. "On WH-movement" is 1977a.
42. The "cleft" example in (30c) doesn't contain a WH-word, but the construction falls under the same generalizations.
43. WH is a place-holder marking an anaphoric relationship between an empty position within the sentence and a position external to the sentence. Not all languages have WH, and such relationships in English extend to other operators as well as WH.
44. There is disagreement in the literature as to whether NP-movement is bounded or unbounded (like WH-movement). Chomsky's position has consistently been that it is unbounded. What is important is that all movement can ultimately be unified. See McCloskey, 1988, for discussion.
45. Technically the WH-phrase moves to the Specifier of the CP; for details, see Radford, 2004a; Adger, 2003.
46. For the Afrikaans evidence, see du Plessis, 1977 (on so-called partial WH-movement in a variety of other languages, see Pesetsky, 2000; Karimi, 2003); for Scottish Gaelic, see Adger, 2003: 362. The Spanish examples here are based on Adger, 2003: 382f.; I am grateful to Rosa Vega-Moreno for help with the examples.
47. More accurately, inversion is obligatory if there is a WH-word in the Specifier of CP.
48. For "raising" see chapter 3 below; Adger, 2003; Radford, 2004a.

49. On the elimination of PS rules, see Chomsky, 1995b: 25, where it is suggested that "they may be completely superfluous." For general discussion, see Rooryck & Zaring, 1996.
50. The radical revisions became the *Barriers* framework: 1986b.
51. X-bar theory first appeared in 1970c. The bar refers to the notation used to describe X-bar constituents intermediate in size between X and XP.
52. The treatment of *student* and *fond* as transitive ignores a number of problems, as is suggested by the appearance in (42a) and (43a) of *of*.
53. The generalization of X-bar to all categories is one of the innovations of the *Barriers* framework alluded to above; see 1986b; for discussion see Webelhuth, 1995b.
54. For Government and Binding theory, see especially 1981b. The clearest introduction to the theory is Haegeman, 1994.
55. The quotation on terminology is from 1995f: 32.
56. On the disappearance of "government" see e.g. 1995b: 10; for discussion, see Marantz, 1995: 365.
57. For binding theory, see 1981b; Haegeman, 1994; Harbert, 1995.
58. The example (45) is from Harbert, 1995: 202; (46) is from 1987b: 8 and (47) from 1986a: 167–168.
59. The examples in (48) are from Smith, 1987: 62.
60. For general discussion of locality, see Manzini, 1992.
61. For theta theory, see 1981b, 1986a; Williams, 1995.
62. The theta criterion is from 1981b: 36. This version of the criterion is problematic for examples related to (50e); for discussion see Willliams, 1995. For the acceptability of (50e), see Cormack & Smith, 1996.
63. For pro-drop languages, see chapter 3.
64. For PRO, see 1981b: 6.
65. For theta theory within the Minimalist Program, see 1995e; for the disappearance of the theta criterion, see 1995b: 188.
66. More accurately, Nominative is assigned by finite INFL; the difference is irrelevant here.
67. The phenomenon illustrated in (55a) is known as Exceptional Case Marking, and *expect* is called an ECM verb; see e.g. Haegeman, 1994: 167.
68. The analysis of Quechua is from Cole & Hermon, 1981. Their argument was aimed at Chomsky's 1973c. The classic treatment of raising is Postal, 1974.
69. For empty categories, see e.g. 1986a: 114ff.
70. For traditional use of "understood elements", see e.g. Chalker & Weiner, 1994.
71. For a historical overview of treatments of *wanna* contraction, see Pullum & Zwicky, 1988.
72. The first discussion of trace theory is in 1973c; the most detailed treatment is in 1981b.
73. For the ECP, see 1981b: 250; subsequent revisions and general discussion can be found in Haegeman, 1994: 441ff.; Hornstein & Weinberg, 1995.
74. The position after *elected* is a position to which a theta role is assigned.
75. The reference to "transformational" versus "non-transformational" is p.c., April 1998; for discussion, see 1995b: 223. It is relevant to point out that Harris's (1951) use of transformations was non-derivational; one of Chomsky's innovations was precisely to construe the notion derivationally. A typical example of a

"non-transformational" theory in this sense is provided by Categorial Grammar; see e.g. Steedman, 1993, 2000.

76. A representative selection of other positions on the representational/derivational divide is provided in Epstein & Seely, 2002c. The clearest discussion is Lasnik, 2001.

77. A number of arguments for a derivational approach are dissected in Brody, 2002: 36f.

78. Ockham's razor states that "theoretical entities should not be multiplied beyond necessity" (William of Ockham, also spelt "Occam," flourished in the fourteenth century).

79. The quotation on Chomsky's "mixed" position is p.c. April 1998. On Chomsky's maintenance of a "mixed" theory including derivations, see 1995b: 223; for discussion, see Brody, 1998. On "interfaces" see below, p. 84.

80. For the coverage of transformations, see 1995b; p.c. April 1998.

81. A clear statement of notions of simplicity can be found in 1972e: 67; for discussion, see Tomalin, 2003, and references therein.

82. On transformations in first language acquisition, see e.g. Crain & Thornton, 1998; Thornton, 1991.

83. For alternatives to generative grammar, see *inter alia* Borsley, 1996; Pollard & Sag, 1994; Steedman, 1993; Bresnan, 1994; Hudson, 1990. On the terminology, see note 4 above.

84. The simplest introduction to parametric variation is Baker, 2003; see also his 2001.

85. On parameters as switches, see 1988b: 62; the metaphor is originally due to Jim Higginbotham.

86. On Plato's problem, see chapters 3 and 5.

87. On parallels with immunology, see 1980a: 136; for discussion see Piattelli-Palmarini, 1989, and chapter 3.

88. The quotation about "belong[ing] to the genotype" is from Anderson & Lightfoot, 2002: 36.

89. On the number of languages, see Comrie et al., 1997: 16. From an I-language perspective, everyone's language is different, raising the number to 6 billion: see Kayne, 1996. Not all differences between languages are a function of parametric variation.

90. For "twenty questions" see Janet Fodor, 1998, 2001. Whether all choices really are binary is an open question. Nothing in the discussion depends on it.

91. The term "marked" refers to the abnormal case that has to be marked in some way, whereas the "unmarked" case can be left inexplicit. The usage goes back to pre-generative linguistics; for its use in generative grammar, see 1981d.

92. For the epigenetic landscape, see Wolpert, 1991: 92.

93. For discussion of what happens when the data are not deterministic, see Smith & Cormack, 2002.

94. The clearest introduction to functional categories is Radford, 1997a. The technical details – like all technicalities – are both controversial and likely to change.

95. For discussion of the special status of prepositions, see Froud, 2001.

96. CP and IP were introduced in 1986b.

97. Depending on one's analysis of small clauses, it may be the case that not all sentences require I(NFL).

98. On WH *in situ*, as in Chinese, see 1995b: 68; Cheng, 2003.

99. A clear treatment of the more recent view of parametric variation is provided by Roberts, 1997, esp. ch. 5.

100. Minimalism is encapsulated in 1995b; a brief overview is given by Marantz, 1995; the most accessible introductions are 2002b; Lasnik, 2002; Radford, 2004a. A sustained critique of the Minimalist Program is provided by Lappin et al., 2000, which gave rise to heated debate in subsequent issues of *Natural Language and Linguistic Theory*.

101. The "most interesting" quotation is from 1996b: 3.

102. The "central role" of government is from 1981b: 1.

103. On the "elimination" of Phrase Structure, see 1995e: 433.

104. The "end of syntax" is suggested by Marantz, 1995: 380.

105. The quotation on "formulating [interesting] questions" is from 1995b: 9.

106. On legibility, see 2000b: 94f., 2002b: 107ff; the quotation is from a recent paper, to appear: 2. "L" is shorthand for the computational device linking representations of sound and meaning.

107. On "design specifications," see 1995b: Introduction; 2000b: 94. A refinement of these ideas appears in Hauser et al., 2002. See p. 94 below.

108. On binding as an "external system," see 1995f: 32. A more plausible position is that binding is divided between a purely syntactic part and an external "pragmatic" part, along lines suggested by Reinhart & Reuland, 1993. For discussion, see Perovic, 2003.

109. On the effects of communication and style, see Sperber & Wilson, 1986/95.

110. The "optimal solution" is from 2000b: 96. On optimal design, see 2002b: 90, 96.

111. On economy see 1991e, 1995b. For an accessible overview of economy in syntax, see Collins, 2001.

112. Introductory treatment of recent developments in Minimalism can be found in Radford, 2004a, Adger, 2003. There are three relevant papers by Chomsky: "Minimalist inquiries" (2000b), "Derivation by phase" (2001c) and "Beyond explanatory adequacy" (to appear).

113. Strictly speaking, the constraint on sequences of /n/ followed by /p/ or /b/ holds of morphemes rather than words.

114. On *anyway* and similar terms, see Blakemore, 1987, 1992; Carston, 1999.

115. On Shortest Movement, see 1995b: 185.

116. On Full Interpretation, see 1995b: 151.

117. The examples in (81) are from 1986a: 99.

118. For the expression "crash," see e.g. 1995b: 220.

119. For discussion of expletives and economy, see 1995b: 340ff.

120. For free variables, see 1995b: 152.

121. On a minimalist ontology, see especially 2000b: 49ff.

122. For "internal merge" see to appear: 7–8; for its relation to copy theory, see 2003c: 307. Move(ment) is often conceptualised as Attract(ion); see e.g. 1995b: 297f.

123. For "indispensable" and design conditions, see 2000b: 101.

124. On "imperfection" see to appear: 8.

125. The French examples in (83) are from 1995b: 148; the examples in (84) are from Radford, 2004a.

126. Chomsky discusses the linking of probes and goals to the elimination of uninterpretable features in a recent paper, to appear: 11.

127. For the technical details, see to appear or, more accessibly, Radford, 2004a.
128. For "binary merge," see to appear: 12; for the early history of binarity, see Miller & Chomsky, 1963.
129. On the early history of devising computationally tractable theories, see Miller & Chomsky, 1963.
130. For "phase," see 2002b; Radford, 2004a. The formulation "in small chunks" is from Adger, 2003: 376. There is a further contrast between weak and strong phases (2002b: 12), but the details are irrelevant for present purposes.
131. "active memory" is from 2002b: 12 – scare quotes in the original.
132. "minimizing memory" is from to appear: 14.
133. On cyclicity, see 2002b: passim; on island effects, 2002b: 26. There are also implications for compositionality and a variety of other issues: to appear: 18. For general discussion of cyclicity, see Freidin, 1999.
134. On having a "natural characterization" see to appear: 22. Strictly, it is vP which is a phase rather than VP. For technical details, see 2002b.
135. Adger, 2003: 386.
136. On "perfect syntax," see 1995a: 18; 1995b: 9; 1995f: 31–32. In their discussion of grammaticalization, Roberts & Roussou, 2003: 1, make the interesting observation that "perfect systems do not vary over time." Despite this apparent problem for the Minimalist Program they argue at length that historical change (and synchronic variation) are compatible with Chomsky's position and even provide a basis for explaining the existence of functional categories and parametric variation.
137. Galileo – see 2002b: 57; to appear: 2. See 2000b: 111 for whether complexity matters for a cognitive system.
138. On snowflakes, see 2002b: 136. On tinkering, see 2002b: 139. The analogy comes originally from François Jacob, 1977.
139. On the requirements of the perceptual and articulatory systems, see 1995b: 317; see Brody, 1998, for discussion.
140. On a "pretty law" (actually Prout's hypothesis that atomic weights were multiples of that of hydrogen) see 2002b: 137.
141. On "changing reality," see 2002b: 136.
142. On "general properties," see to appear: 1.
143. Relevant works are Thompson, 1942; Turing, 1952. Chomsky refers to both regularly, see e.g. 1993c: 84; 2002b: 57.
144. Assigning appropriate structure was "strong generation." The "weak" generation of the set of sentences was never of central importance.
145. On parametrized principles, see Rizzi, 1982, especially for discussion of this particular example.
146. For locality, see 1995b, 2000b, 2001c; there is useful discussion in Manzini, 1992.
147. "efficient computation" is from to appear: 6; "restricts search" is from to appear: 5.
148. For evolution, see e.g. 1965: 59; 1980a: 99ff., 1996a: 15ff.; 1996c; etc.
149. On Chomsky's putative denial of the evolution of language, see e.g. Dennett, 1995; Pinker, 1994. Jenkins, 2000, discusses the literature in detail. For additional comment, see Smith, 2002b: ch. 15.
150. The quotation on "well adapted" is from 1996a: 16.
151. See Hauser et al., 2002. For related remarks, see also 2002b.
152. All quotations are from Hauser et al., 2002.

CHAPTER 3   PSYCHOLOGICAL REALITY

1. The acceptance of the basic claim that we have grammars in our heads is explicit in the titles of innumerable articles: for instance "The representation of grammatical categories in the brain" (Shapiro & Caramazza, 2003).
2. For *John was too clever to catch*, see 1997c: 7.
3. For discussion of the limitations of imaging, see O'Connor et al., 1994.
4. Ullman's rigidity principle is discussed in e.g. 1986a: 263f., 1996a: 5. See Ullman, 1979, 1996.
5. The quotation on "sparse stimulation" is from 1996a: 5.
6. Chomsky thinks that chemistry is a far better model for the sciences than physics. See 1995a for examples and discussion.
7. On the second dimension of time, see Walker, 1997: 41.
8. For electron spin and the quotation from Pauli, see Matthews, 1998.
9. On causality, see Salmon, 1989: 180ff.; for an opposed viewpoint see van Fraassen, 1980. See also 1998c: 116, 2000b: 94, where Chomsky describes the language faculty as providing "instructions" to the performance systems.
10. For implicature, see chapter 1, p. 34.
11. For the Pasteur–Pouchet debate, see Collins & Pinch, 1993.
12. In Pais's words (1982: 22) "Einstein was canonized" when prediction about light was confirmed in 1919. The quotation about "pure mathematical construction" is from Pais, 1982: 172. The ignored experiments were a re-run of the Michelson–Morley experiments determining the speed of light.
13. For "the ghost in the machine," see Ryle, 1949; or Quine, 1990a, for a more recent recapitulation.
14. For "objective," and "observable," see Byrne, 1994: 134.
15. In fact even bar-pressing by pigeons is somewhat more complex than was thought. What psychologists took to be a single behavior has been decomposed by later work into independent actions that happen to look alike, but have different instinctual origins. See e.g. Gallistel, 1994.
16. The review of B. F. Skinner, 1957, is Chomsky, 1959.
17. For "built-in structure," see 1959: 578.
18. On "click" experiments, see Fodor, Bever & Garrett, 1974, and pp. 106–107 below.
19. For Chomsky, linguistic evidence *is* psychological evidence, so the distinction between the linguistic and the psychological is either "arbitrary" or "senseless" (p.c. April 1998).
20. On notational variants, see Harman, 1980; Sober, 1980; Chomsky, 1980c; see also chapter 4 for discussion of a range of examples.
21. On the contrast between theoretical entities and hypotheses about them, see 1980c: 56.
22. For an early discussion of intuitional variation, see Carden, 1970; book-length treatments are provided by Schütze, 1996; Cowart, 1997. Chomsky's commitment to objectivity is made explicit in 2000h: 20.
23. For discussion of intuitional disagreement, see Smith, 2003b.
24. See Hintikka, 1989: 48; Hintikka & Sandu, 1991: 67.
25. For Xhosa, see Smith, 1989: 103.
26. On meaning and truth, see chapter 4. See 1955/75: 509; 1957: 100–101; Katz & Postal, 1964: 72.

27. The "standard theory" is that encapsulated in 1965 and Katz & Postal, 1964.
28. On theories not being falsified by mere data, see 1980d: 2.
29. For *many arrows* sentences, see also Jackendoff, 1972: 326.
30. On surface structure interpretation, see 1971e, 1972c.
31. On scope of negation facts, see Carden, 1970; Beghelli & Stowell, 1997. On scope more generally, see Szabolcsi, 2001.
32. Concentration on I-language does not relieve one of the need for using rigorous statistical analysis of the relevant data. In that area linguists have much to learn from psychologists. For further discussion, see Smith, 2003b.
33. On causal convergence, see Salmon, 1989. Cladistics is a method for grouping animals by measuring their observable likenesses.
34. On psycholinguistic experimentation, see Tanenhaus, 1988.
35. For a discussion of click experiments, see e.g. Fodor & Bever, 1965.
36. For experiments on "causal" verbs, see Fodor et al., 1980.
37. On *running and buying*, see Cormack & Smith, 1994, 1996, 1997.
38. On the logic of the argument, see 1981b: 148; 1980c: 57. See also the discussion of Quechua in chapter 2.
39. The quotation is from Joos, 1957: 96.
40. On language as "part of psychology," see e.g. 1987b: 27.
41. The new syntactic paradigm was seen first in Chomsky, 1957, but importantly also in his 1958/64 and then in 1965.
42. See Chomsky & Miller, 1963; Miller & Chomsky, 1963.
43. The quotation is from Darwin, 1859: 125.
44. For relevant discussion on historical linguistics, see e.g. Lightfoot, 1991; Roberts & Roussou, 2003. An interesting use of the generative framework in the historical domain is provided by Tony Kroch and his colleagues (see e.g. Kroch, 1989, 2001, 2002; Haeberli, 2002; Pintzuk, 2002; etc.), who have exploited regression analysis to illuminate historical syntax.
45. Advances in imaging technology include "functional magnetic resonance imaging" (fMRI), "positron emission tomography" (PET), and "event-related potentials" (ERP), etc. For introductory discussion, see e.g. Fromkin, 1997; for detailed discussion, see Rugg, 1999; for a recent overview, see Billingsley & Papanicolaou, 2003.
46. Strictly speaking, all sentences involved the application of at least one transformation, but the technical details are even more irrelevant now than they were fifty years ago. Sentences like (6a), to which no transformations applied (strictly, to which only obligatory transformations applied) constituted the class of "kernel" sentences.
47. The quotation is from 1969c: 134.
48. See Miller, 1962, Savin & Perchonock, 1965, for representative experiments, and Fodor & Garrett, 1966, for early critical discussion.
49. For discussion of the reaction of psychologists to theory change, see Bever, 1988.
50. For later remarks on the derivational theory of complexity, see 1987c.
51. On chess, see 1994g: 7.
52. On parsers "incorporating" the I-language, see e.g. 1986a: 25.
53. On "minimal attachment," see Frazier, 1988.
54. On levels referred to by the parser, see van de Koot, 1991; on rule-based or principle-based parsers, see e.g. 1986a: 151.

55. On whether parsers should be the "same" for all languages, see 1995b: 28.

56. The claim that parsers and grammars should be the same has been argued by Phillips, 1996. The conclusion about grammaticality versus parsability is on p. 274. I am grateful to him for helpful correspondence on the issues involved.

57. The quotation on the incoherence of denying the competence–performance distinction, is p.c. April 1998.

58. Phillips, to appear.

59. On computational complexity for a cognitive system, see 2000b: 111; the remark that it "might be correct" is 2000b: 112.

60. For a further potential basis for the unification of grammars and parsers, see the discussion on phases in chapter 2.

61. Berwick & Weinberg, 1984.

62. For discussion of the direction of explanation, see Smith, 1986. This may well be an area where "design specifications" of the external system have been evolutionarily operative in fixing the properties of the language faculty. See the discussion of Minimalism in chapter 2.

63. On the denial that parsing is "quick and easy," see 1995a: 19; compare e.g. Gazdar, 1981: 276.

64. Steiner, 1978: 147.

65. Example (11) is from Montalbetti, 1984, and is cited in Phillips, to appear. The designation "seductively natural" is from Phillips.

66. Example (12) is from 1986a: 11; (13) is from Smith, 1989: 58; (14) is from Pritchett, 1988: 570.

67. On accessibility to the central system, see 1986a: 262.

68. On perceptual strategies and deciding between the grammar and the parser, see Smith & Wilson, 1979: 42f.

69. Pritchett, 1988; the quotation is from p. 575. This account is greatly simplified and, of course, controversial; see Pritchett, 1988, for discussion.

70. For economy, see 1998c. Recent discussion occurs in 2000b.

71. On "least commitment," see Marr, 1982: 106.

72. On back-tracking, see Marcus, 1980: 34.

73. The quotation "the least costly derivation be *used*" is from 1995b: 145 (my emphasis).

74. For earlier versions of the theory, see e.g. 1991e, 1995b: 139.

75. Technically, the verb moves to AGRS. The insight about the difference between French and English illustrated in (15) and (16) goes back to Emonds, 1978.

76. For "procrastination" see 1991e, 1995b. For relevant discussion of comparable examples, see Roberts, 1997: 100. In more recent work "the principle Procrastinate is no longer formulable" (2000b: 132), and the notion of feature strength is likewise eliminated from the theory. Replacements for these concepts are matters of ongoing research, and will hopefully have beneficial effects on the properties of the parser.

77. *John is likely* . . . is a case of "super-raising"; *What did you persuade* . . . shows "superiority effects." See e.g. 1995b: 296f.

78. Føllesdal, 1990: 102.

79. On *Pygmalion*, see 1977b: 89.

80. "Grammar grows in the mind," 1980a: 134.

81. For parameter setting, see 1981e; for classic exemplification and discussion, see Hyams, 1986, Roeper & Williams, 1987. For a useful early overview, see A. Smith, 1988. For more recent discussion, see e.g. 2002b; Roberts, 1997; Uriagereka, 1998; Belletti & Rizzi, 2002; Baker, 2003.
82. Chomsky discusses (17) and (18) in 1986a: 78.
83. The observation that theories are not refuted by data is not original with Chomsky, cf. e.g. Koyré (1968) on Galileo, but he has done more than most to make its relevance obvious to cognitive scientists.
84. Neeleman & Weerman, 1997. The examples in (19) and (20) are from p. 145.
85. For the child data corpus, see MacWhinney, 1995.
86. On the immune system, see 1980a: 136ff.; Piattelli-Palmarini, 1989.
87. The quotations are from Piattelli-Palmarini, 1989: 12. Chomsky quotes approvingly the work of Niels Kaj Jerne (1985), who was pre-eminently responsible for the intellectual breakthrough: see 1980a: 136; 1992d: 15.
88. On multiple critical periods, see Eubank & Gregg, 1996.
89. Lenneberg, 1967; for discussion, see Hurford, 1991. For further kinds of evidence for the critical period, see Smith, 1998.
90. On first versus second language acquisition, see e.g. Strozer, 1994.
91. The claim about lateralization is simplistic, see chapter 1, note 34 above.
92. On the evidence from aphasia, see Bishop, 1993.
93. Vargha-Khadem et al., 1997, present an interesting, but inconclusive, case of a boy who underwent hemidecortication at eight and a half years of age and began to speak shortly thereafter.
94. On Down's syndrome, see Rondal, 1995, and especially Rondal & Comblain, 1996. A comprehensive recent overview with new results can be found in Perovic, 2003.
95. On word learning, see Carey, 1978. Bloom & Markson (1998) suggest that the rate of word learning drops off only because most of the relevant words have been learned.
96. Mayberry, 1993: 1258.
97. For Genie, see Curtiss, 1977; Curtiss et al., 1974; Rymer, 1993.
98. On the "imperfection" of parametric variation, see 2001c: 2.
99. On learning and modularity, see Fodor, 1989.
100. On conditions imposed by the mind–brain, see 1997g: last page.
101. Baker, 2003, makes the intriguing suggestion that parametric differences among languages have the advantage of allowing the concealment of information.
102. On maturation, see Radford, 1990; Tsimpli, 1992/96.
103. Null-subject languages were formerly referred to as "pro-drop" languages: see 1981b; the term "null subject" is due to Rizzi, 1982.
104. Greek examples from Tsimpli, 1992; English examples from Radford, 1990; French and Italian examples from Tsimpli, 1991.
105. The structure of the VP, like everything in current theory, is contested; see e.g. Kayne, 1994.
106. The quotation is from Tsimpli, 1992: 160; 1996: 159.
107. The analysis of the alternative word orders of Irish is replete with complexities; see e.g. Borsley & Roberts, 1996: 19ff. Current research at the University of Ulster casts considerable doubt on the validity of the argument about word-order acquisition in Irish.

108. On evidence for the anatomical and functional organization of the language faculty in general, see Saffran, 2003. The *Journal of Neurolinguistics* is a good source of evidence.
109. On commisurotomy, see e.g. Gazzaniga, 1994.
110. On agenesis of the corpus callosum, see Tappe, 1999. "Word naming" involves giving the appropriate word for a stimulus picture, such as a *brush*.
111. The "computational system" is the "CS" of 1995b: 6; or the "C_{HL}" of 1995b: 221.
112. On the polyglot *savant*, see Smith & Tsimpli, 1995; Morgan et al., 2002, and references therein.
113. The correlation between the possibility of having a null subject and postposing that subject is not absolute; see Smith & Tsimpli, 1995: 92.
114. On lexical acquisition not being subject to a critical period, see Bloom & Markson, 1998.
115. On the K family (also known as the KE family), see Gopnik, 1990, 1994; Gopnik & Crago, 1991; Hurst et al., 1990; and especially Paradis, 1997.
116. The family tree in (28) is modified from Gopnik, 1994: 112. See also Paradis, 1997. For the affected gene being FOXP2, see Lai et al., 2001; Enard et al., 2002; Newbury & Monaco, 2002; Marcus & Fisher, 2003.
117. On the K family members' problems with abstract features, see Gopnik & Crago, 1991: 34.
118. The quotations are from Gopnik, 1994: 127, 132.
119. On alternative interpretations of the K family data, see e.g. Vargha-Khadem et al., 1995. For the "Chomskyan" interpretation, see Gopnik & Goad, 1997. There has been a huge amount of research on the K family in the last five years. A balanced summary of the case, which does justice to both sides in the debate, is provided by Marcus & Fisher, 2003.
120. Van der Lely, 1997a.
121. A useful summary of connectionism appears in Bechtel, 1994; more detailed treatment can be found in Bechtel and Abrahamson, 1991. Critical analysis occurs in Fodor & Pylyshyn, 1988; Pinker & Prince, 1988; and especially Rey, 1997.
122. Rey, 1997: 227.
123. On "automaticity," see Elman et al., 1996: 386.
124. Quotations from Elman et al., 1996: 39 and 388.
125. The array in (29) is from Elman, 1993: 87. For further discussion, see Smith, 1997; and especially Marcus, 1998. If the correct hypothesis involves "even parity," (30) should receive "1"; if it involves a "1" in fifth position, it should receive "0" and so on.
126. Smith & Tsimpli, 1995: 137ff.
127. On the connectionist anathema, see Elman et al., 1996 *passim*.
128. Chomsky's remark is from 1993c: 86.
129. For further discussion see Smith & Tsimpli, 1997, and references therein. Christiansen & Chater, 2001, and Plaut, 2003, provide useful summaries of applications of connectionist networks to linguistic problems. On poverty-of-the-stimulus arguments in general, see Ritter, 2002. Culicover, 1999, defends the claim that parasitic gaps can be acquired inductively, a position which Janke, 2001, attacks. Smith, 2003c, suggests a further use for networks in the acquisition of phonology.

CHAPTER 4 PHILOSOPHICAL REALISM: COMMITMENTS AND CONTROVERSIES

1. For one philosopher's comments on the obtuseness of philosophers vis-à-vis Chomsky, see Horwich, 2003: 175.
2. On realism, see 1980a: 189ff. *et passim*; 1986a: 256; 1988c: 237; etc.
3. An instrumentalist stance is adopted by Dennett, 1978, 1987.
4. Chomsky's historical discussion is in e.g. 1995a: 5ff.
5. The quotation about traces is from 1988b: 81; see chapter 2.
6. The quotation about quarks is from 1995a: 38, citing Quine, 1992.
7. The best-known proponents of Platonism are Jerrold Katz, 1981, 1985, 1996; Richard Montague (Thomason, 1974: 2); and Bas van Fraassen, 1980: 134–135.
8. For dragons, see Yang et al., 1989: 214.
9. On I-language, see 1986a: 21; 1987b: 36. For recent discussion, see Egan, 2003; Ludlow, 2003, and Chomsky's replies, 2003c: 269ff.
10. "Mind–brain" is the usual short-hand term Chomsky uses (e.g. 1995b: 2) to refer to what is "in our minds, ultimately in our brains" (1980a: 5).
11. The "internalized" quotation is from 1965: 8.
12. In philosophy, "intentional" refers to the property of "aboutness" in virtue of which sentences containing e.g. the word "cat" are about cats; "intensional" refers to the meaning, as opposed to the reference, of particular expressions, so that "evening star" and "morning star" have different meanings even though they both refer to Venus.
13. On squeaking doors, see 1987b: 37; and chapter 1 above for discussion. It is worth putting on record that Chomsky is not advancing the theory that the I-language interprets squeaking doors. He is committed to the I-language strongly generating expressions and assigning them various kinds of status. There is a possibility that it may further assign a structure to "every event," including coughs, squeaking doors, bleating, and so on. If the latter is correct then the implication would be that speakers of different languages would interpret these events differently. "I have no idea whether it's true, and nothing turns on it" (p.c. April 1998).
14. For discussion of computationalism, see Smolensky, 1994. For representationalism, see Egan, 2003; Rey, 2003, and Chomsky's reply, 2003c: especially p. 285 for the various meanings of "represent."
15. On the hardware–software distinction, see 1996a: 12.
16. "what is actually represented . . ." is from 1981b: 8; "the brain uses such notations . . ." is from 1981b: 35.
17. "something akin to deduction . . ." is from 1986a: 270.
18. The best-worked-out inferential model of cognition is Relevance theory, see Sperber & Wilson, 1986/95.
19. On Chomsky's computationalism, see e.g. 1988b: 2; 1994e *passim*.
20. On "representation of," see 1995a: 53. For discussion of the difference between "representation" and "representation of," see Burton-Roberts et al., 2000; Carr, 2003.
21. On the weakness of non-representational theories, see 1986a: 245.
22. On the act of faith, see 1994e: 206.
23. Following Hockney, 1975, Quine's position has become known as the "bifurcation" thesis.

24. On the "fact of the matter," see 1980a: 15. Chomsky points out that what makes no sense is the notion of "extensional equivalence," when it is predicated of human language, as it falsely presupposes the existence of a set of well-formed formulae (the expressions of the language).

25. On fitting but not guiding, see Quine, 1972/74: 442. The ABC example is from p. 448.

26. The claim of empirical falseness is made in 1975a: 181.

27. On weak equivalence, see 1955/75: 5; 1995b: 16.

28. For the notion "constituent," see chapter 2.

29. The quotation is from Montague, 1970/74: 223. Montague's work has no bearing on real semantics on the traditional interpretation, as the existence of the world is irrelevant to his mathematical results. Even on the construal of "semantics" that he presumably intended, as pertaining to the meaning of expressions, it is worth noting that Chomsky's early work (1955/75) explicitly motivated syntactic theory in terms of its providing the basis for an analysis of the meanings of expressions and their use. Elsewhere (1979: 72), he describes work on model-theoretic semantics as "promising."

30. For Chomsky's mentalism, see e.g. 1995a: 1. The quotation is from 1988b: 8.

31. On tacit knowledge, see e.g. 1975a: 24.

32. On "Procrastinate," see chapter 3 p. 118; 1995b: 198.

33. The quotation is from Quine, 1972/74: 442.

34. Searle is quoted in 1980a: 129.

35. Dummett et al. are discussed in 1994e: section 5. See 1990c on Searle and the discussion of blindsight.

36. "Cognize" appears in 1975a: 164, 1980a: 69. Chomsky writes caustically that "I used the word 'cognize' just to avoid pointless debates caused by irrational ideologies" (p.c. April 1998).

37. On the formulability of the mind–body problem, see 1988b: 145; 1994a: 157; 1995a: 5. On Newton's exorcizing the machine, see 2002b: 71. For recent discussion, see Lycan, 2003; Poland, 2003; Strawson, 2003, Egan, 2003; and Chomsky's response, 2003c.

38. The quotation about Priestley is from 1995a: 10.

39. The quotations are from Montague, 1969/74: 188; 1970/74: 223. The aim for "complete coverage" is enjoying a revival in Construction grammar; see e.g. Goldberg, 2003, and p. 8 above.

40. See e.g. Katz, 1981, 1996.

41. For the "Chomsky hierarchy," see Levelt, 1974.

42. The only empirical result of much interest is the strong equivalence of Context-free grammars and non-deterministic Pushdown storage automata, which basically underlies most parsers (Chomsky, p.c. April 1998).

43. An example of an attack on Chomsky for woolliness is Pullum, 1989.

44. "You can always do that" is from 1982c: 101; see also 1990a.

45. On the disanalogy between I-language and formal languages, see 1991c: 10.

46. It is perhaps worth making explicit a possible equivocation in the use of the term "abstract object." All science studies objects in the real world, but we can understand their real nature only by abstracting away from irrelevancies like friction or sentence length. For Katz and other Platonists, "abstract objects" are real things but not part of the physical world at all.

47. On infinity, see Langendoen & Postal, 1984; Katz, 1996. A denumerably infinite set is one whose members can be put into a one-to-one correspondence with the natural numbers; a non-denumerably infinite set is one whose members cannot. For instance, the real numbers are not denumerably infinite, but are "larger" (have greater cardinality), because there is an injective map from the natural numbers to the real numbers, but no such map in the reverse direction.

48. George, 1996.

49. On Katz's awareness, see Katz, 1996: 278.

50. The quotations are from Katz, 1996: 270 and 277.

51. On communication, see Armstrong, 1971; Searle, 1972/74. The "essential purpose" is from Searle, 1972/74.

52. Davidson, 1994: 234.

53. On the "theory of meaning," see Dummett, 1989: 210.

54. On public language, see Egan, 2003; Millikan, 2003; and Chomsky's response 2003c.

55. The "entire vocabulary of English" is in fact not well-defined: even major dictionaries omit huge swathes of the technical vocabulary of domains as varied as punk rock and core science.

56. Dummett, 1989: 192.

57. Grice, 1975; Sperber & Wilson, 1986/95.

58. For detailed discussion of inference, see Sperber & Wilson, 1986/95; Smith & Wilson, 1992; Carston, 2002, and references therein.

59. The philosophical presuppositions about semantics are implicit in the title of Quine's seminal *Word and Object* (Quine, 1960). Chomsky has repeatedly stressed that no such relation should be assumed, hence the use of "alleged."

60. Chomsky points out (p.c.) that even the use of the word *who* in *who I am referring to* presupposes the notion of "person," which is already philosophically problematic.

61. For more on hints, see Sperber & Wilson, 1986/95; Smith, 1989. Interesting corroboration of the claim comes from work on language processing, e.g. Sanford & Sturt, 2002.

62. For Chomsky's views on the evolution of language, see Hauser et al., 2002. A useful overview of the issues appears in Christiansen & Kirby, 2003; see also Nowak & Komarova, 2001, and the papers in Briscoe (ed), 2002.

63. On the usability of language, see 1994a: 161.

64. For Chomsky's views on pragmatics, see 1999i; for discussion, see Carston, 1999, 2002. Given the success of Relevance theory (Sperber & Wilson, 1986/95; Carston, 2002), one might consider Chomsky's comment that "[t]here are no theories about use" (Winston, 2002: 32) unduly pessimistic.

65. On Dummett's "absurd" view, see 1989: 205.

66. This guarantee is essentially Sperber & Wilson's (second) principle of relevance, see their 1986/95: 260f.

67. An "utter mystery" is from Bilgrami, 1992: 4; see also Chomsky, 1995a: 47f.

68. On the "more-or-less" nature of communication, see 1996a: 14.

69. On arthritis, see Burge, 1979; Bilgrami, 1992: 67f.; on yawls and ketches, see Davidson, 1984: 196.

70. On convention, see Lewis, 1969; Millikan, 2003; and Chomsky's response, 2003c: 308.

71. On *likely* and *probable*, see Smith, 1989: 194.

72. On language as ill-defined, see e.g. Hockett, 1968.
73. It should be noted that I am referring to variation across individuals rather than variation within a single individual.
74. On private language, see Wittgenstein, 1953: paragraph 269; cf. Kripke, 1982; Budd, 1994. For detailed discussion, see 1986a: ch. 4.
75. "Intrinsically social" and "public availability" are from Davidson, 1990: 314. Cf. "Linguistics is the study of what the members of a speech community have in common" (Lycan, 1986: 247).
76. The status of rules is the same whether these pertain to the principles of binding theory, the regularities of aspiration in phonology, or the meaning of lexical items such as *know* or *house*.
77. On Robinson Crusoe, see Kripke, 1982: 96.
78. For "taking him in to our community," see Kripke, 1982: 110. On the "right," see ibid. fn. 85. Chomsky's main discussion of Kripke appears in his 1986a.
79. "Kripkensteinian" is the rebarbative adjective standardly used to describe Kripke's (1982) interpretation of Wittgenstein.
80. On a person "in isolation," see again Kripke, 1982: 110. As Chomsky puts it: "The argument against private language is defanged" (1986a: 233).
81. For Genie, see Curtiss, 1977; chapter 3 above.
82. For discussion of rules in this context, see 1986a: ch. 4; Smith, 1988.
83. The quotation about "completely foreign" is from 1993c: 18–19; see also 1986a: 226.
84. For Chomsky's discussion of a private language, see 1986a: 232ff.; and Budd, 1994.
85. Bilgrami, 1992: 75.
86. The quotation on Wittgenstein's skeptic is from 1986a: 225.
87. On foundationalism, see Bracken, 1993: 59.
88. For the "best theory," see 1986a: 245.
89. "skeptical arguments can be dismissed" is from 1994e: 182.
90. On "justified true belief," see e.g. Moser, 1995.
91. On being so constituted ("I have no grounds . . . I just do it"), see 1986a: 225, 235, 244.
92. On "unconscious knowledge," see 1977b: 97. For "cognize," see note 36 above.
93. Chomsky's demurral is p.c. April 1998.
94. On necessary limitations, see 1994a: 156; 1986a: 237. As he picturesquely puts it "if you're a great weight-lifter, you're going to be a rotten butterfly" (2002h: 220).
95. On echolocation, see e.g. the *Encyclopaedia Britannica*.
96. On "problems and mysteries," see 1975a, esp. ch. 4; 1980a: 6–7; cf. Winston, 2002: 38.
97. The quotation on human science-forming capacities is from 1975a: 25.
98. For a more detailed account of reference, see any of the standard text-books: Heim & Kratzer, 1998; Larson & Segal, 1995. On Chomsky's view, these books are examples of "syntax"; see further 2003c: 304f.
99. On intentionality, see Rey, 2003, and Chomsky's response, 2003c.
100. "beyond the reach of our minds" is from 1980a: 6 (Chomsky was not discussing intentionality).
101. "only syntax and pragmatics" is from 1995a: 26; "pure syntax" is from 1995a: 19.

102. On "representing the world" is from 1995a: 27.
103. The quotation about "everything falling within semantics" is p.c. April 1998. "LSLT" is 1955/75.
104. On formal semantics as internalist, see Winston, 2002: 17.
105. "causal connection" is from Putnam, 1989: 219; cf. Devitt, 1981. Putnam has revised his position more recently: see his 1993. For discussion, see Chomsky, 1995a: 43.
106. *a hard bed for a dwarf* is from 1988c; *tea* or *polluted water* is from 1996a: 50.
107. On Chomsky on truth, see e.g. 1980a: 116ff. He is sympathetic to "deflationary" accounts.
108. Chomsky himself has been somewhat skeptical about pragmatics, though he believes that certain aspects are amenable to research, unlike the Cartesian problems, which remain mysteries. See, in particular, 1992d; for discussion, see Carston, 2002.
109. For compositionality, see Horwich, 2003: 174–175, and Chomsky's reply, 2003c.
110. In recent work (to appear) Chomsky discusses the nature of semantic representation in some detail, replacing the earlier "LF" with the level "SEM." Importantly, this is still syntactically defined.
111. Chomsky's position on the analytic/synthetic distinction (see e.g. 1980c: 45, 1996a: 52) is anti-Quine, and anti-most other people, but see Grice & Strawson, Moravcsik and the extensional circle, Moravcsik, 1990: 134, etc. For recent discussion, see Pietroski, 2003, and Chomsky's reply, 2003c.
112. For Chomsky's position on reference, see 1988b: 33. The examples are from 1992d: 114. For recent discussion, see Ludlow, 2003; Horwich, 2003, and Chomsky's replies, 2003c.
113. On London, see e.g. 1993c: 22; 1995a: 21; 1996a: 22. As always, his position is actually more complex than this: see 1995a: 43.
114. Frege, 1956.
115. On nearness, see 1996a: 47, and chapter 1 above.
116. On innateness, see e.g. 1988b: 134, 190. For recent discussion, see Gopnik, 2003; Horwich, 2003; and Chomsky's reply, 2003c.
117. "expression of the genes" is from 2000a: 187. Chomsky explicitly avoids the term "innateness hypothesis" (see e.g. 1975a: 13) which is frequently used by those arguing the alternative position. For a useful summary but hostile and uncomprehending critique of Chomsky's position, see Sampson, 1989, 1999. For discussion, see Smith, 2001.
118. Chomsky's earliest discussion of his rationalist forebears is 1966a; there is a sustained defense and elaboration of his position in 1975a. See especially, pp. 146ff., and for Quine, pp. 200ff.
119. On universals and the poverty of the stimulus, see e.g. 1993d: 6. For recent discussion, see Gopnik, 2003, and Chomsky's response, 2003c. Further debate is provided in Ritter, 2002.
120. Virtually all Chomsky's linguistic work is about universals.
121. On learning, see 1986a: 263–264, and on general properties of learning, see 1980a: 135, 244ff.
122. The quotation is from Smith, 1989: 65, paraphrasing Fodor, 1975.
123. Chomsky even suggests (1992d: 116) that the argument carries over to examples like *carburetter* and *bureaucrat*.

124. On selection rather than instruction, see 1980c: 58, 1991d: 33; and Piattelli-Palmarini, 1989.
125. The quotation on learning having little place is from 1991c: 17. For doubts about the innateness of the language of thought, see Spelke & Tsivkin, 2001.
126. Chomsky's puzzlement is expressed frequently; the quotation is in p.c. April 1998. For discussion, see Smith, 2001.
127. On dispositions, see Quine, 1969; cf. 1975a: 204.
128. On "input" versus "uptake" (or "intake"), see e.g. White, 1981: 271.
129. On motherese, see 1988c: 259; Smith, 1989: ch. 13. For enlightened discussion, see Cattell, 2000.
130. On the relative success of first and second language learning, see Strozer, 1994; Eubank & Gregg, 1996; Birdsong, 1992.
131. On negative evidence, see e.g. Bowerman, 1987, from whom the examples in (12) are taken.
132. On retreat, see e.g. Randall, 1990. On reformulation, see Chouinard & Clark, 2003.
133. Putnam, 1967: 21.
134. On general intelligence as enough for language acquisition, see Quine, 1972/74; Halliday, 1975; Elman et al., 1996.
135. The quotation is from Elman et al., 1996: 117.
136. On rigidity, etc., see 1986a: 72, 264; 1988b: 160.
137. On monogenesis, see Putnam, 1967: 18.
138. On what precisely is innate, it is worth emphasizing that Minimalism of the sort described in chapter 2 seeks to minimize those properties which are exclusive to language.
139. On unification and reduction, see Boakes & Halliday, 1970; for general discussion, see Kitcher, 1989; Fodor, 1974/81; Poland, 2003: 39–42. For extensive discussion of unification, see 1995a; 1996a: 34; 2003c, especially p. 264.
140. J. J. Thomson discovered the electron in 1897.
141. For Gresham's law, see Fodor, 1974/81: 133–134.
142. Lewis, 1994: 412. The promissory notes are from 1994: 418, 412.
143. For discussion of connectionism, see Rey, 1997, Smith, 1997.
144. Chomsky's remarks about electrical activity are from 1995a: 11.
145. The remark about "current imaging" is from 2002b: 160. See also 1999j.
146. The term "system of ideas" is the title of D'Agostino, 1986.

CHAPTER 5   LANGUAGE AND FREEDOM

1. Chomsky puts the point in the epigraph more forcefully when he says that "in the sciences at least, people have to be trained for creativity and disobedience" (2002h: 237).
2. "the task of a scientific analysis . . ." is from 1972d: 161.
3. On common sense, see 1994a: 155.
4. On genetics, see 1978/87: 199.
5. On the benevolence of governments, see 1994d: 40. On language learning, see 1980a: 134.

6. The quotation on the morality of states is from 1988c: 695.
7. On Palestinians, the PLO, and Israel, see 1991a: 187.
8. On external infiltration, see 1992a: 87.
9. The Trilateral Commission, founded in 1973 with money from David Rockefeller and with Zbigniew Brzezinski as executive secretary and director, is a linkage of elite groups from North America, Europe, and Japan, whose stated goals include "managing the world economy."
10. "the normally passive general population . . ." is from Herman & Chomsky, 1988: 237.
11. On "the science-forming faculty," see 1994a: 155.
12. On understanding and changing the world, see 1971b, c.
13. A similar point about overwhelming documentation is made by Roy, 2003.
14. "Plato's problem" and "Orwell's problem" are from 1986a: xxv *et passim*.
15. On the tenuous relation between the strands of his work, see e.g. 1992b: 1; 2003b: 40.
16. The "essential human need" is from 1992b: 2.
17. The quotation about Skinner is from 1959: 547.
18. "[Reason] is all we have" is from Peck, 1987: 48. "irrational belief" is from 1988c: 773; 1992b: 158.
19. "drowning in hypocrisy" is from 1992b: ix. Elsewhere Chomsky puts "an end to hypocrisy" at the top of his wish list (Vidal-Hall, 2003: 261).
20. For Chomsky on Rorty, see Burchill, 1998: 10f.
21. On rationality, see Nagel, 1997: 15 *et passim*.
22. The quotations from Foucault are from Wilkin, 1997: 77ff.
23. The quotation on "a future science of mind" is from 1996a: 12.
24. For references on the emotions, see Smith, 2002d.
25. The "painful void" is from Levi, 1988: xi.
26. For "problems" and "mysteries," see 1975a: ch. 4; 1980a: 6.
27. For Fodorian modularity, see Fodor, 1983; chapter 1 above.
28. The quotation about "a subsystem dedicated to language" is from 1994a: 155; see also 1980b: 46. On face recognition, see 1979: 51f.
29. On moral judgment, see Cohen & Rogers, 1991: 10; the quotation is from 1988c: 469. For further discussion, see Burchill, 1998: 8f.
30. The quotation about a "rich, intricate system" is from 1988c: 241; for general discussion see also Premack & Premack, 1994.
31. On a "theory of justice," see 1988c: 241.
32. The quotation about David Hume is from 2003b: 40–41; Chomsky elaborates on this idea in his 2002h: 359ff.
33. On moral objectivity, see Nagel, 1997: ch. 6.
34. On the absence of any ethical theory, see Winston, 2002: 69.
35. The quotation is from Damasio, 1994: 10–11.
36. The quotation about "moral barriers to coercion . . ." is from 1988c: 244. See also Burchill, 1998: 12.
37. Cf. Chomsky, 1971d, 1972d.
38. The quotation "intrinsic to human nature . . ." is from 1988c: 245.
39. On arguing from plasticity, see e.g. Elman et al., 1996; Bates, 1997.
40. On hemispherectomy, see chapter 3 and the references cited there.

41. On modularity as emergent, see Karmiloff-Smith, 1992a; for discussion, see Smith, 1994b.
42. Dehaene, 2003: 30, observes that "the architecture of our brain is limited by strong genetic constraints, though it retains a fringe of flexibility." His article emphasizes the fact that the "visual word form region" is consistently located within the brain of all individuals investigated.
43. On human limitations, see e.g. 1988c: 466; and the discussion of echolocation in chapter 4.
44. On our lack of understanding of human behavior, see e.g. 1988c: 404, 416.
45. The quotations on "mental organization" and the "defining property of man" are from 1973b: 185, 171.
46. The quotation from Rousseau is from his *Discourse on Inequality*, 1755.
47. The quotations about Descartes are from 1973b: 173, 175.
48. For background on Chomsky's anarchism, see 2002h; Barsky, 1997; Winston, 2002: ch. 4.
49. The quotation about Proudhon is from Zeldin, 1973: 345.
50. The quotations about Humboldt are from 1973b: 177.
51. The quotations are from Rocker, 1938: 7, 26.
52. For Chomsky's first article, see Rai, 1995: 8.
53. The countries bombed by the United States include (in chronological order): China, Korea, Guatemala, Indonesia, Cuba, Congo, Peru, Laos, Vietnam, Cambodia, Lebanon, Grenada, Libya, El Salvador, Nicaragua, Panama, Bosnia, Sudan, Former Yugoslavia, Iraq and Afghanistan.
54. Chomsky's view of corporations can be deduced from his description of them as "rabid raccoons" (2002h: 345).
55. On the patenting of sterile seeds, see Edwards, 1998.
56. "Rollback" features in 1995d; largely reproduced in 1996b: ch. 2; see also 1999g. The quotation is part of their statement of purpose. *Z Magazine* and its associated website, *ZNet*, http://www.zmag.org is an excellent source for Chomsky's political essays.
57. The quotation about free enterprise is from 1995c: 12.
58. The quotation about "giving suggestions" is from 1996b: 79.
59. The quotation about the "vision of a future society" is from 1973b: 183.
60. The case of the kibbutzim differs from the other examples cited: rather than establishment repression causing their failure, it was "their trade-off with the state" whereby they "received lots of subsidies and support for their (I'm sorry to say) extreme racist policies," p.c. April 1998. Chomsky spent a few weeks on a kibbutz in 1953; for discussion see 2002h: 196–199; Barsky, 1997: 82; Peck, 1987: 9.
61. "optimism of the will" is from the masthead of the journal *Ordine nuovo*, edited by Gramsci immediately after the First World War.
62. "Being alone . . ." is from 1994b: 105–106.
63. "An organizer's dream" is from 2002h: 399.
64. "the intensive study . . ." is from 1973b: 186.
65. "I don't have faith . . ." is from Peck, 1987: 48.
66. The quotation about "providing a service" is from 1992b: 161. On the inclusion of universities in this list, see 1997a.

67. The quotation about "ideological disciplines" is from 1982b: 110.
68. On propaganda, see 2002f; 2003f. Corroboration of many of Chomsky's claims can be found in e.g. Pilger, 2002; Winston, 2002; Curtis, 2003.
69. I had originally written Denmark and Canada in lieu of Norway and Finland, but both these former countries appear in both the 1995 and 1996 editions of the Amnesty International annual report.
70. For documentation by Liberty, see Foley, 1995, especially chapter 9.
71. On the case of Fatih Tas, see e.g. Turgut, 2002.
72. On his responsibility as an American, see e.g. 1988c: 767.
73. On Danchev, see 1986a: 276.
74. On Ienaga, see Parry, 1997; Ienaga, 1998.
75. Some of the most extreme attacks on Chomsky, many involving Alan Dershowitz, are documented in 1992b: 346ff. Strikingly, the issue of his perceived anti-Semitism virtually never arises in Israel, where he receives "extensive and quite sympathetic media coverage . . . in mainstream press and national TV," p.c. April 1998. For discussion, see Rai, 1995: 132.
76. "outside the pale" is cited in 1993e: 85. His perversity is mentioned in e.g. Searle, 1972/74.
77. Stimson's remark is quoted in 1987a: 57.
78. Publications on Vietnam include: 1969a, 1971a, 1973a, 1973b, 1981a, 1982b, 1985, 1993a, 2000f, 2002a, 2002h, and especially 1993b.
79. On the "American invasion," see e.g. 1992b: 66. Major American involvement in Vietnam dates from the withdrawal of the French after the battle of Dien Bien Phu in 1954.
80. On the "doveish" view, see 1993b: 54; Chomsky is citing Hilsman, 1967.
81. On East Timor, see 1981a: 85; 1982b: ch. 13; 2002h:294ff. and especially 1996a: ch. 8. On the British role, see Curtis 2003: ch. 21.
82. The figure of 10 percent of the population is cited by Moynihan (see below). When Bishop Belo and Jose Ramos-Horta were awarded the Nobel Peace Prize in 1996, figures between a quarter and a third of the population were cited by the United Nations.
83. Moynihan is cited in 1982b: 339 and 1996a: 209.
84. The quotation on the "responsibility of the writer" is from 1996a: 56.
85. On "crimes against humanity," see e.g. 1996a: 56f.
86. On the lies and exaggeration about Cambodian atrocities, see Chomsky & Herman, 1979a: 130. Here as elsewhere, the massive documentation that they have provided has been largely ignored.
87. On "ignoring crimes," see 1996a: 63.
88. The "high level of dishonesty" is from Rai, 1995: 27ff.
89. On the coda, see Chomsky & Herman, 1979a. The quotation is p.c. April 1998. The object of their criticism was François Ponchaud.
90. The "defining moment" is from 2002c: 23.
91. On the use of the events of 9–11 as an excuse, see e.g. 2002a: 157.
92. *9–11* (2001a) is the only political book of Chomsky's to have enjoyed commercial success in the United States.
93. "monstrous crimes" comes from 2002d: 66.
94. "horrifying atrocities" comes from 2001a: 11.

95. On Chomsky being an "apologist" for terror, see e.g. 2003b: 15. On the need to understand (e.g.) Osama bin Laden's putative motives – to get infidels out of Saudi Arabia and other Muslim countries – see 2001a: 60, and the observation (ibid.: 78) that the "clash of civilizations" "makes little sense."
96. On rational responses, see e.g. 2001a: 26.
97. "moral truism" is from 2002g: 77.
98. On double standards, see 2003b:28f.; on the manipulation of the historical record – Orwell's memory hole – see 2001a: 47.
99. On definitions of "terror," etc. see 2001a, 2000f, etc. The definition cited here is from 2002f: 79; for a slightly different version, see 2001a: 16.
100. For the US as a terrorist state, see 2001a: 40, 43f., 89–90; 2000f: 79. For a comparable analysis of the British role in terror, see Curtis, 2003: ch. 3 "Explaining the 'war against terrorism.'"
101. On the UN resolution (A/RES/42/159), see 2001a:73. (Details may be found at the UN website: http://www.un.org/Depts/dhl/res/resa42.htm.)
102. On condemnation by the World Court, see 2002f: 86; 2002h: 86. (For documentation, see the on-line footnotes to the latter book, esp. ch 3 fnn. 43, 44, 45.)
103. On comparisons with Iraq, see 2001a: 42, 56, 66, 84.
104. On Albright's remark, see 2001a: 72–73.
105. On the "redeclaration" of the war, see 2002g: 70; cf. 2001a: 68.
106. On the "choice of victims," see 2002a: 1.
107. On the "universality" of double standards, see 2002f: 80.
108. On comparisons of counter-insurgency manuals, see 2001a: 57; 2003b: 24. Chomsky's original comparison appeared in his 1969a.
109. On the Al-Shifa pharmaceutical plant, see 2001a: 45; Curtis, 2003: 110–111.
110. On the tie-up with al-Qaeda, see 2001a: 53f. On the comparability of "worthy and unworthy victims," see below, p. 202.
111. On torture, see e.g. Vallely, 2003; Gillan, 2003. Gillan cites the killing under interrogation of two men from Afghanistan, where the official cause of death was given as "homicide"; and in the same article reports that an MI5 expert in terrorism "has admitted that the security service would use information extracted from tortured prisoners as evidence" (Gillan, 2003: 2).
112. The A. J. Muste quotation is from 2002a:144.
113. On protests *before* the war, see 2002j.
114. On health insurance, see 1993e; on free trade 1994b; on fruit growing in Guatemala 1992a: 47, 1985: 154; on pig farming in Haiti 1993a: 222.
115. "Private structures . . ." is from 1995f: 33.
116. "concentration of power" is from 1988c: 744.
117. The "economic role of terror" and the headline about Indonesia are from Chomsky & Herman, 1979a: 54, 205.
118. On tax reform, see Herman, 1992: 178–179.
119. *Year 501* was published in 1993, 501 years after Columbus's "discovery" of America. See now, 2003a. For an account of American history to which Chomsky is sympathetic, see Zinn, 1996.
120. On Liberia, see 1993a: 222.
121. On Guatemala, see 1983b: 283–284; 2000f; 2002h. On the recurrent pattern of American intervention, see Curtis, 2003: 346.

122. On drugs, see 1991a: ch. 4; 1992a: 82; 1994b: 34; 1992b: 221; 1994c: 198; 2002h: 152f.
123. The quotation from the Surgeon General is from 1991a: 123.
124. The threat of trade sanctions came under Super 301 (section 301 of the 1974 Trade Act) which is frequently invoked to ensure appropriate markets for American exports.
125. On the radar installation, see 1991a: 132.
126. On the banking industry, see 1991a: 116.
127. On companies which are off limits, see 1991a: 117.
128. The prison at the center of the report was Featherstone jail in Wolverhampton, UK.
129. The pamphlet is 1997b (updated as 2002f). The later edition has a few notes.
130. The most relevant collaboration with Herman is Herman & Chomsky, 1988.
131. The "purpose of the media . . ." is from Herman & Chomsky, 1988: 298. See also 1993b, 1993f, 1994d; Chomsky & Herman, 1979a, 1979b. A comparably scathing analysis of the US media appears in von Hoffman, 2003. For interesting parallel discussion see Carey, 1995; Chomsky's (1995g) introduction; and especially Rai, 1995: ch. 1.
132. The filters are introduced in Herman & Chomsky, 1988: ch. 1. The quotation is from p. 31.
133. The *Daily Herald* is discussed in Herman & Chomsky, 1988: 15; the US Air Force's newspapers on p. 20.
134. On the World Wide Web, see Burchill, 1998: 20.
135. On self-censorship, see e.g. 2001a: 113.
136. For the discussion of Orwell, see 2002h: 111ff.
137. The editors of Chomsky's 2002h have done a comparable task of reference-checking, providing 450 pages of notes substantiating the various claims made.
138. For Popiełuszko, see Herman & Chomsky, 1988: ch. 2.
139. Oscar Romero is now commemorated as a Christian martyr in Westminster Abbey.
140. On "indoctrination," see 1986a: 286.
141. The terms "legitimize" and "meaningless" are from Herman & Chomsky, 1988: ch. 3.
142. For some academic discussion of the propaganda model, see Rai, 1995.
143. Chomsky's first major political essay appeared originally in *Mosaic* in 1966 and is reprinted in revised form in 1969a.
144. See Rai, 1995: ch. 9.
145. Waldegrave was speaking in the House of Commons in February 1993. One might have hoped that a former Fellow of All Souls College Oxford would have greater regard for the truth.
146. "States are not . . ." is from 1993b: 45.
147. For "murdering history," see 1993a: ch. 10.
148. Schlesinger is discussed in 1981a: 147f. For detailed dissection of a comparable "web of deceit" in the activities of the British government, see Curtis, 2003.
149. The page chosen at random was 1991a: 135. The "Unsettling Specter of Peace" is from p. 108.
150. NSC68 is cited in e.g. 1992a: 8–9.
151. The target of the irony was Dixon, 1963. See 1966b: 30. McGilvray, 1999: 19 notes that Chomsky uses irony more in his political than his academic writing; and

MacFarquhar (2003: 75) contrasts his current "vicious sarcasm" with his earlier fierce, but relatively unsarcastic, criticism of government.

152. "benign bloodbaths" is from Chomsky & Herman, 1979a: 96 *et passim*. "mere genocide" is from 1969a: 255.
153. The documentation is in Peck, 1987: 270 *et passim*. On comparable destruction of dikes in North Korea, see 2000h: 302.
154. The figures for bombs dropped on Laos are from Chance, 1997. The quotation about "the rebel economy" is from Peck, 1987: 265.
155. The quotation about the "moral level" is from Peck, 1987: 266.
156. On the comparisons between East Timor and Cambodia, see e.g. Peck, 1987: 309ff.; Chomsky 1993a: 134ff.; 1996a: ch. 8; 2002h: 206.
157. "Our country right or wrong" is from Stephen Decatur, a US naval officer at the beginning of the eighteenth century.
158. On Saddam Hussein, see 1994d: 193.
159. On Noriega, see 1992a: 50f. The quotation is from p. 51.
160. On Pearl Harbor, see 1993b: 22.
161. On Hamlet, see 1985b: 32. Several examples of "what is left unsaid" are documented in "Objectivity and liberal scholarship", which appears in 1969a.
162. The US government papers are cited in 1993b: 95.
163. On the attempted heroization of Kennedy, see 1993b, *passim*. It could be argued that Kennedy's only deviation from his predecessors was to escalate the war dramatically: Eisenhower was relatively moderate.
164. On the Israeli invasion of Lebanon, see 1991a: 188. In Israel, it was pointed out at once that the Israeli attack was in reaction to the PLO adherence to the July 1981 cease-fire in the face of repeated attacks. For discussion and extensive documentation, see 1994d: ch. 3.
165. On Frankfurt airport, see 1983b: 303–304.
166. Herman's book is his 1992, updating Bierce, 1911/58.
167. On "communists," see e.g. Peck, 1987. This and the following quotation are from pp. 319 and 320.
168. On "terror," see 1986a: ch. 5. "retaliation" is from 1986c: 25; "counter-terror" from 1993b: 51, 61. Since the events of 9–11, Chomsky has returned repeatedly to the subject; see e.g. 2003b.
169. "internal aggression" is cited in Peck, 1987: 329; "subversion" is from 1993b: 41.
170. "preventing the spread of violence" and "stable regimes" are from Chomsky & Herman, 1979a: 86, 90.
171. The quotation from the *Economist* is cited in e.g. 1986a: 277.
172. On "peace" and "moderates," see 1983b: 271, 304, 288. On "profits," see 1993e: 68.
173. "I doubt that there are moral absolutes . . ." p.c. April 1998. For elaboration, see 2002h: 274, where he makes explicit that not being an axiom system allows for contradictions.
174. "a moral monster" is from 1988c: 748.
175. "I support the right . . ." is from 1992b: 349–350; "any form of authority . . ." is quoted by Alexander Cockburn in 1992b: xiii.
176. For useful summaries of the Faurisson affair, see Hitchens, 1985/90; Rai, 1995; and Barsky, 1997.

177. The "morass of insane rationality" and "lost one's humanity" are from 1969a: 11; comparable remarks appear on p. 294.
178. "conclusions of standard Holocaust studies" is quoted in Rai, 1995: 201–202.
179. "know very little" is cited in Barsky, 1997: 180.
180. The title of Faurisson's memoir translates as: "Memoir in my defense against those who accuse me of falsifying history: the question of the gas chambers."
181. The quotation is from Barsky, 1997: 183.
182. On compromise, see 1992b: 49.
183. Chomsky emphasizes (1996a: 165–166) that the term "fundamentalist" is code for "independent," only one of whose interpretations is fundamentalist in the sense of strict adherence to a literal interpretation of religious texts, be these Christian or Islamic. He has not to my knowledge written about Hizb-ut-Tahrir.
184. In England the law of blasphemy is an exception to the generalization. Moreover, it has the invidious property of defending only Christianity and not other religions.
185. "incitement to imminent lawless action" is cited in 1993d: 18; "a reasonable line," p.c. April 1998.
186. The quotation about Marx is from Rai, 1995: 135.
187. The quotation appeared in the paper *Al-Khilafah*, February 23, 1990.
188. Nagel's observation is from his 1991: 157. On the rationality of religion, see Nagel, 1997.
189. "I think you can give an argument . . ." is from 1992b: xiv.
190. His "personal reactions" are from 1992b: 248. Note that, even if ingenuous, his reactions are never simplistic. For instance, he believes that institutions like the World Bank are "illegitimate," but that to close them down "would be a catastrophe" (Winston, 2002: 80); what is needed is reform. Elsewhere (2002h: 201), he describes himself as "conservative" in his views on social change.
191. The remark "to change [the world] for the better" is from an endorsement for *Le Monde Diplomatique* in *Index on Censorship* 208: 87 (July 2003).
192. "Poor people . . ." is from 1992b: 324. "Get to work on it" is from 1996b: 114. See also 2002h: ch. 6.
193. "Provide the kind of service" is from 1992b: 161.

CONCLUSION

1. On problems and mysteries, see especially 1975a: ch. 4.
2. On the evolution of language, see 1996c; Newmeyer, 1997, and Hauser et al., 2002.
3. "No ordinary genius" is the title of Sykes, 1994.

ENVOI

1. On talking to rap-metal bands, see 1997f.
2. "something decent" is from 1992b: 292.

Bibliography

As is customary, I include here all the items I have referred to. In addition, I have included all those items by Chomsky, and a few by other authors, that I have used, directly or indirectly, in the preparation of the book. This is partly because some of the ideas clearly emanate from Chomsky, even if I have not ascribed them to him in detail, and partly because this will give the reader a clear indication of the extent of Chomsky's published output. I should emphasize that this part of the bibliography does not aim to be complete; it does aim to be representative.

Works which are of basic importance, either historically or currently, are marked with an asterisk.

Aarts, B. (2004) "Conceptions of gradience in the history of linguistics." *Language Sciences* 26.

Achbar, M. (ed.) (1994) *Manufacturing Consent: Noam Chomsky and the Media.* London, Black Rose Books.

Adger, D. (2003) *Core Syntax: A Minimalist Approach.* Oxford, Oxford University Press.

Alperovitz, G. (1967) *Atomic Diplomacy: Hiroshima and Potsdam.* New York, Vintage Books.

Altmann, G. (1998) "Ambiguity in sentence processing." *Trends in Cognitive Sciences* 2: 146–152.

Amnesty International Report 1995. London, A. I. Publications.

Amnesty International Report 1996. London, A. I. Publications.

Amnesty International Report 1997. London, A. I. Publications.

Amnesty International Report 2003. London, A. I. Publications.

Anderson, S. & D. Lightfoot (2002) *The Language Organ: Linguistics as Cognitive Physiology.* Cambridge, Cambridge University Press.

*Antony, L. & N. Hornstein (eds.) 2003. *Chomsky and his Critics.* Oxford, Blackwell.

Armstrong, D. (1971) "Meaning and communication." *Philosophical Review* 80: 427–447.

Atkinson, M. (2001) Review of N. Smith (1989) *Chomsky: Ideas and Ideals* (Cambridge University Press). *Journal of Linguistics* 37: 644–645.

Baker, G. P. & P. M. S. Hacker (1984) *Language, Sense and Nonsense.* Oxford, Blackwell.

Baker, M. (2001) *The Atoms of Language.* New York, Basic Books.

(2003) "Linguistic differences and language design". *Trends in Cognitive Sciences* 7: 349–353.

Baron-Cohen, S., A. Leslie & U. Frith (1985) "Does the autistic child have a theory of mind?" *Cognition* 21: 37–46.

Baron-Cohen, S. & J. Harrison (eds.) (1997) *Synaesthesia: Classic and Contemporary Readings.* Oxford, Blackwell.

Barrett, R. & R. Gibson (eds.) (1990) *Perspectives on Quine.* Oxford, Blackwell.

*Barsky, R. F. (1997) *Noam Chomsky: A Life of Dissent.* Cambridge, MA, MIT Press.

Bates, E. (1997) "On language savants and the structure of the mind: a review of Neil Smith & Ianthi-Maria Tsimpli, *The Mind of a Savant: Language Learning and Modularity." The International Journal of Bilingualism* 2: 163–179.

Bechtel, W. (1994) "Connectionism." In Guttenplan: 200–210.

Bechtel, W. & A. Abrahamson (1991) *Connectionism and the Mind: An Introduction to Parallel Processing in Networks.* Oxford, Blackwell.

Beeman, M. & C. Chiarello (eds.) (1997) *Right Hemisphere Language Comprehension: Perspectives from Cognitive Neuroscience.* Hillsdale, NJ, Lawrence Erlbaum Associates.

Beghelli, F. & T. Stowell (1997) "Distributivity and negation: the syntax of *each* and *every*." In A. Szabolcsi (ed.), *Ways of Scope Talking.* Dordrecht, Kluwer. 71–107.

Belletti, A. & L. Rizzi (2002) Editors' introduction to Chomsky, 2002b; pp. 1–44.

Bellugi, U., S. Marks, A. Bihrle & H. Sabo (1993) "Dissociation between language and cognitive functions in William's syndrome." In Bishop & Mogford: 177–189.

Berlinski, D. (1988) *Black Mischief: Language, Life, Logic, Luck.* Boston, Harcourt Brace Jovanovich.

Berwick, R. & A. Weinberg (1984) *The Grammatical Basis of Linguistic Performance.* Cambridge, MA, MIT Press.

Bever, T. (1988) "The psychological reality of grammar: a student's eye view of cognitive science." In W. Hirst (ed.), *The Making of Cognitive Science: Essays in Honor of George A. Miller.* Cambridge, Cambridge University Press. 112–142.

Bierce, A. (1911/58) *The Devil's Dictionary.* New York, Dover.

Bilgrami, A. (1992) *Belief and Meaning.* Oxford, Blackwell.

Billen, A. (2002) "How right can one man be?" *The Times,* 19.8.2002; pp. 4–5.

Billingsley, R. & A. Papanicolaou (eds) (2003) *Functional Neuroimaging Contributions to Neurolinguistics.* Special Issue of *Journal of Neurolinguistics,* 16: 251–456.

Birdsong, D. (1992) "Ultimate attainment in second language learning." *Language* 68: 706–755.

Bishop, D. (1993) "Language development after focal brain damage." In Bishop & Mogford: 203–219.

Bishop, D. & K. Mogford (eds.) (1993) *Language Development in Exceptional Circumstances.* Hove, Lawrence Erlbaum Associates.

Blackburn, S. (1984) *Spreading the Word.* Oxford, Oxford University Press.

Black, M. (1970) "Comment" on Chomsky, 1970. In Borger & Cioffi: 452–461.

Blakemore, D. (1987) *Semantic Constraints on Relevance.* Oxford, Blackwell.
    (1992) *Understanding Utterances.* Oxford, Blackwell.

Bloom, P. & L. Markson (1998) "Capacities underlying word learning." *Trends in Cognitive Sciences* 2, 2: 67–73.

Bloomfield, L. (1933) *Language.* New York, Holt.

Boakes, R. A. & M. S. Halliday (1970) "The Skinnerian analysis of behaviour." In Borger & Cioffi: 345–374.

Boole, G. (1854) *An Investigation of the Laws of Thought: On Which Are Founded the Mathematical Theories of Logic and Probabilities.* London, Walton & Maberley.

Borger, R. & F. Cioffi (eds.) (1970) *Explanation in the Behavioural Sciences.* Cambridge, Cambridge University Press.

Borsley, R. (1996) *Modern Phrase Structure Grammar.* Oxford, Blackwell.

Borsley, R. & I. Roberts (1996) "Introduction" to R. Borsley & I. Roberts (eds.), *The Syntax of the Celtic Languages.* Cambridge, Cambridge University Press. 1–52.

Botha, R. (1989) *Challenging Chomsky: The Generative Garden Game.* Oxford, Blackwell.

Bowerman, M. (1987) "The 'no negative evidence' problem: how do children avoid constructing an overly general grammar?" In J. Hawkins (ed.), *Explaining Language Universals.* Oxford, Blackwell. 73–101.

Bracken, H. (1984) *Mind and Language: Essays on Descartes and Chomsky.* Dordrecht, Foris.

(1993) "Some reflections on our sceptical crisis." In Reuland & Abraham: 59–70.

Braine, M. D. S. (1994) "Is nativism sufficient?" *Journal of Child Language* 21: 9–31.

Braithwaite, R. B. (1953/68) *Scientific Explanation: A Study of the Function of Theory, Probability and Law in Science.* Cambridge, Cambridge University Press.

Bresnan, J. (1994) "Locative inversion and the architecture of universal grammar." *Language* 70: 72–131.

Briscoe, T. (ed) (2002) *Linguistic Evolution through Language Acquisition.* Cambridge, Cambridge University Press.

Brodsky, J. (1987) *Less than One: Selected Essays.* Harmondsworth, Penguin.

Brody, M. (1987) Review of Chomsky, 1986a. *Mind & Language* 2: 165–177.

(1995) *Lexico-Logical Form: A Radically Minimalist Theory.* Cambridge, MA, MIT Press.

(1998) Review of Chomsky, 1995b. *Mind & Language* 13: 205–214.

(2002) "On the status of representations and derivations". In S. Epstein & D. Seely (eds.) *Derivation and Explanation in the Minimalist Program.* Oxford, Blackwell; pp. 19–41.

Brown, J. (1994) "Moving target guides drivers round the bend." *New Scientist* 1936: 17 (paraphrasing M. F. Land & D. N. Lee (1994) "Where we look when we steer," *Nature* 369: 742–74).

Budd, M. (1994) "Wittgenstein, Ludwig." In Guttenplan: 617–622.

Burchill, S. (1998) "Human nature, freedom and political community: an interview with Noam Chomsky." *Citizenship Studies* 2: 5–21.

Burge, T. (1979) "Individualism and the mental." *Studies in Philosophy* 4: 73–121.

Burkhardt, F. (ed.) (1996) *Charles Darwin's Letters: A Selection.* Cambridge, Cambridge University Press.

Burton-Roberts, N., P. Carr & G. Docherty (eds.) (2000) *Phonological Knowledge: Conceptual and Empirical Issues.* Oxford, Oxford University Press.

Byrne, A. (1994) "Behaviourism." In Guttenplan: 132–140.

Carden, G. (1970) "A note on conflicting idiolects." *Linguistic Inquiry* 1: 281–290.

Carey, A. (1995) *Taking the Risk out of Democracy: Propaganda in the US and Australia.* Sydney, University of New South Wales Press.

Carey, D. (2001) "Do action systems resist visual illusions?" *Trends in Cognitive Sciences* 5: 109–113.

Carey, S. (1978) "The child as word learner." In M. Halle, J. Bresnan & G. Miller (eds.), *Linguistic Theory and Psychological Reality*. Cambridge, MA, MIT Press. 264–293.

Carr, P. (2003) "Innateness, internalism and input: Chomsky's rationalism and its problems." *Language Sciences* 25: 615–636.

Carruthers, P. (1996) *Language, Thought and Consciousness: An Essay in Philosophical Psychology*. Cambridge, Cambridge University Press.

Carston, R. (1999) "The relationship between generative grammar and (relevance-theoretic) pragmatics." *University College London Working Papers in Linguistics* 11: 21–39.

(2002) *Thoughts and Utterances: The Pragmatics of Explicit Communication*. Oxford, Blackwell.

Cattell, N. R. (2000) *Children's Language: Consensus and Controversy*. London, Cassell.

Chalker, S. & E. Weiner (1994) *The Oxford Dictionary of English Grammar*. Oxford, Oxford University Press.

Chance, M. (1997) "Secret war still claims lives in Laos." *The Independent*, June 27, 1997.

Cheng, L. L.-S. (2003) "*Wh*-in situ." *Glot International* 7: 103–109.

Chiarello, C. (2003) "Parallel systems for processing language: Hemispheric complementarity in the normal brain." In M. Banich & M. Mack (eds.) *Mind, Brain and Language: Multidisciplinary Perspectives*. Mahwah, NJ, Lawrence Erlbaum. 229–247.

Chomsky, C. (1969) *The Acquisition of Syntax in Children from Five to Ten*. Cambridge, MA, MIT Press.

(1986) "Analytic study of the Tadoma method: language abilities of three deaf-blind subjects." *Journal of Speech and Hearing Research* 29: 332–347.

Chomsky, N. (1951/79) *Morphophonemics of Modern Hebrew*. University of Pennsylvania Master's thesis. New York, Garland Publishing.

(1954) Review of E. Rieger, *Modern Hebrew*. *Language* 30: 180–181.

(1955a) "Logical syntax and semantics: their linguistic relevance." *Language* 31: 36–45.

(1955b) "Semantic considerations in grammar." *Georgetown University Monograph Series in Linguistics* 8: 140–158.

*(1955/75) *The Logical Structure of Linguistic Theory*. New York, Plenum Press. [The foundation of nearly all Chomsky's subsequent linguistic work. It remained unpublished for twenty years.]

(1956) "Three models for the description of language." *Institute of Radio Engineers Transactions on Information Theory*, IT-2: 113–124.

*(1957) *Syntactic Structures*. The Hague, Mouton. [The book which traditionally marks the beginning of the Chomskyan revolution.]

(1958/64) "A transformational approach to syntax." In A. A. Hill (ed.), *Proceedings of the Third Texas Conference on Problems of Linguistic Analysis in English, 1958*. Austin, Texas, University of Texas Press, 1962. Reprinted in Fodor & Katz, 1964: 211–245.

*(1959) Review of Skinner, 1957. *Language* 35: 26–58. Reprinted in Fodor & Katz, 1964: 547–578. [This review sounded the knell of behaviorism.]

(1961) "Some methodological remarks on generative grammar." *Word* 17: 219–239.

(1962) "Explanatory models in linguistics." In E. Nagel, P. Suppes & A. Tarski (eds.), *Logic, Methodology and Philosophy of Science: Proceedings of the 1960 International Congress*. Stanford, Stanford University Press. 528–550.

(1962/64) "The logical basis of linguistic theory." In H. Lunt (ed.), *Proceedings of the Ninth International Congress of Linguists*. The Hague, Mouton. 914–978.

(1963) "Formal properties of grammars." In R. D. Luce, R. Bush & E. Galanter (eds.), *Handbook of Mathematical Psychology*. Vol. II: 323–418. New York, Wiley.

(1964) *Current Issues in Linguistic Theory*. The Hague, Mouton.

*(1965) *Aspects of the Theory of Syntax*. Cambridge, MA, MIT Press. [This book encapsulates what became known as the "Standard Theory."]

*(1966a) *Cartesian Linguistics*. New York, Harper & Row. [The first systematic attempt to identify the intellectual antecedents of generative grammar.]

(1966b) *Topics in the Theory of Generative Grammar*. The Hague, Mouton.

(1967a) "The formal nature of language." In E. Lenneberg, *Biological Foundations of Language*. New York, Wiley. 397–442.

(1967b) "Recent contributions to the theory of innate ideas." *Boston Studies in the Philosophy of Science*. Vol. III: 81–90. New York, The Humanities Press. Reprinted in J. Searle (ed.), *The Philosophy of Language*. Oxford University Press, 1971. 121–144. Also in *Synthèse* (1967) 17: 2–11.

(1967c) "Some general properties of phonological rules." *Language* 43: 102–128.

*(1968) *Language and Mind*. New York, Harcourt, Brace & World. Enlarged edition 1972b.

*(1969a) *American Power and the New Mandarins*. Harmondsworth, Penguin. (New edition with a foreword by Howard Zinn, 2002.) [The first collection of political essays, including "The responsibility of intellectuals."]

(1969b) "Linguistics and philosophy." In S. Hook (ed.), *Language and Philosophy*. New York, New York University Press.

(1969c) "Language and the mind." *Psychology Today*. Reprinted in *Language in Education*. London and Boston, Routledge & Kegan Paul and the Open University Press, 1972. 129–135.

(1970a) "Problems of explanation in linguistics." In Borger & Cioffi: 425–451.

(1970b) "Reply" to Black, 1970. In Borger & Cioffi: 462–470.

*(1970c) "Remarks on nominalization." In R. Jacobs & P. Rosenbaum (eds.), *Readings in English Transformational Grammar*. Waltham, MA, Ginn & Co. 184–221. [The initial counter-attack to Generative Semantics.]

(1971a) *At War with Asia*. London, Fontana.

(1971b) "On interpreting the world." *Cambridge Review* 92: 77–93. [This and the following were the Russell memorial lectures.]

(1971c) "On changing the world." *Cambridge Review* 92: 117–136.

(1971d) Review of Skinner, 1971. *New York Review of Books*, December 30, 1971.

(1971e) "Deep structure, surface structure, and semantic interpretation." In D. Steinberg & L. Jakobovits (eds.), *Semantics: An Interdisciplinary Reader in Philosophy, Linguistics, Anthropology and Psychology*. Cambridge, Cambridge University Press. 183–216.

(1972a) *Problems of Knowledge and Freedom*. New York, Pantheon.

(1972b) *Language and Mind*. (Enlarged edition.) New York, Harcourt Brace Jovanovich.

(1972c) *Studies on Semantics in Generative Grammar.* The Hague, Mouton.

(1972d) "Psychology and ideology." In Peck, 1987: 157–182. [A longer version is also in 1973b.]

(1972e) "Some empirical issues in the theory of transformational grammar." In S. Peters (ed.), *Goals of Linguistic Theory.* Englewood Cliffs, NJ, Prentice-Hall. 63–130.

(1973a) *The Backroom Boys.* London, Fontana.

*(1973b) *For Reasons of State.* London, Fontana. (New edition with a foreword by Arundhati Roy, 2002.)

*(1973c) "Conditions on transformations." In S. Anderson & P. Kiparsky (eds.), *A Festschrift for Morris Halle.* New York, Holt, Rinehart & Winston. 232–286.

*(1975a) *Reflections on Language.* New York, Pantheon. [A classic statement of his philosophical position, including discussion of modularity.]

(1975b) *Peace in the Middle East?* London, Fontana. (New edition with Rowman & Littlefield Publishers, 2003.)

(1975c) "Questions of form and interpretation." *Linguistic Analysis* 1: 75–109.

(1976) "Conditions on rules of grammar." *Linguistic Analysis* 2: 303–351.

(1977a) "On WH-movement." In P. Culicover, T. Wasow & A. Akmajian (eds.), *Formal Syntax.* New York, Academic Press. 71–132.

(1977b) Interview with David Cohen. In D. Cohen, *Psychologists on Psychology.* London, Routledge and Kegan Paul. 72–100.

(1977c) *Essays on Form and Interpretation.* New York, North Holland.

(1978) "Language development, human intelligence, and social organization." In W. Feinberg (ed.), *Equality and Social Policy.* Champaign, University of Illinois Press. Reprinted in Peck, 1987: 183–202.

(1979) *Language and Responsibility (Interviews with Mitsou Ronat).* New York, Pantheon.

*(1980a) *Rules and Representations.* Oxford, Blackwell. [A classical statement of his philosophical position.]

(1980b) "Rules and representations." *Behavioral and Brain Sciences* 3: 1–15.

(1980c) "The new organology." *Behavioral and Brain Sciences* 3: 42–61.

(1980d) "On binding." *Linguistic Inquiry* 11: 1–46.

*(1981a) *Radical Priorities.* Montreal, Black Rose Books.

*(1981b) *Lectures on Government and Binding.* Dordrecht, Foris. [The source of Government and Binding theory; still presupposed in much current research.]

(1981c) "Knowledge of language: its elements and origins." *Philosophical Transactions of the Royal Society of London* B 295: 223–234.

(1981d) "Markedness and core grammar." In A. Belletti et al. (eds.), *Theory of Markedness in Generative Grammar. Proceedings of the 1979 GLOW Conference.* Pisa, Scuola Normale Superiore. 123–146.

(1981e) "Principles and parameters in syntactic theory." In N. Hornstein & D. Lightfoot (eds.), *Explanations in Linguistics.* London, Longman. 123–146.

(1982a) "A note on the creative aspect of language use." *The Philosophical Review* 91: 423–434.

(1982b) *Towards a New Cold War: Essays on the Current Crisis and How We Got There.* New York, Pantheon Books.

(1982c) *The Generative Enterprise: A Discussion with Riny Huybregts and Henk van Riemsdijk.* Dordrecht, Foris.

(1982d) *Some Concepts and Consequences of the Theory of Government and Binding.* Cambridge, MA, MIT Press.

*(1983a) *The Fateful Triangle: The US, Israel and the Palestinians.* Boston, South End Press.

(1983b) "Interventionism and nuclear war." In M. Albert & D. Dellinger (eds.), *Beyond Survival: New Directions for the Disarmament Movement.* Boston, South End Press. 249–309.

(1984) *Modular Approaches to the Study of Mind.* San Diego, San Diego State University Press.

(1985a) *Turning the Tide: US Intervention in Central America and the Struggle for Peace.* London, Pluto Press.

(1985b) "Visions of righteousness." In J. C. Rowe & R. Berg (eds.), *The Vietnam War and American Culture.* New York, Columbia University Press. 21–51.

*(1986a) *Knowledge of Language: Its Nature, Origin and Use.* New York, Praeger. [Partly accessible, partly technical state of the art.]

*(1986b) *Barriers.* Cambridge, MA, MIT Press.

(1986c) *Pirates and Emperors: International Terrorism in the Real World.* Brattleboro, VT, Amana Books.

(1987a) *On Power and Ideology: The Managua Lectures.* Boston, South End Press.

(1987b) *Language in a Psychological Setting.* Special issue of *Sophia Linguistica* 22, Sophia University, Tokyo.

(1987c) *Generative Grammar: Its Basis, Development and Prospects.* Studies in English Linguistics and Literature. Kyoto University of Foreign Studies.

(1987d) "Reply" [to reviews of his 1986a by A. George and M. Brody]. *Mind & Language* 2: 178–197.

(1988a) *The Culture of Terrorism.* London, Pluto Press.

(1988b) *Language and Problems of Knowledge: The Managua Lectures.* Cambridge MA, MIT Press.

*(1988c) *Language and Politics*, ed. C. P. Otero. Montreal, Black Rose Books.

*(1989) *Necessary Illusions: Thought Control in Democratic Societies.* Boston, South End Press.

(1990a) "On formalization and formal linguistics." *Natural Language and Linguistic Theory* 8: 143–147.

(1990b) "Language and mind." In D. H. Mellor (ed.), *Ways of Communicating.* Cambridge, Cambridge University Press. 56–80.

(1990c) "Accessibility 'in principle.'" *Behavioral and Brain Sciences* 13: 600–601.

*(1991a) *Deterring Democracy.* London, Verso.

(1991b) *Terrorizing the Neighbourhood.* Stirling, AK Press.

(1991c) "Linguistics and adjacent fields: a personal view." In Kasher: 3–25.

(1991d) "Linguistics and cognitive science: problems and mysteries." In Kasher: 26–53.

(1991e) "Some notes on economy of derivation and representation." In R. Freidin (ed.), *Principles and Parameters in Comparative Grammar.* Cambridge, MA, MIT Press. 417–454.

(1991f) "Language, politics, and composition: a conversation with Noam Chomsky." *Journal of Advanced Composition* 11: 4–35.

*(1992a) *What Uncle Sam Really Wants.* Berkeley, Odonian Press.

*(1992b) *Chronicles of Dissent: Interviews with David Barsamian.* Stirling, AK Press.

(1992c) "Explaining language use." *Philosophical Topics* 20: 205–231. Reprinted in 2000a: 19–45.

(1992d) "Language and interpretation: philosophical reflections and empirical inquiry." In J. Earman (ed.), *Inference, Explanation and Other Philosophical Frustrations*. Berkeley, University of California Press. 99–128. Reprinted in 2000a: 46–74.

(1992e) "A minimalist program for linguistic theory." *MIT Occasional Papers in Linguistics*: 1–71.

*(1993a) *Year 501: The Conquest Continues*. London, Verso.

*(1993b) *Rethinking Camelot: JFK, the Vietnam War, and US Political Culture*. London, Verso.

*(1993c) *Language and Thought*. London, Moyer Bell.

(1993d) "Mental constructions and social reality." In E. Reuland & W. Abraham (eds.), *Knowledge and Language*, vol. 1: *From Orwell's Problem to Plato's Problem*. Dordrecht, Kluwer. 29–58.

(1993e) *The Prosperous Few and the Restless Many*. Berkeley, Odonian Press.

(1993f) *Letters from Lexington: Reflections on Propaganda*. Edinburgh, AK Press.

*(1994a) "Chomsky, Noam." In Guttenplan: 153–167.

(1994b) *Secrets, Lies and Democracy*. Berkeley, Odonian Press.

(1994c) *Keeping the Rabble in Line: Interviews with David Barsamian*. Edinburgh, AK Press.

*(1994d) *World Orders, Old and New*. London, Pluto Press.

(1994e) "Naturalism and dualism in the study of language and mind." *International Journal of Philosophical Studies* 2: 181–209. Reprinted in 2000a: 75–105.

(1994f) "Sweet home of liberty." *Index on Censorship* 23.3: 9–18.

(1994g) "Language as a natural object." The Jacobsen lecture. Reprinted in 2000a: 106–133.

(1994h) "Language from an internalist perspective." Lecture given at King's College, London, May 24, 1994. Revised version in 2000a: 134–163.

*(1995a) "Language and nature." *Mind* 104: 1–61. [The most important statement of his philosophical position.]

*(1995b) *The Minimalist Program*. Cambridge, MA, MIT Press. [The classical statement of his current linguistic theory: formidably difficult.]

(1995c) "The free market myth." *Open Eye* 3: 8–13, 51.

(1995d) "Rollback II: 'Civilization' marches on." *Z* 8.2: 20–31; "Rollback IV: towards a utopia of the masters." *Z* 8.5: 18–24.

(1995e) "Bare Phrase Structure." In Webelhuth, 1995a: 383–439.

(1995f) "Language is the perfect solution." Interview with Noam Chomsky by Lisa Cheng & Rint Sybesma. *Glot International* 1, 9.10: 1–34.

(1995g) "Foreword" to Carey, 1995: vi–xiii.

(1995h) "Letter from Noam Chomsky." *Covert Action Quarterly*. n.p., n.d.

*(1996a) *Powers and Prospects: Reflections on Human Nature and the Social Order*. London, Pluto Press. [Probably the best overview of his work in both academe and politics.]

(1996b) *Class Warfare: Interviews with David Barsamian*. London, Pluto Press.

(1996c) "Language and evolution." Letter in the *New York Review of Books*. February 1, 1996: 41.

(1997a) "The cold war and the university." In A. Schiffrin (ed.), *The Cold War and the University: Towards an Intellectual History of the Postwar Years*. New York, The New Press. 171–194.

(1997b) *Media Control: The Spectacular Achievements of Propaganda*. New York, Seven Stories Press.

(1997c) "Internalist explorations." In 2000a: 164–194.

(1997d) "New horizons in the study of language." In 2000a: 3–18.

(1997e) "Serial veto." *Index on Censorship* 26.6: 155–161.

(1997f) "Rage against the Machine." An interview with Tom Morello. Available on the Internet: http://www.worldmedia.com/archive/rage/rage.html

(1997g) "Language and mind: current thoughts on ancient problems." University of Brasilia.

(1998a) "Domestic constituencies." Z 11.5: 16–25.

(1998b) "Comments: Galen Strawson, *Mental Reality*." *Philosophy and Phenomenological Research* 58: 437–441.

(1998c) "Some observations on economy in generative grammar." In P. Barbosa, D. Fox, P. Hagstrom, M. McGinnis & D. Pesetsky (eds.), *Is the Best Good Enough? Optimality and Competition in Syntax*. Cambridge MA, MIT Press.

(1998d) *The Common Good: Interviews with David Barsamian*. Odonian Press.

(1999a) "Derivation by phase". See 2001c.

(1999b) "Language and the brain" MS. Address at the European Conference on Cognitive Science, Siena. Reprinted in 2002b: 61–91.

(1999c) *Latin America: From Colonization to Globalization. In Conversation with Heinz Dieterich*. New York, Ocean Press.

(1999d) *The Umbrella of United States Power: The Universal Declaration of Human Rights and the Contradictions of United States Policy*. The Open Media Pamphlet Series; New York, Seven Stories Press.

(1999e) *The New Military Humanism: Lessons from Kosovo*. Monroe ME, Common Courage Press.

(1999f) *Fateful Triangle: The United States, Israel and the Palestinians*. Updated edition. London, Pluto Press.

(1999g) *Profit over People: Neoliberalism and Global Order*. New York, Seven Stories Press.

(1999h) Introduction to: G. Slapper, *Blood in the Bank: Social and Legal Aspects of Death at Work*. Aldershot, Ashgate. xi–xv.

(1999i) "An on-line interview with Noam Chomsky: On the nature of pragmatics and related issues." *Brain and Language* 68: 393–401.

(1999j) "Linguistics and brain science." LAUD Linguistic Agency University GH Essen, Paper no. 500.

*(2000a) *New Horizons in the Study of Language and Mind*. Cambridge, Cambridge University Press. [A collection of seminal philosophical essays.]

*(2000b) "Minimalist inquiries: the framework". In R. Martin, D. Michaels & J. Uriagereka (eds.) *Step by Step: Essays on Minimalist Syntax in Honor of Howard Lasnik*. Cambridge, MA. MIT Press. 89–155. [The basis of recent developments in Minimalism.]

(2000c) "States of concern". In "Manufacturing Monsters." *Index on Censorship* 29.5: 44–48.

(2000d) "Foreign policy: the Colombian plan, April 2000." *Z Magazine* 13.6: 26–34.

*(2000f) *Rogue States: The Rule of Force in World Affairs.* London, Pluto Press.

(2000g) *A New Generation Draws the Line: Kosovo, East Timor and the Standards of the West.* London, Verso.

(2000h) *Chomsky on MisEducation.* Edited and introduced by D. Macedo. Lanham, Rowman and Littlefield Publishers.

*(2001a) *9–11.* New York, Seven Stories Press.

*(2001b) *Propaganda and the Public Mind: Interviews by David Barsamian.* London, Pluto Press.

(2001c) "Derivation by Phase." In M. Kenstowicz (ed.), *Ken Hale. A Life in Language.* Cambridge, MA: MIT Press. 1–52.

(2002a) *Pirates and Emperors, Old and New.* London, Pluto Press. (Updated and expanded edition of 1986c.)

*(2002b) *On Nature and Language.* Cambridge, Cambridge University Press. [An overview of his current thought.]

(2002c) "Terror and just response." In M. Rai, *War Plan Iraq: Ten Reasons against War on Iraq.* London, Verso. 23–35.

(2002d) "September 11 aftermath: where is the world heading?" In P. Scraton (ed.), *Beyond September 11: An Anthology of Dissent.* London, Pluto Press. pp. 66–71.

(2002e) "An interview on Minimalism" with Adriana Belletti & Luigi Rizzi. In 2002b: 92–161.

(2002f) *Media Control: The Spectacular Achievements of Propaganda.* New York, Seven Stories Press. (Second enlarged edition.)

(2002g) "The journalist from Mars". In 2002f: 67–100. (Notes appear on pp. 65–66.)

*(2002h) *Understanding Power: The Indispensable Chomsky*, ed. P. Mitchell and J. Schoeffel. New York, The New Press. (Explanatory footnotes available at www.understandingpower.com.) [A massively documented survey.]

(2002i) "An interview with Chomsky." December 28, 2002. *ZNet.* http://www.zmag. org/content/Activism/chomsky_interview.cfm

(2002j) "Human rights week 2002". December 28, 2002. *ZNet.* http://www.zmag. org/content/showarticle.cfm?SectionID=11 &ItemID=2805

(2003a) "Torturing democracy." *ZNet Foreign Policy* (January 25, 2003).

(2003b) *Power and Terror: Post-9/11 Talks and Interviews.* New York, Seven Stories Press.

(2003c) "Replies." In L. Antony & N. Hornstein (eds), *Chomsky and his Critics.* Oxford, Blackwell. 255–328.

(2003d) *Middle East Illusions.* Lanham, MD, Rowman & Littlefield Publishers, Inc.

(2003e) "Wars of terror." *New Political Science* 25: 113–127.

(2003f) "Collateral language." An interview with David Barsamian. http://www.zmag. org/ZMagSite/Aug2003/barsamian0803.html

(2003g) "Preventive war 'the supreme crime.'" http://www.zmag.org/content/ showarticle.cfm?SectionID=40 &ItemID=4030

(2003h) *Hegemony or Survival: America's Quest for Global Dominance.* New York, Metropolitan Books.

(to appear) "Beyond explanatory adequacy." In A. Belletti (ed.), *Structures and Beyond: Current Issues in the Theory of Language.* University of Siena.

(forthcoming) "The United States and the 'Challenge of Relativity.'"

Chomsky, N. & D. Barsamian (2003) "Imperial ambition." *Monthly Review* 55. http://www.zmag.org/content/showarticle.cfm?SectionID=40 &ItemID=3627

Chomsky, N., R. Clark & E. Said (1999) *Acts of Aggression: Policing "Rogue" States.* New York, Seven Stories Press.

Chomsky, N. & M. Foucault (1997) "Human nature: justice versus power." In A. Davidson (ed.), *Foucault and his Interlocutors.* Chicago, University of Chicago Press. 107–145.

Chomsky, N., & M. Halle (1964) "Some controversial questions in phonological theory." *Journal of Linguistics* 1: 97–138.

    *(1968) *The Sound Pattern of English.* New York, Harper & Row. [The classic statement of generative phonology.]

Chomsky, N., M. Halle & F. Lukoff (1956) "On accent and juncture in English." In M. Halle, H. Lunt & H. MacLean (eds.), *For Roman Jakobson.* The Hague, Mouton. 65–80.

*Chomsky, N. & E. Herman (1979a) *The Political Economy of Human Rights.* Vol. I: *The Washington Connection and Third World Fascism.* Nottingham, Spokesman.

    *(1979b) *The Political Economy of Human Rights.* Vol. II: *After the Cataclysm – Postwar Indochina and the Reconstruction of Imperial Ideology.* Nottingham, Spokesman.

Chomsky, N. & J. Katz (1974) "What the linguist is talking about." *Journal of Philosophy* 71: 347–367.

    (1975) "On innateness: a reply to Cooper." *Philosophical Review* 84: 70–87.

Chomsky, N. & H. Lasnik (1977) "Filters and control." *Linguistic Inquiry* 8: 425–504.

    (1993) "The theory of principles and parameters." In J. Jacobs, A. von Stechow, W. Sternefeld & T. Vennemann (eds.), *Syntax: An International Handbook of Contemporary Research.* Berlin, de Gruyter. 506–569. [A revised version constitutes chapter 1 of Chomsky, 1995b.]

Chomsky, N. & G. Miller (1963) "Introduction to the formal analysis of natural languages." In R. D. Luce, R. Bush & E. Galanter (eds.), *Handbook of Mathematical Psychology.* Vol. II: 269–322. New York, Wiley.

Chomsky, N. & M. P. Schützenberger (1963) "The algebraic theory of context-free languages." In P. Braffort & D. Hirschberg (eds.), *Computer Programming and Formal Systems.* Studies in Logic Series. Amsterdam, North Holland. 119–161.

Chomsky, W. (1957) *Hebrew: The Eternal Language.* Philadelphia, The Jewish Publication Society of America.

Chouinard, M. & E. Clark (2003) "Adult reformulations of child errors as negative evidence." *Journal of Child Language* 30: 637–669.

Christiansen, M. & N. Chater (2001) "Connectionist psycholinguistics: capturing the empirical data." *Trends in Cognitive Sciences* 5: 82–88.

Christiansen, M. & S. Kirby (2003) "Language evolution: consensus and controversies." *Trends in Cognitive Sciences* 7: 300–307.

Churchland, P. (1994) "Can neurobiology teach us anything about consciousness?" *Proceedings and Addresses of the American Philosophical Association* 67.4: 23–40.

Clahsen, H. & M. Almazan-Hamilton (1998) "Syntax and morphology in children with William's syndrome." *Cognition* 68: 167–198.

Cohen, J. & J. Rogers (1991) "Knowledge, morality and hope: the social thought of Noam Chomsky." *New Left Review* 187: 5–27.

Coker, C. (1987) "The mandarin and the commissar: the political thought of Noam Chomsky." In S. Modgil & C. Modgil (eds.), *Noam Chomsky: Consensus and Controversy*. Sussex, The Falmer Press. 269–278.

Cole, P. & G. Hermon (1981) "Subjecthood and islandhood: evidence from Quechua." *Linguistic Inquiry* 12: 1–30.

Collins, C. (2001) "Economy conditions in syntax". In M. Baltin & C. Collins (eds.), *The Handbook of Contemporary Syntactic Theory*. Oxford, Blackwell. 45–61.

Collins, H. & T. Pinch (1993) *The Golem: What You Should Know about Science*. Cambridge, Cambridge University Press.

Coltheart, M., R. Langdon & N. Breen (1997) "Misidentification syndromes and cognitive neuropsychiatry." *Trends in Cognitive Sciences* 1: 157–158.

Comrie, B., M. Polinsky & S. Matthes (eds.) (1997) *The Atlas of Languages: The Origin and Development of Languages throughout the World*. New York, Checkmark Books.

Cook, V. J. & M. Newson (1996) *Chomsky's Universal Grammar: An Introduction*. 2nd edition. Oxford, Blackwell.

Cormack, A. & N. V. Smith (1994) "Serial verbs." *University College London Working Papers in Linguistics* 6: 63–88.

(1996) "Checking theory: features, functional heads, and checking parameters." *University College London Working Papers in Linguistics* 8: 243–281.

(1997) "Checking features and split signs." *University College London Working Papers in Linguistics* 9: 223–252.

Cowart, W. (1997) *Experimental Syntax: Applying Objective Methods to Sentence Judgments*. London, Sage Publications.

Crain, S. & R. Thornton (1998) *Investigations in Universal Grammar: A Guide to Experiments on the Acquisition of Syntax and Semantics*. Cambridge MA, MIT Press.

Crane, T. & D. H. Mellor (1990) "There is no question of physicalism." *Mind* 99: 185–206.

Culicover, P. (1999) *Syntactic Nuts: Hard Cases, Syntactic Theory and Language Acquisition*. Oxford, Oxford University Press.

Curtis, M. (2003) *Web of Deceit: Britain's Real Role in the World*. London, Vintage.

Curtiss, S. (1977) *Genie: A Psycholinguistic Study of a Modern Day "Wild Child."* London, Academic Press.

Curtiss, S., V. Fromkin, S. Krashen, D. Rigler & M. Rigler (1974) "The linguistic development of Genie." *Language* 50: 528–554.

D'Agostino, F. (1986) *Chomsky's System of Ideas*. Oxford, Clarendon Press. [An excellent but somewhat dated survey of his philosophical position.]

Damasio, A. (1994) *Descartes' Error: Emotion, Reason and the Human Brain*. New York, Putnam.

Darwin, C. (1859/1968) *The Origin of Species by Means of Natural Selection*, ed. J. W. Burrow. Harmondsworth, Penguin.

Davidson, D. (1984) *Inquiries into Truth and Interpretation*. Oxford, Clarendon Press.

(1990) "The structure and content of truth." *Journal of Philosophy* 87: 279–328.

(1994) "Davidson, Donald." In Guttenplan: 231–236.

Davidson, D. & G. Harman (eds.) (1972) *Semantics of Natural Language*. Dordrecht, Reidel.

Davies, M. (1986) "Tacit knowledge, and the structure of thought and language." In C. Travis (ed.), *Meaning and Interpretation*. Oxford, Blackwell. 127–158.

de Beaugrande, R. (1991) "Language and the facilitation of authority: the discourse of Noam Chomsky." *Journal of Advanced Composition* 11: 425–442. [This paper is ostensibly a reaction to an interview with Chomsky in the same journal: "Language, politics, and composition: A conversation with Noam Chomsky," pp. 4–35.]

Dehaene, S. (1997) *The Number Sense*. Oxford, Oxford University Press.

(2003) "Natural born readers." *New Scientist* (July 5), pp. 30–33.

Dehaene, S. & L. Cohen (1997) "Cerebral pathways for calculation: double dissociation between rote verbal and quantitative knowledge of arithmetic." *Cortex* 33: 219–250.

Dennett, D. (1978) *Brainstorms*. Cambridge, MA, MIT Press.

(1987) *The Intentional Stance*. Cambridge, MA, MIT Press.

(1995) *Darwin's Dangerous Idea*. New York, Simon & Schuster.

(1996) *Kinds of Minds*. London, Weidenfeld & Nicolson.

Derbyshire, D. (1985) *Hixkaryana and Linguistic Typology*. Arlington, Texas, Summer Institute of Linguistics.

De Villiers, J. & P. de Villiers (1999) "Linguistic determinism and the understanding of false beliefs." In P. Mitchell & K. Riggs (eds.), *Children's Reasoning and the Mind*. New York, Psychology Press.

Devitt, M. (1981) *Designation*. New York, Columbia University Press.

Dixon, R. M. W. (1963) *Linguistic Science and Logic*. The Hague, Mouton.

Dobbs, B. J. T. (1991) *The Janus Faces of Genius: The Role of Alchemy in Newton's Thought*. Cambridge, Cambridge University Press.

Dummett, M. (1975) "What is a theory of meaning? (1)." In S. Guttenplan (ed.), *Mind and Language*, Oxford, Oxford University Press.

(1976) "What is a theory of meaning? (2)." In G. Evans & J. McDowell (eds.), *Truth and Meaning*, Oxford, Oxford University Press.

(1981/94) "Objections to Chomsky." *London Review of Books* 3: 16, 5–6. Reprinted in Otero, 1994, vol. II: 391–7.

(1989) "Language and communication." In George: 192–212.

(1993) *The Seas of Language*. Oxford, Clarendon Press.

du Plessis, H. (1977) "*Wh* movement in Afrikaans." *Linguistic Inquiry* 8: 723–726.

Duranti, A. (1997) *Linguistic Anthropology*. Cambridge, Cambridge University Press.

Edgley, A. (2000) *The Social and Political Thought of Noam Chomsky*. London, Routledge.

Edwards, R. (1998) "End of the germ line." *New Scientist* 2127: 22.

Egan, F. (2003) "Naturalistic inquiry: where does mental representation fit in?" In L. Antony & N. Hornstein (eds.), *Chomsky and his Critics*. Oxford, Blackwell: 89–104.

Ellis, H. & M. Lewis (2001) "Capgras delusion: a window on face recognition." *Trends in Cognitive Sciences* 5: 149–156.

Elman, J. (1993) "Learning and development in neural networks: the importance of starting small." *Cognition* 48: 71–99.

Elman, J., E. Bates, M. Johnson, A. Karmiloff-Smith, D. Parisi & K. Plunkett (1996) *Rethinking Innateness: A Connectionist Perspective on Development*. Cambridge, MA, MIT Press.

Emonds, J. (1978) "The verbal complex V'-V in French." *Linguistic Inquiry* 9: 151–175.

Enard, W., M. Przeworski, S. Fisher, C. Lai, V. Wiebe, T. Kitano, A. Monaco & S. Pääbo (2002) "Molecular evolution of FOXP2, a gene involved in speech and language." *Nature* 418: 869–872.

Engdahl, E. (1983) "Parasitic gaps." *Linguistics & Philosophy* 6: 5–34.

Epstein, S. & D. Seely (2002a) "Introduction: on the quest for explanation." In Epstein & Seely: 1–18.

(2002b) "Rule applications as cycles in a level-free syntax". In Epstein & Seely: 65–89.

eds. (2002c) *Derivation and Explanation in the Minimalist Program.* Oxford, Blackwell.

Eubank, L. & K. R. Gregg (1996) "Critical periods and (S)LA." *Working Papers in English and Applied Linguistics.* Research Centre for English and Applied Linguistics, University of Cambridge. 3: 1–21.

Evans, G. (1982) *The Varieties of Reference.* Oxford, Oxford University Press.

Fillmore, C. J., P. Kay & M. C. O'Connor (1988) "Regularity and idiomaticity in grammatical constructions: the case of *let alone*." *Language* 64: 501–538.

Fodor, J. D. (1998) "Unambiguous triggers." *Linguistic Inquiry* 29: 1–36.

(2001) "Setting syntactic parameters". In M. Baltin & C. Collins (eds.), *The Handbook of Contemporary Syntactic Theory.* Oxford, Blackwell. 730–767.

Fodor, J. (1974/81) "Special Sciences." *Synthèse* 28: 77–115. Reprinted in J. Fodor, *Representations: Philosophical Essays on the Foundations of Cognitive Science.* Brighton, Harvester Press. 127–145.

(1975) *The Language of Thought.* New York, Crowell.

*(1983) *The Modularity of Mind.* Cambridge, MA, MIT Press.

(1989) "Why should the mind be modular?" In George: 1–22.

(1994a) *The Elm and the Expert.* Cambridge, MA, MIT Press.

(1994b) "Fodor, Jerry A." In Guttenplan: 292–300.

(2000) *The Mind Doesn't Work that Way.* Cambridge MA, MIT Press.

Fodor, J. & T. Bever (1965) "The psycholinguistic validity of linguistic segments." *Journal of Verbal Learning and Verbal Behavior* 4: 414–420.

Fodor, J., T. Bever & M. Garrett (1974) *The Psychology of Language: An Introduction to Psycholinguistics and Generative Grammar.* New York, McGraw-Hill.

Fodor, J. & M. Garrett (1966) "Some reflections on competence and performance." In J. Lyons & R. Wales (eds.), *Psycholinguistics Papers.* Edinburgh, Edinburgh University Press.

Fodor, J., M. Garrett, E. Walker & C. Parkes (1980) "Against definitions." *Cognition* 263–367.

Fodor, J. & J. Katz (eds.) (1964) *The Structure of Language: Readings in the Philosophy of Language,* Englewood Cliffs, NJ, Prentice-Hall.

Fodor, J. & Z. Pylyshyn (1988) "Connectionism and cognitive architecture: a critical analysis." In S. Pinker & J. Mehler (eds.), *Connections and Symbols.* Cambridge, MA, MIT Press; Bradford Books.

Foley, C. (1995) *Human Rights, Human Wrongs: The Alternative Report to the United Nations Human Rights Committee.* London, Rivers Oram Press.

Føllesdal, D. (1990) "Indeterminacy and mental states." In Barrett & Gibson: 98–109.

Fox, J. (2001) *Chomsky and Globalisation.* Cambridge, Icon Books.

Frampton, J. & S. Gutmann (2002) "Crash-proof syntax." In Epstein & Seely: 90–105.

Franz, V. (2001) "Action does not resist visual illusions". *Trends in Cognitive Sciences* 5: 457–459.

Frazier, L. (1988) "Grammar and language processing." In F. Newmeyer (ed.), *Linguistics: The Cambridge Survey*. Cambridge, Cambridge University Press. Vol. II: 15–34.

Frege, G. (1956) "On sense and reference." In M. Black & P. Geach (eds.), *Philosophical Writings of Gottlob Frege*. Oxford, Blackwell.

Freidin, R. (1997) Review of Chomsky, 1995b. *Language* 73: 571–582.

(1999) "Cyclicity and Minimalism." In S. D. Epstein & N. Hornstein (eds.), *Working Minimalism*. Cambridge MA, MIT Press. 95–126.

Freidin, R. & J.-R. Vergnaud (2001) "Exquisite connections: some remarks on the evolution of linguistic theory." *Lingua* 111: 639–666.

Frith, U. (1989) *Autism: Explaining the Enigma*. Oxford, Blackwell. (Second edition, 2003.)

Fromkin, V. (1988) "Grammatical aspects of speech errors." In F. Newmeyer (ed.), *Linguistics: The Cambridge Survey*. Cambridge, Cambridge University Press. Vol. II: 117–138.

(1997) "Some thoughts about the brain/mind/language interface." *Lingua* 100: 3–27.

Froud, K. (2001) "Linguistic Theory and Language Pathology: Evidence for the Morphology Interface from a Case of Acquired Language Disorder." Ph.D. thesis, University College London.

Gallistel, R. (1994) "Space and Time." In N. J. Mackintosh (ed.), *Animal Learning and Cognition. Handbook of Perception and Cognition* 9: 221–253. New York, Academic Press.

Garfield, J., C. Peterson & T. Perry (2001) "Social cognition, language acquisition and the development of theory of mind." *Mind & Language* 16: 494–541.

Gazdar, G. (1981) "On syntactic categories." *Philosophical Transactions of the Royal Society of London* B 295: 267–283.

Gazzaniga, M. (1994) *Nature's Mind*. London, Penguin.

(2002) "The split brain revisited." In *The Scientific American Book of the Brain*. 129–138.

George, A. (ed.) (1989) *Reflections on Chomsky*. Oxford, Blackwell.

(1996) "Katz astray." *Mind & Language* 11: 295–305.

Gillan, A. (2003) "Torture evidence 'acceptable.'" *Guardian* 22.07.03; p. 2.

Gleick, J. (1992) *Richard Feynman and Modern Physics*. London, Abacus.

Goldberg, A. (2003) "Constructions: a new theoretical approach to language." *Trends in Cognitive Sciences* 7: 219–224.

Goldman-Eisler, F. (1968) *Psycholinguistics: Experiments in Spontaneous Speech*. London, Academic Press.

Goldsmith, J. (1994) *Handbook of Phonological Theory*. Oxford, Blackwell.

Gopnik, A. (2003) "The theory theory as an alternative to the innateness hypothesis." In Antony & Hornstein: 238–254.

Gopnik, M. (1990) "Feature-blindness: a case study." *Language Acquisition* 1: 139–164.

(1994) "Impairments of tense in a familial language disorder." *Journal of Neurolinguistics* 8: 109–133.

(ed.) (1997) *The Inheritance and Innateness of Grammars*. New York, Oxford University Press.

Gopnik, M. & M. Crago (1991) "Familial aggregation of a developmental language disorder." *Cognition* 39: 1–50.

Gopnik, M. & H. Goad (1997) "What underlies inflectional error patterns in genetic dysphasia?" *Journal of Neurolinguistics* 10: 109–137.

Grice, P. (1975) "Logic and conversation." In P. Cole & J. Morgan (eds.), *Syntax and Semantics 3: Speech Acts*. New York, Academic Press. 41–58.

(1986) "Reply to Richards." In R. Grandy & R. Warner (eds.), *Philosophical Grounds of Rationality: Intentions, Categories, Ends*. Oxford, Clarendon Press. 45–106.

Grice, P. & P. Strawson (1956) "In defence of a dogma." *The Philosophical Review* 65. Reprinted in part in Nagel & Brandt, 1965: 246–254.

Grossenbacher, P. & C. Lovelace (2001) "Mechanisms of synesthesia: cognitive and physiological constraints." *Trends in Cognitive Sciences* 5: 36–41.

Guttenplan, S. (ed.) (1994) *A Companion to the Philosophy of Mind*. Oxford, Blackwell.

Haeberli, E. (2002) "Analyzing Old and Middle English V2: evidence from the distribution of subjects and adjuncts." Paper presented at the LAGB, UMIST; September 2002.

Haegeman, L. (1994) *Introduction to Government and Binding Theory*. 2nd edition. Oxford, Blackwell.

Hale, K. (1982) "On the position of Warlpiri in a theory of typology." Circulated by Indiana University Linguistics Club, Bloomington.

Hale, S. (2002) *The Man who Lost his Language*. London, Allen Lane.

Haley, M. C. & R. F. Lunsford (1994) *Noam Chomsky*. New York, Twayne Publishers.

Halle, M. (1959) *The Sound Pattern of Russian*. The Hague, Mouton.

Halliday, M. A. K. (1975) *Learning How to Mean*. London, Arnold.

Harbert, W. (1995) "Binding theory, control and *pro*." In Webelhuth, 1995a: 177–240.

*Harman, G. (ed.) (1974) *On Noam Chomsky: Critical Essays*. New York, Anchor Books.

(1980) "Two quibbles about analyticity and psychological reality." *Behavioral and Brain Sciences* 3: 21–22.

Harris, R. A. (1993) *The Linguistics Wars*. Oxford, Oxford University Press.

Harris, Z. S. (1951) *Methods in Structural Linguistics*. Chicago, University of Chicago Press.

(1952) "Discourse analysis." *Language* 28: 1–30.

(1957) "Co-occurrence and transformation in linguistic structure." *Language* 33: 283–340.

(1965) "Transformational theory." *Language* 41: 363–401.

*Hauser, M., N. Chomsky & W. Tecumseh Fitch (2002) "The faculty of language: what is it, who has it, and how did it evolve?" *Science* 298: 1569–1579 (November 22).

Heim, I. & A. Kratzer (1998) *Semantics in Generative Grammar*. Oxford, Blackwell.

Hempel, C. G. (1966) *Philosophy of Natural Science*. Englewood Cliffs, NJ, Prentice-Hall.

Herman, E. S. (1992) *Beyond Hypocrisy*. Boston, South End Press.

*Herman, E. S. & N. Chomsky (1988) *Manufacturing Consent: The Political Economy of the Mass Media*. New York, Pantheon (page references to 1994 Vintage edition).

Hilsman, R. (1967) *To Move a Nation: The Politics of Foreign Policy in the Administration of John F. Kennedy*. New York, Doubleday.

Hintikka, J. (1989) "Logical form and linguistic theory." In George: 41–57.

Hintikka, J. & G. Sandu (1991) *On the Methodology of Linguistics*. Oxford, Blackwell.

Hirschfeld, L. & S. Gelman (eds.) (1994) *Mapping the Mind: Domain-specificity in Cognition and Culture*. Cambridge, Cambridge University Press.

Hitchens, C. (1985/90) "The Chorus and Cassandra." In *Prepared for the Worst*. London, Hogarth Press. 58–77.

Hjelmslev, L. (1961) *Prolegomena to a Theory of Language*. Madison, University of Wisconsin Press.

Hockett, C. F. (1942) "A system of descriptive phonology." *Language* 18: 3–21.

(1968) *The State of the Art*. The Hague, Mouton.

Hockney, D. (1975) "The bifurcation of scientific theories and indeterminacy of translation." *Philosophy of Science* 42: 411–427.

Hoffman, N. von (2003) "In the war whorehouse". *Index on Censorship* 32.3: 36–43.

Hookway, C. (1994) "Quine, Willard van Orman." In Guttenplan: 520–525.

Hornstein, N. & A. Weinberg (1995) "The empty category principle." In Webelhuth, 1995a: 241–296.

Horwich, P. (1990) *Truth*. Oxford, Blackwell.

(2003) "Meaning and its place in the language faculty". In Antony & Hornstein: 162–178.

Howe, M. J. A. (1989) *Fragments of Genius*. London, Routledge.

Hudson, R. A. (1990) *English Word Grammar*. Oxford, Blackwell.

Hughes, S. (2001) "Speech". *The Pennsylvania Gazette, July/August 2001*, pp. 39–45.

Hurford, J. (1991) "The evolution of the critical period for language acquisition." *Cognition* 40: 159–201.

Hurst, J. A., M. Baraitser, E. Auger, F. Graham & S. Norell (1990) "An extended family with an inherited speech disorder." *Developmental Medicine and Child Neurology* 32: 347–355.

Hyams, N. (1986) *Language Acquisition and the Theory of Parameters*. Dordrecht, Reidel.

Hymes, D. (1972) "Models of the interaction of language and social life." In J. Gumperz & D. Hymes (eds.), *Directions in Sociolinguistics*. New York, Holt, Rinehart & Winston. 35–71.

Ienaga, S. (1998) "Turning the page." *Index on Censorship* 27.3: 48–49.

Jackendoff, R. (1972) *Semantic Interpretation in Generative Grammar*. Cambridge, MA, MIT Press.

(1997) *The Architecture of the Language Faculty*. Cambridge, MA, MIT Press.

Jacob, F. (1977) "Evolution and tinkering". *Science* 196: 1161–1166.

Jakobson, R. (1941) *Kindersprache, Aphasie und allgemeine Lautgesetze*. Uppsala, Almqvist & Wiksell. English translation: A. Keiler (1968) *Child Language, Aphasia and Phonological Universals*. The Hague, Mouton.

Janke, V. (2001) "Syntactic nuts and parasitic gaps." Unpublished term paper, University College London.

Jenkins, L. (2000) *Biolinguistics: Exploring the Biology of Language*. Cambridge, Cambridge University Press.

Jerne, N. K. (1985) "The generative grammar of the immune system" (Nobel lecture). *Science* 229: 1057–1059.

Johnson, D. & S. Lappin (1997) "A critique of the Minimalist Program." *Linguistics and Philosophy* 20: 272–333.

Johnson, M. & J. Morton (1991) *Biology and Cognitive Development: The Case of Face Recognition*. Oxford, Blackwell.

Joos, M. (ed.) (1957) *Readings in Linguistics*. Chicago, University of Chicago Press.

Kager, R. (1999) *Optimality Theory*. Cambridge, Cambridge Univeristy Press.

Karimi, S. (ed) (2003) *Word Order and Scrambling*. Oxford, Blackwell.

Karmiloff-Smith, A. (1992a) *Beyond Modularity*. Cambridge, MA, MIT Press.

(1992b) "Abnormal phenotypes and the challenges they pose to connectionist models of development." *Technical Report PDP.CNS.92.7* Carnegie Mellon University.

Karmiloff-Smith, A., E. Klima, J. Grant & S. Baron-Cohen (1995) "Is there a social module? Language, face processing, and theory of mind in individuals with Williams syndrome." *Journal of Cognitive Neuroscience* 7: 196–208.

Kasher, A. (1991) *The Chomskyan Turn*. Oxford, Blackwell.

Katz, J. J. (1965/74) "The relevance of linguistics to philosophy." *Journal of Philosophy* 62: 590–602. Reprinted in Harman, 1974: 229–241.

(1981) *Language and Other Abstract Objects*. Oxford, Blackwell.

(ed.) (1985) *The Philosophy of Linguistics*. Oxford, Oxford University Press.

(1996) "The unfinished Chomskyan revolution." *Mind & Language* 11: 270–294.

Katz, J. J. & P. M. Postal (1964) *An Integrated Theory of Linguistic Descriptions*. Cambridge, MA, MIT Press.

Kayne, R. (1994) *The Antisymmetry of Syntax*. Cambridge, MA, MIT Press.

(1996) "Microparametric syntax: some introductory remarks." In J. Black & V. Motapanyane (eds.), *Microparametric Syntax and Dialect Variation*. Amsterdam, John Benjamins. ix–xvii.

Kenstowicz, M. (1994) *Phonology in Generative Grammar*. Oxford, Blackwell.

Kitcher, P. (1989) "Explanatory unification and the causal structure of the world." In P. Kitcher & W. Salmon (eds.), *Scientific Explanation; Minnesota Studies in the Philosophy of Science* XIII: 410–505. Minneapolis, University of Minnesota Press.

Klima, E. & U. Bellugi (1966) "Syntactic regularities in the speech of children." In J. Lyons & R. Wales (eds.), *Psycholinguistics Papers*. Edinburgh, Edinburgh University Press.

Koster, J. (1987) *Domains and Dynasties*. Dordrecht, Foris.

Koyré, A. (1968) *Metaphysics and Measurement: Essays in Scientific Revolution*. London, Chapman & Hall.

Kripke, S. (1982) *Wittgenstein on Rules and Private Language*. Cambridge, MA, Harvard University Press.

Kroch, A. (1989) "Function and grammar in the history of English periphrastic *do*." In R. Fasold & D. Schiffrin (eds.), *Language Variation and Change*. Philadelphia, John Benjamins. 199–244.

(2001) "Syntactic change." In M. Baltin & C. Collins (eds.), *The Handbook of Contemporary Syntactic Theory*. Oxford, Blackwell. 699–729.

(2002) "Variation and change in the historical syntax of English." Paper presented at the LAGB, UMIST, September 2002.

Labov, W. (1972) "The logic of nonstandard English." *Language in the Inner City: Studies in the Black English Vernacular*. Philadelphia, University of Pennsylvania Press. 201–240.

Lai, C. et al. (2001) "A novel forkhead-domain gene is mutated in a severe speech and language disorder." *Nature* 413: 519–523.

Langendoen, D. & P. Postal (1984) *The Vastness of Natural Languages*. Oxford, Blackwell.

Lappin, S., R. Levine & D. Johnson (2000) "The structure of unscientific revolutions". *Natural Language and Linguistic Theory* 18: 665–671.

Larson, R. & G. Segal (1995) *Knowledge of Meaning*. Cambridge, MA, MIT Press.

Lasnik, H. (2001) "Derivation and representation in modern transformational syntax." In M. Baltin & C. Collins (eds.), *The Handbook of Contemporary Syntactic Theory*. Oxford, Blackwell. 62–88.

(2002) "The minimalist program in syntax." *Trends in Cognitive Sciences* 6: 432–437.

Lau, J. (2001) "Onkel Noam aus dem Netz." *Die Zeit*, July 26, 2001.

*Lees, R. (1957) Review of Chomsky, 1957. *Language* 33: 375–408.

(1960) *The Grammar of English Nominalizations*. Bloomington, Indiana University Press.

Lenneberg, E. (1967) *Biological Foundations of Language*. New York, Wiley.

Leonard, L. (1996) "Characterizing specific language impairment: a crosslinguistic perspective." In M. Rice (ed.), *Towards a Genetics of Language*. Hillsdale, NJ, Lawrence Erlbaum. 243–256.

Levelt, W. J. M. (1974) *Formal Grammars in Linguistics and Psycholinguistics*. Vol. 1: *An Introduction to the Theory of Formal Languages and Automata*. The Hague, Mouton.

Levi, P. (1988) *The Drowned and the Saved*. London, Michael Joseph.

(1990) *The Mirror Maker*, trans. R. Rosenthal. London, Minerva.

Lévi-Strauss, C. (1964–71) *Mythologiques*. 4 volumes. Paris, Plon.

Lewis, D. (1969) *Convention: A Philosophical Study*. Cambridge MA, Harvard University Press.

(1994) "Reduction of mind." In Guttenplan: 412–431.

Lieberman, P. (2001) "On the subcortical bases of the evolution of language." In J. Trabant and S. Ward (eds.), *New Essays on the Origin of Language*. The Hague, Mouton.

Lightfoot, D. (1991) *How to set Parameters: Arguments from Language Change*. Cambridge, MA, MIT Press.

Ludlow, P. (2003) "Referential semantics for I-languages?" In Antony & Hornstein: 140–161.

Lycan, W. (1986) "Semantics and methodological solipsism." In E. Lepore (ed.), *Truth and Interpretation: Perspectives on the Philosophy of Donald Davidson*. Oxford, Blackwell. 245–261.

Lycan, W. (2003) "Chomsky on the mind–body problem". In Antony & Hornstein: 11–28.

*Lyons, J. (1970) *Chomsky*. Fontana Modern Masters Series. London, Fontana-Collins.

MacFarquhar, L. (2003) "The Devil's accountant." *The New Yorker,* March 31, 2003, pp. 64–79.

MacWhinney, B. (1995) *The CHILDES Project: Tools for Analyzing Talk*. Hillsdale, NJ, Lawrence Erlbaum.

Mailer, N. (1968) *The Armies of the Night*. London, Weidenfeld & Nicolson.

Manzini, R. (1992) *Locality: A Theory and Some of its Empirical Consequences*. Cambridge, MA, MIT Press.

Marantz, A. (1995) "The minimalist program." In Webelhuth, 1995a: 349–382.

Marcus, G. (1998) "Can connectionism save constructivism?" *Cognition* 66: 153–182.

Marcus, G. & S. Fisher (2003) "*FOXP2* in focus: what can genes tell us about speech and language?" *Trends in Cognitive Sciences* 7: 257–262.

Marcus, M. (1980) *A Theory of Syntactic Recognition for Natural Language*. Cambridge, MA, MIT Press.

Marr, D. (1982) *Vision*. New York, W. H. Freeman.

Marshall, P. (1990) "Chomsky's anarchism." *Bulletin of Anarchist Research* 22: 22–27.

Matthews, R. (1998) "Take a spin." *New Scientist* 2123: 24–28.

Mayberry, R. (1993) "First-language acquisition after childhood differs from second-language acquisition: the case of American Sign Language." *Journal of Speech and Hearing Research* 36: 1258–1270.

McCloskey, J. (1988) "Syntactic theory." In F. Newmeyer (ed.), *Linguistics: The Cambridge Survey*. Cambridge, Cambridge University Press. Vol. I: 18–59.

McGilvray, J. (1998) "Meanings are syntactically individuated and found in the head." *Mind & Language* 13: 225–280.

*(1999) *Chomsky: Language, Mind, and Politics*. Cambridge, Polity Press.

Meisel, J. (1995) "Parameters in acquisition." In P. Fletcher & B. MacWhinney (eds.), *The Handbook of Child Language*. Oxford, Blackwell. 10–35.

Miller, G. (1962) "Some psychological studies of grammar." *American Psychologist* 1: 748–762.

*Miller, G. & N. Chomsky (1963) "Finitary models of language users." In R. D. Luce, R. Bush & E. Galanter (eds.), *Handbook of Mathematical Psychology*. New York, Wiley. Vol. II: 419–492.

Millikan, R. (2003) "In defense of public language." In Antony & Hornstein: 215–237.

Milsark, G. (2001) Review of N. Smith (1999) *Chomsky: Ideas and Ideals* (Cambridge University Press). *Language* 77: 599–600.

*Modgil, S. & C. Modgil (eds.) (1987) *Noam Chomsky: Consensus and Controversy*. New York, The Falmer Press.

Montalbetti, M. (1984). "After Binding: On the Interpretation of Pronouns." Ph.D. dissertation, MIT.

Montague, R. (1969/74) "English as a formal language." In Thomason, 1974: 188–221. (1970/74) "Universal grammar." *Theoria* 36: 373–98, reprinted in Thomason, 1974: 222–246.

Moravcsik, J. (1990) *Thought and Language*. London, Routledge.

Morgan, G., N. V. Smith, I.-M. Tsimpli & B. Woll (2002) "Language against the odds: the learning of British Sign Language by a polyglot *savant*." *Journal of Linguistics* 38: 1–41.

Moser, P. K. (1995) "Epistemology." In R. Audi (ed.), *The Cambridge Dictionary of Philosophy*. Cambridge, Cambridge University Press: 233–238.

A. Motluk, A. (1996) "Brain detectives see memories in their true colours." *New Scientist* 2040: 16. (1997) "The inner eye has sharper vision." *New Scientist* 2087: 18.

Nagel, E. & R. Brandt (eds.) (1965) *Meaning and Knowledge: Systematic Readings in Epistemology*. New York, Harcourt, Brace & World.

Nagel, T. (1969/74) "Linguistics and epistemology." In S. Hook (ed.), *Language and Philosophy*. New York, New York University Press. Reprinted in Harman, 1974: 219–228.

(1991) *Equality and Partiality*. Oxford, Oxford University Press.

(1997) *The Last Word*. Oxford, Oxford University Press.

Neeleman, A. & F. Weerman (1997) "L1 and L2 word order acquisition." *Language Acquisition* 6: 125–170.

Neidle, C., J. Kegl, D. MacLaughlin, B. Bahan & R. Lee (2000). *The Syntax of American Sign Language: Functional Categories and Hierarchical Structure*. Cambridge, MA: MIT Press.

Newbury, D. F. & A. P. Monaco (2002) "Molecular genetics of speech and language disorders." *Current Opinion in Pediatrics* 14: 696–701.

Newmeyer, F. (1983) *Grammatical Theory*. Chicago, Chicago University Press.

(1997) "Genetic dysphasia and linguistic theory." *Journal of Neurolinguistics* 10: 47–73.

Nowak, M. & N. Komarova (2001) "Towards an evolutionary theory of language." *Trends in Cognitive Sciences* 5: 288–295.

O'Connor, N., N. Smith, C. Frith & I.-M. Tsimpli (1994) "Neuropsychology and linguistic talent." *Journal of Neurolinguistics* 8: 95–107.

*Otero, C. (ed.) (1994) *Noam Chomsky: Critical Assessments*. 4 volumes. London, Routledge. [An excellent sourcebook of articles and reviews.]

(ed.) (2003) *Chomsky on Democracy and Education*. New York, RoutledgeFalmer.

Owen, U. (1998) "The speech that kills." *Index on Censorship* 27.1: 32–39.

Pais, A. (1982) *Subtle is the Lord . . . : The Science and the Life of Albert Einstein*. Oxford, Oxford University Press.

(1994) *Einstein Lived Here*. Oxford, Clarendon Press.

Papafragou, A. (1998) "The acquisition of modality: implications for theories of semantic representation." *Mind & Language* 13: 370–399.

(2002) "Mindreading and verbal communication." *Mind & Language* 17: 55–67.

Papineau, D. (1994) "Content (2)." In Guttenplan: 225–230.

Paradis, M. (ed.) (1997) *Genetic Dysphasia*. Special issue of *Journal of Neurolinguistics* 10: 45–249.

Parry, R. L. (1997) "Japan rejects professor's fight for freedom of speech." *The Independent*, August 8.

Partee, B. H. (1971) "On the requirement that transformations preserve meaning." In C. Fillmore & T. Langendoen (eds.), *Studies in Linguistic Semantics*. New York, Holt, Rinehart & Winston. 1–21.

(1975) "Comments on C. J. Fillmore's and N. Chomsky's papers." In R. Austerlitz (ed.), *The Scope of American Linguistics*. Lisse, Peter de Ridder Press. 197–209.

*Peck, J. (1987) *The Chomsky Reader*. New York, Pantheon. [An outstanding sourcebook.]

Perovic, A. (2003) "Knowledge of Binding in Down Syndrome: Evidence from English and Serbo-Croatian." Ph.D. thesis, University College London.

Pesetsky, D. (2000) *Phrasal Movement and its Kin*. Cambridge MA, MIT Press.

Phillips, C. (1996) "Order and Structure." Ph.D. thesis, MIT.

(in press) "Parsing: Psycholinguistic aspects". *International Encyclopaedia of Linguistics*, Oxford, Oxford University Press.

(to appear) "Linguistics and linking problems." In M. Rice & S. Warren (eds.), *Developmental Language Disorders: From Phenotypes to Etiologies*. Mahwah, NJ: Lawrence Erlbaum Associates.

Piaget, J. & B. Inhelder (1966) *The Psychology of the Child*. London, Routledge.

*Piattelli-Palmarini, M. (1980) *Language and Learning: The Debate between Jean Piaget and Noam Chomsky.* Cambridge, MA, Harvard University Press.

(1989) "Evolution, selection and cognition: from learning to parameter setting in biology and in the study of language." *Cognition* 31: 1–44.

Pierrehumbert, J., M. Beckman & R. Ladd (2000) "Conceptual foundations of phonology as a laboratory science." In Burton-Roberts et al.: 273–303.

Pietroski, P. (2003) "Small verbs, complex events: analyticity without synonymy." Antony & Hornstein: 179–214.

Pilger, J. (2002) *The New Rulers of the World.* London, Verso.

Pinker, S. (1994) *The Language Instinct.* New York, William Morrow.

Pinker, S. & A. Prince (1988) "On language and connectionism: analysis of a parallel distributed processing model of language acquisition." *Cognition* 28: 73–193.

Pintzuk, S. (2002) "Verb-object order in Old English: variation as grammatical Competition". In D. W. Lightfoot (ed.), *Syntactic Effects of Morphological Change,* Oxford, Oxford University Press. 276–299.

Plaut, D. (2003) "Connectionist modelling of language: Examples and implications." In M. Banich and M. Mack (eds.), *Mind, Brain, and Language: Multidisciplinary Perspectives.* 143–167.

Plunkett, K. (1995) "Connectionist approaches to language acquisition." In P. Fletcher & B. MacWhinney (eds.), *The Handbook of Child Language.* Oxford, Blackwell. 36–72.

Poizner, H., U. Bellugi & E. Klima (1987) *What the Hands Reveal About the Brain.* Cambridge, MA, MIT Press.

Poland, J. (2003) "Chomsky's challenge to physicalism". In Antony & Hornstein: 29–48.

Pollard, C. and I. Sag. (1994) *Head-Driven Phrase Structure Grammar.* Chicago, University of Chicago Press, and Stanford, CSLI Publications.

Post, E. (1944) "Recursively enumerable sets of positive integers and their decision problems." *Bulletin of the American Mathematical Society* 50: 284–316.

Postal, P. (1974) *On Raising: One Rule of English Grammar and its Theoretical Implications.* Cambridge MA, MIT Press.

Powell, M. (2002) "An eminence with no shades of gray". *The Washington Post,* May 5.

Premack, D. & A. Premack (1994) "Moral belief: form versus content." In L. Hirschfeld & S. Gelman (eds.), *Mapping the Mind: Domain Specificity in Cognition and Culture.* Cambridge, Cambridge University Press. 149–168.

Pritchett, B. L. (1988) "Garden path phenomena and the grammatical basis of language processing." *Language* 64: 539–576.

Pullum, G. K. (1979) *Rule Interaction and the Organization of a Grammar.* New York, Garland.

(1989) "Formal linguistics meets the boojum." *Natural Language and Linguistic Theory* 7: 137–143.

Pullum, G. K. & B. Scholz (2003) "Linguistic models." In M. Banich and M. Mack (eds.) *Mind, Brain, and Language: Multidisciplinary Perspectives.* Mahwah, NJ, Lawrence Erlbaum. 113–141.

Pullum, G. K. & A. Zwicky (1988) "The syntax-phonology interface." In F. Newmeyer (ed.), *Linguistics: The Cambridge Survey.* Cambridge, Cambridge University Press. Vol. I: 255–280.

Putnam, H. (1967) "The 'innateness hypothesis' and explanatory models in linguistics." *Boston Studies in the Philosophy of Science.* New York, Humanities Press.

Vol. III: 91–101. Reprinted in Searle, 1971: 121–144. Also in *Synthèse* (1967) 17: 12–22.

(1989) "Model theory and the 'factuality' of semantics." In George: 213–232.

(1993) "Replies." In J. Tomberlin (ed.), *Philosophical Topics* 20: 347–408.

Quine, W. v. O. (1960) *Word and Object*. Cambridge, MA, MIT Press.

(1969) "Linguistics and philosophy." In S. Hook (ed.), *Language and Philosophy*. New York, New York University Press. 95–98.

(1972/74) "Methodological reflections on current linguistic theory." In Davidson & Harman: 442–454. Reprinted in Harman, 1974: 104–117

(1990a) *Pursuit of Truth*. Cambridge, MA, Harvard University Press.

(1990b) "Three indeterminacies." In Barrett & Gibson: 1–16.

(1992) "Structure and nature." *Journal of Philosophy* 89.1: 5–9.

Radford, A. (1990) *Syntactic Theory and the Acquisition of English Syntax*. Oxford, Blackwell.

(1997a) *Syntactic Theory and the Structure of English*. Cambridge, Cambridge University Press.

(1997b) *Syntax: A Minimalist Introduction*. Cambridge, Cambridge University Press.

(2004a) *Minimalist Syntax: Exploring the Structure of English*. Cambridge, Cambridge University Press.

(2004b) *English Syntax: An Introduction*. Cambridge, Cambridge University Press.

*Rai, M. (1995) *Chomsky's Politics*. London, Verso. [An excellent overview.]

(2002) *War Plan Iraq: Ten Reasons against War on Iraq*. London, Verso.

Ramsey, W., S. Stich & J. Garon (1990) "Connectionism, eliminativism and the future of folk psychology." *Philosophical Perspectives* 4: 499–533.

Randall, J. (1990) "Catapults and pendulums: the mechanics of language acquisition." *Linguistics* 28: 1381–1406.

Reinhart, T. & E. Reuland (1993) "Reflexivity." *Linguistic Inquiry* 24: 657–720.

Reuland, E. & W. Abraham (1993) *Knowledge and Language*. Vol. 1: *From Orwell's Problem to Plato's Problem*. Dordrecht, Kluwer.

Reuland, E. & M. Everaert (2001) "Deconstructing binding". In M. Baltin & C. Collins (eds.), *The Handbook of Contemporary Syntactic Theory*. Oxford, Blackwell. 634–669.

Rey, G. (1997) *Contemporary Philosophy of Mind: A Contentiously Classical Approach*. Oxford, Blackwell.

(2003) "Chomsky, intentionality, and a CRTT." In Antony & Hornstein: 105–139.

Ritter, N. (ed.) (2002) *A review of "the poverty of stimulus argument."* Special issue of *The Linguistic Review* 19: 1–223.

Rizzi, L. (1982) *Issues in Italian Syntax*. Dordrecht, Foris.

Roberts, I. (1997) *Comparative Syntax*. London, Arnold.

Roberts, I. & A. Roussou (2003) *Syntactic Change: A Minimalist Approach to Grammaticalization*. Cambridge, Cambridge University Press.

Robins, R. H. (1989) *General Linguistics: An Introductory Survey*. 4th edition London, Longman.

Roca, I. (ed.) (1992) *Logical Issues in Language Acquisition*. Dordrecht, Foris.

Roca, I. & W. Johnson (1999). *Course in Phonology*. Oxford, Blackwell.

Rocker, R. (1938) *Anarcho-syndicalism*. London, Secker & Warburg.

Roeper, T. & E. Williams (eds.) (1987) *Parameter Setting*. Dordrecht, Reidel.

Rondal, J. (1995) *Exceptional Language Development in Down's Syndrome*. Cambridge, Cambridge University Press.

Rondal, J. & A. Comblain (1996) "Language in adults with Down's Syndrome." *Down's Syndrome: Research and Practice* 4.

Rooryck, J. & L. Zaring (eds.) (1996) *Phrase Structure and the Lexicon*. Dordrecht, Kluwer.

Rosemont, H. (1978/94) "Gathering evidence for linguistic innateness." *Synthèse* 38: 127–48. Reprinted in Otero, 1994, vol. II: 362–380.

Ross, J. R. (1967/86) "Constraints on Variables in Syntax." Ph.D. thesis, MIT. Published in 1986 as *Infinite Syntax*. Norwood, NJ, Ablex Publishing Corporation.

Rousseau, J.-J. (1755/1964) *Discourse on the Origins and Foundations of Inequality among Men*. Translated in R. D. Masters (ed.), *The First and Second Discourses*. New York, St. Martin's Press.

Roy, A. (2003) "The loneliness of Noam Chomsky." http://www.zmag.org/content/showarticle.cfm?SectionID=11 &ItemID=4116

Rugg (1999) "Functional neuroimaging in cognitive neuroscience". In C. Brown & P. Hagoort (eds.), *The Neurocognition of Language*. Oxford, Oxford University Press. 15–36.

Russell, B. (1948) *Human Knowledge: Its Scope and Limits*. London, Allen & Unwin.
   (1950) "An outline of intellectual rubbish." In *Unpopular Essays*. London, Allen & Unwin. 82–123.

Ryle, G. (1949) *The Concept of Mind*. London, Hutchinson.
   (1961) "Use, usage and meaning." *Proceedings of the Aristotelian Society, Supplementary Volume* 35: 223–242. Reprinted in part in A. Cashdan & E. Grugeon (eds.), *Language in Education: A Source Book*. London, Open University Press. 5–8.

Rymer, R. (1993) *Genie: A Scientific Tragedy*. New York, Harper Perennial.

Sacks, O. (1985) *The Man who Mistook his Wife for a Hat*. New York, Summit Books.

Saffran, E. (2003) "Evidence from language breakdown: Implications for the neural and functional organization of language." In M. Banich & M. Mack (eds.), *Mind, Brain and Language*. Mahwah, NJ, Lawrence Erlbaum. 251–281.

Salmon, W. (1989) "Four decades of scientific explanation." In P. Kitcher & W. Salmon (eds.), *Scientific Explanation. Minnesota Studies in the Philosophy of Science* 13: 3–219.

Sampson, G. (1989) "Language acquisition: growth or learning?" *Philosophical Papers* XVIII 3: 203–240.
   (1999) *Educating Eve: The "Language Instinct" Debate*. London, Cassell.

Sanford, A. & P. Sturt (2002) "Depth of processing in language comprehension: not noticing the evidence". *Trends in Cognitive Sciences* 6: 382–386.

Sapir, E. (1929) "The status of linguistics as a science." *Language* 5: 207–214.

Savin, H. & E. Perchonock (1965) "Grammatical structure and the immediate recall of English sentences." *Journal of Verbal Learning and Verbal Behavior* 4: 348–353.

Schacter, D. L., E. Reiman, T. Curran, L. S. Yun, D. Bandy, K. B. McDermott & H. L. Roediger III (1996) "Neuroanatomical correlates of veridical and illusory recognition memory: evidence from Positron Emission Tomography." *Neuron* 17: 267–274.

Schoenman, R. (1967) *Bertrand Russell: Philosopher of the Century*. London, Allen & Unwin.

Schütze, C. T. (1996) *The Empirical Basis of Linguistics. Grammaticality Judgments and Linguistic Methodology.* Chicago, Chicago University Press.

Searchinger, G. (1995) *The Human Language Series. Part I Discovering the Human Language: "Colorless green ideas."* New York, Equinox Films Inc.

Searle, J. (ed.) (1971) *The Philosophy of Language.* Oxford, Oxford University Press.

(1972/74) "Chomsky's revolution in linguistics." *The New York Review of Books.* Reprinted in Harman, 1974: 2–33.

(1990) "Consciousness, explanatory inversion, and cognitive science." *Behavioral and Brain Sciences* 13: 585–642.

Sgroi, S. C. (1983) *Noam Chomsky: Bibliografia 1949–1981.* Padova, CLESP Editrice.

Shallice, T. (1988) *From Neuropsychology to Mental Structure.* Cambridge, Cambridge University Press.

Shapiro, K. & A. Caramazza (2003) "The representation of grammatical categories in the brain." *Trends in Cognitive Sciences* 7: 201–206.

Skinner, B. F. (1948) *Walden Two.* New York, Macmillan.

(1957) *Verbal Behavior.* New York, Appleton Century Crofts.

(1971) *Beyond Freedom and Dignity.* New York, Knopf.

Smith, A. (1988) "Language acquisition: learnability, maturation and the fixing of parameters." *Cognitive Neuropsychology* 5: 235–265.

Smith, N. V. (1967) *An Outline Grammar of Nupe.* London, School of Oriental and African Studies.

(1973) *The Acquisition of Phonology: A Case Study.* Cambridge, Cambridge University Press.

(ed.) (1982) *Mutual Knowledge.* London, Academic Press.

(1983) *Speculative Linguistics.* (An inaugural lecture delivered at University College London, published by the College.)

(1985) "Chomsky, Noam." In A. Kuper & J. Kuper (eds.), *The Social Science Encyclopaedia.* London, Routledge & Kegan Paul. 105–106.

(1986) Review of Berwick & Weinberg, 1984. *Journal of Linguistics* 22: 222–229.

(1987) "Universals and typology." In Modgil & Modgil: 57–66.

(1988) "Principles, parameters and pragmatics." Review article on Chomsky, 1986. *Journal of Linguistics* 24: 189–201.

(1989) *The Twitter Machine: Reflections on Language.* Oxford, Blackwell.

(1990) "Can pragmatics fix parameters?" In Roca: 277–289.

(1994a) "Competence and performance." In the *Pergamon Encyclopaedia of Linguistics*, vol. 2: 645–648.

(1994b) Review article on A. Karmiloff-Smith, 1992. *European Journal of Disorders of Communication* 29: 95–105.

(1996) "Godshit." *Glot International* 2.5: 10. [Reprinted in Smith, 2002b.]

(1997) "Structural eccentricities." *Glot International* 2.8: 7. [Reprinted in Smith, 2002b.]

(1998) "Jackdaws, sex and language acquisition." *Glot International* 3.7: 7. [Reprinted in Smith, 2002b.]

(2001) "Backlash." *Glot International* 5: 169–171.

(2002a) "Frogs, parrots, grooming, the basal ganglia and language." *Glot International* 6: 168–170.

(2002b) *Language, Bananas and Bonobos: Linguistic Problems, Puzzles and Polemics.* Oxford, Blackwell.

(2002c) "Modules, modals, maths & the mind". *Glot International* 6: 248–250.

(2002d) "Wonder." *Glot International* 6: 55–57.

(2002e) "Personal history." In K. Brown & V. Law (eds.), *Linguistics in Britain: Personal Histories.* Publications of the Philological Society, 36. Oxford, Blackwell. 262–273.

(2003a) "Dissociation and modularity: reflections on language and mind." In M. Banich & M. Mack (eds.), *Mind, Brain and Language.* Mahwah, NJ, Lawrence Erlbaum. 87–111.

(2003b) "Linguistics by numbers." *Glot International* 7: 110–102.

(2003c) "Are gucks mentally represented?" *Glot International* 7: 164–166.

Smith, N. V. & A. Cormack (2002) "Parametric poverty." *Glot International* 6: 285–287.

Smith, N. V., B. Hermelin & I.-M. Tsimpli (2003) "Dissociation of social affect and theory of mind in a case of Asperger's syndrome". *University College London Working Papers in Linguistics* 15: 357–377.

Smith, N. V. & I.-M. Tsimpli (1995) *The Mind of a Savant: Language-learning and Modularity.* Oxford, Blackwell.

(1997) "Reply to Bates' review of Smith & Tsimpli, 1995." *The International Journal of Bilingualism* 2: 180–186.

*Smith, N. V. & D. Wilson (1979) *Modern Linguistics: The Results of Chomsky's Revolution.* Harmondsworth, Penguin.

(1992) "Introduction to *Relevance Theory.*" Special Issue of *Lingua*, ed. D. Wilson & N. Smith. 87: 1–10.

Smolensky, P. (1994) "Computational models of mind." In Guttenplan: 176–185.

Soames, S. (1985) "Semantics and psychology." In Katz: 204–226.

Sober, E. (1980) "Representation and psychological reality." *Behavioral and Brain Sciences* 3: 38–39.

Spelke, E. & S. Tsivkin (2001) "Initial knowledge and conceptual change: space and number". In M. Bowerman & S. Levinson (eds.), *Language Acquisition and Conceptual Development.* Cambridge, Cambridge University Press. 70–97.

Sperber, D. (1994) "Understanding verbal understanding." In J. Khalfa (ed.), *What Is Intelligence?* Cambridge, Cambridge University Press. 179–198.

*Sperber, D. & D. Wilson (1986/95) *Relevance: Communication and Cognition.* Oxford, Blackwell.

Steedman, M. (1993) "Categorial Grammar." *Lingua* 90: 221–258.

Steedman, Mark. 2000. *The Syntactic Process.* Cambridge, MA, MIT Press.

Steiner, G. (1978) *On Difficulty and Other Essays.* Oxford, Oxford University Press.

Stich, S. (1978) "Beliefs and subdoxastic states." *Philosophy of Science* 45: 499–518.

Strawson, G. (2003) "Real materialism". In Antony & Hornstein: 49–88.

Strawson, P. F. (1952) *Introduction to Logical Theory.* London, Methuen.

Stromswold, K. (2001) "The heritability of language: a review and meta-analysis of twin, adoption and linkage studies." *Language* 77: 647–723.

Strozer, J. (1994) *Language Acquisition after Puberty.* Washington, DC, Georgetown University Press.

Suppes, P. (1986) "The primacy of utterer's meaning." In R. Grandy & R. Warner (eds.), *Philosophical Grounds of Rationality: Intentions, Categories, Ends.* Oxford, Clarendon Press. 109–129.

Sutton-Spence, R. L. & B. Woll. (1999). *An Introduction to the Linguistics of BSL.* Cambridge, Cambridge University Press.

Sykes, C. (ed.) (1994) *No Ordinary Genius: The Illustrated Richard Feynman.* London, Weidenfeld & Nicolson.

Szabolcsi, A. (2001) "The syntax of scope." In M. Baltin & C. Collins (eds.), *The Handbook of Contemporary Syntactic Theory.* Oxford, Blackwell. 607–633.

Tanenhaus, M. (1988) "Psycholinguistics: an overview." In F. Newmeyer (ed.), *Linguistics: The Cambridge Survey.* Cambridge University Press. Vol. 3: 1–37.

Tappe, H. (1999) *Der Spracherwerb bei Corpus-Callosum-Agenesie: eine explorative Studie.* [Language acquisition in agenesis of the corpus callosum: an exploratory study.] Tübingen: Narr.

Thomas, M. S. C. & A. Karmiloff-Smith (in press). "Modelling language acquisition in atypical phenotypes."

Thomason, R. (ed.) (1974) *Formal Philosophy: Selected Papers of Richard Montague.* New Haven, Yale University Press.

Thompson, D'A. W. (1942) *On Growth and Form.* 2 vols. Cambridge, Cambridge University Press.

Thompson, R. F. (1993) *The Brain: A Neuroscience Primer.* 2nd edition. New York, Freeman.

Thornton, R. (1991) "Adventures in Long-distance Moving: The Acquisition of Complex Wh-Questions." Ph.D. thesis, University of Connecticut.

Tomalin, M. (2002) "The formal origins of syntactic theory." *Lingua* 112: 827–848.

  (2003) "Goodman, Quine, and Chomsky: from a grammatical point of view." *Lingua* 113: 1223–1253.

Tomasello, M. (2003) *Constructing a Language.* Cambridge, MA, Harvard University Press.

Tovée, M. J. (1996) *An Introduction to the Visual System.* Cambridge, Cambridge University Press.

Townsend, D. & T. Bever (2001) *Sentence Comprehension: The Integration of Habits and Rules.* Cambridge, MA, MIT Press.

Tsimpli, I.-M. (1991) "Functional categories and maturation: the prefunctional stage of language acquisition." *University College London Working Papers in Linguistics* 3: 123–148.

  (1992/96) *The Prefunctional Stage of Language Acquisition.* New York, Garland.

Tsimpli, I.-M. & N. V. Smith (1998) "Modules and quasi-modules: language and theory of mind in a polyglot savant." *Learning and Individual Differences* 10: 193–215.

Turgut, P. (2002) "Turkish judge in Chomsky case frees publisher." *The Independent,* February 14, p. 15.

Turing, A. (1952) "The chemical basis of morphogenesis". *Philosophical Transactions of the Royal Society of London*: 37–72.

Tynan, K. (ed.) (1994) *Kenneth Tynan: Letters.* London, Weidenfeld & Nicolson.

Ullman, S. (1979) *The Interpretation of Visual Motion.* Cambridge, MA, MIT Press.

  (1996) *High Level Vision.* Cambridge, MA, MIT Press.

Uriagereka, J. (1998) *Rhyme and Reason: An Introduction to Minimalist Syntax.* Cambridge, MA, MIT Press.

Vallely, P. (2003) "The invisible." *The Independent,* June 26 (*Review*) pp. 2–5.

Van de Koot, J. (1991) "Parsing with principles: on constraining derivations." *University College London Working Papers in Linguistics* 3: 369–395.

Van der Lely, H. K. J. (1997a) "Language and cognitive development in a grammatical SLI boy: modularity and innateness." *Journal of Neurolinguistics* 10: 75–107.

(1997b) "SLI in children: movement, economy and deficits in the computational-syntactic system." MS, Birkbeck College, University of London.

Van Fraassen, B. (1980) *The Scientific Image*. Oxford, Clarendon Press.

Vargha-Khadem, F., K. Watkins, K. Alcock, P. Fletcher & R. Passingham (1995) "Praxic and nonverbal cognitive deficits in a large family with a genetically transmitted speech and language disorder." *Proceedings of the National Academy of Sciences, USA*. 92: 930–933.

Vargha-Khadem, F., L. Carr, E. Isaacs, E, Brett, C. Adams & M. Mishkin (1997) "Onset of speech after left hemispherectomy in a nine-year-old boy." *Brain* 120: 159–182.

Vidal-Hall, J. (ed.) (2003) *The A–Z of Free Expression*. London, Index on Censorship.

Walker, G. (1997) "Here comes hypertime." *New Scientist* 2106: 40–41.

Waller, B. (1977/94) "Chomsky, Wittgenstein and the behaviourist perspective on language." *Behaviorism* 5: 43–59. Reprinted in Otero, 1994, vol. II: 341–361.

Webelhuth, G. (1995a) *Government and Binding Theory and the Minimalist Program*. Oxford, Blackwell.

(1995b) "X-bar theory and case theory." In Webelhuth, 1995a: 15–95.

Weinberg, A. (1999) "A minimalist theory of human sentence processing." In S. D. Epstein & N. Hornstein (eds.), *Working Minimalism*. Cambridge, MA, MIT Press. 283–315.

Weiskrantz, L. (1986) *Blindsight: A Case Study and Implications*. Oxford, Clarendon Press.

Wells, R. S. (1947) "Immediate constituents." *Language* 23: 81–117.

White, L. (1981) "The responsibility of grammatical theory to acquisitional data." In N. Hornstein & D. Lightfoot (eds.), *Explanations in Linguistics*. London, Longman. 241–271.

Wilkin, P. (1997) *Noam Chomsky: On Power, Knowledge and Human Nature*. London, Macmillan Press.

Williams, E. (1995) "Theta theory." In Webelhuth, 1995a: 97–123.

Wilson, D. S. M. (1994) "Concepts: their structure and functions." Unpublished lectures on the Philosophy of Language, University College London.

(2003) "New directions for research on pragmatics and modularity." *University College London Working Papers in Linguistics* 15: 105–127.

*Winston, M. (2002) *On Chomsky*. Wadsworth Philosophers Series. Belmont, CA, Wadsworth/Thomson Learning, Inc.

Wittgenstein, L. (1953) *Philosophical Investigations*, trans. G. E. M. Anscombe. Oxford, Blackwell.

Wolpert, L. (1991) *The Triumph of the Embryo*. Oxford, Oxford University Press.

(1992) *The Unnatural Nature of Science*. London, Faber & Faber.

Yang, X., Y. Li & N. Xu (1989) *Art of the Dragon*. London, Studio Vista.

Zeldin, T. (1973) *France 1848–1945*. 2 volumes. Oxford, Clarendon Press.

(1988) *Happiness*. London, Collins Harvill.

(1994) *An Intimate History of Humanity*. London, Sinclair-Stevenson.

Zinn, H. (1996) *A People's History of the United States: from 1492 to the Present*. London, Longman.

Index